Leadership for the Common Good

Leadership for the Common Good

Tackling Public Problems in a Shared-Power World

Second Edition

Barbara C. Crosby

John M. Bryson

JOSSEY-BASS
A Wiley Imprint
www.josseybass.com

Published by Jossey-Bass
A Wiley Imprint
989 Market Street, San Francisco, CA 94103-1741   www.josseybass.com

Jossey-Bass books and products are available through most bookstores. To contact Jossey-Bass directly call our Customer Care Department within the U.S. at 800-956-7739, outside the U.S. at 317-572-3986 or fax 317-572-4002.

Jossey-Bass also publishes its books in a variety of electronic formats. Some content that appears in print may not be available in electronic books.

Library of Congress Cataloging-in-Publication Data

Crosby, Barbara C., 1946–
  Leadership for the common good : tackling public problems in a shared-power world / Barbara C. Crosby, John M. Bryson.– 2nd ed.
      p. cm.
  Bryson's name appears first on the earlier edition.
  Includes bibliographical references and index.
  ISBN 0-7879-6753-X (alk. paper)
  1. Leadership. 2. Political leadership. 3. Common good. 4. Public administration. I. Bryson, John M. (John Moore), 1947– II. Title.
  JF1525.L4B79 2005
  303.3'4–dc22

                                                              2004025833

Printed in the United States of America
FIRST EDITION
HB Printing   10 9 8 7 6 5 4 3 2 1

Contents

Preface   xiii

Acknowledgments   xxv

The Authors   xxix

Part One: Understanding Leadership in Shared-Power Settings   1

1   When No One Is in Charge: The Meaning of Shared Power   3

2   Leadership Tasks in a Shared-Power World: Leadership in Context, and Personal Leadership   34

3   Leadership Tasks in a Shared-Power World: Team and Organizational Leadership   64

4   Leadership Tasks in a Shared-Power World: Visionary, Political, and Ethical Leadership   108

5   Policy Entrepreneurship and the Common Good   156

Part Two: The Process of Policy Entrepreneurship   195

6   Forging an Initial Agreement to Act   197

7   Developing an Effective Problem Definition to Guide Action   216

8   Searching for Solutions in Forums   242

9   Developing a Proposal That Can Win in Arenas   267

10   Adopting Policy Proposals   290

11   Implementing and Evaluating New Policies, Programs, and Plans   312

12 Reassessing Policies and Programs 340

Summary and Conclusion 359

References 365

Resource A: Conflict Management 393

Resource B: A Guide to Oval Mapping 395

Resource C: Seven Zones 399

Resource D: Forums, Arenas, and Courts 401

Resource E: Future Search 427

Resource F: Initial Policy Retreats 433

Name Index 437

Subject Index 445

List of Exhibits

Exhibit 1.1.   Tackling Public Problems in a Shared-Power
               World: Some Definitions   22

Exhibit 5.1.   Policy Entrepreneurship and the
               Common Good: Some Definitions   158

Exhibit 6.1.   Characteristics of Effective Coordinating
               Committees and Other Policy-Making Bodies   209

Exhibit 7.1.   Generic Problem Statement Format   238

Exhibit 11.1. Guidance for Pilot Projects, Demonstration
               Projects, and Transfer to Entire
               Implementation System   337

Exhibit D.1.   The Three Dimensions of Power   402

Exhibit D.2.   Designing and Using Forums   410

Exhibit D.3.   Designing and Using Arenas   416

Exhibit D.4.   Designing and Using Courts   421

List of Exercises

Exercise 1.1. Understanding Public Problems in a
Shared-Power World   21

Exercise 2.1. Discovering Cares and Concerns   38

Exercise 2.2. Assessing the Context for Leadership   43

Exercise 2.3. Assessing Global Trends   45

Exercise 2.4. Assessing Cultural Differences   48

Exercise 2.5. Exploring Personal Highs and Lows   50

Exercise 2.6. Assessing Additional Strengths and
Weaknesses   60

Exercise 2.7. Analyzing Social Group Membership
and Means of Bridging Differences   62

Exercise 3.1. Using "Snowcards" to Identify and Agree
on Norms   72

Exercise 3.2. Assessing Your Team   78

Exercise 3.3. Stakeholder Identification and Analysis   83

Exercise 3.4. Mission Development   85

Exercise 3.5. Constructing an Organizational Vision
of Success   88

Exercise 3.6. Assessing Your Organization   103

Exercise 4.1. Outlining and Constructing Personal Visions   116

Exercise 4.2. Using a Power-Versus-Interest Grid   121

Exercise 4.3. Analyzing Interpretive Schemes,
or Problem Frames   124

Exercise 4.4. Assessing Visionary Leadership Capacity   130

Exercise 4.5. Laying the Groundwork for a
Winning Coalition   137

Exercise 4.6 Assessing Political Leadership Capacity   144

Exercise 4.7. Identifying Ethical Role Models, and
Overcoming Barriers to Ethical Leadership   147

Exercise 4.8. Analyzing Ethical Principles, Laws,
and Norms   152

Exercise 4.9. Assessing Ethical Leadership Capacity   153

Exercise 5.1. Thinking About a Public Problem   166

Exercise 5.2. Thinking About the Public Interest and
the Common Good   191

Exercise 6.1. The Basic Stakeholder Analysis Technique
for a Policy Change Effort   203

Exercise 6.2. Constructing a Stakeholder Influence
Diagram   204

Exercise 6.3. Participation Planning Matrix   204

Exercise 6.4. Assessing Stakeholder Attitudes Toward
the Status Quo   211

Exercise 7.1. Developing Objectives from Preferred
Solutions for a Problem   233

Exercise 7.2. Constructing a Diagram of Bases of Power
and Directions of Interest (Goals)   234

Exercise 7.3. Constructing a Map of the Common Good
and Structure of a Winning Argument   235

Exercise 8.1. Undertaking a Solution Search Within
Specified Areas   254

Exercise 8.2. Constructing a Stakeholder-Issue
Interrelationship Diagram   257

Exercise 8.3. Using a Multicriteria Assessment Grid   259

Exercise 9.1. Pursuing a Big-Win or a Small-Win Strategy   276

Exercise 9.2. Constructing a Stakeholder-Support-Versus-
Opposition Grid   283

Exercise 9.3. Conducting a Stakeholder Role Play   284

Exercise 9.4. Constructing a Grid of Policy Attractiveness
Versus Stakeholder Capability   285

Exercise 11.1. Tapping Stakeholder Interests and
Resources for Policy Implementation   327

Preface

*Our world is so complex, interdependent, and interrelated
that the old paradigms of singular leadership will not
work and cannot work.*
SUZANNE W. MORSE

*Remember that leaders come in both genders, all sizes,
[all] ages, [and] from all geographic areas and
neighborhoods.*
MARIAN WRIGHT EDELMAN

Several times over the last few years, we've asked ourselves about
our own call to leadership in a world beset by unprecedented challenges and crises, from the AIDS pandemic to global warming to
the destruction and fear wrought by terrorism and state responses
to it. We have joined particular initiatives to respond to these challenges, but we always return to the conviction that our best contribution is teaching and writing about how the world's citizens can
work together for the common good in their organizations and
communities.

In particular, we realized it was high time to respond to the
many users of the original *Leadership for the Common Good* who asked
for more practical guidance in how to lead in a shared-power environment, and for more recent and varied examples of how others are striving to achieve the common good. The new *Leadership
for the Common Good* is our effort to update and make our leadership framework more accessible to a variety of audiences, to connect it with the challenges of the twenty-first century, and to draw
on the best of recent research on leadership and public problems.

We take heart (and guidance) from the many other leadership
scholars and practitioners who also have turned their attention to
the importance of shared leadership and the need for collaboration

among diverse groups during recent years. It's common now to hear that leadership can and should be exercised by people with many kinds of formal and informal authority and responsibility. Leadership analysts and educators in many parts of the world are preaching openness to more diverse leaders by agreeing with Marian Wright Edelman (1993) that leaders come from a multiplicity of backgrounds.

We began our original book by noting that today's citizens live in a world where no one is in charge, where the needed resources for coping with most important public problems extend well beyond the capacity of any group or organization, and often beyond the scope of national governments. To make progress in tackling those problems, people in a variety of roles—from citizen to elected official, from business executive to nonprofit advocate, from educator to public manager—must take on the leadership challenge of building shared-power arrangements of lasting value.

What was true a decade ago is even truer now. We agree with Suzanne Morse (1991) that singular models of leadership don't match the needs of the twenty-first century. Shared and widespread leadership is required for dealing with the effects of global complexity and interdependence, from economic shifts to climate change to terrorism. The same is true for remedying problems that might seem to be local or national: AIDS, homelessness, rural outmigration, urban brownfields, drug abuse, domestic violence, and a host of other public problems.

Many individuals, groups, organizations, and institutions have a stake in each of these problems. They are directly affected, or have some responsibility to act on the problem, or have information or other resources necessary to make improvements; yet each of these stakeholders has only some of the information, resources, and authority needed to remedy the problem. They operate in a "shared-power world," a world in which they must share objectives, activities, resources, or authority to achieve collective gains or minimize losses (Bryson and Einsweiler, 1991; Healey, 1997; Peters, 1996a, 1996b; Bardach, 1998).

Achieving beneficial policy change in such a world requires heroic individuals, groups, and organizations (Kennedy, 2002) but also quiet or invisible leaders (Sorenson and Hickman, 2002; Badaracco, 2002; Mintzberg, 2002). To make headway, leaders and supporters have to work with great persistence, often over a long period of time to institute new policy regimes and often dismantle old ones. These leaders have to be what Nancy Roberts and Paula King (1996) call policy entrepreneurs.

The second edition of *Leadership for the Common Good* offers policy entrepreneurs a wealth of practical guidance grounded in the most recent research about leadership effectiveness. The book also highlights important new contributions of leadership and public policy theorists. We draw extensively on four new minicases of leadership for the common good, and each chapter includes exercises to help you the reader apply concepts and tools to your own leadership cases. The original single chapter on leadership capabilities has been expanded to three chapters, and we have added a substantial section (in Chapter Five) on the common good. Greater attention is given to the methods and tools of stakeholder involvement in public policy change efforts.

The minicases focus on (1) the early campaign against AIDS; (2) the work of the World Business Council for Sustainable Development; (3) the African American Men Project in Hennepin County, Minnesota; and (4) development of the Vital Aging Network, a pioneering initiative based at the University of Minnesota. Of necessity, we mention by name only a handful of the leaders connected to each case but recognize that we could have mentioned many, many more.

We concede that shared-power arrangements can be used to thwart change for the common good; indeed, we cite examples in which such arrangements slowed the fight to stop the spread of AIDS. In the face of this reality, we offer practical and ethical arguments for doing otherwise. Those who ignore the well-being of their fellow humans in today's interdependent world risk damage to their own groups in the long run. We also think that all human endeavors, including leadership, should be judged on ethical grounds; that is, they should promote widely held principles such as human dignity and equal opportunity (Crosby, 1999).

Who Should Read This Book?

We assume you're reading this because you want to do something about an issue, improve your organization or your community, or make the world a better place. You are seeking to match your passions and skills with significant social needs.

This book is for people around the world who care about governance and policy change, people providing formal and informal leadership in nonprofit organizations, government agencies, elected office, businesses, schools and universities, foundations, and mass media. It is for the seasoned veteran of the world of public affairs as well as the citizen who is just getting involved in community issues. It is for those who want to be change agents and catalysts, reshapers of old arrangements and midwives for new ones. It is for those who want to operate effectively across organizational or jurisdictional boundaries, understand power and shared-power arrangements, and wrestle with public issues so the common good can be achieved.

We also present concepts, tools, and guidance that can be useful to those who educate or support community activists, public administrators, policy analysts, elected officials, and nonprofit and business executives and managers. The book should be useful as a text for university courses in leadership, public affairs, public administration, planning, and public policy. It can also be a resource for community educators, organizational consultants, and researchers.

We offer our leadership framework to people seeking to promote significant policy change and community reform in a democratic context, even as we recognize that an understanding of how policy change really occurs can at least temporarily aid those who wish to thwart democratic action. The framework offers promising possibilities for democratic citizenship and change by drawing critical attention to what often remains hidden or assumed, enumerating and naming access points for influencing policy and highlighting the moments of change in a shared-power world. Indeed, revealing the dynamics of shared power makes democratic change more likely, because wider awareness means many more people know how to join the action and forestall abuses of power. As former Vice President Hubert Humphrey observed, "Democracy is based on the premise that extraordinary things are possible from ordinary people." We hope our leadership framework contributes to the continuous regeneration of a democratic, just, free, and sustainable world.

We acknowledge legitimate skepticism about such terms as *democracy* and *the common good*. Although we recognize that the common good necessarily embraces some moral principles, we are definitely not endorsing any predetermined, unified, rigid vision of the common good. We also recognize that democracy is a means as well as an end; in the hope of being relevant for diverse societies, we are not committed to a particular mode of democratic government and are well aware that any form of government can easily take on antidemocratic methods.

Can the book be useful to people living under an authoritarian government? We think it can and must be. There are always free spaces in which to work; witness the overt and covert citizen activism that contributed to the downfall of the USSR and of the apartheid regime in South Africa. Witness the recent progress, however uneven, of democratic forces in Iran.

Where Do Our Ideas Come From?

Our attempt to understand leadership in today's shared-power world is part of a worldwide intellectual endeavor. Over the last dozen years, other authors have made valuable contributions through books exhorting and guiding ordinary citizens to act courageously, claim their power, and demand decision-making authority over policies and programs that affect them (Sirianni and Friedland, 2001; Boyte and Kari, 1996; Daloz, Keen, Keen, and Parks, 1996; Loeb, 1999; Roy, 2001). Several of these writers also ask professionals to use their expertise in a fashion that empowers fellow citizens rather than objectifying and alienating them.

Other authors offer new guidance for elected officials and public managers, for nonprofit groups, and for businesspeople who want to lead innovative and responsible companies—for example, Jean Lipman-Blumen's *Connective Leadership* (1996), Jeff Luke's *Catalytic Leadership* (1998), Kathleen Allen and Cynthia Cherrey's *Systemic Leadership* (2000), Robert Terry's *Seven Zones for Leadership* (2001), Donald Kettl's *Transformation of Governance* (2002), and James MacGregor Burns's *Transforming Leadership* (2003). A literature has developed on public deliberation and consensus building (Innes, 1994; Roberts, 2002; Susskind, McKearnan, and Thomas-Larmer, 1999); alternative dispute resolution (Thompson, 2000); governance as relationship in contrast to principal-agent theory (Feldman and Khademian, 2002); collaboration (Innes, 1994; Healey, 1997; Margarum, 2002; Ray, 2002; Huxham, 2003); and advocacy coalitions

(Sabatier and Jenkins-Smith, 1993). Some of this new literature contributes to the notion of policy entrepreneurship (Roberts and King, 1996; Henton, Melville, and Walesh, 1997; Osborne and Plastrik, 1997; see especially Krieger, 1996). Helpful research and theory building have also been published in periodicals such as *The Leadership Quarterly*, the *Journal of Leadership and Organizational Studies* (formerly the *Journal of Leadership Studies*), and *Leader to Leader* as well as in proceedings of International Leadership Association conferences.

In this book we try to pull together these contributions, along with the insights we've gained in the last decade as we helped others use the Leadership for the Common Good framework. Since publication of the first edition of *Leadership for the Common Good*, we've used the framework in classes, workshops, and consultations in the United States, the United Kingdom, and Eastern Europe. Participants in these sessions have ranged from college undergraduates to midcareer professionals from around the world. They have helped us develop and refine our ideas and methods and thus contributed indirectly to this book and others, especially *Strategic Planning for Public and Nonprofit Organizations,* Third Edition (Bryson, 2004a) and *Leadership for Global Citizenship* (Crosby, 1999). In recent years our own research has concentrated on use of the Leadership for the Common Good framework in diverse settings, on use of specific tools and methods to help groups achieve their goals, and on leadership education.

Our main goal in writing this book is to help ordinary citizens, elected officials, business people, nonprofit activists, and public managers work with diverse stakeholder groups to develop and implement new regimes of mutual gain—that is, policy regimes serving the common good. We present the theoretical underpinnings of our framework, along with considerable guidance for putting it to use.

What Is the New Leadership for the Common Good?

Most writing about leadership, even the most recent spate, focuses on individual development and efficacy, or on organizational performance. Much of this writing deepens the understanding of how individuals develop leadership passions and capabilities, how they learn, and how they can (and sometimes fail to) serve others while caring for themselves. A few leadership scholars focus on inter-organizational leadership and policy change; examples are Jeffrey Luke (1998), Siv Vangen and Chris Huxham (Huxham and Vangen, 2000; Vangen and Huxham, 2003), and David Chrislip and Carl Larson (1994). Additionally, multiple contributions have emerged from the growing body of research into modes of organizational leadership suited to the complex, networked, fast-moving social environment of the early twenty-first century (Wheatley, 1999; Allen and Cherrey, 2000; Terry, 2001; Drath, 2001; Brown and Gioia, 2002; Gronn, 2002; Nelson, Kaboolian, and Carver, 2003). Meanwhile, scholars and practitioners continue to refine analysis of politics, public policy, social innovation, and citizenship. We attempt to bring these strands together in a comprehensive, dynamic approach that offers practical guidance for leadership, which we define as *inspiring and mobilizing others to undertake collective action in pursuit of the common good.*

The new Leadership for the Common Good framework emphasizes the importance of eight leadership capabilities:

1. *Leadership in context:* understanding the social, political, economic, and technological givens
2. *Personal leadership:* understanding self and others
3. *Team leadership:* building effective work groups
4. *Organizational leadership:* nurturing humane and effective organizations
5. *Visionary leadership:* creating and communicating shared meaning in forums
6. *Political leadership:* making and implementing decisions in legislative, executive, and administrative arenas
7. *Ethical leadership:* adjudicating disputes in court and sanctioning conduct
8. *Policy entrepreneurship:* coordinating leadership tasks over the course of a policy change cycle

These capabilities are rooted in a model of power, a model of policy change, and an approach to the common good. We emphasize the importance of stakeholder analysis and involvement throughout policy change efforts. Although we offer a general framework that should apply across contexts, we also recognize the need for specific adaptations of the framework in differing contexts—a need emphasized by a recent Harvard University Leadership Roundtable chaired by Ronald Heifetz and Philip Heyman (Pruyne, 2002).

The new edition of *Leadership for the Common Good* presents an overview of the complex fields of leadership and policy change, and although it gives practical guidance it does not present a simple recipe or cookbook. Instead, we seek to offer what Chris Huxham calls "handles for reflective practice" (Huxham, 2003, p. 420). We are guided by the wisdom of Albert Einstein, who said, "Things should be made as simple as possible, but no simpler."

In a very real sense this book is about planning, if planning is viewed as what Stephen Blum calls "the organization of hope" (Forester, 1989, p. 20; Baum, 1997). Planning, in other words, is what makes hope reasonable. The planning process in a shared-power situation, however, is quite different from the process many organizational theorists have recommended. Planning in a shared-power situation hardly ever follows a rigidly structured sequence from developing problem definitions and solutions to adopting and implementing proposals. Serious difficulties arise when people try to impose any rigidly sequential approach on a situation in which no one is in charge. Nonetheless, to be steadily effective, leaders must have an organized approach of some sort (Abramson and Lawrence, 2001). Their challenge is to instill political, technical, legal, and ethical rationality into these difficult situations; that is, they must effectively link knowledge to action (Friedmann, 1987). Therefore, we describe the kind of *procedural* rationality that can be used to effectively address *substantive* public problems, and we define the conditions and leadership actions that will support this rationality (March and Simon, 1958; Stone, 2002).

The new *Leadership for the Common Good* is chiefly concerned with enhancing practice; it draws on and develops theory in the service of practice. The four minicases highlighted in this book are used mainly to illustrate elements of the Leadership for the Common Good framework. At the same time, our study of the cases has enriched the framework and the guidance we offer for applying it. We have been personally involved in the African American Men Project and the Vital Aging Network as action researchers and educators. Our research on the AIDS and World Business Council cases draws mainly on secondary sources. We selected these cases because they involve complex public problems (AIDS, global warming, and social exclusion) that affect communities around the world, and because they involve policy entrepreneurs from business, government, and the nonprofit or voluntary sectors. If you want to update yourself on what has become a global campaign against AIDS, we suggest consulting http://www.unaids.org. Updated information about the World Business Council for Sustainable Development may be found at http://www.wbcsd.org, for the African American Men Project at http://www.aamp-mn.org, and for the Vital Aging Network at http://www.van.umn.edu.

Outline of Chapters

Part One is devoted to understanding leadership in a shared-power setting.

Chapter One introduces the idea of a shared-power world with no one in charge and contrasts two organizational forms: hierarchy and networks. In hierarchical organizations, someone or a small group is recognized as being in charge, whereas in a network of organizations and individuals many people are partly responsible for acting on important public problems and must share power if they are to find and implement effective remedies for the problems. The chapter also contrasts the rational planning model with the political policy-making model of the shared-power world and explains the importance of developing a new appreciation of public problems and potential solutions. Shared power and shared-power arrangements are defined and their causes and consequences are discussed, leading to a call for leadership for the common good. Finally, we introduce the four examples of public problem solving that are used throughout the book to illustrate our points. The campaign to eradicate AIDS highlights the need for leadership at many levels, from local to supranational. The work of the World Business Council for Sustainable Development highlights networking among business executives, and among these executives and multiple stakeholder groups to build support for environmental protection coupled with economic growth. The African American Men Project, sponsored by elected officials in Hennepin County, Minnesota, highlights collaborative leadership by public officials and community partners, and the Vital Aging case highlights a university-based response to a major demographic change, the "graying" of the baby boom generation.

Chapters Two, Three, and Four describe the eight key leadership capabilities in a shared-power world. Chapter Two focuses on leadership in context and on personal leadership; Chapter Three focuses on team and organizational leadership. Chapter Four explores visionary, political, and ethical leadership and the shared-power settings associated with them (respectively, forums, arenas, and courts). The design and use of these settings affects dramatically how public issues are framed and how public policies can deal with them. We tie these settings to a holistic view of power.

Chapter Five outlines the policy change process in shared-power settings and links the process to the common good. The process, or cycle, comprises seven phases played out as interconnected activities with shifting purposes and actors in shifting forums, arenas, and courts. Policy entrepreneurship is the label we give to the leadership work of navigating the policy change cycle.

Part Two elaborates the process of policy entrepreneurship. Chapters Six through Twelve describe in detail how to work through the policy change cycle. Each chapter describes one phase of the cycle in terms of desired outcomes; benefits; the roles of forums, arenas, and courts; and leadership guidelines, with special attention to stakeholder involvement. Chapters Six through Eight together consider the process of creating public issues, which we define as linked problems and solutions, and placing them on the public agenda. Chapter Six covers the initial agreement to do something about an undesirable condition, Chapter Seven explores the nature of public problems and presents a practical approach to formulating these problems so they can be addressed, and Chapter Eight presents effective methods for developing solutions or remedies that can ameliorate the problems. This chapter also describes how the nature of issues affects the politics of doing something about them.

Chapter Nine discusses proposal development, presents the characteristics of winning proposals, and highlights the differences between "big win" and "small win" solutions. Chapter Ten covers proposal review and adoption. This phase requires a "coupling" of change cycle elements: a recognized problem, a viable solution, a favorable political climate, reduced barriers to effective action, and a policy decision. Because political manipulation is involved, the chapter also covers agenda control, strategic voting, and alteration of an issue's dimensions in order to build or break a coalition. Chapter Eleven considers the process of policy implementation, and Chapter Twelve concludes the detailed description of the policy change cycle with a discussion of policy maintenance, modification, and termination.

Chapter Twelve also includes guidelines for getting started with leadership for the common good. The book ends with five resource sections.

The new *Leadership for the Common Good* offers a comprehensive approach to leadership as a shared-power phenomenon that embraces many individuals, organizations, and institutions. Our basic premise is that sharing power to resolve public issues is a fortunate, rather than unfortunate, necessity because it ensures that diverse voices and needs receive attention, and that implementation of solutions is more likely to succeed. Also, and fortunately, no one can give direct orders and dictate terms in a shared-power world with any assurance of compliance, but leaders do have many effective indirect methods at their disposal.

If the world's people are to survive and prosper, and if our children and grandchildren—and their children and grandchildren—are to enjoy the benefits of our ability to make the world better, all of us need ways to think and act more effectively in a shared-power context. We must deepen our understanding of the interrelated phenomena of power, change, and leadership.

Acknowledgments

Harlan Cleveland and Robert Terry—two men of big ideas—contributed greatly over the years to our understanding of leadership and power. We were privileged to work with them and receive their warm friendship and encouragement. We were deeply saddened by Bob's death from ALS two years ago and constantly miss his ability to keep us laughing in the midst of a weighty conversation.

We began the revised version of *Leadership for the Common Good* during our recent sabbatical year in Glasgow, Scotland, and are grateful to all who helped make that year an amazing time of personal renewal and intellectual stimulation for us. Gayle McPherson, Malcolm Foley, David Andersen, and Deborah Andersen were often close at hand for good conversation, food, and exchange of friendship, ideas, and household tools. We also appreciate all the others who contributed to the "stair" community in our apartment building overlooking Queens Park.

Our colleagues at the University of Strathclyde were gracious hosts who tied us into professional networks, gave us a chance to test our ideas on European audiences, and put up with our endless shipments of book boxes. Special thanks to Colin Eden, Fran Ackermann, Chris Huxham, Nic Beech, Alf Hatton, George Burt, George Cairn, Phyl Johnson, Gerry Johnson, John Bothams, Jill Shepherd, Val Turner, Sharon Gribben, Peter McInnes, Shima Barakat, Paul Hibbert, and Aiden McQuade. Other colleagues in the United Kingdom—Steve Cropper, Stephen Osborne, Kate McLaughlin, Jim Bryant, Michael Barzelay—gave us helpful feedback on our ideas about leadership and the common good. Thanks, too, to old friends Sue Richards, Roger Colori, Katherine Bradley, and Richard Bradley for welcoming us again to England and their homes.

Back at the University of Minnesota, we benefited tremendously from the interest, feedback, and support of many colleagues. John

Brandl (former Humphrey Institute dean), Sharon Anderson, Gary DeCramer, Katherine Fennelly, Donna Rae Scheffert, and Joyce Hoelting helped us think about what should be included in the revised *Leadership for the Common Good*. Melissa Stone, Marsha Freeman, Aijun Nie, Sharon Anderson, Julia Classen, and Karen Zentner Bacig have helped us probe more deeply into leadership and collaboration as part of our mutual work in developing the Humphrey Institute's new Center for Leadership of Nonprofits, Philanthropy, and the Public Sector. We also appreciate the support of Dean Brian Atwood and former Associate Dean Sandra Archibald (now dean of the Evans School of Public Policy at the University of Washington) in arranging the sabbatical that enabled us to do much of the research and writing of this book. Other university colleagues who continuously keep us exploring how best to describe and teach leadership are Stuart Albert, Rosita Albert, Ragui Assaad, Iman Ghazalla, Harry Boyte, Zbigniew Bochniarz, Arthur Harkins, Susan Atwood, June Nobbe, and Karen Lokkesmoe. During our work on this book, we've been especially blessed by having the assistance of highly dedicated and talented research assistants: Ruth Bowman, Meredith Anderson, Aaron North, and Thompson Ivory. We are constantly stimulated and challenged by the participants in our classes and workshops, from twenty-year-old undergraduates to ninety-year-old "vital agers."

Many people helped us learn about the cases featured in this book. We especially appreciate the time contributed by Gary Cunningham, Jan Hively, Kevin Winger, and Lawrence Gikaru.

A host of other scholars and practitioners have strongly influenced our thinking about leadership and public affairs over the years, notably Anthony Giddens, Beverly Stein, David Reimer, David Osborne, Jeffrey Luke, Robert Denhart, André Delbecq, Robert Einsweiler, Jerry Kaufman, Mark Moore, Judith Innes, Nancy Roberts, Brint Milward, Hal Rainey, Kimberly Boal, Ron Heifetz, James MacGregor Burns, James Kouzes, Barry Posner, Barbara Kellerman, and Jean Lipman-Blumen. Thank you, Jerry Hunt, for asking us to serve on the editorial board of *The Leadership Quarterly*, the leading scholarly journal in the field, and thus helping us to keep our fingers on the pulse of the developing field of leadership studies. We also want to single out three circles of collegiality and friendship: the Thinkle Peepers Institute (Colin Eden, Fran Ackermann, David Andersen, Charles Finn, and George

Richardson), the Missing Page Club (Michael Winer, Michael Hopkins, Ronnie Brooks, Lonnie Helgeson, Milne Kintner, and George Dow), and Women Who Talk (Yvonne Cheek, Deb Clemmensen, Milne Kintner, and Gloria Winans).

At Jossey-Bass, Dorothy Hearst has been encouraging and supportive all along the way. Allison Brunner and Xenia Lisanevich have provided superb support, and our hats go off to our copy editor, Tom Finnegan.

Finally, we want to thank John Kee Crosby Bryson and Jessica Ah-Reum Crosby Bryson for continuing to cheer us on and for putting up with our inability to quit talking about leadership and public affairs. We treasure your insights and love.

To Jessica Ah-Reum Crosby Bryson and John Kee Crosby Bryson, whose cares and concerns for the world sustain us and prompt us to think anew

The Authors

Barbara C. Crosby is an associate professor at the Hubert H. Humphrey Institute of Public Affairs, University of Minnesota, and has taught and written extensively about leadership and public policy, women in leadership, media and public policy, and strategic planning. She is the author of *Leadership for Global Citizenship* and coauthor with John M. Bryson of the first edition of *Leadership for the Common Good: Tackling Public Problems in a Shared-Power World* (Jossey-Bass, 1992). The volume won the 1993 Terry McAdam Award from the Nonprofit Management Association and was named the Best Book of 1992–93 by the Public and Nonprofit Sector Division of the Academy of Management. She serves on the editorial board of *The Leadership Quarterly*.

She is a member of the Humphrey Institute's Center for Leadership of Nonprofits, Philanthropy, and the Public Sector and former coordinator of the Humphrey Fellowship Program at the University of Minnesota. During the 2002–03 academic year, Crosby was a visiting fellow at the Graduate School of Business, University of Strathclyde, in Glasgow. For the 1992–93 academic year, she lived and studied in Oxford, England, where she was a visitor in the School of Planning, Oxford Brookes University.

A frequent speaker at conferences and workshops, she has conducted training for senior managers and educators in nonprofit, business, and government organizations in the United States, the United Kingdom, Poland, and Ukraine. Formerly, she was press secretary for Gov. Patrick Lucey of Wisconsin, speechwriter for Gov. Rudy Perpich of Minnesota, vice president of a nonprofit community development organization, and a newspaper reporter and editor.

Crosby has a B.A. degree, with a major in political science and a minor in French, from Vanderbilt University and an M.A. degree in journalism and mass communication from the University of Wisconsin-Madison. She has a Ph.D. in leadership studies from the Union Institute, where she concentrated on leadership, political philosophy, international relations, social movements, and intercultural communication.

John M. Bryson is a professor of planning and public affairs at the Hubert H. Humphrey Institute of Public Affairs at the University of Minnesota, where he also serves as associate dean for research and centers. He has been a visiting professor at the London Business School, University of Strathclyde, University of Oxford, and Oxford Brookes University.

Bryson's interests include public leadership and policy change, strategic planning, and designing participation processes. His research explores ways to improve the theory and practice of policy change and planning, particularly through situationally sensitive approaches. He has received numerous awards for his work, among them the General Electric Award for Outstanding Research in Strategic Planning from the Academy of Management and awards for best articles in the *Journal of the American Planning Association* and the *Journal of Planning Education and Research*. The second edition of *Strategic Planning for Public and Nonprofit Organizations* was named the Best Book of 1995 by the Public and Nonprofit Division of the Academy of Management. His most recent book (with Fran Ackermann, Colin Eden, and Charles Finn) is *Visible Thinking: Unlocking Causal Mapping for Practical Business Results* (2004). He serves on the editorial boards of *The Leadership Quarterly, Journal of Public Administration Research and Theory, Public Management Review,* and *Journal of Public Affairs Education.*

Bryson is a regular presenter in many practitioner-oriented training programs. He has served as a strategic planning and leadership consultant to a variety of public, nonprofit, and for-profit organizations in North America and Europe. He received a B.A. degree (1969) in economics from Cornell University and three degrees from the University of Wisconsin-Madison: an M.A. (1972) in public policy and administration, his M.S. (1974) in urban and regional planning, and his Ph.D. (1978) in urban and regional planning.

Leadership for the Common Good

Understanding Leadership in Shared-Power Settings

The Leadership for the Common Good framework is presented, along with numerous exercises to help you progress in your own leadership work. Chapter One elaborates our understanding of leadership and change in today's shared-power, no-one-in-charge world. We explain what we mean by shared power, public problems, and public problem solving. You will be introduced to leaders in the early fight against AIDS in the United States, to the initiators of the African American Men Project, to the founder of what would become the World Business Council for Sustainable Development, and to the founders of the Vital Aging Initiative (now the Vital Aging Network).

Chapter Two introduces eight leadership capabilities that are necessary for remedying public problems in a shared-power world. Two of these capabilities are explored in depth: leadership in context (understanding social, political, economic, and technological givens as well as potentialities) and personal leadership (the work of understanding and deploying personal assets on behalf of beneficial change). Chapter Three presents the elements of team leadership (building effective work groups) and organizational leadership (nurturing humane and effective organizations). Chapter Four describes forums, arenas, and courts, the main shared-power settings in which leaders and followers tackle public problems. It also focuses on visionary leadership (creating and communicating shared meaning in forums), political leadership (making and implementing policy decisions in legislative, executive, and administrative arenas), and ethical leadership (sanctioning conduct and adjudicating disputes in courts).

Chapter Five introduces the eighth leadership capability, policy entrepreneurship, or coordination of leadership tasks over the course of a policy change cycle. We describe the seven phases of the cycle, in which policy entrepreneurs work in multiple forums, arenas, and courts to remedy public problems. Finally, we suggest how policy entrepreneurs can discern and enact the common good in the policy change process.

Chapter One

When No One Is in Charge
The Meaning of Shared Power

If there is no struggle, there is no progress. . . . Power concedes nothing without a struggle. It never did and it never will.
FREDERICK DOUGLASS

We live in an era in the history of nations when there is a greater need than ever for coordinated political action and responsibility.
GRO HARLEM BRUNDTLAND

Anyone who tries to tackle a public problem or need sooner or later comes face to face with the dynamics of a shared-power world. Consider the public health officer or physician picking up the signs of a new disease affecting gay men. Or perhaps you're an elected official concerned about all the unemployed men congregating on the streets of your district. Perhaps you're a successful business-person who realizes the environmental destruction caused by industry will ultimately lead to disaster. Perhaps you're a university teacher or administrator who believes the university isn't prepared to serve the growing numbers of retirees who could have many years of productive life ahead of them.

Or you may have no professional role related to these issues; you may be the sister of a man dying of AIDS, you may have lost your job, you may be the homeowner who finds out your water supply has been contaminated by a nearby factory, or you may be someone wondering how to have a satisfying life after sixty in an ageist world.

When any of these people, whether professionals or concerned citizens, try to do something about these public problems, they may soon have the feeling of being stuck in a quagmire. They clearly cannot wave a magic wand and make everything better. Today, anyone who's involved in the fight against AIDS realizes that a host of groups and organizations need to be part of any new initiative to reduce the incidence of the disease or deal with its effects. Anyone who digs deeply into the causes of local unemployment soon finds that causes of the problem (and therefore the solutions) are tied to governmental systems, specific employers, economic institutions, schools, individual experiences and aspirations, and voluntary organizations. Anyone who tries to attack environmental destruction, reform a university, or help a society become more humane likewise soon realizes that many individuals, groups, and organizations have contributed to or are affected by the problem or need at hand, and somehow these individuals, groups, and organizations, as well as many others, will have to be part of any significant beneficial change.

This chapter elaborates our understanding of this complex, no-one-in-charge, shared-power world. To begin, we describe two contrasting types of organizational structure, planning, and decision making: what might be called an "in-charge" model, and the shared-power model. Then we explain more fully our view of public problems and shared power. We explore the causes and consequences of today's shared-power world and highlight some leadership opportunities and responsibilities in this world. Along the way, we introduce some people who have been engaged in leadership for the common good as they wrestle with public problems such as AIDS and environmental destruction. You will also have a chance to think about a public problem that is important to you and begin analyzing it in light of a shared-power view of its context.

Two Types of Organizations, Planning, and Decision Making

An enduring "ideal" organizational structure is the hierarchical pyramid, or bureaucratic model, which might be called the "in-charge organization." At the apex of such an organization resides an individual (president, CEO, director) or small group (board or top management team) that establishes organizational direction, determines guiding policies, and sends directives downward to a group of middle managers, who in turn translate policies and orders into more specific orders that are passed down to the large number of lower-level workers. Embedded in this ideal type is the assumption that the organization "contains" a problem area, or need, and engages in highly rational, expert-based planning and decision making to resolve it. The organization efficiently and effectively handles the problem or fulfills the need (Weber, 1947). Peter Marris talks about this form as a means of managing uncertainty and displacing risk downward (Marris, 1996).

Increasingly, however, this organizational structure is proving inadequate, both as a reflection of how organizations really operate and as a model of the forms most suited for today's interconnected, interdependent world. Thus another ideal type, the networked organization, has emerged. In this view, the organization itself is often a network of units, departments, and individuals; moreover, the organization is part of a variety of external networks that are fluid and chaotic. Organizations viewed in this way are part of a "multi-organizational field," or "multiactor network," of overlapping domains and conflicting authorities (Feldman and Khademian, 2000; Klandermans, 1992). Anyone who wants to influence an organization's behavior has to understand and design these internal or external networks. See Figure 1.1 for representations of an in-charge organization and of two types of networked organization.

Let's consider the example of U.S. physicians who detected unusually virulent forms of skin cancer and pneumonia among gay patients in their clinics and hospitals in the early 1980s—notably Linda Laubenstein in New York City; Marcus Conant, a dermatologist affiliated with the University of California at San Francisco; and Michael Gottlieb, an immunologist and assistant professor at the University of California at Los Angeles. The physicians soon realized as they talked with local colleagues that other physicians were encountering similar patients, who were dying because no treatments worked. Already Laubenstein, Conant, and Gottlieb were operating within a professional network. They spread their net further, however, as they sought to learn more and alert others to their observations—turning to local public health officials, the

Figure 1.1. Hierarchical and Networked Organizations.

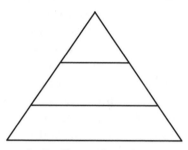

An In-Charge Organization

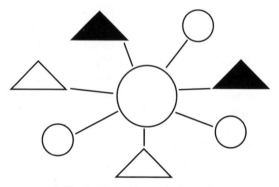

A Single-Node Network Organization

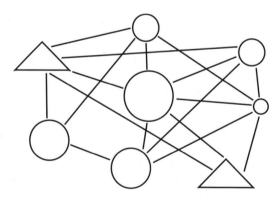

A Multinode Network Organization

national government's Centers for Disease Control, and medical journals. Now the relevant network extended to doctors' offices, clinics, university departments, journals, and public health departments. The network expansion continued, as these and other doctors worked with gay rights activists to help raise money for research into the cause of what appeared to be a new, lethal, sexually transmitted disease. New gay-led organizations emerged to support the people suffering from the new disease and promote needed research and education. The gay press began covering what their writers called the "gay plague."

The network grew even more as evidence emerged that the disease was affecting drug addicts and Haitian New Yorkers, and that it was being transmitted to hemophiliacs through the blood products they received. Now hemophiliac organizations and the blood bank industry were involved. Before long, the physicians became part of local-to-national networks, what Robert Quinn (2000) would call an adhocracy, of clinicians, infectious disease researchers, local elected officials, and gay activists who were putting pressure on members of Congress, top officials in the Reagan administration, and even the president himself to channel resources toward the effort to identify the disease and control its spread.

The organizational structure that best fit the developing AIDS crisis is illustrated in Figure 1.2, in which the problem is represented by the amorphous large blob. Within the blob are many individuals, groups, and organizations, represented by the dots, circles, and triangles—in other words, the stakeholders in the problem. (Of course, in the case of the AIDS crisis, the actual picture would be immensely more complicated since a tremendous number of people, groups, and organizations were involved.) The solid and dotted lines between some of the stakeholders represent respectively the formal and informal connections, or networks, among groups and organizations. As time went on, newly created or newly involved groups and organizations would be added to the picture.

Note that the problem spills far beyond the boundary of even the existing networks. No single person, group, or individual is "in charge" of the problem, yet many organizations are affected or have partial responsibility to act. In effect, they have a share of the power that is required for remedying the problem. Of course, this

Figure 1.2. Public Problems in a
No-One-in-Charge, Shared-Power World.

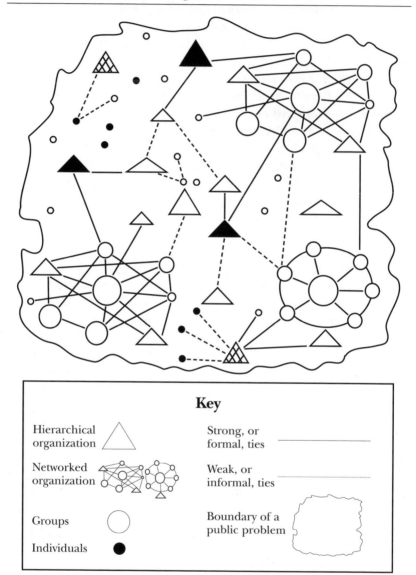

Key

Hierarchical organization △	Strong, or formal, ties ———
Networked organization	Weak, or informal, ties ·········
Groups ○	Boundary of a public problem
Individuals ●	

is not to say that all organizations have equal power (they don't) or that power is shared equally (it isn't). The organizations come in various sizes and structures, from large hierarchies to loose networks. In such a shared-power situation, part of the battle is just gaining rough agreement on what the problems are. Indeed, some of the organizations may have radically conflicting aims. The physicians trying to marshal resources to combat AIDS would have encountered some groups and organizations, such as conservative "family values" groups, that they might have wished were not involved. To the conservative groups, the real problem was gay lifestyles. In another example, public health officials who realized that practices at bathhouses frequented by gay men were a major contributor to the rapid spread of the disease faced intense resistance from bathhouse owners against any restrictions on the operation of their businesses.

In addition to coping with supportive, neutral, or hostile organizations, change advocates encounter existing networks that may be supportive, neutral, or resistant to their proposed changes. The AIDS crisis developed in the midst of a formidable set of networks, including those of officials in the Reagan administration, scientific and public health associations, groups of bathhouse owners, the gay press, and the blood bank industry. Some of the networks were political alliances, such as those between gay activists and politicians in San Francisco or among some U.S. senators and the right-wing Moral Majority.

To coordinate action and make headway on resolving a complex public problem, the organizations involved need to be aware of the whole problem system and recognize that it has to undergo significant change. The change advocates have to engage in political, issue-oriented, and therefore messy planning and decision making, in which shared goals and mission are being developed as the process moves along. New networks must be created, old ones coopted or neutralized. These networks range from the highly informal, in which the main activity is information sharing, to more organized shared-power arrangements (which are described more fully in the next section).

Further (as with the AIDS crisis, which has now reached global proportions), no matter what is done the problem is not likely to be "solved" so much as "re-solved" (Wildavsky, 1979), "dissolved" (Ackoff, 1981; Alexander, 1982), "redefined" (Mitroff and Featheringham, 1984), "continued" (Nadler and Hobino, 1998), or "finished" (Eden, 1987). Many people have power to thwart action in such a world, but few have the will, faith, hope, and courage to say yes to new initiatives. The result is that even powerful people can feel frustrated and impotent.

In a no-one-in-charge world, planning and decision making are often very different from the "rational planning" approach associated with bureaucratic hierarchy (Simon, 1947). The rational planning model, presented in Figure 1.3, begins with well-informed experts' setting goals (for example, eliminating AIDS by the year 2000, or cutting industrial air pollution by 10 percent). Policies, programs, and actions are then developed to achieve the goals. The assumption is that once the actions are taken, programs and policies will be implemented, the goals will be achieved, and the problem solved. The model makes sense, but it works well only when there is consensus on the goals, policies, programs, and actions needed to solve a problem. Moreover, it presumes agreement on how a problem should be defined, as well as what causes it.

The consensus and agreement implicit in the rational planning model are very hard to come by in a no-one-in-charge, shared-power world. The dynamics of this world accord more closely with the political decision-making model articulated by Charles Lindblom in a series of classic articles and books (Lindblom, 1959, 1965,

Figure 1.3. Rational Planning.

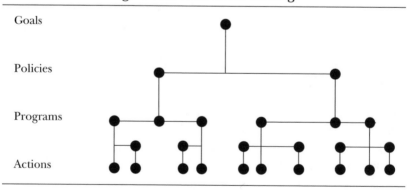

1977; Braybrooke and Lindblom, 1963). This model (Figure 1.4) begins with issues, which almost by definition involve conflict, not consensus. The conflict may be over ends, means, timing, location, political advantage, or philosophy—and it may be severe. If the effort to resolve the issue produces policies and programs, they will be *politically* rational; that is, they are acceptable to a dominant group of stakeholders (Stone, 2002; Flyvbjerg, 1998). Over time, more general policies may be formulated to capture, shape, or interpret the policies and programs initially developed to deal with the issues. These various policies and programs are, in effect, treaties among the various stakeholders, and although they may not record a true consensus at least they represent a reasonable level of agreement (Sabatier and Jenkins-Smith, 1993).

To illustrate the political decision-making model and its difference from the rational planning model, let's consider the experience of Mark Stenglein, a county commissioner for the Minnesota county containing Minneapolis; and Gary Cunningham, the county's planning director, as they wrestled with the issue of unemployment among young African American men in the county.

Stenglein's Hennepin County district includes the northwestern part of the city, one afflicted by concentrated unemployment

Figure 1.4. Political Decision Making.

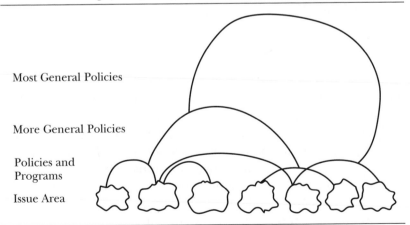

Most General Policies

More General Policies

Policies and Programs

Issue Area

and poverty. In recent years, the area also has become home for many African American residents of Minneapolis. As he drove through the area in 1999, Stenglein wondered about all the African American men he saw standing on street corners in the middle of the day. At the time the state's economy was doing very well, and he questioned why these men weren't working. He approached Gary Cunningham and asked him for an explanation.

One might have predicted a confrontation between the two men—a conservative Euro-American raising questions about the behavior of African American men with a public servant who himself was African American and had a long history of working on behalf of that community. Cunningham did remark that he had recently been in an area of Minnesota hard hit by shutdowns in the mining industry and had seen lots of white guys standing around on the streets there.

Nevertheless, Cunningham saw a chance for fact finding and proposed a formal inquiry. He already knew that although many African American men in Hennepin County were doing very well in terms of employment, financial success, and leadership roles, a substantial number were in trouble. He already knew many of the statistics:

- Each year 44 percent of the county's African American men between eighteen and thirty were arrested, mainly for minor offenses.
- Only 28 percent of male African Americans in the Minneapolis public schools were graduating on time.
- The death rate among young African American men was twice that of their white counterparts.

Moreover, a host of goals, objectives, policies, and programs had been established for these men over the years. Schools had set graduation targets, public health agencies had programs aimed at improving health care for African Americans, the court system had specific objectives for processing cases, and so on. Already, an array of government and nonprofit organizations were involved, as well as some businesses participating in hiring and retention programs. Yet none had made a real dent in the group's high unemployment, low education level, and terrible health conditions. Moreover, given the conflictual history of U.S. race relations, almost any proposed solution to problems affecting African American men was likely to invoke old and acrimonious debate over civil rights, the legacy of slavery, racism, affirmative action, welfare policy, and personal morality.

Cunningham well knew that any solutions to the problems affecting African American men would have to be multifaceted and would require contributions from a multitude of stakeholders—including African American men themselves, county commissioners and employees, businesspeople, African American families, education officials and teachers, other government bodies, and journalists. He consulted his staff, African American community leaders, other county commissioners, business leaders, and university faculty. Stenglein and fellow commissioner Peter McLaughlin persuaded the county board to authorize an in-depth study of the status of African American men in the county. Cunningham's department organized a thirty-seven-member steering committee that would guide the study and final report. Herman Milligan Jr., a vice president at Wells Fargo, agreed to chair the committee. Working teams including committee members, community advisers, and academic researchers were assembled to research issues affecting African American men and develop recommendations. These teams collected information about the issues, participated in a process to clarify the issues, and then moved to specific goals.

Even though we have drawn a sharp distinction between the rational and political decision-making models, we actually see them as complementary, rather than antithetical. They may simply need to be sequenced properly. In the typical sequence, political decision making is necessary to determine the issues and the politically acceptable policies and programs that resolve them. Rational planning can then be used to recast that agreement into technically and administratively workable goals, policies, programs, and actions. As the work teams studying the condition of African American men in Hennepin County held conversations with stakeholders, they had no clear idea of what policy changes were needed. The aim of their initial research was to understand more about the reasons these men had such a high unemployment rate or such poor health. As they consulted diverse stakeholders, the work teams encountered a number of perspectives and were caught up in sometimes heated debate over the causes of problems and the efficacy of specific solutions. Various stakeholder analysis techniques were used to array the perspectives and find common interests that could be the basis of acceptable policies and programs (Bryson, Cunningham, and Lokkesmoe, 2002). (These techniques are described in detail in Part Two of this book.) The preliminary and final reports created a unifying framework that was based on the theme "What is good for young African American men is good for the county, and vice versa" (Hennepin County, 2002). A rich array of data were presented, to support:

- Deeper understanding of African American men's lives and the social and economic conditions affecting them
- Recognition of the link between the well-being of African American men and the well-being of the broader community
- Specific recommendations for an initiative sponsored by the county board

Appreciating Problems and Solutions

It may be helpful at this point to describe more fully our view of public problems. Our understanding of public problems is expansive, moving well beyond the realm of government responsibility. To us, a public problem is one that affects diverse stakeholders and cannot be remedied by a single group or organization. Indeed, extensive collaboration and consultation among numerous stakeholders is necessary to achieve significant improvements. These problems resist any short-term, piecemeal solution because they are embedded in a complex system of interconnection and feedback effects.

Our emphasis is on large, difficult, even seemingly intractable public problems, or what Wilfred Drath (2001) calls *emergent problems*: complex problems that are as yet ill-defined and for which no clear solutions exist. Other authors have called them developmental problems (Jantsch, 1975; Bryson, 1981; Nutt, 2001). Emergent, or developmental, problems are most suitably addressed through what Geoffrey Vickers (1995) calls "acts of appreciation." Appreciation, in Vickers's usage, merges judgment of what is *real* with judgment of what is *valuable*. Recognizing and naming a new problem involves new *appreciation* of how a part of the world works, and what is wrong with it, or how it might be considerably better. This appreciation subsequently shapes the way a public problem is defined, the solutions considered, and the accommodation of stakeholder interests.

In 1990, Swiss industrialist and multimillionaire Stephan Schmidheiny was invited by Maurice Strong, secretary general of the 1992 U.N. Conference on Environment and Development (UNCED), to be the principal adviser on global business perspectives on sustainable development at the conference, to be held in Rio de Janeiro. As he and a group of like-minded businesspeople began a global campaign to change the prevailing business mentality, it was clear that destruction of the natural environment was still an emergent problem in the eyes of many business owners and managers. To the extent these people linked business practices to environmental problems, they were likely to question the severity of the problems or identify the real challenge as combating forces that would stifle economic growth. They had yet to appreciate that business success and their own future prosperity and well-being might depend on environmental protection (Schmidheiny, 1992).

Emergent or developmental problems are one of three closely linked problem types (the other two are *programming* and *operational* problems). Programming problems are created once emergent problems are understood and applicable values, norms, goals, and directions are articulated. To make progress on a programming problem, change advocates must create an effective strategy embedded in policies and programs that can resolve the problem in light of desired values, norms, goals, and directions. Once a strategy is set, the problem becomes operational; the question becomes how the strategy can best be implemented. Change agents dealing with an operational problem focus on priority setting, budgets, timetables, regulations, standard procedures, and so on.

The rational planning model would suggest addressing problems in the order presented—namely, emergent problems first, programming problems second, and operational problems third. This was the approach taken by Schmidheiny as he tried to make businesspeople aware of the threat that environmental degradation posed to business success. It was also the approach taken by the physicians who raised the alarm about the mysterious disease that would later be identified as AIDS. Often as not, however, in the real world of public policy making the process begins with operational failure. The Rio Conference on Environment and Development was convened because existing government regulations and modern business practices were failing to stem pollution and the loss of natural resources. Wildlife, seacoasts, and local fishing industries continued to be destroyed by oil spills. Reforestation programs were driving out native species. Modern food production and dissemination systems were contributing to increased obesity among U.S. and European citizens while millions of people in Africa faced famine. Fossil fuel consumption fostered global warming. Production using outmoded technologies left former Soviet countries with innumerable polluted waterways and denuded forests.

Operational failure can lead to reviewing and rehashing appropriate strategies and programming problems; rethinking appropriate and politically acceptable values, norms, or goals; or redefining appreciation of emergent or developmental problems. For example, the World Business Council has recommended a host of alternative strategies as a result of its stakeholder consultations and other research. Among them are more reliance on underused economic tools, such as full-cost pricing and polluter-pays principles. The council also has objected to setting radically different goals, and it has developed new ways of understanding the problem of environmental degradation through a call for sustainable consumption and "eco-efficiency."

We return to this discussion in Chapter Five, when we describe in more detail the process of tackling public problems. For now, we simply emphasize that change advocates can begin with operational problems and political decision making, or with emergent problems and rational planning. To be effective, however, they need to adopt a shared-power approach that includes elements of both political decision making and rational planning. At some point in the policy change process, they have to create shared-power networks of groups and organizations that engage in issue-oriented political decision making aimed at developing widely shared appreciation of what the problems are and what can be done about them. They also need to help their constituents develop shared understanding of why it is important to solve the problems, and what vision of the future they want to achieve. Additionally, change advocates face the ongoing challenge of how to establish incentives and systems of mutual accountability that keep the participants in a shared-power network working together.

Some readers may consider our focus on public *problems and needs* to be unduly negative. They might prefer that we emphasize instead *challenges,* or else the *assets* of an organization or community and how they might serve the aspiration for a better future. Indeed, we direct attention to assets and how they can be multiplied in shared-power arrangements. We will prompt policy entrepreneurs to focus on desired outcomes and better futures. We think of *problem* in keeping with its Greek roots, as something thrown forward for citizens to work with. (See Chapter Seven for elaboration of our view of public problems.)

What Do We Mean by Shared Power?

Our conception of the shared-power world began developing in the early 1980s and was influenced considerably by a 1984 Humphrey Institute conference on shared power, inspired by Harlan Cleveland and organized by John Bryson and Robert Einsweiler (see Bryson and Einsweiler, 1991, for selected conference presentations). The conference theme reflected an atmosphere of disillusionment with the grand U.S. government schemes of the 1960s and growing recognition of global interdependence and complexity. Old notions of leaders who were in charge of situations, organizations, and even nations seemed not to apply.

We were convinced that a new understanding of power was required to explain why some groups and organizations were able to accomplish significant change in such a world. Moreover, we hoped to enable many more groups and organizations to make beneficial progress on difficult public problems. As we studied successful change efforts, we realized that organizations had to find a way to tap each other's resources (broadly conceived) in order to work effectively on public problems. That is, they had to engage in sharing activities, which vary in level of commitment and loss of autonomy. Moving from least to most commitment and loss of autonomy, these are the methods of sharing:

1. Information sharing and informal coordination
2. Formal coordination through shared activities or resources to achieve a common objective

3. Shared power
4. Shared authority

We focus on shared power because this level of sharing is usually most effective in tackling difficult public problems and because it does not require the tremendous effort and cost of merging authority. (Merging authority is difficult because participants can be expected to resist the massive loss of autonomy that merger entails.) We define *shared power* following Giddens (1979, p. 90; 1984) and Bryson and Einsweiler (1991, p. 3) as *actors jointly exercising their capabilities related to a problem in order to further their separate and joint aims.* The actors may be individuals, groups, or organizations working together in order to achieve joint gains or avoid losses. Power sharing requires a common or mutual objective held by two or more actors, whether or not the objective is explicitly stated, agreed upon, or even clearly understood. Yet shared-power arrangements remain a "mixed-motive" situation, in which participants reserve the right of "exit" (Hirschman, 1970) to protect their other, unshared objectives. Of course, exit may not be easy or even possible, as when the shared-power arrangements have been mandated by a government body, foundation, or other powerful organization.

Viewed another way, shared-power arrangements exist in the midrange of a continuum of how organizations work on public problems. At one end of the continuum are organizations that hardly relate to each other or are adversaries, dealing with a problem that extends beyond their capabilities. At the other end are organizations merged into a new entity that can handle the problem through merged authority and capabilities. In the midrange are organizations that share information, undertake joint projects, or develop shared-power arrangements such as collaborations or coalitions (see also Himmelman, 1996). Particular policy change efforts are likely to involve all the relationship types along the continuum (see Figure 1.5).

To adapt a phrase from the international relations literature, leaders can think of an enduring, multiparty shared-power arrangement as a "policy regime." Stephen Krasner defines regimes as "sets of implicit or explicit principles, norms, rules, and decision-making procedures around which actors' expectations converge in a given area" (Krasner, 1983, p. 2; see also Lauria, 1997). A regime

Figure 1.5. Continuum of Organizational Sharing.

What is Shared	Mechanism for Sharing			
Authority				Merger
Power			Collaboration	
Activities & resources		Coordination		
Information	Communication			
Nothing	**None**			

is a system embracing many groups, organizations, and one or more institutions (when an institution is defined as a persistent pattern of social interaction).

Just as Krasner found the concept of the regime critical to understanding stability, change, and creation of desirable outcomes in international relations, we find it helpful in understanding how interorganizational networks can tackle complex public problems. A policy regime embodies ways of appreciating these problems and implementing strategies for remedying them. The most useful policy regime is likely to be a *regime of mutual gain,* which will tap and serve people's deepest interests in, and desire for, a better world for themselves and those they care about. A regime of this kind achieves widespread, lasting benefit at reasonable cost (Ostrom, 1990; Bellah and others, 1991; Cleveland, 1993). It is also vital to attend to those who aren't benefited by a regime of mutual gain, if it is to be truly sustainable, and to consider that differing regimes may be in destabilizing conflict with each other. Thomas Friedman describes the emergence of a "globalization" regime that has produced benefits for a large number of people of diverse backgrounds (Friedman, 2000); yet for many others, the disruption caused by this regime has been painful, even deadly (Klein, 2002; Roy, 2001). Samuel Huntington, meanwhile, describes other contemporary expansive regimes, which he calls civilizations, constituting opposing blocs that define themselves through differing cultural and political traditions (Huntington, 1996).

Let's consider how a Minnesota leader helped create a shared-power arrangement that she hopes can foster a regime of mutual gain. In 1998 Jan Hively, who has a lengthy record of public service in Minnesota, became concerned about the "graying" of her state's rural communities. Young people were migrating away from small towns, just as so-called baby boomers were nearing retirement age. Hively was working in rural Minnesota as part of her outreach job in the University of Minnesota's College of Education and Human Development. She soon joined a project sponsored by the Minnesota Board on Aging that was studying how to help older adults lead productive and satisfying lives. She was especially interested in how new technologies might be used to connect older adults with employment and service opportunities. With encouragement from an assistant commissioner in the Minnesota Department of Human Services, Hively joined Hal Freshley, from the Minnesota Board on Aging, and Darlene Schroeder, from the Elder Advocacy Network in rural Minnesota, in launching the Vital Aging Initiative, an effort to gather information about older adults' activities and interest in further education. Hively also worked with educators in the University of Minnesota Extension Service on a proposal to bolster the Vital Aging Initiative with a program that would "connect older adults across the state with education programs that support their employability, self-sufficiency, community participation, and personal enrichment" (Hively, 2002, p. 3). The university provost approved funding for the program, which sponsored forums around the state, issued publications, and started several collaborative education programs.

These efforts were the impetus for founding the Vital Aging Network (VAN), which grew out of a meeting convened by Freshley in fall 2000. The network was a shared-power arrangement; participants came from several parts of the University of Minnesota (Extension Service, Continuing Education, and other departments), the Minnesota Board on Aging, the Department of Human Services, and nonprofit senior organizations and networks. The participants began meeting regularly to share information and plan specific projects, such as a Vital Aging Summit and a VAN Website. The university supplied funds, staffing, and technical support for starting the Website; other organizations provided planning assistance and convened meetings. Following the summit, the VAN organizers developed an ambitious plan to promote a "strengths-based perspective" on aging instead of "the traditional needs-based perspective" (Hively, 2002, p. 7). Hively, Freshley, and Schroeder clearly envisioned a new regime of mutual gain, which Hively described as a "grassroots liberation movement" breaking down stereotypes and linking older adults with resources that help them be productive citizens (Hively, 2002).

You may now want to analyze a public problem that concerns you in light of the shared-power model. Exercise 1.1 poses some questions that should help. You may also want to consult Exhibit 1.1, which defines the main concepts introduced so far in this chapter. The next section continues the discussion of a shared-power world by considering why shared-power regimes are increasingly necessary.

Causes and Consequences of a Shared-Power World

Today's shared-power world arises from a number of interconnected causes and produces many interconnected consequences. At the outset of the twenty-first century, many wise observers have described the growing interdependence, complexity, and diversity of human societies, which is due to the information revolution, the

Exercise 1.1. Understanding
Public Problems in a Shared-Power World.

1. Identify a need or problem in your organization, community, nation, or beyond that requires cooperation or collaboration among diverse individuals, groups, or organizations.

2. Who are the main stakeholders (those affected by the problem; those with responsibility for resolving it; those with resources, including knowledge, that relate to the problem)?

3. Describe the existing connections among these stakeholders:
   - Which networks and coalitions exist?
   - Which policy regimes are important?

4. In what ways is this an emergent, programming, or operational problem?

5. Which individuals and groups might have a passion for remedying the problem?

**Exhibit 1.1. Tackling Public Problems
in a Shared-Power World: Some Definitions.**

Term	Definition
Public problem	Affects diverse stakeholders Cannot be solved by single organization Likely to demand extensive collaboration Resists short-term, piecemeal solution
Emergent or developmental problem	Complex problem that is as yet ill-defined and for which no clear solutions exist
Programming problem	Created once emergent problems are understood and applicable values, norms, goals, and directions are articulated
Operational problem	Concerns how strategies can best be implemented
Stakeholders	Individuals, groups, or organizations that are affected by a public problem, have partial responsibility to act on it, or control important resources
Shared power	Actors jointly exercising their capabilities related to a problem in order to further their separate and joint aims
Shared-power world	Highly networked policy environment in which many individuals, groups, and organizations have partial responsibility to act on public problems, but not enough power to resolve the problems alone; power is fragmented; decision making is messy and seemingly chaotic; shifting coalitions form and dissipate

**Exhibit 1.1. Tackling Public Problems
in a Shared-Power World: Some Definitions, Cont'd.**

Term	Definition
Shared-power arrangements	Partnerships, coalitions, collaborations, regimes
Policy regimes	Sets of implicit or explicit principles, norms, rules, and decision-making procedures around which actors' expectations converge in a given policy area (based on Krasner, 1983, p. 2)
Regimes of mutual gain	Achieve widespread lasting benefit at reasonable cost; tap and serve people's deepest interest in, and desire for, a better world for themselves and those they care about

burgeoning global arms trade and terrorist threats, the dominance of the global market economy, the scale of environmental problems, massive refugee flows within continents and across oceans, rising demands for human rights, and a declining capacity to govern. The result is a world in which rapid, often unpredictable, change is ubiquitous and not always beneficent.

The Wired and Wireless World

In April 2002, the one billionth personal computer was shipped from a manufacturer. About half of the first billion are actually installed, and most are connected to the Internet. Another billion are expected to be shipped by 2007 (Blasko, 2002).

The explosion in computing power, the spread of personal computers, and the advance of wired and wireless telecommunications technologies have produced a massive and rapid flow of information around the world. Because the Internet can permit access to a host of networks and because centralized authorities have difficulty controlling it, in some ways it allows individuals or small groups to become more powerful political and economic actors. This marriage of computers and communications technology (Cleveland, 2002) has led to what some observers call the knowledge economy, which is increasingly supplanting the manufacturing economy and which requires a labor force of knowledge workers. In this wired world, "virtual teams" and "virtual organizations" are not only possible but often required.

The explosion of computing and communications technology has a host of benefits, but it also brings new difficulties. For example, many of us are burdened by the expectation that we will be constantly hooked up and available. We can see danger in the assumption that because information is more quickly obtainable, decisions will be made and implemented more quickly. We also find it difficult to assess the reliability of some of the information that is so accessible. We struggle to manage relationships, teams, and organizations without much face-to-face interaction. Our tendency toward short-term thinking and a desire for instant gratification may be reinforced (Hutton, 2003).

Social critics highlight the division between those who have access to the new technologies and those who don't. If the new dominant theme is "I am connected, therefore I exist" (Rifkin, 2000, p. 208), then to be disconnected is to not exist. Of those billion computers, 63.4 percent went to buyers in the United States; Japan received 9 percent of the shipments. Only 4.1 percent went to buyers in all of Latin America. "In a society built around access relations," Jeremy Rifkin says, "whoever owns the channels of communication and controls the passageways into the networks determines who is a player and who sits out" (2000, p. 178). Additionally, those who have knowledge skills are far more attractive employees in a wired world than those without such skills.

Global Arms Trade and the Threat of Terrorism

Scientific advances of the twentieth century gave human beings tremendous collective power to make the world better (through, for example, vaccines against terrible diseases such as smallpox, or systems for delivering safe drinking water) as well as frightening power to destroy it (through, for example, nuclear warfare). As we noted in our earlier version of this book, over the last several decades supposedly advanced nations have used technological breakthroughs to build enough nuclear and chemical weaponry to destroy virtually every living thing. Now people worry that a relatively small group of terrorists affiliated with political or religious factions will also gain access to some of these weapons. Meanwhile, vast numbers of "conventional" arms are produced (mainly by U.S., European, and Russian companies) and help to fuel ongoing conflict in some of the world's poorest nations. (For extensive information on global arms production and trade, see the Website of the Stockholm International Peace Research Initiative, http://www.sipri.se.)

Global Economy

The global market economy has risen to ascendance in the wake of the dissolution of the Soviet empire. Thomas Friedman's *The Lexus and the Olive Tree* (2000) offers statistics and stories to demonstrate the tremendous recent growth in the flow of capital, goods, services, and information in the global marketplace. The growth of transportation systems and advanced telecommunications and computing facilitates this flow. In *The Age of Access*, Rifkin argues that networks are in a sense replacing markets in this economy; he identifies a shift away from actual exchange of tangible property to "short-term access between servers and clients operating in a network relationship" (2000, p. 4).

The global economy brings both expanded opportunities and threats. New communications technology, for example, makes it possible for a technical adviser in India to efficiently serve computer users in the United States; improved transportation contributes to the global spread of AIDS. Workers in one country may lose their jobs when a factory relocates halfway round the world, bringing jobs to another group of people; meanwhile, international mechanisms for preventing worker exploitation and destruction of natural resources are weak. Local cultures may be threatened by the influx of multinational food chains and entertainment media.

Several observers worry about the effect global economic forces have on social cohesion. Rifkin describes the emerging world as a place in which "virtually every activity outside the confines of family relations is a paid-for experience, a world in which traditional reciprocal obligations and expectations—mediated by feelings of faith, empathy, and solidarity—are replaced by contractual relations in the form of paid memberships, subscriptions, admission charges, retainers, and fees" (Rifkin, 2000, p. 9).

Environmental Degradation

Such environmental problems as global warming, acid rain, and pollution of waterways and seas know no national boundaries. The pollutants spewed from a factory's smokestack in one country may destroy forests in another country. CO_2 emissions from cars in an urban center contribute to climate change for the entire world. (Meanwhile, the oxygen produced by rainforests in Brazil benefits people in other countries as well.) In November 2002 a crippled oil tanker spilled thousands of tons of fuel oil near Spain's Galician coast, damaging one of Europe's richest coastal habitats and devastating the local fishing industry. The boat, on its way from Latvia, had been built in Japan, was flagged in the Bahamas, was piloted by a Greek captain and owned by a Greek company, and was insured by a British company. A Dutch company tried to salvage oil from the wreckage.

The need to reduce environmental damage also causes tension between the industrialized nations and poor nations. Representatives of poor nations question the fairness of international efforts to control pollution from their developing industries, when the nations that are already industrialized did not face such restrictions as their economies developed, and when some of those nations are still unwilling to do their part to cut pollution.

Population Shifts

The number of refugees fleeing their home country because of war, famine, or oppression has grown tremendously in recent years. The Office of the U.N. High Commissioner for Refugees estimates that about twenty million of the world's people are refugees and another thirty million have been displaced within their own country (http://www.unhcr.ch/un&ref/numbers/numbers.htm). Additionally, immigrants seeking better economic opportunity continue flowing across national borders. The receiving countries gain workers and increased ethnic diversity, but they also experience tension between old and new cultures, and social services may be overtaxed. Our own state of Minnesota is a prime example. The aftermath of the Vietnam War brought an influx of refugees from Vietnam, Laos, and Cambodia; according to 2000 census data, the state is home to 42,000 Hmong Americans, 18,500 Vietnamese Americans, and 5,500 to 6,500 Cambodian Americans. Recently, Somalian refugees have settled in the state, along with smaller groups from Sierra Leone, Zaire, and Sudan. The state also continues to attract a sizeable number of immigrants from Central and South America.

Another important population shift is migration within a country from rural to urban areas, a movement that in many cases overwhelms the urban infrastructure. City residents thus find they have an interest in improving business opportunities in rural areas in order to decrease the exodus from the countryside.

Growth in the Demand for Human Rights and Democratic Governance

An international human rights regime has taken hold in the last three decades. Comprising most of the world's nations, a series of U.N. treaties, U.N. conferences, a host of civil society organizations, and various (often weak) enforcement mechanisms, this regime in a sense makes the citizens of every country responsible for all the other citizens of the world. The regime is also a force for democratization and thus for the spread of power to many more of the world's people, since it supports everyone's right to participate in the decisions that affect his or her life.

Other forces contributing to democratization are the downfall of the Soviet Union, the information revolution, the demands of a market economy, and the spread of education (Cleveland, 2002). New and emerging democracies (South Africa, Nigeria, Poland, the Czech Republic, and others) still are struggling to build sustainable democratic systems, but they have made tremendous progress. Even in China, the last remaining major Communist power, the state has considerably loosened control over citizens' lives.

Decline in Capacity to Govern, Blurred Boundaries

Interconnectedness, speed, and complexity have reduced the capacity of any single organization, especially a government, to manage and to govern (Peters, 1996b; Kettl, 2000). Management professor Peter Vaill expresses this state vividly when he describes today's organizations as operating in "permanent whitewater" (Vaill, 1996). The shared-power, no-one-in-charge world is one of shifting currents, impermanent coalitions, seemingly chaotic decision making, and what Janowitz (1978) calls "weak regimes." Moreover, the distinctions between domestic and global affairs are eroding. The same is true for distinctions among the responsibilities of local, state, or provincial governments and national governments; among business, government, and civil society; and between policy areas (Kellerman, 1999; Kettl, 2000, 2002). The United States may have emerged as the world's sole superpower, but this does not mean that unilateral action by the United States is well received or even effective (Sarder and Davies, 2002). The United States will continue to need allies in pursuing its goals. Meanwhile, China and regional groupings, notably the European Union, continue to gather strength.

Charles Handy, another well-known management professor, predicts more federalist structures will be developed to cope with this turbulent world: "Societies will break down into smaller units but will also regroup into even larger ones than now for particular purposes. Federalism, an old doctrine, will become fashionable once again, in spite of its inherent contradictions" (1996, p. 7). He believes that businesses too need to be more federalist. Jean Lipman-Blumen, a professor of organizational behavior and management, echoes his view as she heralds "the connective era" characterized by "loosely structured global networks of global organizations and nations tied to multiple subnetworks, living in a clumsy federated world (and sharing space in the archetype of interdependence, the natural environment). These networks link all kinds of groups, with long chains of leaders and supporters who communicate, debate, negotiate, and collaborate to accomplish their objectives" (Lipman-Blumen, 1996, p. 9).

In such a world, governance is increasingly shared among governments, civil society organizations, and businesses (Peters, 1996b;

Rifkin, 2000; Cleveland, 2002; Holliday, 2002). Handy adds, "The softer words of leadership and vision and common purpose will replace the tougher words of control and authority because the tougher words won't bite any more" (1996, p.7).

In other words, the demand for shared-power arrangements is growing. Such arrangements are designed to increase governance and management capacity in this world that is *functionally* interconnected but *structurally* divided, and in which structural separations are often based on strongly held ideological beliefs. Such shared-power arrangements are not easy solutions to easy problems. Instead, they are usually difficult-to-implement-and-manage responses to thorny problems.

The Need for Leadership

For some people, attention to the shared-power world may evoke cynicism and despair. They say this is just more of what we already knew: powerful elites have their shared-power arrangements, from interlocking corporate directorships to organized crime. These elites make the rules, control the resources, and even determine what counts as knowledge and rationality (see Flyvbjerg, 1998).

This perspective is refuted by the cases of policy change we have studied and the complex, comprehensive view of leadership we have developed. In our view, potential for effective leadership lies alike with those who do and do not have formal positions of power and authority. Indeed, this view of leadership may be most useful in reminding those with little formal authority how powerful they can be through collaboration (Marris, 1996), and in reminding those in a supposedly powerful position just how much they rely on numerous stakeholders for any real power they have. Ours is not a zero-sum view. A shared-power arrangement enhances the power of the participants beyond the sum of their separate capabilities. Moreover, our view is based on an expansive model of what constitutes power. We see power as not just the ability to make and implement decisions (a traditional view) but also the ability to sanction conduct and, most important, to create and communicate shared meaning (an understanding that is elaborated in Chapter Three).

Leaders who focus on building shared-power arrangements enhance the power of the groups involved by reducing the risk for the participants and by sharing responsibility. If things go well, no person or group gets all the credit, but if things go badly they won't get all the blame either. Second, leaders of a change effort can use a shared-power arrangement simply to manage complexity and interconnectedness—as in a policy network, interorganizational or intergovernmental agreement, federation, business-government partnership, or a variety of other collaborations.

Finally, leaders can change how they view interconnectedness. A perception of risk and complexity may be more a consequence of a particular worldview than of a changed reality (Luke, 1991). For people in societies (such as the United States) that value autonomy and capacity for unilateral action, interconnectedness often means undesirable complexity and risk. It is possible, however, to value interconnectedness as a good in itself because it is a reflection of our situation in societies and in the natural environment (Wheatley, 1999, 2002; Youngblood, 1997). In *Bowling Alone,* Robert Putnam highlights research that indicates people who have multiple social connections are likely to be healthier and happier than people with few connections (Putnam, 2000). He also argues persuasively that rich social networks (social capital) benefit the societies in which they are embedded—by, for example, establishing a culture of reciprocity and helping people be more productive.

Using and creating social networks was crucial for the progress that change advocates such as Marcus Conant and Michael Gottlieb were able to make in California during the early years of the AIDS crisis. These and other physicians, public health officials, and gay activists teamed up in 1982 to generate resources for research and for support of AIDS sufferers. Tangible results included creation of the Kaposi's Sarcoma Research and Education Foundation (later the AIDS Foundation); funding from San Francisco's board of supervisors for an AIDS clinic, a nonprofit program supporting people with AIDS, and an education program to be conducted by the new foundation; and funds from the California legislature for AIDS research. Cooperative arrangements among medical researchers also contributed to progress in identifying the AIDS virus. In 1985, when Rock Hudson's death and a growing number of nongay deaths (along with a horrifying level of deaths among gay men) finally made it impossible for citizens and their elected representatives to ignore the disease, the preexisting collaborations among AIDS activists, medical professionals, congressional staff, and others were a foundation for concerted progress on a number of fronts.

By approving the African American Men Project, Hennepin County commissioners were establishing a shared-power arrangement that brings leaders from community and nonprofit groups together with elected officials, university researchers, and public professionals to break an oppressive cycle that has trapped African American men and deprived their families and the broader community of their potential as citizens, workers, and fathers. The arrangement has produced public conferences, impressive research studies, and commitment from the county board and community partners to a host of specific actions.

The corporate executives who have joined the World Business Council for Sustainable Development not only are participating in a shared-power arrangement (the council) but are promoting numerous additional shared-power arrangements—for example, an international system of quality standards and binding international agreements to reduce emissions of greenhouse gases—that are good for business and the environment.

The founders of the Vital Aging Network have maximized their impact by creating a network of networks. Some of those networks—such as university campuses, libraries, and senior centers—have considerable resources that can be marshaled on behalf of VAN. Other networks may have little money and minimal infrastructure, but they bring the energy of active citizens who can supply firsthand knowledge of community needs, as well as personal experience and hope for the future. The VAN Website is a powerful tool for making the resources of these networks accessible to older adults throughout the state; the Website also attracts users from elsewhere in the United States and even outside the country. Aging activists in other states have created Websites based on the VAN design and linked them to that site.

Our view of leadership speaks to people's yearning for empowerment and improved prospects for themselves and their children (Burns, 2003). It is democratic work of the type championed by political philosophers Mary Dietz (2002) and Harry Boyte (1989). Both are interested in a revitalized citizenship, or democratic work, that "entails the collective and participatory engagement of historically situated and culturally constituted persons-as-citizens in the determination of the affairs of their polity" (Dietz, 2002, p. 35).

Notions of a shared-power world and the desire to revitalize or expand democracy have caused the old image of the leader as the one in charge of a hierarchical organization to diminish considerably since we wrote the first version of this book. At the start of the twenty-first century, images such as "catalytic leader," "co-leader," "connective leader," "quiet leader," and even "invisible leader" have become prominent. Shared, collaborative, collective, and distributed leadership are recognized and lauded.

Leaders rooted in a networked world may or may not have positions of authority. They inspire and motivate constituents through persuasion, example, and empowerment, not through command and control. They lead up and out rather than down, to borrow imagery from Mark Moore (1995) and Dee Hock (2002). Such leaders foster dialogue with their constituents and the situations in which they find themselves, and they encourage collective action to tackle real problems. Further, they claim and make use of the powers they do have to push for changes in a world often resistant to their demands. As the antislavery leader Frederick Douglass found, leaders must forcefully wield their own power if they expect to overcome entrenched power.

All this does not mean that the in-charge leadership image has disappeared or completely lost its usefulness. The connective or quiet leader sometimes has to make a decision and implement it using whatever powers and controls he or she has. Similarly, leaders who are formally in charge know they often must consult and compromise with other powerful people before acting. In a shared-power situation, however, leadership that encourages the participation of others must be emphasized because only it has the power to inspire and mobilize those others. In the effort to tackle public problems, leadership and power must be consciously shared with a view to eventually creating power-sharing institutions within a regime of mutual gain. As Robert Bellah and his coauthors argue, "The public lives through those institutions that cultivate a constituency of conscience and vision. To achieve the common good, leaders and citizens create and sustain such institutions and use them to change other institutions" (Bellah and others, 1991, p. 271).

Summary

If you seek to bring about major social change—whether it be halting the spread of AIDS or improving economic opportunities in your community—you need to understand and act in accordance with the dynamics of today's shared-power world. In this world, public problems such as AIDS or poverty are embedded in a complex system of diverse, interconnected parts. Many individuals, groups, and organizations have some stake in the problem, but no one of them has enough power to resolve it alone.

In such a world, leaders cannot rely on hierarchic bureaucratic models to bring about needed change. Rational planning on its own is ineffective. Instead, leaders must increasingly focus on building and altering shared-power arrangements within and among organizations, and they must engage in political decision making. These strategies should be aimed at developing a widely shared understanding of a public problem and potential solutions, and at building coalitions to support proposed changes and eventually establish a regime of mutual gain. To foster understanding of a complex public problem, leaders should promote an appreciative approach that helps participants delve into multiple causes and consequences of the problem and develop a sense of desired improvements.

The heightened importance of a shared-power perspective stems from several interrelated developments: the effects of advanced telecommunications and computer technology, the proliferation of nuclear and conventional arms and fear of terrorism, the ascendance of the market economy, continued degradation of the natural environment, a massive flow of refugees across national borders along with an exodus from rural to urban areas, increased demand for human rights, and a decline in the capacity to govern. These developments and the complexity of the shared-power model can be daunting for those undertaking major change efforts, but they can also be viewed as offering multiple opportunities and levers for an expansive and inclusive style of leadership. The next chapter considers several of the leadership capabilities encompassed by this new approach.

Chapter Two

Leadership Tasks in a Shared-Power World

Leadership in Context, and Personal Leadership

*Human progress is neither automatic nor inevitable.
Even a superficial look at history reveals that no social
advance rolls in on the wheels of inevitability. Every step
towards the goal of justice requires sacrifice, suffering,
and the tireless exertions and passionate concern of
dedicated individuals.*
MARTIN LUTHER KING JR.

*It always takes a group of people working together
with a common purpose in an atmosphere of trust
and collaboration to get extraordinary things done.*
JAMES KOUZES AND BARRY POSNER

In a shared-power world, beneficial change doesn't happen without committed, concerted action by groups of people. To be effective, these change agents must draw on a variety of leadership capabilities:

- *Leadership in context:* understanding the social, political, economic, and technological givens as well as potentialities
- *Personal leadership:* understanding and deploying personal assets on behalf of beneficial change
- *Team leadership:* building effective work groups

- *Organizational leadership:* nurturing humane and effective organizations
- *Visionary leadership:* creating and communicating shared meaning in forums
- *Political leadership:* making and implementing decisions in legislative, executive, and administrative arenas
- *Ethical leadership:* sanctioning conduct and adjudicating disputes in courts
- *Policy entrepreneurship:* coordinating leadership tasks over the course of a policy change cycle

The first two of these capabilities (leadership in context and personal leadership) are especially important at the outset of any effort to achieve the common good in a shared-power world. This chapter focuses on those two capabilities; the next chapter turns to team and organizational leadership. Chapter Four describes forums, arenas, and courts (the three key settings for tackling public problems in a shared-power world) and the types of leadership (visionary, political, and ethical) associated with each. Policy entrepreneurship is covered in Chapter Five. Even though the capabilities build on each other and all are vital to a change effort, we recognize that some leaders are better at certain ones. A leader may have a "home base" among the eight but need some understanding of the others.

The eight capabilities are distilled in part from the main approaches to leadership in scholarly and popular literature. Over the last two decades, we have worked with Robert Terry and other colleagues at the Reflective Leadership Center (now the Center for Leadership of Nonprofits, Philanthropy, and the Public Sector) to deepen our understanding of these capabilities and their connection to power and to social change. The guidance we offer here draws on our work with individuals, groups, and organizations aspiring to lead for the common good, as well as on case studies and recently published research by ourselves and others. The guidance expands on the original version of *Leadership for the Common Good* and on *Leadership for Global Citizenship* (Crosby, 1999).

We could write a book about each capability. Indeed, many books have been written about most of them, especially on particular aspects of personal, team, and organizational leadership. Here we merely highlight what we consider the most vital aspects for leadership in a shared-power world and point toward sources of further guidance. Don't be surprised if some of our advice seems contradictory. As Chris Huxham and Nic Beech (Beech and Huxham, 2003) point out, those who engage in collaborative leadership live with tension among "best practices." Now more than ever, leaders must become adept at dealing with ambiguity and paradox (Terry, 2001; Drath, 2001).

We also could write an extended essay on the debate over the meaning of leader and leadership. We are among those arguing that the label *leader* is fluid; it may suitably be applied to all kinds of people, regardless of position or background. Some people practice leadership so habitually that those who know them refer to them as leaders. Some people may lead less frequently. Certainly the person who leads in one situation may not lead in another. We agree with Harlan Cleveland (2002) that all of us are followers most of the time.

Some people are surrounded by expectations that they will provide leadership, and they may or may not live up to those expectations. Additionally, expectations about who leads, and how, are greatly influenced by culture.

Distinguishing between leader and leadership is important. We generally see leadership as a broader concept because it implies a number of people leading at different times and in varying ways over the course of a policy change effort. Leadership is a relational practice, embracing those who lead and those who follow (also called followers, constituents, disciples, citizens; see Burns, 1978; Rost, 1991; Burns, 2003). Leadership for the common good requires a high degree of mutuality among leaders and followers. As Wilfred Drath notes: "Leadership happens when people who acknowledge shared work use dialogue and collaborative learning to create contexts in which that work can be accomplished across the dividing lines of differing perspectives, values, beliefs, cultures, and more generally what I refer to as differing worldviews" (Drath, 2001, p. 15). This definition leaves open the possibility that leadership may be happening within a community that itself is in conflict with other communities that do not seek collaboration to accomplish shared work.

The meaning of follower and followership is also worth exploring. We tend to use *follower, constituent, citizen, participant,* and other synonyms interchangeably and take the active view of followership explicated by Robert Kelley in *The Power of Followership* (1992). In other words, leaders and followers are mutually empowering. For us, the follower label also is fluid. As Cleveland (2002) points out, citizens often lead their titular leaders. For example, at the end of 2002, Turkish Cypriots rose up in protest to inform their resistant president that it was time to make peace with Greek-controlled Cyprus. The people wanted to benefit from participation in the European Union, and they knew continued division of their island was preventing that. Similarly, public officials have often had to be convinced by outraged citizens and concerned professionals that offenses such as drunk driving or child abuse had to be stopped. Citizen pressure was a prime force in finally convincing senior Reagan administration officials to live up to their leadership responsibilities by channeling resources to prevention and treatment of AIDS. In a relational, reciprocal view of leadership, influence flows both ways among leaders and followers, and distinctions are blurred.

Yet, as Drath argues, despite the increased need for leadership explicitly based on mutuality and shared work (that is, participatory leadership), more traditional modes of leadership can still be effective. Command and control (what Drath calls dominance) or reliance on the influence of a central figure may be most effective in some situations. An individual leader may find she uses all three of these approaches (participation, dominance, and influence) in the course of a day, depending on what type of problem her group or community is trying to solve and how she and other participants view leadership.

Starting Places for Leadership for the Common Good

Leadership erupts at the intersection of personal passion and public need. The call to leadership arises from the conjunction of intense personal concern and the urgent demands or needs of the world. Thus leaders respond to both an inner and an outer call. They develop what the authors of *Walking the Talk* describe as a "deeper anticipation of the silent currents that move the world and a commitment to make a lasting contribution to society" (Holliday, Schmidheiny, and Watts, 2002, p. 128). They are practicing leadership in context and personal leadership.

As a starting place for understanding your own call to leadership, we recommend the "cares and concerns" exercise included here. Exercise 2.1 prompts you to focus on what you deeply care about in your context and to think about how this "public passion" might call you to leadership. Our experience is that people lead around what matters to them. Indeed, if you do not care about a mission, a goal, or an activity, you can hardly be expected to inspire others to care about it.

The personal leadership section focuses further on understanding yourself and others in relation to the cares and concerns that emerge from your context. For now, let's delve further into leadership in context. (Indeed, analyzing your context may help you decide what your cares and concerns really are.)

Leadership in Context

The work of leadership in context is understanding social, political, economic, and technological "givens," and identifying the latent or inherent potentialities and opportunities for change. By *givens* we mean those taken-for-granted systems and practices that shape social activities. We put quotes around the term here to signify the possibility that even the most solid tradition can crumble.

Exercise 2.1. Discovering Cares and Concerns.

---

1. What do I deeply care about in my family, occupational, and community (or public) life? What are my main concerns connected to my family, occupational, and community (or public) life? In other words, what truly matters to me?

2. What is the extent of my commitment to acting on these cares and concerns? Is there a gap between what I really care about and how I spend my time?

3. How do or might my cares and concerns summon me to leadership?

By *potentialities,* we mean the scope for possible change, the opportunity spaces that may open up (Bryson, 1981).

A prime skill for leading in context is *awareness of continuity and change.* Some aspects of human social, political, and economic systems have endured for centuries—family and tribal arrangements, nations, cities, trade. Ancient stories from Greek, Chinese, Egyptian, or aboriginal cultures still resonate today; they are not about an alien race on an alien planet. Specific practices and systems may have shorter duration, yet still acquire a taken-for-granted status. They become part of the givens of our existence. In the United States, a federal form of representative government and a market economy are taken for granted. In other parts of the world, a parliamentary system, a religious state, or an informal economy might be the dominant tradition.

Those who seek to tackle major social problems can't afford to ignore traditional systems, but they can't afford to assume that they are static either. The breakup of the former Soviet Union, the institution of a common currency among European states, the move to a global economy, a permanent space station, advances in human rights, the information revolution, global warming—all are examples of change in taken-for-granted conditions. Moreover, these changes are bringing additional changes in their wake.

If you are working at the local level—and most of us are—it's important to consider the forces of continuity and change in your community. Perhaps a political and economic elite has dominated local politics for as long as anyone can remember. Signs of change may be emerging. Perhaps the old "bosses" are growing old; new ethnic groups may be settling in; old industries may be struggling, while new technologies foster opportunities for aspiring entrepreneurs.

Let's consider some forces of continuity and change that are context for the change efforts highlighted in this book. In the case of the early AIDS crisis, physicians, health officials, and gay activists operated in a society in which prejudice and discrimination against gay and lesbian people were still a strong force, but where gay and lesbian activists had also won significant political gains. Ironically, the understandable desire (among gay activists and their supporters) to protect hard-won rights in the face of continued prejudice contributed to unwillingness to confront practices that helped AIDS spread.

As physicians such as Linda Laubenstein, Marcus Conant, and Michael Gottlieb sought resources for treating AIDS patients and preventing the spread of the disease, they had to deal with a federal political system of partly separated and partly overlapping powers (among executive, legislative, and judicial branches and among local, state, and national governments). Gottlieb and Conant also had to negotiate the public university systems of which they were a part.

The U.S. AIDS crisis also emerged in a market economy, wherein businesses (whether bathhouses or blood banks) operate with great freedom. The business sector also provides much of the nation's health care, drugs, and other medical products.

Additionally, the United States has a tradition of developing nonprofit, or civil society, organizations for handling what markets and governments won't or can't. Advocacy and service organizations with an interest in the emerging AIDS crisis included "religious right" affiliates, gay rights groups, some hospitals and clinics, nonprofit blood banks, and medical research foundations. Public health officials and physicians were also part of national and global professional associations.

As for technological systems, those trying to understand and prevent the spread of AIDS could benefit from newly developed equipment such as cell sorters. Yet massive funding would be needed to build research labs to identify the cause of AIDS and develop tests and treatments for the disease, as well as a vaccine against it.

Some epidemiologists studying the disease that would be known as AIDS realized the potential for its becoming a global epidemic. They and other health professionals believed that some of the same structures set up to fight major public health threats—structures such as the National Institutes of Health in the United States and the World Health Organization—could launch the immense research and education campaigns that would be needed to curb the disease.

In the World Business Council case, advocates of sustainable development had to be aware of population trends, the dominance of industrialized nations in many international governance systems, and political trends within nations. For example, prospects for U.S.

ratification of the Kyoto protocols were considerably diminished by the outcome of the nation's 2000 presidential and 2002 congressional elections. Advocates of sustainable development also need to understand the structure of local and national economies and implications of the growth of global markets. They are aware of the potential for worse destruction on the one hand and for great improvements through development of renewable energy sources and through smarter management and consumption on the other.

In the African American men case, Mark Stenglein, Gary Cunningham, Herman Milligan, and many other leaders needed to understand shifts in family structures in African American communities. They needed to recognize the continued force that racial prejudice exerted on individuals and institutions. They needed to understand the distinctive, yet overlapping, responsibilities of county, municipal, state, and federal governments and local school districts. They had to attend to economic and technological trends that devalued unskilled labor. They grasped the potential of a large group of citizens for contributing to the economy and to their families.

Jan Hively and her colleagues focused on the graying of the population—a social trend affecting not just Minnesota but the nation and other industrialized societies. In many rural areas, the trend is especially problematic, because so many young people are leaving for urban areas. Meanwhile, advances in medical technology help people who have reached retirement age remain in good health. Fewer younger workers might mean there will be continued demand for older workers' skills. Additionally, the so-called young-old may be a market for new kinds of educational programs that offer ways to update their expertise and put it to use. The founders of VAN also needed awareness of government programs on aging, of advocacy and service groups focusing on aging, and of the existing role of universities and other educational institutions in serving older citizens. They were alert to the potential of new communications technology that could help retirees connect with opportunities.

In addition to analyzing forces of continuity and change and hidden potentialities, change advocates should consider whether they are seeking major reform or a revolution—that is, a whole new way of thinking and dramatic change in social, political, economic, or technological systems. If a revolution is required, leaders have to organize a social movement to carry it out. The revolution may also begin with a coup d'état, replacing a controlling group that opposes change; but eventually a social movement has to be developed to support any far-reaching, lasting change. Change efforts often combine reform and revolution. That is, a series of reforms guided by revolutionary thinking can add up eventually to revolution.

Hively, Hal Freshley, Darlene Schroeder, and others saw the need for a radically different way of thinking about people in their sixties and beyond. They envisioned new systems for connecting and serving these people and for deploying their expertise. They seeded a vital aging movement in Minnesota. In effect, by addressing a public problem (the graying of the population, combined with ageism), they created a movement that is likely to create resources for resolving many other public problems.

Stephan Schmidheiny and his colleagues are promoting a drastically different worldview and practices in the business sector. To a certain extent, they are calling businesspeople to develop or join a movement within the larger environmental movement. They are calling on businesses to adopt eco-efficiency as an operating principle and become part of the solution to environmental degradation and the gap between rich and poor communities as well as between rich and poor countries.

As the AIDS crisis developed in the United States, systems were in place to deal with the disease, if public officials and others could be convinced to deal with it as a medical or public health problem. Thus reform might have seemed the best approach. Yet as time went on, it became clear that the virulence of the disease, its global reach, and its devastating impact on particular communities and nations could not be dealt with by reforming existing systems. Massive change in resource allocation and major reorientation of existing systems, as well as reduction of formidable cultural barriers, were needed to manage the disease, care for the sick and their families, and stop practices that spread the disease.

In the African American men case, change advocates decided that a revolution in thinking was required to improve conditions for young African American men. They offered several new perspectives: the view that what was good for African American men was good for Hennepin County; the view that this group had considerable existing and potential contributions to make as workers, fathers, and citizens; and the view that the various conditions leading to poor outcomes for young African American men were interrelated. The diverse African American Men Commission might be seen as a minisocial movement that will champion the broadly based and coordinated reforms in several systems needed to add up to the "revolution in practice" necessary to create better outcomes for these men.

Before we offer more guidance for leadership in context, we suggest you do Exercise 2.2, which prompts you to consider the social, political, economic, and technological conditions affecting your public passions. It also prompts you to consider possibilities for change.

Exercise 2.2. Assessing the Context for Leadership.

1. Thinking of your own cares and concerns, what social, political, economic, and technological givens might be important?

   - Social
   - Political
   - Economic
   - Technological

2. What changes in social, political, economic, and technological conditions might provide opportunities for leadership around what you care about?

   - Social
   - Political
   - Economic
   - Technological

3. What are the less obvious potentialities in these conditions that might support future changes?

4. What kind of reform or revolution will be needed to accomplish the type of change you seek?

Further Guidance for Leadership in Context

Leaders in context should also seek insights from history, trends analysis, personal experience, and cultural anthropology.

1. *Become a student of history.* Don't forget, though, that the prominent texts and biographies are often written from the point of view of great men, or the "winners," of major conflicts. Seek out less prominent views, perhaps by visiting a local historical society, collecting oral accounts, and reading authors such as Barbara Tuchman (1984), Andrew Delbanco (1999), Howard Zinn (2001), or Dipesh Chakrabarty (2000). Novels and plays may be especially useful for understanding what an era was like. For example, Larry Kramer's hard-hitting play *The Normal Heart,* about the early AIDS crisis, may be better than any history in conveying the human toll of the epidemic in the United States.

2. *Analyze trends and get involved in the debates that surround them.* Some scholars urge everyone to think about how current societal trends or shifts signal an "emergent reality" that offers opportunities for—and even demands—leadership (Quinn, 2000). Exercise 2.3 prompts you to think about the emergent reality signaled by several global trends, those mentioned in Chapter One and others that are important in the early years of the twenty-first century. Cleveland (2002) suggests that the most important overarching trend is what has been variously called the Information Revolution, the informatization of society, the explosion of knowledge, and the Age of Access. He argues that the melding of high-speed computers and advanced telecommunications is "creating societies where the dominant resource is information" and the emphasis is on "the production and sharing of symbols" rather than goods. In the face of this trend, the world's citizens need to "rethink an economics based on scarcity, rethink laws based on ownership, rethink leadership based on hierarchy" (p. 138). The knowledge explosion has also produced earth-shaking advances in biotechnology, especially genetic engineering. Francis Fukuyama (2002) writes about a "post-human future" in which human nature itself is drastically altered. Both Cleveland and Fukuyama argue that existing modes of governance are terribly inadequate to ensure that the fruits of the information revolution are nourishing

Exercise 2.3. Assessing Global Trends.

1. Consider these important trends seen in the early years of the twenty-first century:

   - Global interdependence and the shift toward a global market economy
   - The continued importance of the nation state
   - Increased democratization around the world
   - Post–Cold War politics, use of terrorism, continued nuclear threat
   - Burgeoning telecommunications and computer technology
   - The emergence of international organizations
   - Growing cleavage between rich and poor populations
   - Citizen disaffection with governments
   - Global warming
   - Increased prominence of human rights
   - The global spread of AIDS
   - Growth of secular culture, diminution of some forms of organized religion, strengthening of evangelical religion, the connection of religious extremism and terrorism
   - Declining social capital and civic activism in industrialized countries

2. What signs of an "emergent reality" can be gleaned from these trends?

3. How does this reality affect what you care about?

4. How does this reality offer opportunities for leadership in the areas you care about?

rather than poisonous to human well-being. Cleveland also reminds analysts to resist the temptation of mistaking "current trends for future destiny" (2002, p. 131).

3. *Get involved in an important part of civil society, politics, the economy, or technology.* For example, you could become active in a political party, work for a nonprofit organization, become more adept at using the Internet, or explore your own company's connections to the global economy.

4. *Become a student of culture.* Nations, subnational regions, ethnic groups, cities, neighborhoods, organizations, and other groups

can be said to have a culture, a distinctive way of ordering relationships and responding to their environment. In addition to a prominent, or dominant, culture, these entities also often have one or more "co-cultures" (see Samovar and Porter, 1994). Most fundamentally, a group's culture is a set of shared assumptions about reality and truth, time, space, and human nature. Here is guidance for thinking about each of these cultural dimensions, adapted from *Leadership for Global Citizenship* (Crosby, 1999):

> *Reality and truth.* Scholars distinguish "low-context" and "high-context" cultures (Hall, 1980). In a low-context culture, such as the dominant U.S. culture, reality and truth are conveyed in written and verbal messages. In a high-context culture, people are more likely to consider the context of the message as well—for example, nonverbal behavior and the status of the person sending the message. In some cultures, reality and truth are established by moral authority; in others, reality and truth are determined by pragmatic experimentation.
>
> *Time.* A low-context culture tends to view time as segmented and linear, susceptible to scheduling. In a high-context culture, time is full of simultaneous happenings; an activity, rather than a schedule, may dictate how much time is devoted to it. Some societies are oriented toward the past; others focus on the present; still others are more future-oriented (Kluckhohn and Strodtbeck, 1961).
>
> *Space.* Cultures have their own norms about appropriate interpersonal space or the best way to design work and living spaces.
>
> *Human nature.* Cultures differ in their basic assumptions about the human condition. They may assume that human beings are essentially good, essentially bad, or a mix of good and bad. They may think of human beings as being at the mercy of the natural environment, superior to it, or at one with it. If a culture views humans basically as victims of natural forces, it is likely to reinforce acceptance of one's fate; if the culture views humans as lords of the earth, the culture will reinforce efforts to tame nature. If a culture deems human beings to be com-

pletely a part of nature, then it prompts them to attempt to harmonize their lives with nature (Schein, 1992). Societies also establish social hierarchies on the basis of assumptions about which groups are superior to others. Common hierarchies are based on gender, age, sexual orientation, ethnicity, religion, and class.

A group's assumptions about each of these dimensions are woven together to form a distinctive worldview (Schein, 1992). To understand cultures different from yours (whether a co-culture in your own society or outside it), you might visit them for an extended period, talk to astute observers of the culture, or read cultural analyses. Perhaps the most difficult culture to understand is one in which you are a long-time participant. Leaving the culture may help you achieve some perspective on it.

In general, Edgar Schein's approach (1992) to understanding organizational culture may be helpful. He advises studying a group's artifacts: language, art, dress, eating habits, arrangement of space, technology. Then try to discern what those artifacts tell you about the group's shared assumptions about the cultural dimensions as we have described them. Looking at the group's espoused values may also be helpful, but there is often a mismatch between what a society says it values and the values embedded in its basic, shared assumptions. Since cultures are dynamic, you may also want to delve into layers of artifacts and values and consider the mix of layers from the distant and recent past. You might consider how major changes in political arrangements or demographic patterns, for example, are affecting the culture. Also vital is understanding cultural norms and practices about leadership and change. A culture's worldview affects what kind of change is valued, what kinds of people are in formal leadership positions, and which leadership styles are valued. At the same time, analysis conducted as part of a major global project focusing on cross-cultural leadership does indicate almost universal support for transformational leadership behaviors—personal consideration and intellectual stimulation of followers, future focus, and inspirational communication (House, Wright, and Aditya, 1998). Exercise 2.4 prompts you to analyze cultures that are important for you to understand in relation to your cares and concerns.

Exercise 2.4. Assessing Cultural Differences.

Focus on a culture that is important for you to understand, given your cares and concerns. You may want to complete the exercise for several cultures in your community and nation. One option is interviewing knowledgeable informants and adding their insights to your own.

You will be prompted to think about several dimensions of cultural difference.

Reality and Truth

1. Do people in the culture rely primarily on the *content* of written or verbal messages?
2. Or do people in the culture rely primarily on the *context* of written or verbal messages?
3. What are the implications for leadership and change?

Time

1. Do people think of time as linear—something to be scheduled or parceled out for specific activities?
2. Or do people think of time as cyclical—holding many activities and concerns simultaneously?
3. Do people focus mainly on the past, the present, or the future?
4. What are the implications for leadership and change?

Space

1. What places are sacred to people in this culture?
2. How far apart do people stand when they talk with each other?
3. How do people design and locate their homes, offices, and public spaces?
4. What are the implications for leadership and change?

Human Nature

1. Do people think humans control nature?
2. Or do they think humans are controlled by nature?
3. Or do they think humans should strive to live in harmony with nature?
4. Is a person's value or importance determined by a connection to a family or other group?
5. Or is a person's importance determined mainly by what the person does?
6. Is social hierarchy or egalitarianism valued?
7. What are the proper activities for women? for men?
8. Are people viewed as basically evil, basically good, or a mix and able to improve if they choose?
9. What are the implications for leadership and change?

Personal Leadership

The work of understanding oneself and others and using this understanding to achieve beneficial change is a lifelong process. We suggest three especially helpful practices for achieving such understanding in relation to leadership for the common good:

1. Discerning the call to leadership
2. Assessing other personal strengths and weaknesses
3. Appreciating diversity and commonality

These practices should help aspiring leaders focus on what many scholars, researchers, and philosophers have found helpful in responding to the highest hopes and deepest needs of leaders, as well as of their constituents and colleagues.

Discerning the Call to Leadership

As we suggested earlier in this chapter, leadership begins with being in touch with what truly matters to you. Identifying your cares and concerns and attending to the larger world around you can assist with this work. You may also want to create (or review) your personal credo (see Kouzes and Posner, 1993). In many of our courses and workshops, we have used a self-assessment tool called "Exploring Personal Highs and Lows," which prompts participants to review their lives and reflect on patterns of success and failure (the peaks and pits). Exercise 2.5 is loosely patterned on a more elaborate charting exercise described in *The Leadership Challenge* (Kouzes and Posner, 2002). You may want to take time now to do the exercise yourself, in order to reflect more deeply on your own leadership call. Like Parker Palmer, we believe analyzing your mistakes as well as your achievements can help you discern your calling (Palmer, 2000).

Reviewing your own history may reveal that you have grasped opportunities for leadership—or, as Bob Terry was fond of saying, that they may have grasped you! Randy Shilts's book about the early AIDS crisis is full of examples of people who were propelled into leadership by the experience of caring for those with AIDS, or of contracting the disease themselves (Shilts, 1988). As you consider your history, you may find that you set out to make great changes in your organization or community. You may also find that

Exercise 2.5. Exploring Personal Highs and Lows

Create a Personal Timeline

1. Take out a sheet of paper, turn it sideways, and draw a line from left to right that divides the paper into top and bottom halves of equal size.

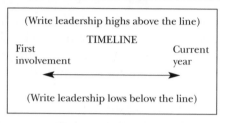

(Write leadership highs above the line)

TIMELINE

First involvement

Current year

(Write leadership lows below the line)

2. At the right-hand end of the line, write in the current year. At the left-hand end of the line, write in the date of your first involvement in dealing with organizational or societal problems.

Identify Leadership Highs and Lows

1. Think about the organizational or societal problems you have worked on over the time span you have marked out.
2. Leadership highs: in the appropriate place above the timeline, mark, date, and label times when your leadership helped remedy these problems. The distance of each mark above the timeline should represent just how successful the experience was.
3. Leadership lows: in the appropriate place below the timeline, mark, date, and label times when you were unable to help remedy these problems. The distance of each mark below the timeline should represent just how unsuccessful the experience was.

Add Other Personal Events

1. At the appropriate points on the timeline, fill in as highs or lows any important events that have occurred in your personal life, such as weddings, births, divorces, deaths of relatives or friends, the establishment or breakup of important relationships, graduations, layoffs, and so forth.

Identify Themes

1. Note themes that are common to the highs.
2. Note themes that are common to the lows.

Discover Lessons

1. What lessons do you learn from this analysis? What guidance would you give yourself for the future?

Share Results

1. Share these results with someone who knows you well and whose friendship, support, and insights you value. Ask for observations and feedback.

you are gripped by some unexpected need: the organization is falling apart and you are in a position to help. Drug dealers are taking over the neighborhood, and one day you've had enough and phone your friends and start talking about what all of you might do together to fight back.

You might reflect on what has made you receptive to the call to lead. Physicians such as Conant, Gottlieb, and Laubenstein made serious professional commitments to care for ill human beings, and when they encountered a mysterious and deadly disease in their patients they began doing everything in their power to mobilize professional networks and governmental agencies to give priority to understanding and treating the disease. Gay filmmaker and writer Kramer worked fiercely to wake up the New York gay community and the broader citizenry to the dimensions of the AIDS crisis, because he had already developed a deep concern for the effects of the sexual excesses of gay liberation—a concern presented in unvarnished detail in a controversial novel he had written previously.

People who attend our semesterlong seminars sometimes make dramatic career or life changes during or just after the program so as to act on their own call to leadership. Although we might like to claim credit for these changes, we think the seminar was simply an occasion for them to listen to their call and act on it. They probably had done considerable work identifying what they cared about and building commitment to it. They may have taken our seminar because they already were aware of a big gap between their deep commitment and their ongoing activities. Each of these participants was ready to pay attention to what unique contribution he or she could make to achieving the common good.

Note that at the conclusion of the "personal highs and lows" exercise we urge you to share the results with someone you trust, and listen to his or her observations. Obtaining other people's views can deepen your understanding of the passion that energizes your leadership. The reflections of others may also help you delve into the shadow side of passion. Commitment to a just cause may blind us to the truth in another perspective. We may feel the righteousness of our own conviction so much that we're blind to our own shortcomings. We may become so intent on helping strangers that we ignore the needs of the people around us. Robert Quinn (2000) advises us to keep in mind that we're all hypocrites. We need to recognize that even as we aspire to high ideals of continuously caring for others or fighting for social good, we have spells of spitefulness, misdirected anger, and outrageous selfishness. Our evil twins emerge and stun us with their vitality.

Once you are fairly clear about the public passion that summons you to leadership, you can continue the discernment process by exploring how it matches the ethical principles that you deem most important. Additionally, you might want to assess your leadership commitment by using questions drawn from the main ethical categories identified by Robert Terry in *Authentic Leadership* (1993):

- To what extent does my commitment affirm human existence and development, as well as ecological diversity and survival?
- To what extent does my commitment help ensure that everyone has the necessities of living and is allowed to fulfill his or her potential?
- To what extent does my commitment promote fairness, especially in the distribution of resources?
- To what extent does my commitment affirm every member's participation in the decisions that shape a group or society?
- To what extent does my commitment foster love—that is, care, respect, and forgiveness toward oneself and others?
- To what extent does my commitment promote personal responsibility and promote a thriving future for the earth and its inhabitants?

By reflecting on your life's commitments, you are engaged in soulwork, the process of staying in touch with the deep center that resides in each of us and is connected to the creative spirit of the universe (Bolman and Deal, 2001; Quinn, 2000; Loeb, 1999). Soulwork both clarifies and sustains passion and probes the personal shadow: "Though soulwork can be thought of as a spiritual journey, it is not about separating from the mundane material world. . . . It is about seeking the mysterious in the ordinary. It is experiencing our unity or connection with the humblest object, as well as the most dazzling. It is not about leaving the earth, but about knowing deeply the cycles of earthly life. It is about releasing our desire to laugh and cry about the human condition" (Crosby, 1999, p. 44).

Soulwork helps us claim power as co-creators of the universe and discern the unique gift we can make to the world (Becker,

1973). It helps us answer the question, What will I live for? Sometimes the question is put in a contrasting way: What am I willing to die for? The first question, however, is probably more helpful, since people working for the common good should hope for a long life, and since necessary sacrifices may be easier to deal with in the context of what we seek to embody.

Discerning the call to leadership may be helped by going on a retreat, or simply taking a break from normal pursuits. In 1990, Schmidheiny had time to reflect, because he was taking a break from his business career. He spent some time worrying about the future of the planet and made a speech in Norway about the possibility of creating "a world in which what was good for the planet was good for business" (Holliday, Schmidheiny, and Watts, 2002). Maurice Strong was in the audience and pressed Schmidheiny to act further on his concern by spreading the idea of sustainable development among business leaders and coordinating a business response for the 1992 U.N. Conference on Environment and Development.

Reflection may come more easily and be more necessary at life's transition points, as was the case with Schmidheiny. Transitions are a time when reviewing commitments makes sense (Bridges, 1980).

Aids for reflection include journal writing, religious or spiritual practice, artistic endeavor (photography, drawing, painting, singing, dancing, writing poetry). Insight and guidance can come from nonfiction books, notably *Leading with Soul* (Bolman and Deal, 2001); *The Critical Journey: Stages in the Life of Faith* (Hagberg and Guelich, 1995); *Change the World* (Quinn, 2000); *Leadership from the Inside out* (Cashman, 1999). Novels, plays, and films can also awaken an audience to social concern and self-knowledge.

You may want to write your autobiography as a way of reflecting on your commitment. Include your highest hopes and deepest fears; successes and failures; people and events that have shaped you; cultural, economic, political, and technological forces that have affected you. You might convene a conversation to tap your own and others' wisdom. Margaret Wheatley's *Turning to One Another* (2002) suggests some questions to get people talking about what matters to them. Pasquale Pistorio, CEO of the Swiss company STMicroelectronics, reports that conversation with his son caused him to accept a "moral responsibility for protecting the environment" and commit his company to sustainable development (Holliday, Schmidheiny, and Watts, 2002, p. 127).

Assessing Other Personal Strengths and Weaknesses

Your public passion, or commitment to lead, is a fundamental leadership asset. Other vital strengths are integrity and a sense of humor; awareness of your preferred or habitual ways of learning and interacting with people; a sense of self-efficacy and courage; cognitive, emotional, and behavioral complexity; commitment to nonstop learning; authority and other resources; supportive personal networks; balance; and awareness of how leadership is strengthened and weakened by your location in major social hierarchies. (The focus here is on general leadership strengths and weaknesses. Certain aspects of each apply to specific leadership tasks and change efforts.)

Integrity and a Sense of Humor
People trust those they believe will behave in accordance with espoused values that are based on ethical principles. Integrity demands that you know what your guiding ethical principles are, and that you generally live by them across your multiple social roles. It requires being honest with yourself and others. This does not mean, however, that you should constantly worry about perfection, but simply seek to be perfected by a commitment to acting on your beliefs (Quinn, 2000; hooks, 2000). You'll also need the ability to forgive yourself and those who don't manage to fully walk their talk. You'll also need a sense of humor about your own foibles and those of others. James Hillman reminds us: "The laughing recognition of one's own absurdity in the human comedy bans the devil as effectively as garlic and the cross" (1997, p. 222). Jeffrey Luke offers a helpful discussion of integrity and notions of virtue and character in *Catalytic Leadership* (1998). Also helpful is David Shapiro's *Choosing the Right Thing to Do* (1999).

Ways of Learning and Interacting
You may want to use such formal self-assessments as the Myers-Briggs Type Indicator (http://www.cpp-db.com/index.html) or the Dimensions of Leadership Profile (http://inscapepublishing.com)

to help clarify your preferred or habitual ways of learning and interacting with people. Both of these instruments are administered by facilitators who have been trained in helping you interpret the results. Other assessments can be self-administered and interpreted. For example, the Keirsey Temperament Sorter is available online at http://keirsey.com. These assessments are best used as hypotheses to guide further observation, reflection, and desired change, not to place yourself or others in a rigid category. They can help you understand why it's easier to relate to some people than to others, what helps you learn, or why you don't seem to fit in certain groups or work environments. The assessments also help you think about the strengths and weaknesses of your own approaches and of quite different approaches.

Sense of Self-Efficacy, Optimism, and Courage

Helping others pursue major change is likely to be a scary, risky, protracted business requiring a large amount of determination, persistence, and resilience. Martin Krieger's book *Entrepreneurial Vocations* underlines this point (1996). Self-efficacy, optimism, and courage are crucial assets in this work. Self-efficacy essentially is the confidence that one's efforts will produce desired results, or at least make a significant difference. Optimism is closely connected to self-efficacy. Many authors emphasize the importance of an optimistic, though pragmatic, outlook for those who would inspire and mobilize others. James Kouzes and Barry Posner call for "flexible optimism" (1993); James Collins and Jerry Porras call for "pragmatic idealism" (Jacobs, 1994). Cleveland goes further and recommends "unwarranted optimism" (2002). He says leaders need "a mindset that crises are normal, tensions can be promising, and complexity is fun" (Cleveland, 2002, p. 8). Using some of the self-assessment methods mentioned earlier in this section can help you recognize your own strengths, which constitute a base for feelings of self-efficacy and optimism. Martin Seligman (1998) and Albert Bandura (1997) offer further insights about how to develop optimism and self-efficacy. We'd like to reinforce the notion of restrained self-efficacy and practical optimism. Yes, leaders need great self-confidence and optimism, but they need to recognize their limitations as well. As the authors of *Common Fire* put it, leaders need to "balance hubris and humility" (Daloz, Keen, Keen, and Parks, 1996, p. 226).

Self-efficacy and optimism enhance courage—the willingness to venture into the unknown, to go against the prevailing wisdom, to be vulnerable, to be radically innovative, to keep on in the face of adversity. Moving through fear or letting go of it is often not easy, but it's vital to overcome the barrier to connecting authentically with others (Terry, 1993, 2001). We recommend looking back over your life to find occasions when you've been courageous (the highs-and-lows exercise might reveal some of these). We also recommend sharing personal stories of courageous action with a group of friends or colleagues.

Cognitive, Emotional, and Behavioral Complexity

Cognitive complexity includes the capacity to see systems, to identify the interconnections among ideas, people, and organizations. It often refers to the ability to gather and organize many strands of information, to reenvision systems, to carve out new paths or directions, to take the long-term as well as the short-term view. Rosabeth Moss Kanter talks about "kaleidoscopic thinking—a way of constructing patterns from the diverse fragments of data available and then manipulating them to form different patters" (Kanter, 2002, p. 53). Robert Quinn talks about "bold-stroke capacity," the ability to transcend a complex system and see a clear, even simple way forward (Quinn, 2000). Cognitive complexity includes comfort with ambiguity and paradox. Cognitive complexity also requires attention to differing points of view. If you are going to lead diverse people, you need the ability to accept the validity of many perspectives and truths. You'll need to work out your own perspective and, as Drath says, see through and beyond it. In other words, you need to understand your own worldview as "useful, sensemaking and truth giving, but incomplete, not the whole of reality" (Drath, 2001, p. 149). Cognitive complexity is sustained by the habit of reflection—the practice of stepping back from the systems and worldview in which you are enmeshed, thinking about how they work, questioning assumptions, and identifying limitations of the systems and worldview (Kegan, 1994). For another take on cognitive complexity, see Hooijberg, Hunt, and Dodge (1997).

Emotional complexity, or emotional intelligence, complements cognitive complexity. Emotional intelligence includes the ability to recognize and express one's own emotions, practice self-discipline, and understand and respond to the views and feelings of other people (Goleman, 1995; Goleman, Boyatzis, and McKee, 2002; Salovey and Mayer, 1997). It is the basis of empathy, the capacity for experiencing the world as another sees it. Obviously, emotional intelligence is vital for building and sustaining relationships with those we seek to lead. Janet Hagberg (1995) advises would-be leaders that it's especially important to question their negative perceptions of other people. She urges all of us to list the qualities we dislike about someone, and then consider how these are the very qualities we have trouble seeing in ourselves. She doesn't recommend trying to get rid of the despised quality so much as confronting it and trying to learn from it. Megan Boler warns against an unquestioning emphasis on emotional control, noting that "emotions function in part as moral and ethical evaluations" (1999, p. xviii). She points out that power relations affect cultural definition and evaluation of emotions—for example, a greater value put on reason rather than emotion.

Behavioral complexity is the ability to draw on one's cognitive and emotional intelligence in acting appropriately for the demands of a particular situation (Hooijberg, Hunt, and Dodge, 1997; Hooijberg and Schneider, 2001). It requires understanding and comfort in a variety of roles; a leader may need to adeptly balance or integrate the roles of parent, administrator, teacher, community volunteer, and follower. Leaders also need the ability to enact their roles differently according to context; see, for example, Irving Goffman's insights about the "presentation of self" (1959). Behavioral flexibility should not be confused, however, with opportunism and lack of a moral compass. Leaders who hope to sustain integrity (and effectiveness) must adopt behavior that clearly reflects their core values.

Gary Cunningham demonstrated considerable cognitive, emotional, and behavioral complexity in his work with the African American Men Project. As county planning director he has carried out tough, complicated assignments. He had to keep in mind a diverse array of stakeholders: county commissioners, other public officials, businesspeople, community groups, schools, professional organizations, staff, service and advocacy groups. He saw problems affecting African American men as a system. He believed a breakthrough was possible but knew he would have to keep his own emotions in balance as he looked fully at the practices that had kept many of these men from being productive citizens. He had to accomplish a fine balancing act of managing his relations with powerful politicians and businesspeople, quirky academics, and African American community leaders, some of whom didn't hesitate to express their anger, frustration, and skepticism that government initiatives would bring progress.

Authority, Skills, and Connections

Among the assets that each of us brings to our leadership work are authority, specialized skills, and connections. Authority may come from our position in our family or in an organization; it might come from the moral example we present. In the African American men case, Stenglein had significant authority over the time, money, and attention of county commissioners and county departments. Cunningham had authority by virtue of his job title and a lifetime of connection with the African American community, people at the University of Minnesota, and government and nonprofit leaders. Milligan had prestige and connections through his vice presidency of a local bank. The senior academics involved brought a host of analytic tools and synthesizing capabilities. Younger county staff, community activists, and researchers brought particular personal connections and research, writing, and speaking skills. In the AIDS case, an example is Surgeon General C. Everett Koop, who combined medical expertise and conservative credentials to overcome the resistance of others in the Reagan administration to launching a major AIDS prevention campaign.

Commitment to Continuous Learning

An ongoing curiosity and devotion to learning contribute to cognitive and emotional complexity and acquisition of the specific knowledge and skills needed for leadership work. In addition to formal education, consider putting yourself in unfamiliar situations and encouraging fearless, constructive feedback from those who know you well. Find mentors in expected and unexpected places. Janet Hagberg (1995) recommends, for example, that a person who is at home in "mainstream society" seek a mentor from the social fringes.

Supportive Personal Networks and Balance

Leaders need a supportive personal network (including family, friends, counselors, mentors, and coaches) to cheer them on, give honest feedback, hold them accountable, serve as role models, and furnish emotional sustenance and other resources. If your current network is not strong, you can be proactive in seeking out people who can give the support you need. Of course, to sustain a supportive network, you also need to help those who help you.

This reciprocity is one aspect of needed balance. Generally, the advocates of balance recommend that all of us devote a significant amount of our time to personal renewal and family responsibilities, as well as to our job and community activities. Of course, balance may not be the best metaphor, since it implies an exactitude that escapes most of us. We may choose to be sequentially lopsided, though never for too long (Delbecq and Friedlander, 1995). Weaving the aspects of our lives together into a satisfying whole may be a helpful metaphor.

Position in Social Hierarchies

Each of us is situated in several of the social hierarchies described in the "leadership in context" section of this chapter. Our position in these hierarchies may make it easier for us to influence some groups of people and harder to influence others. If we are in a position of relatively low power and status, we are likely to have insights into the modus operandi of the powerful (because we've had to pay attention to them) as well as of our own group. We may have more difficulty understanding the experience of groups when we are in a position of privilege compared to them, and thus able to habitually ignore them.

Exercises 2.6 and 2.7 (part one of the latter) can help you assess the additional strengths and weaknesses described here. Exercise 2.7 lists seven pervasive dimensions of social hierarchy; you may want to add others. A possible resource is the work of Charles Manz and his colleagues on self-leadership (see, for example, Manz and Neck, 1999; and Houghton, Neck, and Manz, 2003). Their methodology suggests how individuals can build on their leadership strengths and overcome their weaknesses. Self-leadership strategies emphasize self-observation, goal setting,

Exercise 2.6. Assessing Additional Strengths and Weaknesses.

Integrity and Sense of Humor

What are my guiding principles? How well does my behavior match them? Am I honest with myself and others? Can I laugh at my own and others' foibles?

Ways of Learning and Interacting

What are my preferred or habitual ways of learning? What are my preferred or habitual ways of interacting with people? What are the strengths and weaknesses of these approaches?

Self-Efficacy, Optimism, and Courage

How confident am I that my efforts to promote beneficial change can be successful? Do I have and convey a generally positive outlook and a realistic optimism about the possibility of people's working successfully together on their common concerns? How willing am I to venture into the unknown, go against the prevailing wisdom, be vulnerable, be radically innovative, keep on in the face of adversity?

Cognitive, Emotional, and Behavioral Complexity

Do I take a systems view? Can I see connections among ideas, people, and organizations? Can I synthesize multiple strands of information? Can I envision new ways of doing things? Am I comfortable with ambiguity and paradox? Do I accept the validity of different perspectives? How good am I at identifying my own feelings? How do I practice self-discipline? How well am I able to understand and respond to the feelings of others? How well do I manage my negative perceptions of other people? How well do I balance and integrate multiple roles? How good am I at enacting my roles according to the context, while still being aligned with my core values?

Continuous Learning

How does my formal and informal training (especially in cross-cultural communication) help or hinder me in exercising leadership around my policy passion? Do I seek and accept frank feedback from others?

Authority, Skills, and Connections

What sources, and what amount, of authority can I apply to my leadership work?

1. Authority based on family position, craft, profession, position in organization or community

Exercise 2.6. Assessing Additional Strengths and Weaknesses, Cont'd.

2. Moral authority rooted in demonstrated integrity or trustworthiness

What general skills and social connections can I apply to my leadership work?

Supportive Spouse, Other Family Members,
Friends, Colleagues, and Mentors

Who among my family, friends, and colleagues can be counted on to support or oppose me in this work? Who can mentor or coach me? Are there people whose example I can follow even if I can't work with them directly?

Balance

What engagements and attachments do I have to balance with my involvement with public work? How do they help and hinder my leadership?

---

self-reward, self-correcting feedback, and practice. Self-leadership also includes "natural reward strategies"—methods of finding intrinsic value in the tasks one undertakes—and "constructive thought pattern strategies" (Houghton, Neck, and Manz, 2003, p. 129).

Appreciating Diversity and Commonality

All human beings have much in common; just to begin with, we are all natal and mortal. Yet each of us is unique, and this will remain true even if scientists are able to produce humans who are genetic clones of each other. Just debriefing an assessment such as the MBTI or the "personal highs and lows" exercise in a small group can reveal numerous commonalities and differences in the group. Sharing autobiographies is also revealing. Since conversation about difference can be extremely uncomfortable (especially when the differences are linked to oppression or discrimination), participants should be especially ready to engage in respectful dialogue characterized by active listening (described in the "team leadership" section of the next chapter) and by other means of ensuring that less powerful participants can safely express their experiences.

Exercise 2.7. Analyzing Social Group Membership and Means of Bridging Differences.

Part One

How do these personal conditions affect your leadership?

	How It Strengthens My Leadership	How It Makes My Leadership Harder
Gender		
Ethnicity		
Nationality		
Religion		
Class		
Sexual orientation		
Physical ability		
Age		

Part Two

Bridging differences:

1. What are the causes of negative stereotypes about members of a group other than one's own?
2. What methods can be used to overcome prejudice and discrimination?
3. What strategies have you found effective for understanding and connecting with people who are different from you?

Prejudice and stereotypes about groups of people we see as different develop out of ignorance and distance, as well as from the desire to feel secure in our own group and to see people like us as good and admirable (Allport, 1954; Stephan, 1985). Prejudice and negative stereotypes also help us rationalize oppression of other groups.

To deepen your appreciation of cultural difference, you may want to visit other cultures, engage in formal intercultural education programs, or join a project that requires culturally diverse people to work together. (Ideally you will plan visits that move beyond the tourist view, and become involved in programs and projects led by people with excellent multicultural competency.)

Exercise 2.7 prompts you to reflect on your own diversity and ways you've found to build bridges between diverse groups. When skillfully debriefed in a group, the exercise can promote considerable learning about participants' diverse experiences and cross-cultural bridging.

Understanding oneself and diverse others is hard but rewarding work. Leaders use this knowledge to put together productive work groups, nurture organizations, and help constituents engage in "public work" (Boyte and Kari, 1996) and achieve regimes of mutual gain.

Summary

People seeking to achieve beneficial change in a shared-power world need to understand and draw on eight main leadership capabilities. This chapter has explored the two capabilities—leadership in context and personal leadership—that are the foundation for all the others. Team and organizational leadership are the focus of the next chapter.

Chapter Three

Leadership Tasks in a Shared-Power World
Team and Organizational Leadership

> *[Leadership is] people taking the initiative, carrying things through, having ideas and the imagination to get something started, and exhibiting particular skills in different areas.*
> CHARLOTTE BUNCH

> *A healthy work community is key to professional happiness, to organizational loyalty, and to the level of cooperation across boundaries that is essential in the Information Age.*
> GIFFORD PINCHOT

Sooner or later, those seeking to accomplish major change need to assemble and sustain productive work groups or teams and develop effective, humane organizations. They require an array of team and organizational leadership skills.

Team Leadership

A team might begin as an informal working group and progress to a more formal arrangement, examples being a task force, steering committee, planning team, or standing committee. They may come together for a relatively brief period of time to complete a specific task, or they may last for years (although the membership might change).

Teams of gay activists and health professionals organized the conferences and public demonstrations aimed at focusing the attention of medical researchers and public officials on the emerging AIDS crisis. Teams organized stakeholder consultations sponsored by the World Business Council on Sustainable Development and put together council publications. A steering committee oversaw the African American Men Project; teams prepared reports and organized events. Teams helped organize the Vital Aging Summit.

Teams may have an appointed leader or leaders, such as a coordinator, project director, or cochairs. They may choose their own coordinator, director, or chair and parcel out other leadership functions among themselves. They may also rotate leadership functions.

To create and sustain productive work groups, leaders should attend to the satisfaction of individual group members, group cohesion, and task achievement (Johnson and Johnson, 2003). Many authors refer to this work as facilitation and coaching (Bacon, 1996; Rees, 1997; Schwarz, 2002). Let's consider how leaders accomplish this through recruitment, communication, empowerment, and leadership development of team members.

Recruitment

Team members should be diverse enough to bring needed perspectives, skills, connections, and other resources to the team's work, yet they should share commitment to the team's purpose and be willing to cooperate to achieve it. An especially important skill in diverse teams is the ability to accommodate various communication and work styles (DiTomaso and Hooijberg, 1996).

When assembling a team to initiate or oversee a change effort, leaders would be wise to conduct a basic stakeholder analysis. The first step is identifying the key individuals and groups affected by proposed changes or having access to needed resources. The second is clarifying what stake these people have in the change. What exactly is their interest? What expectations might they have of any change effort? Team members can then be systematically recruited to represent, or at least connect with, those stakeholders. (Additional advice on using stakeholder analysis to organize groups involved in a change effort is in Chapter Six.)

For example, as Gary Cunningham put together his recommendations for members of the citizen group that would oversee the African American Men Project, he knew he needed African Americans who had rich connections and credibility in their own ethnic community. He needed businesspeople interested in a diverse workforce, representatives of government agencies, executives of nonprofit organizations that worked with African American families, respected academics, and people with political clout. He obtained commitment from accomplished individuals from all these categories. The result was a steering committee that had prestige in the eyes of many stakeholders and access to important networks for implementing project recommendations. As he assembled teams to work on research reports, he sought out academic partners with a reputation for sound research and a commitment to achieving better outcomes for African American men. Members of these teams could be expected to produce research seen as legitimate by many stakeholders.

Of course, leaders cannot always control the membership of their teams. Team membership may be mandated in general terms or quite specifically by law, policy, or someone with authority over the team. Even then, however, it may be possible to add members, or at least bring in consultants when their special perspectives or skills are needed. Regardless of how people are recruited for the team, the leader should take time to build a shared understanding of the group's mission and ways of working together. Sometimes it will become clear that a group member cannot agree with the others on mission or methods, and it is time to part. For example, gay activist Larry Kramer finally resigned from the Gay Men's Health Crisis board in 1983 after his prolonged and unsuccessful effort to convince other board members to be more confrontational in pressuring New York City officials to provide AIDS services.

In general, the size of a working group should be small; seven to nine members is ideal. If the group has to be larger—in order to represent all the key stakeholders, for example—subgroups are needed to carry out many of the team's tasks. Also important is bringing in new members as needed. Team leaders need to ensure that new members are brought up to speed on what the team has accomplished, how it operates, and what it plans to do. They may consciously mentor newcomers for a time.

Communication

The most essential team leadership skill is fostering communication that aligns and coordinates members' actions, builds mutual understanding and trust, and fosters creative problem solving and commitment. Such communication requires an atmosphere of openness, information sharing, and respect (see Kouzes and Posner, 2002). It combines seriousness and playfulness. It requires attention to verbal and nonverbal communication, to message sending and message receiving. We recommend several methods. Regardless of the method chosen, a team leader should be sensitive to right timing and right setting. As an example, a leader should ensure that seating arrangements facilitate free and equal exchange of ideas.

Active Listening and Dialogue

Traditionally, leaders have been advised to concentrate on the messages they send—make them clear, consistent, positive, credible, and tailored to audience members. The advice is still important, but increasingly those who study groups and organizations advise leaders to become exemplary "active listeners" and practitioners of dialogue. Active listeners concentrate more on receiving messages. They use questions, body language, and verbal feedback to encourage others to express their ideas, feelings, and concerns. They check with the speaker to be sure their understanding is accurate. They seek out information about the person's needs, about the team's cohesion, and about the tasks the team is trying to accomplish. They seek to understand how the person's ties to various groups and cultures affect his or her participation (Stivers, 1994).

Practitioners of dialogue set up team conversations with simple ground rules (Schein, 1993; Senge and others, 1994; see also Senge, 1994). First, group members are asked to take turns presenting their ideas or proposals. Second, as an individual participant presents an idea or proposal, the other members are expected to practice *suspension*, hearing a speaker out instead of offering judgment or other reactions. As part of suspension, they also try to reflect on their reactions and examine the assumptions on which they are based. Third, once all the ideas have been presented, group members might be encouraged to talk about the assumptions they found themselves making and seek clarification. Finally, participants are invited to advocate a particular course of action and come to consensus on what should be done.

Joyce Fletcher and Katrin Kaüfer explain how leaders can help groups move to "generative dialogue," in which group members cocreate ideas (Fletcher and Kaüfer, 2003, p. 24). Typically, they say, groups begin by "talking nice" to each other and then move to "talking tough," in which members offer their perspectives and engage in debate. By practicing the skills of "self-in-relation"—empathy, listening, relational inquiry, revelation of personal vulnerability, and tolerance for ambiguity and uncertainty—leaders can move the group through these stages to "reflective dialogue," in which participants reflect on their own perspectives and begin to realize they can learn from the other group members, and then finally to generative dialogue.

The Institute of Cultural Affairs recommends a process that moves from focusing on facts about a situation to reflecting on related emotions, feelings, and associations, thence to considering the values and meaning of the subject, and finally to deciding on a response to the situation. For additional information, see http://www.icaworld.org and http://www.icaworld.org/usa/usa.html.

Managing Conflict

Leaders of diverse teams can expect conflict to occur within the group. Indeed, leaders will want to encourage a clash of views and ideas, with the aim of developing the most effective and synergistic problem solutions. What they don't want is personalized conflict that results in group members' discounting each other's ideas and motives and mistrusting each other. The active listening and dialogue methods presented here can help prevent such destructive conflict. Other methods include Tom Rusk's ethical persuasion process (Rusk and Miller, 1993; Crosby, 1999, p. 68), Marshall Rosenberg's nonviolent communication process (1999), simulations and role plays (Mikolic and others, 1992), and the reconciliation process developed by the National Coalition Building Institute in Washington, D.C. (see Brown and Mazza, 1991; Crosby, 1999). The NCBI process should be especially helpful for teams that include members from social groups with widely differing power and status. Tom Fiutak, our colleague at the University of Minnesota, recommends a multistep process that begins with airing of perspectives on the source or causes of the conflict; it progresses to examination of underlying assumptions and expression of feelings about the conflict, then focuses on option building, and finally moves on to development of an action plan (Crosby, Bryson, and Anderson, 2003).

Oval Mapping

Another method of helping team members freely share and explain their ideas for accomplishing a task or resolving problems is the oval mapping technique described in Resource B. The technique can be used to help a team or organization decide on strategies, goals, missions, and action plans. It promotes effective intragroup communication through several features:

- Everyone's ideas are included.
- Linkages with other ideas are made visible.
- Consequences of pursuing the ideas are identified.
- Requirements for implementing the ideas are identified.

With the help of an able facilitator, the process allows a group to separate ideas from individuals and discuss them as part of a system of options, issues, and goals.

The methods we have introduced, when practiced with patience and honest engagement, promote equality and connection; honor thoughts, opinions, and feelings; foster mindfulness of one's own mental processes and group dynamics; and increase group creativity and learning. They are part and parcel of the empowerment work described later in this chapter. The increasingly prevalent virtual teams—that is, groups mostly linked together by electronic communication—are likely to require even more attention to communication (Antonakis and Atwater, 2002). Wherever possible, at least some face-to-face interaction should supplement electronic forms (see Kostner, 1994).

Some team members—especially those from an individualistic culture that prizes quick action—may object to the patience and time required for these methods. They may have to be reassured that efforts to garner diverse ideas and align team members around a shared purpose will pay off with higher-quality group decisions and products (see Wheelan, 1999).

Matching Communication Style
and Content to Group Type and Needs

Team leaders need to remember that every group is unique and full of unpredictable behavior. At the same time, leaders should be sensitive to common stages of group development.

As Susan Wheelan points out, fledgling teams with a designated leader are likely to respond best if the leader uses a somewhat directive communication style; as the team moves toward greater cohesion and shared leadership, the style should become far more participative (Wheelan, 1999). The leader also should provide basic understanding of group process and development—for example, by noting that the group should expect conflict and that conflict handled constructively helps the group become more cohesive. Some teams, however, do not have a designated leader and may choose to share leadership roles from the outset. Some groups also come together with a relatively high level of trust (on the basis of prior relationships, reputation, or long experience with teamwork). These groups may resist directive communication and explanations about group process; the challenge with these groups is to try new working habits or to welcome and educate newcomers.

Team leaders are also often responsible for communicating with groups outside the team. They may need to report to someone or a group that authorized the team in the first place. They may need to promote the group or highlight its progress to several external audiences in order to garner support and resources for the team.

Empowerment

We define empowerment as helping each group member claim and develop his or her power in service of the group's mission and promoting a sense of shared leadership in the group. To do so, team members need a shared understanding of the team's mission, goals, decision-making procedures, rules, norms, work plan, and evaluation methods. They also need to know which roles and responsibilities they are expected to carry out. They need to see leaders and followers as mutually empowering.

A team may have an assigned mission; even some goals, roles, and norms may be specified in advance. The team, however, should decide for itself how to modify, supplement, or supplant its assignments. In the case of a team established by some outside authority, a key early task of a designated team leader is to ensure that the team has enough authority to carry out its work (see Houghton, Neck, and Manz, 2003). An important leadership task is ensuring that the group begins with at least a general sense of what its mission is. Full-fledged goal setting and role clarification may be postponed until group members have worked together awhile, but "group norming" should happen early. The "snowcard" technique for establishing or revisiting group norms is offered in Exercise 3.1. In preparation for doing the exercise, a team leader may want to mention that productive work groups establish norms related to innovation, task achievement, and mutual support (Wheelan, 1999). Examples of norms related to innovation include "open to quirky ideas," "OK to fail," "learn from failures," "open to different practices," "laughter and fun encouraged." As with methods described in the previous section, snowcards allow everyone's ideas to be considered; they give a picture of which ideas are most supported by the group. Snowcards are a quick method too for gathering and organizing team members' proposals for mission, goals, and subtasks.

When a group initially comes together, the norms are more aspirations than genuinely accepted unwritten rules. What is helpful about explicitly identifying desired norms early on is that they are likely to be constructive; almost all the groups we have facilitated, for example, identify norms related to openness, sharing of information, mutual respect, safety for risk taking and disagreement, and cooperation. Those constructive norms are a touchstone that a leader can emphasize as the group continues; importantly, they are a means whereby a leader can activate team members' self-concepts tied to openness and self-transcendence (see Lord and Brown, 2001). One of the most important leadership tasks is to consistently model the norms the group has adopted.

Team leaders should also encourage group members to agree on basic decision-making procedures. Considerable evidence supports the value of consensus as a method of ensuring that group support for a decision is high (L. Thompson, 2001; Johnson and Johnson, 2003). Since achieving full-blown consensus can be extremely time consuming, the wisest route may be reserving consensus for decisions about mission and overarching goals and

Exercise 3.1. Using "Snowcards" to Identify and Agree on Norms.

1. Ask the group the question, What norms or standards would be good for us to establish to help us accomplish our work together? Think of the "unwritten rules" that might improve performance, inspire commitment, or enhance satisfaction.
2. Have individuals in the group brainstorm as many ideas as possible and record each idea on a separate "snowcard," such as a Post-it note, 5" x 7" card, or oval or square of paper.
3. Have individuals share their ideas in round-robin fashion.
4. Tape the ideas to the wall. As a group, remove duplication and cluster similar ideas in categories. Establish subcategories as needed. The resulting clusters of cards may resemble a "blizzard" of ideas—hence the term snowcards.
5. Clarify ideas.
6. Once all the ideas are on the wall and included in categories, re-arrange and tinker with the categories until they make the most sense. Place a card giving the category name above each cluster.
7. If needed, help the group decide which clusters or individual norms have strong group support (for example, by giving each person a certain number of sticky dots to apply to the norms he or she deems most important).
8. As a group, decide how to monitor and reinforce the norms.
9. After the exercise, distribute a copy of the norms listed by categories to all members of the group.

strategies, and even then using methods that define consensus as the wholehearted support of the many and acquiescence of a few. For decisions that are not subject to consensus, executive decision making by one person or a small group with consultation is usually best (Johnson and Johnson, 2003).

Although it's certainly logical that groups would clarify their mission and set achievable goals before they agree on strategies, they may actually be able to agree more easily on strategies and action plans. Often people do not fully know what their mission and goals ought to be until they create viable strategies and actions (Eden and Ackermann, 1998; Huxham, 2003). Regardless of the sequencing of these decisions, an action plan is needed. An action plan should include attention to stakeholders, the means of acquiring needed resources, assignment of team member roles and responsibilities, a timeline for task completion, and evaluation methods. Assigned roles and responsibilities should relate to individual team members' skills and other resources; they should be challenging, but not so challenging that team members feel overwhelmed. Cooperative work (by the entire team or subgroup) should be built into the plan to foster creativity, synergy, and mutual support. If team members are representing stakeholder groups, the timelines should include time for consulting stakeholders and apprising the team of stakeholder feedback. In many cases, the team needs a strategy for relating to other teams and to a larger organization of which it is a part (Zaccaro, Rittman, and Marks, 2001).

Often a team realizes that members need to upgrade their skills or develop new ones. The action plan then should include opportunities for training, including training in group process skills. Evaluation of the team's work should be ongoing through built-in opportunities for constructive feedback on individual and group performance. Many experts on group dynamics recommend taking time at the end of every group meeting to review how well the group observed its own norms and offer ideas for improvement (Wheelan, 1999). It may be helpful to appoint at least one team member to monitor the group's communication patterns to report on how closely the team approaches optimal interaction, in which about two-thirds of verbal comments focus on task achievement and most of the remaining third on support of group members (see Wheelan, 1999). To be constructive, both individual and group feedback should focus on specific behavior, highlight accomplishment as well as failure, avoid blaming and personal attacks, be tied to group tasks, and emphasize specific remedies for problems.

Groups undertaking complex, long-term projects are likely to benefit from one or more retreats to help focus on their mission, vision of success, and action plan (see, for example, Weisman, 2003). These groups should also schedule celebrations to mark attainment of milestones.

Leadership Development

To maximize the contributions of team members, the team leader(s) should seek to develop leadership capacity in everyone, so that leadership tasks such as recruiting new team members, modeling active listening, and reinforcing norms of openness and self-transcendence can be taken on by many if not all group members. Tasks such as planning and conducting meetings or coordinating specific projects can be rotated among group members. Task sharing fosters a more egalitarian atmosphere, allows people to contribute particular expertise, and enables everyone to be in a supportive follower role at least part of the time. Sharing leadership tasks may also help a diverse group become more cohesive, since members from differing cultures have a chance for prominence (Chen and Van Velsor, 1996). Building leadership capacity among team members is also a means of grooming successors for the time when those who have had prominent leadership roles in the team move on to other responsibilities. A team that is expected to last for some time may benefit from crafting a leadership development plan for itself.

To foster shared leadership, Fletcher and Kaüfer emphasize the importance of developing relational skills. They suggest building on the skills team members have learned through family or community involvement, examples being "a welcoming stance toward change; an ability to focus long-term versus short-term goals; and an ability to integrate thinking, feeling, and acting into practice" (Fletcher and Kaüfer, 2003, p. 33). Charles Manz and his colleagues offer techniques of self-leadership that foster shared leadership (Manz and Sims, 2001; Houghton, Neck, and Manz, 2003). Of course, it is also important to remember that more egalitarian societal cultures are more supportive of shared leadership than other cultures.

Trust and Spirit

The recruitment, communication, empowerment, and leadership development methods discussed so far all contribute to the trust building that so many team leadership analysts identify as one of the most important ingredients of a productive team (Useem,

1998; Kouzes and Posner, 2002). When a group first comes together, trust may hardly exist among the group members unless
they have previous connections. (In some cases, of course, previous connections might actually undermine trust!) Team leaders
should constantly assess the level of trust in a group and tailor communication and other activities accordingly. James Kouzes and
Barry Posner suggest a number of ways in which leaders build trust:

• Making their values, ethics, and standards clear, and then
  living by them
• Keeping their commitments and promises
• Trusting those from whom they seek trust
• Going first
• Being open and sensitive to the needs of others
• Demonstrating competence

Team spirit grows in the medium of trust, but it also refers to a
shared enthusiasm for the group's mission and a belief that the
team can accomplish great things together. Leaders foster team
spirit by ensuring that the team has challenging tasks that can be
competently performed (Csikszentmihalyi, 1990). They also let
every individual shine as well as celebrate the team, blend challenge and support, help team members learn from defeat and difficulty, remind everyone of why the team's work is important, and
help the group laugh at itself.

   In a team with a high level of trust and spirit, each member
knows he or she can rely on the others to fulfill their roles competently and reliably, verbal and nonverbal cues are easily deci-
phered, and productivity amazes observers and even the members.
These teams achieve what Mihaly Csikszentmihalyi called a state of
flow (1990).

   The importance of trust and spirit was evident in two teams
connected to the African American Men Project and the Vital
Aging Initiative. Gary Cunningham asked one of us (John) to use
various stakeholder analyses to help devise a viable political strategy for the African American Men Project. John and Gary had
worked together before at the University of Minnesota and re-
mained friends, supporters, and admirers after Gary left to become
head of planning for Hennepin County. Neither Gary nor John

knew exactly how to use stakeholder analyses for the purpose at hand (several new techniques actually had to be invented to help with the effort), but Gary had faith in John's ability to come up with something useful, and John had faith in Gary's ability to manage key stakeholder input, expectations, and commitments. John then recruited Karen Lokkesmoe, a doctoral student at the university, to help, and Gary created a team with whom John and Karen could work. The team consisted of Hennepin County staff members (one was also a former student of John's) and community activists. The team of Euro-Americans and African Americans became a high-performing team, in part by directly confronting racial tensions in the group; it did create a political strategy that won the day with the steering group and the county commissioners. The group was justifiably proud of its accomplishments.

In the Vital Aging case, one of us (Barbara) agreed to work with Jan Hively and two other women to explore how the Humphrey Institute of Public affairs might contribute to the Vital Aging Initiative. The other two women were Sharon Anderson, the institute's director of professional development, and Shelby Andress, an alumnus of a Humphrey Institute seminar and a retired senior member of a Minneapolis research organization. Barbara and Sharon had teamed up many times over the preceding twenty years, and all four women knew each other well and had great respect for each other's skills. In an initial meeting, the women engaged in free-flowing information exchange about the initiative, possible connections with Humphrey programs, and personal perceptions of vital aging. In subsequent meetings, we agreed to take on a specific project: organizing focus groups in preparation for the Vital Aging Summit. We parceled out roles and responsibilities and agreed on timelines. We stayed in touch between meetings via e-mail, phone calls, and face-to-face conversations. The focus groups were completed, and results were compiled and submitted to the summit organizers.

Team meetings were not perfect by group process standards; not everyone was able to be on time, and we seldom reviewed the quality of each meeting. The group did, however, coalesce around a task, laid groundwork for future work together on the challenging Vital Aging project, and supported each other in actually carrying out the task. We checked periodically on how satisfied each person was with the group's progress. We laughed a lot, sympathized with each other, and celebrated by having tea together at a local restaurant. The team rated high on individual satisfaction, cohesion, and task accomplishment. We fit Susan Wheelan's profile of a high-performing work group (Wheelan, 1999).

There is a wealth of guidance on developing and sustaining productive work groups. Among the best are *Facilitation Resources* (Anderson and others, 1999), developed by a team at the University of Minnesota; the classic *Joining Together* (Johnson and Johnson, 2003); *The Skilled Facilitator* (Schwarz, 2002); *Creating Effective Teams* (Wheelan, 1999); *Super-Leadership* (Manz and Sims, 1989); *The Leadership Challenge* (Kouzes and Posner, 2002); *Encouraging the Heart* (Kouzes and Posner, 1999); and *The Change Handbook: Group Methods for Shaping the Future* (Holman and Devane, 1999). The books by Wheelan and Johnson and Johnson are especially helpful in tailoring leadership style and activities to the stages of a group's development. Several chapters in *Shared Leadership,* by Craig Pearce and Jay Conger (2003), highlight the benefits of shared leadership in teams and the environmental and task conditions that promote shared leadership (Houghton, Neck, and Manz, 2003; see also Hooker and Csikszentmihalyi, 2003). You can also use the team assessment in Exercise 3.2 to highlight leadership tasks that need attention.

By building a productive work group, change advocates are able to harness individual energies to accomplish much more than team members could achieve separately. The power of a team, however, is often constrained by the organization to which it is connected. An organization is a means of coordinating individual and group efforts around some purpose, such as producing a set of goods or services or promoting an innovation. Organizations are typically larger, more formal, more enduring, and more powerful than teams. They become even more powerful by linking with other organizations in networks. The next section focuses on the main tasks of organizational leadership.

Organizational Leadership

Advocates of major policy change must ensure that effective and humane organizations are created, maintained, or restructured as needed. In the AIDS case, gay activists, concerned physicians and

Exercise 3.2. Assessing Your Team.

Rate your team.

	Good	Average	Poor

Membership

1. Team members have shared purpose.
2. Team members contribute needed knowledge, contacts, and skills.
3. Team members represent needed diversity of views and backgrounds.
4. Team size is appropriate.

Effective Communication

1. Team members listen to each other's views.
2. Important messages are expressed clearly.
3. Conflict is managed constructively.
4. Team members laugh together.
5. The setting for a team meeting contributes to the team's effectiveness.
6. Team members are sensitive to their cultural differences.

Empowerment

1. The team has a clear mission and goals.
2. The team has effective strategies for obtaining needed resources.
3. Decision-making rules are clear.
4. Major responsibilities, timelines, and evaluation methods are spelled out in action plans.
5. Team norms support openness, sharing, mutual support, and cooperation.
6. Challenge and support are tailored to members' needs and abilities.

Leadership Development

1. Team leaders groom successors.
2. Leadership responsibilities are shared.
3. Team members organize team training sessions.
4. The team has a comprehensive leadership development program.

Exercise 3.2. Assessing Your Team, Cont'd.

	Good	Average	Poor

Trust and Spirit

1. Achievement is rewarded.
2. Adversity is overcome.
3. Team leaders recognize they are empowered by other team members.

When you are done with the ratings:

1. Identify two or three of the items that you have rated *good*. Bring them to your group, and celebrate!
2. Now identify one or two that you have rated *poor* and for which you have some ideas for improvement. Bring them to your group and develop mutual strategies for improvement.

public health officers, and a few politicians and their aides created new organizations and reoriented existing ones. The AIDS Research and Education Foundation in San Francisco and the AIDS Medical Foundation in New York were examples of new organizations created specifically to fund research into the cause and prevention of the disease. Gay activists in New York launched the Gay Men's Health Crisis in 1982, and before long the organization was a social service agency staffed by hundreds of volunteers who answered a telephone hotline and operated a "buddy program" for people with AIDS. Meanwhile, the emerging AIDS coalition pressured the National Institutes of Health, U.S. Department of Health and Human Services, city health departments, and university research departments to set up new programs and reorder priorities to stop the advance of the disease.

When Stephan Schmidheiny sought to mold a business message for the 1992 Earth Summit, he organized the Business Council for Sustainable Development, which he thought would be a temporary organization of fifty CEOs from around the world. After the summit, however, the members decided that the council should continue, and in 1995 it merged with the World Industry Council for the Environment to become the World Business

Council for Sustainable Development. The council is now a coalition of 170 international companies and has developed a global partnership network of forty-five national and regional councils and other organizations.

In both the African American Men and the Vital Aging cases, change advocates created new programs within existing organizations; their leadership focused on helping their institutions respond to opportunities and threats in their environment. In all four cases, change advocates developed new interorganizational networks; that is the focus of the second part of this book.

Whether leaders are launching a new organization or reshaping an existing one, they must perform three crucial overall leadership tasks:

1. Paying attention to organizational purpose and design
2. Becoming adept in dealing with internal and external change
3. Building inclusive community inside and outside organizations

Each includes several more specific tasks, which are distilled from the vast literature on organizational leadership. The preponderance of research and writing on this subject has focused on hierarchical business organizations, and often on senior executives or managers. Increasingly, scholars are concerned with leadership in nonprofit and government organizations and with development of leadership throughout organizations of varying design. We highlight the leadership tasks that seem to be important regardless of organizational type and recommend sources for information about leadership in specific types. We emphasize the need to create organizations that can thrive in a complex, interdependent world—that is, imbued with leadership capacity at all levels. The approach presented here has much in common with several other contemporary approaches—specifically, servant leadership (Greenleaf, 1977), authentic leadership (Terry, 1993), connective leadership (Lipman-Blumen, 1996), systemic leadership (Allen and Cherrey, 2000), complex leadership (Marion and Uhl-Bien, 2001), and shared leadership (Pearce and Conger, 2003).

Paying Attention to Organizational Purpose and Design

An organization's purpose and connected core values serve as the collective raison d'être for everyone there, as a way of framing reality and as a guiding compass for choosing direction. Continual, explicit attention to purpose and core values is especially important in any large, decentralized organization.

Purpose and core values may be captured in formal mission and philosophy statements. (We've also come across at least one organization that has a "passion statement," expressing the concern or desire that prompts the mission.) To foster the long-term sustainability of the organization, the values should be in some way an expression of the fundamental virtues of justice and mercy (Dutton and others, 2002; Locke, 2003). Organizational purpose is enacted through goals and strategies, vision of success, governance and administrative systems, and a supportive culture. A leader has a special responsibility for being a politician and role model for carrying out the organization's purpose and core values.

Developing Mission and Philosophy Statements

A mission statement succinctly communicates what the organization is, the need to which it responds, whom it serves, its basic strategies, and its uniqueness. The organization's core values and basic principles and standards may be incorporated into the mission statement or else presented in a separate philosophy statement. The mission statement should be action-oriented and aligned with organizational mandates and stakeholder needs and expectations. It should be short and memorable, yet possess "breadth, durability, challenge, and distinction" (Angelica, 2001, p. 6). It should indicate how the organization contributes to the common good and call forth what Rosabeth Moss Kanter (2002) calls the members' "better selves." What's more important than any formal mission statement, however, is that people throughout the organization know what the mission is and, as Collins and Porras say, "live it in their toes" (1997). Robert Terry concludes that mission work is really identity work; the mission should communicate the organization's essence. Although, the mission is a guide for the future, he recommends phrasing it in present tense (2001, pp. 153–156).

David Day (2001) suggests that a successful organization needs multiple, or at least flexible, identities to deal with "an increasingly complex and changing environment" (p. 391).

The World Business Council for Sustainable Development (WBCSD) has a relatively brief mission: "To provide business leadership as a catalyst for change toward sustainable development, and to promote the role of eco-efficiency, innovation, and corporate social responsibility." The mission is presented on a Web page that describes the council as a "coalition of 170 international companies united by a shared commitment to sustainable development via the three pillars of economic growth, ecological balance and social progress" (http://www.wbcsd.org/about us/index.htm). The names of both WBCSD and the Vital Aging Network serve as slogans that communicate their missions.

Leaders are often responsible for clarifying how a part of an organization contributes to the overall mission. For example, Hennepin County government has a general mission to serve individuals, families, and communities in the county, but Cunningham's Office of Planning and Development has to have a clear idea of what it specifically needs to do to support the mission.

Formal mission and philosophy statements can be put together by a small group of founders, a representative team, or the entire membership. It may also be wise to involve representatives of external stakeholders. Involving more people is time consuming but also increases the likelihood of widespread buy-in and allows everyone to contribute ideas. The process we recommend begins with stakeholder analysis and identification of mandates, followed by identification of mission elements. Exercise 3.3 offers guidance for doing a simple stakeholder analysis; Exercise 3.4 offers a process for developing a mission statement. Additional guidance is available in Bryson (2004) and Bryson and Crosby (2003). The use of the oval mapping technique in agreeing on mission is described in Resource B.

Developing Goals and Strategies

Mission and philosophy statements identify organizational directions and ends. A goal is a general statement further specifying the organization's mission. Goals are "obviously good in their own

Exercise 3.3. Stakeholder Identification and Analysis

Step 1. Participants convene in small groups.

Step 2. Each small group brainstorms a list of key internal and external stakeholders and prepares a flipchart that arrays them as illustrated here. (External stakeholders are those over whom the organization has little or no control.)

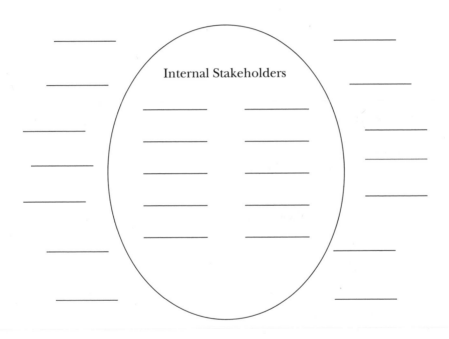

External Stakeholders

Internal Stakeholders

Step 3. After a small group has identified stakeholders, the group should fill out the following worksheet for each stakeholder. In filling out the worksheet, the group should pay attention to different perspectives and needs on the basis of gender, ethnicity, physical ability, age, religious preference, and other characteristics as relevant.

Exercise 3.3. Stakeholder Identification and Analysis, Cont'd.

Stakeholder:			
Criterion or Criteria Used by Stakeholder to Assess Our Performance	**Our Sense of Their Judgment About Our Performance**		
	Very Good	**OK**	**Poor**
How do they influence us?			
What do we need from them?			
How important are they? ☐ Extremely ☐ Reasonably ☐ Not very ☐ Not at all			

Step 4. The group should discuss the implications of the analysis for the organization's mission.

Step 5. The small groups should assemble in plenary session to report to each other.

Based on Bryson, J. M., and Alston, F. K. *Creating and Implementing Your Strategic Plan: A Workbook for Public and Nonprofit Organizations.* San Francisco: Jossey-Bass, 2004.

Exercise 3.4. Mission Development.

Facilitator instructions:

Step 1. Ask participants to answer these six sets of questions silently as individuals, not as a group.

1. Who are we? What is our purpose? What business are we in?
2. In general, what are the basic social and political needs we exist to fill? Or what are the basic social or political problems we exist to address?
3. In general, what do we want to do to recognize or anticipate and respond to these needs or problems?
4. How should we respond to our key stakeholders?
5. What is our philosophy, and what are our core values?
6. What makes us distinct or unique?

Step 2. Ask everyone to record his or her answers on separate large Post-it notes or a half-sheet of paper, one answer apiece. Then aggregate individual answers by placing or taping them to a wall and clustering similar answers. In other words, if an individual has several answers to question one, he or she would use as many Post-its as there are answers (if the person has six answers in total to the six questions, he or she would use six Post-its all told). Alternatively, have people silently brainstorm answers to the questions on prepared worksheets, and then go around the room in round-robin fashion recording answers onto flipchart sheets.

Step 3. Once answers are recorded, either on clustered Post-its on a wall or on flipchart sheets attached to the wall, give each participant eighteen sticky green dots and six sticky red dots (three-quarters or one inch in diameter). Tell people to use three green dots and one red dot per question. For each question, ask everyone to place a green dot by the three answers that he or she deems most important for inclusion in the mission statement. Ask everyone to place a red dot by the one answer—if any—that he or she cannot abide.

If the group is reviewing an existing mission statement, you may not need to ask all of the questions listed above. It may be enough to hand out a copy of the existing mission and use the round-robin process to record answers to the following questions:

1. Is our current mission dated? If so, how?
2. What changes in the mission do I propose?

The material resulting from this exercise can then be turned over to the person charged with drafting a mission statement.

right, and do not seem to need further elaboration. Typically, they are morally virtuous and upright and tap the deepest values and most worthy aspirations of the organization's culture" (Bryson, 1995, p. 269).

Goals are often operationalized as objectives, which are measurable and possibly linked to a timeline. Strategy is the means by which goals are achieved. They therefore link mission, goals, policies, programs, and actions. It is extremely important to ensure that strategies include plans for obtaining necessary resources (staffing, training, equipment, supplies, travel budgets) for the organization to function.

Organizations express goals and strategies in various ways. Here is how the World Business Council for Sustainable Development, for example, refers to its *strategic directions:*

- *Business leadership:* to be the leading business advocate on issues connected with sustainable development
- *Policy development:* to participate in policy development in order to create a framework that allows business to contribute effectively to sustainable development
- *Best practice:* to demonstrate business progress in environmental and resource management and corporate social responsibility and to share leading-edge practices among our members
- *Global outreach:* to contribute to a sustainable future for developing nations and nations in transition (http://www.wbcsd.org/about us/index.htm)

Compared to mission, philosophy, and goal statements, strategy development is more likely to be a source of friction, since mission, values, and goals are usually general enough that diverse people can accept them but the specificity of strategies can generate intense disagreement because of their implications for the organization's image, methods, power distribution, and resource allocation. In the early days of the Gay Men's Health Crisis, for example, board members hotly debated whether the organization should pursue mainly service strategies or add a prominent advocacy role.

Constructing an Inspiring Vision Embodying Organizational Goals and Key Strategies

Leaders help people in the organization develop a clear picture of what it would look and feel like if it were achieving its mission. In Margaret Wheatley's terms, the vision should become a "force field" that runs through the entire organization, generating energy for putting the vision into action (Wheatley, 1999). We talk more about creating and communicating an inspiring vision to guide interorganizational change efforts in the next chapter, and much of what we say there applies to creating and communicating a vision of organizational success. Quite often, development of a full-fledged vision (and even a precise mission statement) is not realistic in the beginning. People in the organization may need to focus on developing and implementing strategies that they can agree on before clarifying a vision to sustain them over the long haul (Bryson, 1995). This approach can help ensure that the vision is what Hively calls "an umbrella within which there are multiple definitions of aspects of success, based on the needs and visions of key stakeholders" (Hively, personal communication, July 2003). The vision can be captured in a written statement or in a variety of media (logos, film, stories, presentations at an annual conference and other events). Exercise 3.5 offers guidance for constructing an organizational vision statement. Other advice and approaches (such as construction of a "vision collage") can be found in our chapter in Carol Weisman's book on retreats (Bryson and Crosby, 2003) and in Burt Nanus's *Visionary Leadership* (1992).

Aligning Design with Organizational Purpose

Leaders ensure that the organization develops flexible, transparent, just, and compassionate governance, administrative, and employee-development systems that develop and sustain the organization's core competencies (Light, 1998; Collins and Porras, 1997). The organizational systems should also allow conflict to surface, so that the organization is able to learn from varying perspectives, support organizational members' efforts to carry out the mission, and respond to stakeholder needs. (Helpful ideas for conflict management systems are available from the Association for Conflict Resolution Website, http://www.acresolution.org.) Training and development programs should include leadership development and be tailored

Exercise 3.5. Constructing an Organizational Vision of Success.

A vision of success should include the organization's:

- Mission
- Basic philosophy and core values
- Basic strategies
- Performance criteria
- Major decision-making rules
- Ethical standards

To develop the vision, assemble participants in small groups to answer the following questions individually. Each group should share and discuss its answers and then develop a group report that can be discussed in a plenary session. After the group reports are presented and discussed in the plenary, someone can be appointed to prepare a draft vision statement. The draft should be circulated to key stakeholders and modifications made as appropriate to achieve general agreement.

The questions:

1. What is the organization's mission?
2. What are the organization's basic philosophies and core values?
3. What are its basic strategies?
4. What are its performance criteria?
5. What are the major decision-making rules followed by the organization?

   - What processes and procedures are followed to make major decisions? to make minor decisions?
   - What is decided centrally?
   - What is delegated?
   - How are exceptions handled?

6. What ethical standards are expected of all members?

to the type of organization and people's role in it. A particularly effective approach to training is to tie it directly to organizational tasks or change efforts (Raelin, 2000).

All too often, internal systems actually undermine mission accomplishment. In the AIDS case, for example, the administrative systems within large government public health agencies such as the National Cancer Institute (NCI) and the Centers for Disease Control (CDC) prevented the agencies from providing substantial resources quickly to understand and fight a new disease. Moreover, these agencies were part of the massive public health bureaucracy overseen by the Department of Health and Human Services. Since the department was headed by a presidential appointee, major policies and budget allocations had to fit the president's agenda, which did not give prominence to health problems affecting gay people.

Medical researchers trying to garner support from their universities for work on AIDS didn't fare much better with their institutions. The application process for research grants was cumbersome and time-consuming. Neither could they persuade academic journals to speed up their process for publishing research results so that the initial findings could be disseminated to other researchers.

At least some public health and medical professionals were able to make headway in the part of the system they did control. By the summer of 1981, James Curran, an epidemiologist at the CDC, was chairing an interdepartmental task force on the emerging disease. The task force allowed experts from several disciplines to trade information and analysis. The NCI finally convened an AIDS task force in April 1983. Marcus Conant persuaded other doctors affiliated with the University of California at San Francisco and San Francisco General Hospital to help him cobble together a clinic that he hoped could attract federal funding.

Monitoring and evaluating results is an important means of checking on how well organizational systems are fulfilling the mission. A key step is establishing reasonable performance measures for the organization as a whole, for subunits, for teams, and for individuals. Useful evaluation processes are 360-degree feedback (Tornow, London, and CCL Associates, 1998), the balanced scorecard (Kaplan and Norton, 1996), program evaluation (Wholey, Hatry, and Newcomer, 1994; Patton, 1997), and responsibility contracts (Behn, 1999). If designed well, these processes should help everyone in the organization focus on what's important. Leaders should also ensure that the evaluation results are used to improve organizational performance.

Ensuring That Organizational Culture Supports Mission and Philosophy

Organizational culture is an organization's greatest cohesive force and often its most formidable barrier to change (Feldman and Khademian, 2002). A culture consists of shared assumptions about how things should be done here, stories we tell about ourselves, the rituals we observe. Founders, of course, have a prime opportunity to shape mission and values; those who attempt to alter an existing culture have to build awareness that old assumptions and approaches are not working and develop understanding of how the best of the old culture can be preserved in new ways of working. To nurture effective and humane organizations, leaders should foster a culture of integrity, inclusion, learning, and productivity.

A *culture of integrity* promotes expectations that everyone will align his or her behavior with the principles and values that the organization professes. It is essential to what Kim Cameron and Arran Caza (2002) call "organizational virtuousness," discussed later in this section. To foster a culture of integrity, leaders:

- Make a public commitment to ethical principles
- Emphasize mission and stewardship
- Emphasize personal responsibility
- Help people in the organization analyze ethical implications of their work and make plans for resolving ethical conflicts
- Make hard decisions supporting ethical principles
- Reward ethical behavior
- Model ethical behavior (Wallace and White, 1988)

Other leadership skills that promote a culture of integrity are included in the ethical leadership section of the next chapter.

In the early years of the AIDS crisis in the United States, a stronger culture of integrity would have helped blood banks respond more quickly to warnings that the AIDS virus had contaminated blood supplies. Nonprofit blood banks objected to the high cost of donor screening and blood testing, and government regulators hesitated to require it. Interestingly, commercial manufacturers of blood products decided early on to screen donors, because they realized that competitors could offer a safer product and therefore lure away their customers. An estimated twelve thousand people became infected with HIV as a result of contaminated blood transfusions administered during the two years that U.S. blood banks and government regulators were dragging their feet over screening and testing (Shilts, 1988, p. 599).

A *culture of inclusion* rests on the assumption that people from diverse backgrounds are valued and supported in the organization. Leaders who seek to build such a culture need to recognize that the organizational culture is strongly influenced by the dominant culture in which it is embedded. As these leaders seek to employ and work with people from diverse cultures (co-cultures within the society, or cultures outside the society), they must understand how the dominant culture operates, and how it influences the organizational culture. They need a comprehensive view of diversity that embraces gender, ethnicity, religion, physical, ability, class, sexual orientation, age, and possibly other characteristics. They require awareness of which cultural competencies organizational members may need and ensure those competencies are developed. Douglas Hicks (2002) suggests that leaders establish an environment of "respectful pluralism" that allows members to negotiate diversity and engage in diverse forms of expression, so long as coworkers do not feel coerced or degraded as a result. Diversity training programs should be selected with care. A promising approach is "diversity self-efficacy" training, which helps people in an organization develop and use strategies for promoting "positive diversity climates" (Combs, 2002). The training emphasizes mastery, modeling, and observational learning.

If diverse people are to be recruited to work in an organization, it must tailor recruitment efforts to different groups—for example, by placing advertisements in media that serve a particular community or using personal connections with a specific group. Leaders also should ensure that those who are a minority within the organization are given the challenging assignments, support, and rewards for achievement that will enable them to perform well (Morrison, 1992). Leaders must work to break down the stereotypes and traditional personnel practices that prevent people in an organizational minority from achieving senior positions.

Advocates of inclusion sometimes argue for special efforts to hire and retain women and members of minority groups on the grounds that these people manage or lead differently from men belonging to the majority culture (Rosener, 1995). Studies of actual managerial and leadership behavior in organizations, however, show only a small difference between men and women;

fewer studies have measured differences other than gender, but there is evidence that management and leadership behavior is affected far more by organizational culture and the nature of the work to be done than by one's gender or minority status (DiTomaso and Hooijberg, 1996; Freeman, 2001; Vecchio, 2002). The case for inclusion rests more soundly on justice and legal grounds and on contribution to organizational image, learning, and networking. Women and members of minority groups can be expected to bring their own experiences and perspectives to bear on the organization's work, and they will have ties to stakeholder groups that may be important to accomplishing the organization's goals.

A *learning culture* prompts people in an organization to undertake the inquiry and analysis that indicate how well activities are advancing the mission and how to improve those activities. A *culture of productivity* prompts members to use this learning efficiently to achieve improvement. In a culture of learning and productivity, people share the assumption that change is to be expected and embraced. Everyone is expected to be a problem solver and learner; experimentation and learning from failure are valued. Current practices are critiqued in order to achieve improvement.

Edgar Schein highlights several additional practices and assumptions that support a culture of learning and productivity (Schein, 1992):

- Viewing the environment as manageable, though not controllable.
- Viewing truth as arrived at, or approximated, through a pragmatic discovery process. The discovery process should aim at discovering tacit knowledge as well as recorded information (Tsoukas, 1996).
- Viewing the world as complex and interconnected.
- Focusing on individuals and groups, tasks and relationships.
- Creating multiple communication channels. In a hierarchical organization, leaders have to pay special attention to opening channels across organizational levels (Crossan, Lane, and White, 1999). Also important is creating means of integrating the learning that comes from these multiple channels—for example, by es-

tablishing cross-functional teams or using tools such as dialogue and cognitive mapping, which were described earlier in this chapter (Crossan, Lane, and White, 1999; Allen and Cherry, 2000).

• Emphasizing diversity and unity (which is also important for fostering a culture of inclusion).

• Focusing on the midterm: long enough to "test whether or not a proposed solution is working but not so much time that one persists with a proposed solution that is clearly not working" (Schein, 1992, p. 369).

These practices and assumptions are nurtured by norms of mutual support and appreciation, openness, humor, inclusion, high expectations, and attention to core values (Fairholm, 1994). Also important (and especially so in a fast-paced dot com environment) is a climate of empowerment, in which frontline employees and teams have the information and flexibility they need to do their jobs well (Quinn, Faerman, Thompson, and Mcgrath, 1996; Brown and Gioia, 2002). Leaders should be especially attentive to the "margin"—a part of the organization that is "renegade," or at least unusual. Edgar Schein argues that vital learning may be occurring in these fringe areas precisely because they are less constrained by organizational norms (Schein, 1992). Russ Marion and Mary Uhl-Bien offer important insights about how to distribute intelligence throughout an organization. They advise leaders to cultivate interdependencies within and outside, to catalyze bottom-up network construction, to seed good ideas in receptive parts of the organization, and to think systematically (Marion and Uhl-Bien, 2001).

Karl Weick, Kathleen Sutcliffe, and David Obstfeld offer guidance for creating a learning culture in "high-reliability organizations"—those operating effectively in a high-pressure, high-stakes environment. Their research indicates that these organizations emphasize five practices:

1. Preoccupation with failure; intense scrutiny of errors and weaknesses
2. Reluctance to simplify interpretation
3. Sensitivity to operations; people have an "integrated picture" of what is going on

4. Commitment to resilience—for example, through use of improvisation
5. Fluidity of decision making (Weick, Sutcliffe, and Obstfeld, 2002)

Stakeholder analysis and involvement can be an especially helpful method of promoting organizational learning. As people listen to diverse stakeholders, they build a much richer understanding of the organization's performance, ideas for improvement, and understanding of the relationships among stakeholders.

The World Business Council on Sustainable Development, for example, has convened focus groups consisting of diverse stakeholders to learn how they view the relationship between business and the environment and to gather ideas for WBCSD projects. The Hennepin County planning office asked diverse stakeholders to participate in the task forces and working groups that developed reports and recommendations for the African American Men Project. The Vital Aging Initiative was a means of connecting the University of Minnesota to a group of stakeholders—the "young old," who had not previously been high on the university's agenda. The initiative has prompted parts of the university to learn about this group and begin incorporating this learning into their programs. When the Vital Aging Initiative became the Vital Aging Network in 2000, the organizers began holding monthly topic meetings (focusing, for example, on financial security or creativity), which attract a variety of people with a stake in vital aging: service providers, children of aging parents, and people going through a midlife or retirement transition, as well as older adults.

Mary Crossan, Henry Lane, and Roderick White also recommend using Joseph Schumpeter's idea of "creative destruction" to stop institutionalized learning from hampering new learning. At times, leaders must set aside established procedures so as "to enact variations that allow intuition, insights and actions to surface and be pursued" (Crossan, Lane, and White, 1999, p. 533). In the monthly VAN meetings, for example, at the beginning—before any experts speak—participants are asked to reveal something about their own experiences and hopes in connection with the meeting topic. Susan Annunzio advises leaders interested in culture change to ask the unaskable and speak the unspeakable (Annunzio, 2001).

Edgar Schein's recommendations for revealing culture are noted in our Chapter Two. Manfred Kets de Vries suggests using exercises that are based on these questions: If your organization were an animal, what would it be? If it were a person, what would it look like? Management scholars Stephen Osborne and Kate McLaughlin ask groups to draw cartoons depicting their current organizational culture and outlining the desired culture.

One important method of shaping culture is ensuring that critical decisions (such as budget allocations, hiring and promotion, and program priorities) support desired principles, norms, and styles. Attention to critical decisions may be especially important in the difficult work of changing a preexisting culture. Whereas people in an organization may discount exhortations and even persuasion, they pay attention to where the money goes and who's being hired, fired, or promoted. Additional advice for shaping culture can be found in Edgar Schein's *Organizational Leadership and Culture* (Schein, 2004), Anne Khademian's *Working with Culture* (Feldman and Khademian, 2002), and Gareth Morgan's *Creative Organizational Theory: A Resourcebook* (Morgan, 1989).

Being a Politician and Role Model

Perhaps the most effective tool a leader can wield for accomplishing an organization's mission is his or her own behavior. Many leadership analysts (prominently, Kouzes and Posner, 2002) note that effective leaders are exemplars of the organization's mission and values. They manifest the behavior they seek from others; they tell stories that reinforce desired norms; they communicate excitement and confidence about the organization and the people in it. They convey a sense of what's important by what they pay attention to (Osborn, Hunt, and Jauch, 2002). As Margaret Wheatley says, they become broadcasters of the organization's vision (Wheatley, 1999).

Leaders also need to stay in touch with other people in the organization (by showing concern or interest in them) to ensure that their efforts to be an exemplar do not turn them into a distant, idealized figure (De Pree, 1992; Sosik, Avolio, and Jung, 2002). It's important to remember that the people being led may have preferences in leadership style; however, three "transformational" leadership styles—charismatic influence, intellectual stimulation, and individual consideration—seem to be generally effective (Zaccaro and Banks, 2001). When cultural change is required, leaders also need to undo old, dysfunctional organizational values and commitments through their behavior. They have to exercise the political skills described in the next chapter so as to achieve adoption and implementation of desirable policies. Jean Lipman-Blumen (1996) urges leaders to deploy every resource they've got, from social skills to positional power on behalf of the organization's mission.

Becoming Adept at Dealing with Internal and External Change

Organizations must change if they are to survive, but they can choose how to cope with change. They might even choose to shape the changes rather than just adapting to them (Terry, 2001). The World Business Council for Sustainable Development is not involved in helping businesses adapt to global warming; the council is trying to help people become more adept in developing eco-efficient businesses. The Vital Aging Network is involving educational institutions, along with older adults and service providers, in redefining a major demographic change.

To help their organizations become adept at dealing with change, leaders:

- Constantly monitor internal and external environments
- Emphasize operating values appropriate to the stage of the organization's life cycle
- Are entrepreneurial and experimental
- Concentrate on team building and collaboration
- Plan for succession

Monitoring Internal and External Environments

Ongoing stakeholder analysis and involvement is an important source of information about developments inside and outside the organization. Information also comes from opinion polls, news media, and expert reports. Leaders may need to set up a continuous formal process of tracking change, but they are also well advised to draw on informal relationships with stakeholders and others who are well situated to observe or predict changes (Osborn, Hunt, and Jauch, 2002).

Emphasizing Operating Values According to the Life-Cycle Stage
In the beginning, an organization is fueled by passion, inspiration, and determination; key values are likely to be initiative, creativity, and all-out effort. At the outset, efficient and reliable systems may not be needed or even possible, but as time goes on people in and outside the organization expect some stability to set in. Thus efficiency and reliability become key values. In maturity, the organization may need shaking up again, and so renewal should become a key value.

For example, in launching the Business Council for Sustainable Development, Schmidheiny didn't waste time trying to establish a permanent organization; he even contributed his own money to pay for convening participants. When physicians and gay activists joined in organizing the Kaposi's Sarcoma Education and Research Foundation in California, several of the physicians themselves initially paid the rent for the foundation office. In both cases, as the organizations grew they needed more formal structures and systems.

For more insight about values and organizational life cycles, see Robert Quinn's *Beyond Rational Management* (1988). For advice about leading and managing in a crisis, see Ian Mitroff and Gus Anagnos's *Managing Crises Before They Happen* (2000) and Karl Weick and Kathleen Sutcliffe's *Managing the Unexpected* (2001).

Being Entrepreneurial and Experimental
Entrepreneurialism and experimentation are likely to come naturally at the beginning of an organization. As the organization stabilizes, leaders may need to make a special effort to sustain some of the same zeal and creativity that contributed to initial success. Developing and sustaining a learning culture is vital, of course. Dedicating resources for experimental projects has been found to be effective in public and nonprofit as well as business organizations (Light, 1998). Preventing management routine from becoming cumbersome and rigid is important. Leaders should be ready to discard routine, and even "core" competencies that are no longer core (Kouzes and Posner, 2002; Leonard and Swap, 2002). Studies conducted by Andrew Van de Ven and his colleagues indicate the importance of involving sponsors, mentors, critics, and "institutional leaders" in innovative projects. (An institutional leader is a top-level power broker who can be counted on

to emphasize the interests of the organization as a whole.) The researchers urge organizers of innovative projects to build in various ways to capture learning from the projects and to guard against overselling the likelihood of success (Brown, 1991; Van de Ven, Polley, Garud, and Venkataraman, 1999). Entrepreneurs also take advantage of new technologies. The Vital Aging Network developed its electronic listserv and Website to help manage the network, link older adults to opportunities for learning and service, and furnish tools for vital aging advocates (social workers, employers, and educators).

Emphasizing Collaboration and Team Building

As the degree of change and instability rises, centralized authority and control become increasingly less functional for organizations. Leaders have to work even harder to be sure that leadership is developed throughout the organization and that teamwork and collaboration are emphasized. They should seek to develop a "constellation of co-stars," rather than a small cadre of top positional leaders (Heenan and Bennis, 1999). They should recognize that power most often resides in "sharing, in compromising and negotiating, in helping and seeking help, in working together, in entrusting others, in altruism and self-sacrifice" (Lipman-Blumen, 1996, p. 241). They may also need to allow some productive individuals to work on their own (Locke, 2003).

In developing collaborative responses to change, leaders help people in the organization focus on what will stay the same as well as what needs changing. Robert Terry (2001) and Peter Drucker (Hesselbein and Johnston, 2002b) urge leaders to emphasize stability of core purpose and values in order to facilitate organizational change. Other analysts note, however, that even the mission may need revising in light of a changed environment; core values may stay the same, but how they are expressed might be altered. As members of the organization focus on needed change, they need the opportunity to express their concern and to participate in shaping the change (O'Toole, 1995). Leaders should recognize the need for a "neutral zone" (Bridges and Mitchell, 2002) between old and new ways of operating. The neutral zone is a place of fluidity and ambiguity where people can come to terms with the loss of old certainties, reassess what is truly important, and become receptive to change (Bridges, 1980; Bridges and Mitchell, 2002).

British businesswoman Anita Roddick is the founder of the Body Shop, a business that exemplifies the attention to social and environmental impact that the World Business Council for Sustainable Development promotes. She reports on her company's collaborative approach to change. When the company had to restructure, "we talked to everyone in the organization. . . . For people who could not continue with the organization, or who didn't want to, we offered retraining packages for the entire family. . . . We set up an Entrepreneur's Club; we provided money to seed people's own ventures, to work with the community, to come back as a consultant to the company. And we worked with everyone in the community—health care workers, social workers, police, psychologists—so they understood the process" (Hesselbein and Johnston, 2002a, p. 25).

Leaders may need to overcome the expectation that power should be concentrated in positional leaders. Raymond Gordon reminds advocates of shared leadership that this expectation is often deeply embedded in the culture of a traditionally hierarchical organization (Gordon, 2002; Drath, 2001). In such a culture, leaders are likely to have to blend directive and shared styles, at least for a time. Furthermore, if the culture places the highest value on individual achievement, then leaders need to communicate the value of collective achievement and combat devaluation of relational leadership styles. As Fletcher and Kaüfer (2003) note, this may be difficult when relational styles are associated with those people (for instance, women) who are less powerful in the organization.

Leaders need to think strategically about how and when to involve external stakeholders in a change effort. Despite pressure from San Francisco health professionals in the early years of the U.S. AIDS crisis, the director of the San Francisco health department deferred launching a crackdown on unsafe sexual practices in bathhouses until he could achieve consensus among the main stakeholder groups on that course of action. The result was a stalemate that contributed to the spread of HIV.

Key stakeholders don't always have to be involved directly. Useful information can be gathered through individual interviews, surveys, and role plays. Forming strategic alliances with like-minded external stakeholders can be a way to develop a shared pool of information and other resources for coping with change (Nanus and Dobbs, 1999).

Planning for Succession

Among the changes that organizational leaders should expect is the likelihood of people in leadership roles moving on to other assignments, retiring, becoming disabled, or dying. Replacement leaders must be mentored and developed if they are to assume additional responsibilities (Dalton and Thompson, 1986; Charan, Drotter, and Noel, 2001). In addition to training programs, an organization may need specific policies aimed at facilitating leadership turnover (Taylor, 1987). The transition from one leader or a group of leaders who founded an organization is likely to be especially difficult; a process such as strategic planning may be required to review the organization's mission and accomplishments, focus on strategic issues, and develop new strategies. A key strategy may well be hiring or promoting a set of leaders who have skills and orientations different from those of the old leaders. Ann Howard (2001) offers advice specifically for identifying, assessing, and selecting senior leaders; it is mainly aimed at the corporate world but applies as well to public and nonprofit organizations.

Jan Hively has a personal policy of moving on from an organizational leadership position when she feels "that a different style of leadership is needed to reinforce the organization's capacity for follow through" (personal communication, July 2003). In 2002, she pressed for electing a formal VAN leadership group that could oversee VAN, and she worked to raise funds to pay for a permanent coordinator and other staff. She also made sure that the relationship of VAN to the University of Minnesota was clarified. She moved out of the role of coordinator and became senior adviser and vice-chair of the leadership group.

Building Inclusive Community Inside and Outside an Organization

As innovation consultant Gifford Pinchot points out, creating a sense of community in the workplace has personal and organizational benefits (2002). Community within an organization resides in the network of supportive, synergistic relationships. Leaders nurture internal community by:

• Caring for self and others. Ultimately, leadership is a matter of the heart. Successful leaders are "in love with leading, with the people who do the work, with what their organizations produce, and with those who honor the organization by using its work" (Kouzes and Posner, 2002, p. 399). This does not mean, however, that they must do all the caring themselves; instead, they should establish social networks and supportive programs (such as health and fitness services, mentoring or coaching programs, grief counseling, outplacement services, or annual celebrations) that institutionalize the work of caring and compassion (see Dutton and others, 2002). Roddick urges leaders to give meaningful praise; she would include the amount of joy in the workplace in any measure of organizational success (Hesselbein and Johnston, 2002a).

• Promoting a shared mission and a culture of integrity, inclusion, learning, and productivity.

• Shaking up the hierarchy. Make people on the periphery more central; reduce markers of rank and privilege.

• Developing a "gift economy" and internal markets. As Pinchot (2002) describes it, this combination rewards people and units for giving resources away and encourages them to offer the best services to other parts of the organization.

• Providing resources, including knowledge of group process and organizational dynamics, to help people work together.

• Starting leadership development programs that are appropriate to the type of organization and to people's roles in it.

Leaders build external community by joining other members of the community in solving common problems and contributing to community well-being. This interorganizational leadership is discussed more fully in Part Two; in general it involves building supportive and synergistic relations with allies and partial supporters, wooing neutrals, and struggling respectfully with opponents in particular issue areas.

Roddick explained earlier in this chapter how her company has fostered internal and external community. Conflict between units of the National Institutes of Health during the early years of the AIDS crisis in the United States demonstrates the harm engendered by lack of communal problem solving. By mid-1983 CDC researchers had gathered considerable specimens and other evidence about the incidence and effects of AIDS, and they needed the help of the National Cancer Institute to analyze specimens for clues to the nature of the retrovirus that was causing AIDS. A leading retrovirologist at NCI was far more interested in protecting his own turf, however, than in cooperating with CDC researchers. Additionally, he undermined external community (and impeded progress on identifying the AIDS virus) by hampering the promising research of AIDS researchers at France's Pasteur Institute (Shilts, 1988).

Helpful Tools for Organizational Leaders

Exercise 3.6 can help you assess how well leadership tasks are being performed. To be most useful, the assessment should be completed and discussed by people from all levels and parts of the organization. The assessment can help you identify and understand strengths and weaknesses that leaders need to keep in mind as they use the tools about to be described.

Strategic planning (Bryson, 2004b) and scenario planning (Van der Heijden and others, 2002) are helpful processes for accomplishing the main tasks of organizational leadership. Both help people reframe change so that it is consistent with (or clearly connected to) the organization's history (Bryson, 1995; Burt, 2002). Both can contribute to community building, by involving people from throughout the organization and from outside. John Kotter (1996) offers a useful process of organizational change consisting of eight stages:

1. Establishing a sense of urgency
2. Creating a guiding coalition
3. Developing a vision and strategy
4. Communicating the change vision
5. Empowering employees
6. Generating short-term wins
7. Consolidating gains and producing more change
8. Anchoring new approaches in the culture

Exercise 3.6. Assessing Your Organization.

Respond to these questions by checking one of the three boxes after each:

	Poor/ Poorly	OK/ Acceptably	Good/ Well
1. How good are the organization's mission and philosophy statements?	☐	☐	☐
2. How well do organizational strategies link mission, goals, policies, programs, and actions?	☐	☐	☐
3. To what extent is the organization animated by an inspiring vision?	☐	☐	☐
4. How flexible and transparent are the governance, administrative, and communication systems?	☐	☐	☐
5. Do critical decisions reinforce organizational purpose?	☐	☐	☐
6. Are organizational ethics emphasized?	☐	☐	☐
7. Does the organization welcome differing ideas and people?	☐	☐	☐
8. Does the organization promote learning and productivity?	☐	☐	☐
9. To what extent does the organization monitor internal and external environments?	☐	☐	☐
10. How entrepreneurial and experimental is the organization?	☐	☐	☐
11. Are management routines and details effectively overseen?	☐	☐	☐
12. Are collaboration and teamwork emphasized?	☐	☐	☐
13. How well does the organization plan for change?	☐	☐	☐
14. How well does the organization plan for turnover of senior managers?	☐	☐	☐
15. How well are social support systems functioning?	☐	☐	☐
16. How would you describe organizational celebrations?	☐	☐	☐

Exercise 3.6. Assessing Your Organization, Cont'd.

Respond to these questions by checking one of the three boxes after each:

	Poor/ Poorly	OK/ Acceptably	Good/ Well
17. How well does the organization manage rewards?	☐	☐	☐
18. To what extent is everyone involved in problem definition and resolution?	☐	☐	☐
19. To what extent does everyone have needed resources and training for doing his or her job?	☐	☐	☐

When you are done with the ratings:

1. Develop a list of organizational strengths on the basis of the items ranked *good/well.* Note a few of the reasons these items were ranked highly.
2. Develop a list of organizational weaknesses on the basis of the items ranked *poor/poorly.* Note a few of the reasons these items were given a low ranking.
3. You might also note which aspects of the items rated *OK/acceptably* need improvement.
4. Referring to the lists can be helpful as people in the organization undertake strategic planning or any other change process.

Ronald Heifetz has developed an approach called "adaptive work," in which leaders help constituents understand and deal with the "adaptive challenges" they face. He offers advice for managing distress, keeping people focused on the challenges, giving the work to the people involved, and protecting "voices of leadership from below" (Heifetz, 1994; Heifetz and Laurie, 1997). The "quality movement" also offers guidance for improving organizational effectiveness (see Cohen and Brand, 1993).

Several organizational leadership analysts recommend using multiple "lenses" or "frames" to diagnose problems and foster creative solutions (Morgan, 1997; Quinn, 1988; Terry 1993; Bolman and Deal, 2003). For example, Lee Bolman and Terrence Deal (2003) suggest four main frames for making sense of an organization: structural, human resource, political, and symbolic. They offer guidance for integrating the four frames and applying them to particular situations. In his *Seven Zones for Leadership* (2001), Terry recommends that the leadership approach depend on the degree to which an organization's environment is "fixable and knowable." His typology is described more fully in Resource C.

The "living systems" frame has received increasing attention from analysts trying to help leaders guide an organization through a chaotic environment (Senge, 1990; Senge and others, 1994, 1999; Eoyang, 1997; Youngblood, 1997; Wheatley, 1999; Allen and Cherrey, 2000; Marion and Uhl-Bien, 2001). Much of their advice is included in our sections on learning culture and adapting to change. Kanter's *Evolve!* and Annunzio's *eLeadership* offer advice for organizations seeking to thrive in the digital age (Kanter, 2001; Annunzio, 2001; see also Brown and Gioia, 2002).

Cameron and Caza promote a "virtues" frame, drawing on research that identifies extraordinary organizations that downsize with "caring and compassion"; recover from crisis with "maturity, wisdom and forgiveness"; and that seek "to do good as well as to do well" (2002, p. 34). These organizations adopt (and exceed) moral codes, establish a values-based culture, perform effectively, and focus on the highest human potential. An especially important virtue in these organizations is forgiveness, the "capacity to foster collective abandonment of justified resentment, bitterness and blame" and adopt in their stead "positive, forward-looking approaches in response to harm or damage" (p. 39). Barbara Nelson, Linda Kaboolian, and Kathryn Carver describe "concord organizations" that can work across diverse communities to be "incubators for larger political settlements or social changes" but that primarily maintain social and political changes in the wake of agreements to settle longstanding conflicts (Nelson, Kaboolian, and Carver, 2003, p. 8).

Many leadership analysts (see, for instance, Zaccaro and Klimoski, 2001; Kets de Vries, 1995) offer advice geared to the demands on people at the top of an organization. Several authors give helpful guidance for leaders in nonprofit organizations (Letts, Ryan, and Grossman, 1998; Nanus and Dobbs, 1999; Brinckerhoff, 1998; Riggio and Orr, 2004). Also helpful are Mark Moore's *Creating Public Value* (1995) for leaders in government and his article "Managing for Value: Organizational Strategy in For-Profit, Nonprofit, and Governmental Organizations" (Moore, 2000). Martin Krieger (1996) offers an intricate model of entrepreneurial leadership that draws on religious notions of creation, tragedy, heroism, virtue, covenant, character, errancy, vision, revelation, and redemption. David Heenan and Warren Bennis (1999) offer advice for people who are second-in-command or a supporting partner of a highly visible leader. Craig Pearce and Jay Conger's *Shared Leadership* offers guidance about when and where shared leadership is appropriate in a team or organization (Pearce and Conger, 2003). David Peterson and Mary Dee Hicks (1996) present strategies for coaching and developing the people in an organization. Robert Kelley's advice in *The Power of Followership* is useful for people who are trying to promote organizational well-being from a less powerful position (Kelley, 1992). Wherever the leaders are in an organization, they must understand the opportunities and constraints that their position entails. As their positional power diminishes, they may need to give more attention to building a broad coalition to champion change efforts. Visa founder Dee Hock directs his leadership advice to managers, wherever they are in an organization. The first responsibility, he says, is to manage oneself, "one's own integrity, character, ethics, knowledge, wisdom, temperament, words, and acts. It is a complex, unending, incredibly difficult, often-shunned task." The second responsibility is "to manage those who have authority over us: bosses, supervisors, directors, regulators, ad infinitum." The third is managing one's peers: associates, competitors, suppliers, customers. The fourth and final is managing people over whom one has authority. This last task need receive only minimal attention if the manager has hired the right people for the job and given them adequate support (Hock, 2002, pp. 67–68). Terry (1993) advises everyone who seeks to lead courageously in an organization to develop a set of "exit cards" that outline options for leaving a current position if necessary.

Summary

Team leadership focuses on recruitment, effective communication, empowerment, and leadership development of team members. The main tasks of organizational leadership are paying attention to purpose and design, becoming adept at dealing with internal and external change, and building inclusive community inside and outside the organization. These leadership tasks track with researchers' attention to transformational and transactional leadership. They have found that effective leaders engage in transformational behavior (being a role model in the service of an inspiring cause; promoting a challenging, meaningful vision; providing intellectual stimulation and individualized attention for followers) along with transactional behavior (specifically rewarding follower productivity; Avolio, 1999).

The next chapter explores how leaders work with individuals, teams, and organizations to create and communicate shared meaning (visionary leadership); to make and implement executive, legislative, and administrative decisions (political leadership); and to adjudicate disputes and sanction conduct (ethical leadership). Considerable attention is given to designing and using forums, arenas, and courts—the shared-power settings for visionary, political, and ethical leadership, respectively.

Chapter Four

Leadership Tasks in a Shared-Power World
Visionary, Political, and Ethical Leadership

*Hope and vision cause us to revalue the world,
reconceiving our situation so that what was once
even beyond hope is now within the realm of reality.*
MARTIN KRIEGER

*It doesn't take courage to shoot a policeman in the back
of the head, or to murder an unarmed taxi driver. What
takes courage is to compete in the arena of democracy,
where the tools are persuasion, fairness, and common
decency.*
GEORGE MITCHELL

Visionary leadership shapes the meaning of public problems and in-spires commitment to proposed solutions. *Political leadership* achieves adoption and implementation of policies, programs, and projects incorporating the solutions. *Ethical leadership* helps settle disputes over those policies, programs, and projects, and it sanctions conduct.

Each type of leadership occurs in a characteristic setting—informal and formal *forums* for visionary leadership, formal and informal *arenas* for political leadership, and formal and informal *courts* for ethical leadership. This chapter describes these settings and the model of power on which they are based, before elaborating the tasks of visionary, political, and ethical leadership.

Forums, Arenas, and Courts

In a policy change effort, forums are likely to be the most important of the three settings, because the operation of forums determine which problems come to the attention of citizens and policy makers and which solutions are considered and which ignored. Examples of forums are a conversation among neighbors and friends, a task force, discussion group, brainstorming session, formal debate, public hearing, political rally, conference, newspaper column, television or radio broadcast, play or other form of dramatization, and a popular or professional journal. All that is required is a speaker, an audience, and a channel of communication.

In an arena, executive, legislative, and administrative decision makers review proposed policies, programs, and projects emerging from a forum and decide whether or not to adopt and implement them. Examples of arenas are a board of directors, city council, cartel, market, legislature, cabinet, and faculty senate. The basic requirements are a policy maker and at least one other participant to negotiate over allocation of resources.

In a court, official and unofficial judges resolve conflicts resulting from the operation of an arena and decide which principles, laws, and norms to enforce and how. Examples of courts are the "court of public opinion" (perhaps the most powerful), a professional licensing body, municipal court, the U.S. Supreme Court, military tribunal, ecclesiastical court, and the International Court of Justice. The basic requirements are two disputants and a third party to help resolve their dispute, plus at least partially shared norms.

Resource D describes how these three shared-power settings operate, interact, and change, on the basis of a holistic model of power. You may wish to review the resource before considering how visionary leaders create and communicate shared meaning in formal and informal forums.

Visionary Leadership

Visionary leaders create and communicate meaning about historical events, current reality, group mission, and prospects for the future. To be effective in tackling public problems and achieving the common good, they need to:

- Seize the opportunity to be an interpreter and direction giver in a situation of uncertainty and difficulty
- Offer a compelling vision of the future
- During a crisis, postpone a full-fledged vision while detailing actions that need to be taken and the anticipated consequences
- Adeptly design and use formal and informal forums

Please note: when we examine the cases featured in this book, we see both visionary individuals and visionary organizations and networks. Larry Kramer, Stephan Schmidheiny, Jan Hively, Gary Cunningham, and numerous colleagues practiced visionary leadership, but the work of creating and communicating shared meaning is often so thoroughly collective that it makes more sense to talk of a team, organization, or network as practicing visionary leadership. Schmidheiny, for example, notes in the preface to *Changing Course* that for practical reasons he is named as the book's author, but "credit for most of the content of this book belongs to others." He acknowledges a raft of individuals and organizations and singles out the council's executive director, Hugh Faulkner, "who managed our entire process with great skill and a rare mix of vision, commitment, and good will," and "our editorial advisor, Lloyd Timberlake, who helped us find words for our findings and conclusions" (Schmidheiny, 1992, p. xxiii). Similar comments could be made about the publications and other messages disseminated by the AIDS organizations, the African American Men Project, and the Vital Aging Network.

Seize the Opportunity to Be an Interpreter and Direction Giver

For people to think something is "real," they must see a correspondence between how they frame a phenomenon, behaviors or actions associated with the phenomenon, and consequences of their behavior (Boal and Bryson, 1987). Visionary leaders help constituents grasp the "reality" of a problem by highlighting consequences that flow from behavior that is based on existing dominant frames, and they propose new frames that entail behavior and action that can be expected to help remedy the problem.

This work of interpretation and direction giving is obviously needed in dealing with emergent problems or issues (as AIDS was in the 1980s, or as the graying of the workforce continues to be for many countries). It is also required when existing solutions to a complex problem are clearly not working well (for example, the situations that prompted the African American Men Project and the creation of the World Business Council for Sustainable Development). In the AIDS case, visionary physicians and public health professionals initially strove to gather evidence about the unusual cancers and pneumonias that were striking gay men. They soon interpreted the problem as a possible health crisis and argued for more resources to investigate the causes, preventive measures, and treatments; they also highlighted the consequences of ignoring the crisis—the rising death rate, the spread of infection, the staggering costs of dealing with a full-blown epidemic. In the Vital Aging case, Hively and her colleagues highlighted opportunities (and, to a lesser extent, threats) associated with the imminent retirement of the baby boom generation. They argued for new programs or projects and redirection of existing ones to develop and employ the human and social capital of older adults. They could point to exemplary programs that had helped older adults become more active in community life.

To engage effectively in interpretation and direction giving, visionary leaders help their constituents reveal and name real needs and real conditions, frame and reframe public issues or problems, and champion new and improved ways of dealing with public issues or problems. Let's explore each of these activities more fully.

Reveal and Name Real Needs and Conditions

Visionary leaders strive to answer the question "What's really going on here?" They scan the environment for more information. They study stakeholders and their relationships. They look for linkages among seemingly disparate events and practices. They use their intuition and integrative thinking to discern and explain patterns. They uncover and exploit contradictions between espoused ideals and practices or outcomes. For example, Schmidheiny and his colleagues at WBCSD have compiled information from diverse sources (numerous consultations with stakeholder groups, reports about many companies and industries, and research about business and consumer practices) and used this information to identify what is helping businesses and consumers adopt environmentally friendly practices and what is preventing them from doing so. They make compelling connections between economic practices in "rich" areas and conditions in "poor" areas of the world. They point up "perverse subsidies," stemming from public policies, for environmentally destructive practices. In the preface to the council's first book, *Changing Course,* Schmidheiny emphasizes that the council members do not "base our hopes for success on radical changes in human nature or on the creation of a utopia. We take humans as we find them, the way we all are made, with all our strengths and weaknesses" (1992, p. xxii). *Changing Course* and its sequel *Walking the Talk* appeal to the audience's cognition (by defining sustainable development and presenting a logical argument for it) and emotions (by using upbeat, optimistic language and personal stories from executives who have become "environmental evangelists"); these and other council publications also highlight specific, consequential behaviors that align with the cognitive and emotional appeals (see Boal and Bryson, 1987).

Visionary leaders often bring to light what power and privilege obscures. In the African American Men Project, Mark Stenglein, Gary Cunningham, Herman Milligan, and others focused attention on a group of stakeholders (African American men aged eighteen to thirty) who were outnumbered by other residents in Hennepin County one hundred to one. Although other members of the county's African American community cared a great deal about these men, their prospects and needs were hardly on the agenda of the majority of stakeholders in the systems that affected these men. In the Vital Aging case, an ongoing challenge is to keep conditions of poor and disabled older adults in the spotlight and to respect diverse perspectives about aging in varied communities.

Of course, commentators—ranging from Niccolò Machiavelli to Robert Kaplan (2002)—have viewed leaders as people who use deception as well as truth to achieve their ends. Leaders, they argue, must manipulate and even mislead the public in the service of worthwhile goals. We argue, however, that deception by leaders is problematic on practical as well as ethical grounds and must be carefully justified (Bok, 1978; Gutmann and Thompson, 1990).

Help Constituents Frame and Reframe Public Issues or Problems
Visionary leaders name and explain problems or issues. Naming and explaining uses one or more frames and interpretive schemes for making sense of the problem and deciding what to do about it. Leaders may evoke a frame that is familiar to their constituents, they may make new linkages among frames, or they may invent new ones. (Sustainable development, for example, was a new frame introduced in the early 1980s.) Frequently, visionary leaders evoke what might be called the "crisis" frame by identifying the problem as critical or urgent. They may be trying to convince their audience that a crisis already exists or that it is imminent. The physicians, epidemiologists, public health workers, and gay activists who picked up the early signs of a terrible new disease affecting gay men wanted to wake up others in their communities as well as the general public, so they offered evidence and language warning of a coming "epidemic," noting that the reported cases of the disease were only the "tip of the iceberg" (Shilts, 1988, p. 90). The gay press summoned "plague" imagery.

The World Business Council publications employ a measured tone and emphasize the positive steps that can be taken to remedy environmental destruction. Yet even they emphasize the urgency of reversing the trends that threaten the earth's carrying capacity. For example, the first chapter of *Changing Course* notes some hopeful global trends but turns quickly to other "alarming" trends. The authors warn, "To overreact to any of [the negative trends] would be dangerous, but to ignore any of them would be irresponsible" (Schmidheiny, 1992, p. 1).

Implicit in the crisis frame is a call to action, but one or more additional frames are needed to generate solutions that can be supported by stakeholders. Thus Schmidheiny and his colleagues have adopted the sustainable development and eco-efficiency frames that can generate solutions to protect the environment and create wealth, thus appealing to businesspeople as well as environmental advocates.

The final report of the African American Men Project emphasized a "shared fate" frame in its description of the critical status of African American men. The report highlighted the authors' sense of urgency, stemming from "a need to address the continuing violence and hopelessness that pervade the neighborhoods where many young African American men live. This sense of urgency exists not just for young African American men, however, but for all Hennepin County residents. When young African American men do poorly, they are not the only ones who suffer; every person, family and business in the county also pays a price in the form of a continued labor shortfall, limited economic development, reduced tax revenues, higher crime, and higher costs for social services, law enforcement, and courts" (Hennepin County, 2002, p. 4). Later, the report casts this theme more positively as "what is good for young African American men is good for the county" (p. 45).

The framing of a problem also suggests desired outcomes, or future states. Sustainable development implies a future in which human beings can achieve economic growth that contributes to the well-being of human communities and the planet. Emphasizing the shared fate of young African American men and other Hennepin County residents implies a future in which outcomes for both groups have improved together.

The reframing process involves breaking with old ways of viewing an issue, problem, or challenge and developing a new appreciation of it. Schmidheiny and colleagues overtly attacked a previous framing of business impacts on the environment as "not our problem." The African American Men Project report highlighted the harmful effects of the tendency of government and nonprofit agencies to define the circumstances of young African American men as "a dilemma to be resolved or eradicated" (p. 39). The old framing too easily implied that African American men were the problem—that they were "dysfunctional people who need to be fixed by others wiser than they are" (p. 40). The Vital Aging Initiative offered an alternative to the prevalent view of older adults as needy dependents or "greedy geezers."

Champion New Ways of Dealing with Public Problems

Visionary leaders gather ideas from many sources for remedying the public problems that concern them. They foster an atmosphere within their organization or network in which innovation flourishes (see the discussion of learning cultures in the organizational leadership section of Chapter Three). Acting in the mode of Donald Schön's "reflective practitioner" (1983), they also champion "improved" ideas, ones that have emerged from practice and been refined by critical reflection. They also keep constituents focused on the general outcomes they seek—outcomes that should be set in consultation with the key stakeholders in the public problem at hand (Nutt, 2002).

For example, when Schmidheiny and colleagues began preparing their report for the 1992 Earth Summit, they first decided what issues to include and then began a series of global meetings and stakeholder consultations to gather ideas for the final report. Hively and her colleagues held focus groups with a variety of older adults, researchers, educators, and others to gather ideas that could be presented at the 2002 Vital Aging Summit. They solicited "informants" who could provide material for the VAN Website. They persistently sought out examples of like-spirited programs from around the United States and organized events featuring speakers who could report on these other programs and seed new ways of thinking about aging.

The focus on outcomes imparts direction to the search for solutions to a public problem or need (Nutt, 2002). Chapter Eight has additional guidance for generating and evaluating these solutions.

Offer a Compelling Vision of the Future

A compelling vision weaves together a hopeful understanding of a public problem and the most promising solutions. Visionary leaders work with others to cocreate such visions—essentially *communal stories* that help diverse stakeholder groups develop a sense of what they have in common with each other and what they might do to tackle common problems and create a better future. These stories are told from a *"we"* perspective to emphasize that the story isn't just about the values and needs of a single leader or small group, but rather about everyone in this community. Martin Luther King Jr., proclaimed "I have a dream," but he emphasized that the dream was a broadly shared dream and required joint action to accomplish. Visionary leaders should be clear about their own needs and values and focus on the subset that overlaps with those of their constituents (Burns, 1978). Exercise 4.1 can help you clarify your own vision and compare it to the visions of other people in your group.

Exercise 4.1. Outlining and Constructing Personal Visions.

Part one: group members outline and construct individual visions.

Outline

1. When you try to picture success in an area you care about—such as your life, family, work, or leadership project—what does it look like?
2. What important outcomes does the picture include?
3. What values, cultural traditions, and experiences from your past will you draw on to achieve these outcomes?
4. What barriers will you have to overcome to achieve these outcomes?
5. How might you make your picture of success a reality? What are the primary strategies and actions you might undertake? Who will support you in this effort?

Construction

(Materials needed: flipchart sheets, bright markers, magazine pictures, stickers, fabric, etc.)

1. Using a flipchart sheet, markers, and other materials, create an imaginative representation of the answers you gave in the first part of this exercise. Show how your desired future is linked to values, traditions, and experiences and to planned strategies and actions. You might include photographs, mission statements, objects (edible or inedible), fabric, poems, strategy documents. Use images rather than words as much as possible. Fill the whole sheet.
2. You might accompany this representation with recordings and aromas.
3. Try to convey how things would look, feel, sound, taste, and smell if you were successful in achieving your goal or dreams.
4. The results will not be subjected to artistic judgment.
5. Sign the sheet and place it on the wall for the group presentation.

Part two: visions are presented to the group. Directions for group presentation:

1. The group assembles in front of each vision. The creator remains quiet while the others say what they think the vision is about.
2. After group members comment, the creator responds.
3. After all visions are presented, the facilitator asks the group to identify any themes in the visions. He or she explains that a common vision might be constructed that is based on such themes; he or she suggests how a team or organizational vision might be created using a similar exercise.
4. The facilitator asks why it is important to use visual imagery. (The exercise taps the left and right brain; visual images may be more real, more memorable; a lot can be communicated with a picture.)
5. Everyone takes his or her vision home to serve as a reminder.

The World Business Council for Sustainable Development and the African American Men Project offer examples of how a vision is presented as something that can and should be embraced by a broad community. Holliday, Schmidheiny, and Watts begin their "business case for sustainable development" by noting: "Sustainable development cannot be achieved by one nation alone. It cannot be achieved in only one sphere, such as the economic sphere. It will require types of partnership never before witnessed in human history" (2002, p. 13). They argue that there will be no real progress "until business, government, and civil society team up in new and dynamic partnerships" (p. 18). The executive summary of the final report of the African American Men Project opens with "*We* are at a crossroads" (italics added) and goes on to describe challenges confronting *all* citizens of Hennepin County, and to relate the circumstances of young African American men to these challenges (Hennepin County, 2002). The authors of the African American Men report summon a vision of what Robert Quinn calls "the productive community," which is characterized by clarity of purpose, high standards of performance, and supportive relationships (2000, p. 29).

At the same time that visionary leaders emphasize the community as a whole, they *personalize* the story by giving illustrative examples from their own lives and others'. *Walking the Talk* offers vignettes explaining how Holliday, Schmidheiny, Watts, and others became advocates of sustainable development. The African American Men report presents survey results and direct quotations from interviews to reflect African American men to themselves and reveal their complexity and humanity to other readers. At the Vital Aging Summit in 2002, diverse groups of older adults told stories about how they have experienced ageism, and about the joy and freedom of being active citizens and learners.

Communal stories attend to past, present, and future. Fundamental values and cultural tradition are honored, while previous mistakes and failings are recognized. The stories evoke a *generative problem frame* (Schön and Rein, 1994), emphasize the disastrous (or at least harmful) consequences of continuing on the current path, and show how values can be realized in the future through specific behaviors; in other words, the stories help people develop a collective identity (Gardner, 1995) and grasp desirable and potentially real futures (Boal and Bryson, 1987; van der Heijden and others, 2002). The specific behaviors do not have to be (and often can't be) guaranteed answers to a problem; rather, they can be the steps in a discovery process (Meadows, 1994). Indeed, visionary leaders should remind their constituents of the need to be flexible and learn along the way, to see themselves as "creative commons" (Snyder and Edwards, 1997).

Walking the Talk illustrates this linkage of past, present, and future. It begins with reflection on the origins of the sustainable development movement, in the 1980s, and offers a potential explanation of why the majority of business leaders did not jump on the bandwagon. The authors note, however, that in the 1990s more and more business leaders realized, partly because of scandals and citizen protests, that they must take a "closer look at sustainable development, particularly its social dimension" (Holliday, Schmidheiny, and Watts, 2002, p. 22). Since the book is aimed at a variety of business stakeholders, the authors honor the traditional business value of wealth creation and highlight how failure on the part of governments and markets to take environmental and social needs into account is undermining future economic growth. They elaborate the problems of environmental destruction and social inequity by using the sustainable development and eco-efficiency frames and offer a host of case studies and examples that delineate specific actions business leaders are already taking or could attempt in order to build a sustainable future.

The final report for the African American Men Project gives some attention to the past. For example, it notes that Hennepin County was considered among the twenty-five best places in the United States to build a business in the recent past but has slipped to fiftieth place. It also cites a thirty-five-year-old regional government report that highlighted some of the same barriers still facing African American men in 2001. Yet the African American Men report mainly focuses on present conditions, emphasizing that although most Hennepin County residents and many young African Americans are doing reasonably well, a large percentage of young African American men—especially those in poor neighborhoods—"are in trouble—with money, with employment, with their families, with their health, with their safety and/or with the criminal justice system" (Hennepin County, 2002, p. 19). The report frames the problem at hand as a complex one, caused by a multitude of social and economic forces and requiring "an aligned and coordinated response—one involving multiple stakeholders and multiple strategies" (p. 3). Additionally, the report emphasizes the "shared-fate" frame, arguing that if conditions affecting African American men are not improved, the whole community will suffer; and if they are improved, then the whole community will benefit. The fundamental cultural values emphasized are community and mutual responsibility, and the report presents specific recommendations for actions that various stakeholders can take to improve conditions for young African American men.

In communicating a communal story, visionary leaders choose their language carefully. They use metaphors that relate to and make sense of people's experience and impel people toward common ground. They use vivid, energetic, and optimistic language, and an expressive style. For example, the final report of the African American Men Project presents statistical portraits of the county's young African American men under the title "How Are Our Neighbors Faring?" The report depicts these men as neighbors, family members, and workers (or potential workers).

Finally, visionary leaders describe a future that is full of immediacy and promise. The African American Men report summons the image of all types of citizens stepping forward and working together to build a better community:

> It is time for our waiting to end; time to choose a new direction. *This is a call for leaders—seasoned and new, old and young, traditional and atypical—to step forward.* [emphasis in original] Many of these leaders may—and, ideally, would be—young African American men. Others may be older African American men and women. Still others may be the wives and partners of young African American men. . . . This is also a call for followers—not just young African American men, but stakeholders from all backgrounds, races, and income levels. It is a call to rediscover citizenship and *public work.* . . . [Hennepin County, 2002, p. 49]

The report concludes with a detailed scenario of "what might actually happen when new and seasoned leaders seize the day, and county government provides the right kind of support" (p. 55).

During a Crisis, Postpone the Full Vision But Detail Actions and Their Anticipated Consequences

Usually visionary leaders elaborate desired outcomes along with the actions needed to achieve them. A crisis, however, may require leaders to emphasize action without clear delineation of a desired future state. If old behaviors are not working and disaster is imminent, followers may wish leaders to prescribe new behavior, and they may even be willing to try that behavior without a full-blown vision of the outcome. Even then, a leader must soon link the recommended course of action to a "higher purpose" (Boal and Bryson, 1987). Establishing causal links between the new behavior and desired outcomes is also critical.

Adeptly Design and Use Forums

The visionary practices listed so far take place in a forum, the setting where leaders and constituents debate various interpretations of public problems, assess potential solutions, and develop specific proposals for enacting favored solutions. The design and use of these settings have a major effect on which problem definitions and solutions are considered and on which proposals are developed. As noted in Resource D, the key considerations that leaders should consider in designing a forum are communicative capability, interpretive schemes, norms of relevance and pragmatic communication, media and modes of argument, and access rules. Leaders who are undertaking a major change effort must also think of numerous forums in relation to each other, orchestrating them as much as possible so they build on each other and generate momentum for change. This orchestration of forums is described more fully in Part Two of this book; here we focus on key design elements of a forum.

Communicative Capability
Visionary leaders should consider, first of all, which stakeholders have the ability to make their voices heard in discussion of a particular public problem. We see this ability as the function of power and interest; those whose voices are most prominent are those who have considerable decision-making power as well as a sense of having an important stake in the problem. Those whose voices are

least prominent are the ones with low decision-making power and a relatively minor stake in the problem.

A tool that can be useful in assessing this aspect of communicative capability is the "power versus interest grid" (Exercise 4.2). This exercise also sets the stage for several other stakeholder analysis methods that we recommend for visionary and political leaders. An individual or group can use the grid to place stakeholders in

Exercise 4.2.   Using a Power-Versus-Interest Grid.

This exercise allows a planning group to map stakeholders in a public problem according to the stakeholder's amount of decision-making power and interest in the problem. A power-versus-interest grid typically helps determine which stakeholders' interests and power bases *must* be taken into account in order to address the problem or issue at hand. It also helps highlight coalitions to be encouraged or discouraged, what behavior should be fostered, and whose buy-in should be sought or who should be "co-opted." Finally, it provides some information on how to convince stakeholders to change their views. Interestingly, the knowledge gained from such a grid can be used to help advance the interests of the relatively powerless (Bryson, Cunningham, and Lokkesmoe, 2002).

Directions for working with a group:

1. Tape four flipchart sheets to a wall to form a single surface two sheets high and two sheets wide.
2. Draw the two axes on the surface using a marking pen. The vertical axis is labeled *interest,* from low to high; the horizontal axis is labeled *power,* from low to high.
3. Participants brainstorm the names of stakeholders by writing names as they come to mind on a 1.5" × 2" (2.5 cm × 5 cm) self-adhesive label, one stakeholder per label. Guided by the deliberations and judgments of the planning group members, a facilitator should place each label in the appropriate spot on the quadrants. Labels should be collected in round-robin fashion, one label per group member, until all labels (other than duplicates) are placed on the grid or eliminated for some reason.
4. Labels should be moved around until all group members are satisfied with the *relative* location of each stakeholder on the grid.
5. The group should discuss the implications of the resulting stakeholder placements. If needed, develop strategies for increasing the power of stakeholders in the subjects category to make their views heard. If needed, develop strategies for increasing the interest of stakeholders in the context-setters category.

one of four categories (Eden and Ackermann, 1998, pp. 121–125, 344–346; see also Bryson, 2004):

1. Players—stakeholders with high power and high interest
2. Context setters—stakeholders with high power and low interest
3. Subjects—stakeholders with low power and high interest
4. The crowd—stakeholders with low power and low interest

Visionary leaders are likely to have to figure out ways to enhance the power of people in the subjects category and how to enhance the interest of context-setter stakeholders in order to build a powerful coalition to achieve broadly beneficial change.

Since powerful social groups strongly influence what is widely held to be "rational," an understanding of power distributions and relations helps account for the legitimacy of rationales for the world as it is (Suchman, 1995; Flyvbjerg, 1998). Altering power distributions and relationships undermines the legitimacy of those rationales. Yet visionary leaders must be thoughtful as to how they go about such efforts, since in a game of power the powerful usually win. It's important to keep conflict at a moderate level so that alternative power relationships have a chance to develop, rather than being stifled at the outset by powerful groups who, if conflict is intense, will move strongly to protect their position.

Communicative capability also includes the skill of delivering a captivating, inspirational message through various media to diverse stakeholder groups. If they do not have all the needed skills themselves (and they usually don't), visionary leaders must recruit others who can craft the reports, write the speeches, plan and produce the videos, and rev up the crowd of demonstrators.

Frames and Interpretive Schemes

Leaders pay attention to which broad frames and interpretive schemes are likely to be applied to the problem that concerns them, and to which interpretive schemes they want to emphasize in promoting a beneficial solution. They emphasize frames that help convince key stakeholders to join a coalition to promote good ideas worth implementing and that reduce the potency of any opposing coalition. In selecting frames, visionary leaders should attend to what they play down as well as to what they play up (Schön and Rein, 1994; Simons, 2001). For example, forums convened to advance the African American Men Project visibly demonstrated the strength and accomplishments of African American men, reinforcing the message that what is good for young African American men is good for the county. The forums presented African American men as contributors, not as a problem. The presence of county commissioners and other powerful people at these forums communicated the importance of the project.

The sustainable development frame adopted by WBCSD, meanwhile, has been a powerful impetus for coalition building among environmentalists, businesspeople, and economists because it merges two other frames—concern for the environment and economic progress—each of which has more narrow support. At the same time, some environmentalists have criticized the sustainable development frame for obscuring the need to reduce wasteful consumption in well-to-do societies (McKibben, 1996). Partly to blunt criticism that supporters of sustainable development are simply trying to protect the right of the affluent to maintain a high level of consumption, WBCSD emphasizes its commitment to conservation, alleviation of poverty, and economic development, which were promoted at the Johannesburg summit as the "three pillars" of sustainable development. One of the council's main programs is called "sustainable livelihoods"; it is developing case studies and pilot projects demonstrating how businesses can help people move out of poverty.

The Vital Aging Network promotes a productive-citizen frame by demonstrating the economic and social contributions that older adults make through paid work; volunteer service; and caring for grandchildren or others who are sick, disabled, or isolated. Jan Hively talks about tapping the resources of older adults to help overstretched communities care for those "on both ends of the lifeline" (personal communication, July 2003).

It's important to be aware that some frames are likely to activate ideologies, which are extremely potent interpretive schemes. For example, a "green" ideology is likely to be evoked in ecologically minded people when the environmental protection frame is applied to an issue. They are then likely to use tenets of this ideology to assess the issue and recommendations for action. The challenge for visionary leaders is to help people draw on the best aspects of their ideologies to build bridges to diverse others (Gerzon, 1996).

Exercise 4.3 helps you analyze the main interpretive schemes connected to a problem that concerns you. Additional guidance about choosing which frames to highlight is in Chapter Seven.

Exercise 4.3. Analyzing
Interpretive Schemes, or Problem Frames.

This exercise can be completed by an individual or a group. If a group is involved, you may want to use the snowcard technique in Exercise 3.1 to organize the results.

1. Brainstorm ways of framing the problem that concerns you. Be sure to include frames that are commonly applied to public problems in general (for example, "not in my backyard") or to problems like this one (for example, if your problem involves what you consider risky behavior—such as handgun use, smoking, unprotected sex— others might defend the behavior by invoking the "freedom of choice" frame).

2. Look at the list of stakeholders you generated in Exercise 4.2. Place a check beside the key stakeholders, those who are most affected or most central to resolving the problem.

3. Now consider the frames you identified in step one. Place a check beside the frame that you think is most closely tied to current solutions to the problem. Identify the stakeholder groups that are likely to support this frame.

4. Place a star beside the frame that incorporates or resonates with the type of solution you seek.

5. Star two or three additional frames that you think have substantial support among key stakeholders in the problem.

6. Now consider how stakeholders are likely to react to your proposals for change, given the different frames. Beginning with the frame that incorporates the changes you seek, array internal and external stakeholders on this diagram.

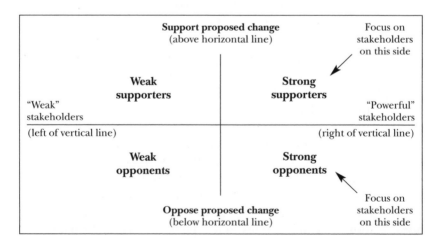

Exercise 4.3. Analyzing
Interpretive Schemes, or Problem Frames, Cont'd.

7. Now consider the other frames that you identified. How can you draw on those frames to develop a new, more comprehensive frame that builds on your own preferred frame but could encourage more key stakeholders to move into the strong-supporter quadrant and allow those who are strong opponents to at least move into the weak-opponent quadrant?

Norms of Relevance and Pragmatic Communication

Visionary leaders must ensure that their messages meet the norms of relevance that prevail in key forums. Schmidheiny and his colleagues know that forums involving businesspeople often consider something to be relevant only if it affects their financial bottom line; thus they devote time to convincing these people that sustainable development is relevant for them. Cunningham and his colleagues recognized that they had to convince the powerful non–African American participants in key forums that measures to help African American men help themselves were important for achieving the non–African Americans' goals.

Visionary leaders need to recognize norms of pragmatic communication—that is, the expectation that a message will be comprehensible, sincere, appropriate to the context, and accurate (Forester, 1989, p. 36). Thus authors of the WBCSD reports acknowledge bad behavior by some businesses and lack of concern on the part of many. They note in the 2002 annual report that many nongovernmental organizations were suspicious of the business community's show of strength (described in the report as a thousand-person presence) at the Johannesburg Summit on Sustainable Development. The annual report indicates, however, that the WBCSD dispelled some of the skepticism by teaming up with Greenpeace to call on governments to implement the Kyoto Protocol on climate change, and organizing a young managers' team that participated in closed and open sessions with nongovernmental representatives. Meanwhile, WBCSD leaders maintain credibility with the business community by having high-profile corporate CEOs in leadership positions and by using language from the business lexicon, such as efficiency, market opportunities, and "business plan for sustainable development" (Holliday, Schmidheiny, and Watts, 2002, p. 12). WBSCD partnered with the International Chamber of Commerce to "project a single voice of business" at the Johannesburg summit, and the partners invited U.N. Secretary General Kofi Annan to keynote their Business Day at the summit (World Business Council for Sustainable Development, 2003, p. 2).

Media and Modes of Argument

Visionary leaders are skilled in using multiple media to convey their arguments—speeches, reports, press releases, advertisements, public service announcements, editorials, books, videos, and Websites. They also time their arguments to connect these media with such highly visible forums as the Johannesburg Summit or the Vital Aging Summit. Although having many ways of communicating a message generally makes sense, it's possible to overdo. At the Johannesburg Summit, nongovernmental suspicion of business representatives may have been stimulated in part by the barrage of WBCSD-sponsored reports and events at the summit.

Visionary leaders should be skilled in using dialogical and persuasive modes of argumentation (the process of formulating reasons and drawing conclusions). Organizing dialogue among stakeholders with differing perspectives on a public problem is especially useful in developing beneficial, comprehensive problem frames and solutions. Several approaches to dialogue have been described. Wilfred Drath endorses using "relational dialogue" when stakeholders have divergent worldviews. Relational dialogue, he explains, is based on acceptance of the worth and validity of those worldviews and the realization that shared work is nonetheless needed. For the dialogue to work, participants must have some willingness to "hold their own truths lightly . . . and appreciate the capacity of other worldviews to make up truths as well" (Drath, 2001, p. 144). Listening to other views, participants can start to "see *through* their worldviews, understand them as useful, sensemaking, and truth giving, but incomplete, not the whole of reality" (p. 149). As noted in Chapter Three, Fletcher and Käufer (2003) suggest ways to foster generative dialogue, in which the members of a group stop seeing themselves as separate individuals and instead as selves in relationship who learn from each other. This type of dialogue is like a "'spiral of growth', in which mutuality, learning, and the creative activity of cocreating solutions, and shared understandings are shared by the collective" (p. 40).

Leaders should be aware of the profound discomfort likely to result from attempting to see through one's worldview and thus becoming "a morally ambiguous self," according to Maxine Boler (1999, p. 182). A philosopher and teacher, Boler suggests that this discomfort may at least be diminished by recognition that it can be better than the pain of separation and alienation from fellow human beings. Participants in relational and generative dialogue may also be heartened by the mutual growth and learning they experience (Fletcher and Kaüfer, 2003).

Persuasion is used both as a supplement to dialogue and alone if dialogue is not feasible. Communication experts offer general guidance for structuring a persuasive argument, but they emphasize that the message must always be tailored to a specific audience. An argument must appeal both to people who assess the message using "cognitive shorthands" and to those who use "central processing"—that is, who ask probing questions about the message and consider additional information and arguments before making a judgment (Simons, 2001, p. 35). Visionary leaders should also prompt central processing as much as possible, since people who develop a policy stance as a result of such critical reflection are more resistant to counterargument (Simons, 2001).

Cognitive shorthand entails frames, association with a likable person or activity, the attractiveness of the person communicating the message, perceived rewards, grievances, and nostalgia (Simons, 2001; Gardner, 1995). For example, U.S. anti-AIDS campaigners scored a significant coup in the mid-1980s when they recruited Elizabeth Taylor to be a visible fundraising supporter. For many of those using cognitive shorthand to process messages about AIDS, her fame summoned up a positive association that would make the message recipients more sympathetic toward people with AIDS and more supportive of efforts to prevent and treat the disease. A similar effect could be counted on when Bill Clinton and Nelson Mandela agreed to cochair the International AIDS Trust. The Vital Aging Network invited Robert Bergland, a former congressman and U.S. commissioner of agriculture, to be cochair of the 2002 Summit. The seventy-eight-year-old Bergland, who also was a regent of the University of Minnesota, was a highly visible exemplar of vital aging.

Appealing to people who use central processing requires use of more formal logic relying on reasoning and evidence. The speaker has to show that a proposed policy change is needed, that it is workable and practical, that it avoids harm (or certainly that the benefits outweigh any harm), and that it is the best available solution (Simons, 2001). If there are well-founded concerns about the proposed change, the speaker should acknowledge and refute them, or concede what can't be refuted and explain why the change is a good idea anyway (Simons, 2001). (See also the elements of policy arguments listed in Resource D.) Even in using reason and evidence, visionary leaders should not lose sight of the story line (Throgmorton, 1991). As Karl Weick notes, "What is necessary in sense making is a good story" (1995, p. 61). Alice Walker adds, "Stories are how the spirit is exercised" (1999, p. 194). Ideally, the story helps listeners integrate the disparate bits of information they have already acquired about the issue at hand (Snyder and Edwards, 1997). Thus the final report of the African American Men Project is filled with evidence about difficulties faced by young African American men, about the achievements of African American men, and about initiatives that are already producing improvement. At the same time, the story line weaving through the report is of a community that is at a crossroads, choosing whether to continue down a destructive and divisive path of decline or down a more hopeful, inclusive path.

Visionary leaders also must shape arguments specifically tailored for the arenas in which policy makers will decide whether to adopt and implement the solutions developed in forums. They must ensure that their groups' good ideas are incorporated into proposals and plans that are shown to be technically and administratively workable, politically acceptable, and legally and ethically defensible.

Access Rules

Leaders ensure that forums are designed so that the right people have access to them. A forum must be held at a time and place that encourages participation by these people. Special services such as child care may be important. The forum should be accessible to people with disabilities. If the conveners are from the majority culture, they probably should ensure that minority members feel welcome. The organizers of the Vital Aging Website, for example, may need to develop an alternative strategy for reaching people who don't have access to the Web.

Helpful Tools

An especially helpful visionary leadership tool is "future search," developed by Marvin Weisbord and colleagues (see Resource E). Herbert Simons's *Persuasion in Society* (2001) and Terry Pearce's *Leading Out Loud* (1995) present useful advice for speech making and presentations. James Throgmorton (1991) presents elements of persuasive storytelling. You can also use Exercise 4.4 to assess the visionary leadership capacity of an individual, group, organization, or network.

Political Leadership

Leaders need visionary skills to develop shared understanding of public problems, build support for beneficial solutions, and develop commitment to collective action. They need political skills to turn a proposed solution into a specific policy, program, or project adopted and implemented by decision makers in executive, legislative, and administrative arenas. These are the main skills of political leadership:

- Mediating and shaping conflict within and among constituencies
- Building a winning, sustainable coalition to convince decision makers to consider the proposed changes, as well as implement them once they are adopted
- Overcoming bureaucratic resistance during implementation
- Adeptly designing and using formal and informal arenas

Mediate and Shape Conflict Within and Among Constituencies

Conflict is necessary and must be used carefully in a policy-making arena if policy makers are to consider multiple options for satisfying diverse constituencies (Burns, 1978; Nutt, 2002; Bryant, 2003); political leaders must possess transactional skills for dealing with individuals and groups with conflicting agendas. Political leaders

Exercise 4.4. Assessing Visionary Leadership Capacity.

You may use this exercise to rate a group, an organization, or an interorganizational network. You may reword the questions to rate your own or another individual's visionary capacity.

If the exercise is done by a group, each member should do the ratings individually; the ratings can then be pooled to produce a group rating.

Respond to the questions by checking one of the three boxes after each.

	Poor/ Poorly	OK/ Acceptably	Good/ Well
1. How good are we in interpreting uncertain or difficult situations and providing directions to pursue? (For example, are we able to diagnose causes of the situation and reveal opportunities arising from it?)	☐	☐	☐
2. How good are we at environmental scanning? (Do we collect information from a variety of sources about trends and new developments in the areas that concern us?)	☐	☐	☐
3. How good are we at using intuitive and integrative thinking to discern connections and patterns? (Are we able to discern how existing power relationships are contributing to a public problem?)	☐	☐	☐
4. Do we uncover and exploit contradictions between espoused ideals and outcomes? (Do we show how the implementation of policies has deviated from policy makers' intent?)	☐	☐	☐
5. Are we able to frame problems so that they make sense to people, and so that beneficial solutions are supported by stakeholders?	☐	☐	☐
6. How good are our strategies for generating good ideas for dealing with the problems that concern us? (Do we use brainstorming to engage in broad searches, gather	☐	☐	☐

Exercise 4.4. Assessing Visionary Leadership Capacity, Cont'd.

	Poor/ Poorly	OK/ Acceptably	Good/ Well
opinions from many kinds of experts, etc.?)			
7. Do we create communal stories that help diverse groups work together to create a better future?	☐	☐	☐
8. Do we use metaphorical language effectively?	☐	☐	☐
9. How skilled are we in developing oral and written presentations?	☐	☐	☐
10. How skilled are we in using a variety of communications media?	☐	☐	☐
11. How skilled are we in needed modes of argumentation?	☐	☐	☐
12. How good are our strategies for making our appeals relevant to key stakeholders?	☐	☐	☐
13. How good are we at ensuring our messages are comprehensible, sincere, appropriate to the context, and accurate?	☐	☐	☐
14. How good are we at using persuasion and dialogue?	☐	☐	☐
15. How well do we design forums to ensure that the right people participate?	☐	☐	☐

When you are done with the ratings:

For Working Alone

1. Develop a list of the visionary strengths of the individual, group, organization, or network on the basis of the items ranked *Good/Well*. Note a few of the reasons these items were ranked highly.
2. Develop a list of the visionary weaknesses of the group, organization, or network on the basis of the items ranked *Poor/Poorly*. Note a few of the reasons these items were given a low ranking.
3. Also note which aspects of the items rated *OK/Acceptably* need improving.

Exercise 4.4. Assessing Visionary Leadership Capacity, Cont'd.

---

4. Identify specific actions you can take to build on the identified strengths and overcome identified weaknesses.

For Working in a Group

1. Develop a list of the visionary strengths of the group, organization, or network on the basis of the items that most group members rated *Good/Well*. Note a few of the reasons these items were ranked highly.
2. Develop a list of the visionary weaknesses of the group, organization, or network on the basis of the items that a majority of the group ranked *Poor/Poorly*. Note a few of the reasons these items were given a low ranking.
3. Identify and discuss aspects of other items that need improvement.
4. Agree on specific actions the group can take to build on the identified strengths and overcome identified weaknesses.

---

must bargain and negotiate, trading the things of value that they control for others' support and developing advantageous positions. These leaders, notes James MacGregor Burns, "use conflict deliberately to protect decision-making options and power, and even more, . . . use conflict to structure the political environment so as to maximize 'constructive' dissonance, thus allowing for more informed decision making" (1978, p. 410). Although Burns is writing mainly about top political officials, his advice is useful for any leader trying to build and sustain an advocacy coalition to affect policy making and implementation. An effective advocacy coalition has multiple channels of access that allow members' conflicts, tensions, and dilemmas to be aired and addressed on the way to full mobilization in support of policy decisions.

The trick is not to be immobilized by conflicting agendas and to maintain the integrity of the vision that is inspiring the proposed policy changes. Burns emphasizes that political leaders play a "marginal" role, avoiding complete assimilation by any one group in order to deal with conflicts outside as well as inside their constituencies: "Their marginality supplies them with a double leverage, since in their status as leaders they are expected by their followers and other leaders to deviate, to innovate, and to mediate between the claims of their group and those of others" (p. 39).

Thus a public official like Stenglein or public manager like Cunningham must encourage numerous constituencies to supply them with their views of what's important, what their needs are, with whom they can work and with whom they can't, and what they can contribute to the change efforts. In working together to improve outcomes for young African American men, they can trade access to Hennepin County's policy-making process for resources (information, expertise, votes, connections to other groups, endorsements) that other individuals and groups control. As a member of the County Board, Stenglein also has a vote on all matters before the board that he can use as leverage to obtain concessions or support from other commissioners. As the head of a county department, Cunningham can direct staff to organize meetings or studies that community groups request.

Bargaining and negotiating have two main desirable outcomes: compromise and copromotion. In compromise, each participant gives up some of his or her desires in exchange for achieving the remainder; everyone, in a sense, loses something but also gains something. In copromotion, or what Leigh Thompson (2001) calls "integrative negotiation," the participants find ways to help each other achieve all or most of each other's aims, and possibly go beyond the parties' initial aims. Copromotion has obvious advantages, but compromise is usually needed too. In its final report, the Steering Committee of the African American Men Project emphasized copromotion as the way forward, rather than setting up a win-lose struggle between ethnic groups. Obviously, some compromise was made as project events and publications were put together, but the overarching approach is copromotion. Of course, total victory by one side is also possible, though hardly advisable because losers may feel so mistreated that they will be more determined and more vicious in future conflict.

Political leaders know that conflict in an arena can generate a lot of heat; policy making at its most basic level is about who gets what, how, how much, when, and where. The *what* can be money, services, contracts, access to opportunity, status and recognition, or campaign contributions; it can also be protection from competing entrepreneurs, corruptors, criminals, and others. Political leaders should never underestimate the ferocity of competition in an arena; those who benefit from the status quo will fight hard to keep and enhance their privileges and those who don't will fight hard for equity.

Political leaders must also be prepared to deal with opponents who reject any gain-gain approach and pursue a win-lose strategy. In such cases, political leaders should develop their own strategies for winning and for returning to a gain-gain strategy at the earliest opportunity. They need to use the resources they have (including credible threats such as leaving the negotiation) to protect their interests (see Bolman and Deal, 2003).

Leaders may have to magnify the voices of a group that is typically ignored or excluded from policy discussion. They must nurture citizen engagement, or what Harry Boyte and Nancy Kari (1996) call "public work." Too frequently, citizens view political conflict as an ugly and unseemly battle over narrow interests, and certainly they have many causes to do so. In a democratic system, however, political conflict is also a means of producing policies that meet a broad array of needs and strengthen community. Citizens cannot leave policy making and implementation to elected and appointed officials and expect this to happen. We would all do well to heed former Vice President Hubert H. Humphrey's call for citizen action: "Quit sitting on the sidelines, whistling and jeering at the people down on the playing field. Get out there and get roughed up a bit and see what it's like to live in this world of reality" (Connell, 1983).

Build a Winning, Sustainable Coalition

The foundation for marshaling a coalition to support a proposed policy change is laid by visionary leadership (see, for example, Hall, 1996). The individuals and groups included in forums focusing on problem definitions and solutions are the potential members of an advocacy coalition (Sabatier and Jenkins-Smith, 1993) that will press policy makers to adopt and implement specific proposals emerging from the forums. If the forums have been well designed and wisely used, key stakeholders will contribute to crafting the problem definition, choosing optimal solutions, and shaping the animating vision for change. They help shape the specific proposals that are to be introduced into the policy-making arenas. As attention shifts to arenas, leaders may seek to formalize the coalition. A formal network with a name and identifiable membership can be an attractor for other interested parties. It can make support for the proposed change seem more formidable than it is, and it amounts to a coordination tool through the signaling and attention that a name provides.

Thus, as WBCSD President Björn Stigson and his colleagues prepared for the 2002 World Summit on Sustainable Development, they joined the International Chamber of Commerce (ICC) in organizing Business Action for Sustainable Development (BASD), a coalition of WBSCD and ICC organizations (both of which are themselves coalitions). BASD then became "the single voice of business at the summit," organizing a Business Day and a virtual exhibit area at the summit (World Business Council for Sustainable Development, 2003, p. 2).

A coalition may be less formal. In the African American men case, a steering committee of community leaders along with Hennepin County commissioners and staff, academic researchers, and community organizations collaborated on the African American Men Project. This formal group acted as an informal coalition that developed the recommendation for a permanent African American Men Commission, consisting of "African American men and community, business, religious, academic, nonprofit, and government leaders." The board was to "provide leadership and advice to policy makers, foundations, nonprofit, organizations and the overall community on issues, programs and policies that impact the lives of young African American men" (Hennepin County, 2002, p. 75). It could be expected to be an attractor for individuals, groups, and organizations supporting particular initiatives that it recommends. It is often easier for public officials or public managers to be part of such an informal coalition since they must emphasize their concern for a multitude of constituencies.

Leaders in a formal coalition should help members develop one or more agreements:

- What each will contribute in the way of information, funds, staff and member energies, and connections
- What each will receive from involvement in the coalition
- General time frame for the coalition's work
- Decision making and coordination methods
- General strategies

One challenge for coalition leaders is to keep the coalition intact or growing once the initial burst of enthusiasm for a campaign or project wears off. Among the applicable strategies are regular, well-run meetings or work sessions, continuous progress reports, periodic conferences and other public events, and sustaining media coverage of the effort to win proposal adoption. To the extent possible, coalition members should be actively involved in the campaign, either by attempting to influence policy makers or by implementing what can be done without policy makers' approval. Once a new policy or program is adopted, coalition members may decide it's time to declare victory and move onto something else, but astute political leaders know that more battles lie ahead in the implementation process. Therefore they try to involve coalition members, whether directly in implementing the policy or indirectly through monitoring and assessing how well implementation is carried out.

The steering committee of the African American Men Project basically ensured continuation and expansion of the project coalition by successfully recommending to the Hennepin County Board that a successor group, the African American Men Commission, should be set up and $500,000 in seed money provided for the next phase of the project. The entire 130-member commission meets quarterly, and an executive committee meets monthly. Additionally, all members are expected to take part on active committees and participate in biweekly training sessions.

More guidance on the care and feeding of coalitions is in Chapter Ten. You may also want to use Exercise 4.5 to help an initial group of change advocates develop a plan for building and sustaining an advocacy coalition to tackle the public problem that concerns you.

Exercise 4.5. Laying the Groundwork
for a Winning Coalition.

1. Return to the list of stakeholders generated for Exercise 4.2. For each one, fill out this worksheet. In doing so, the group should pay attention to perspectives and needs differing by gender, ethnicity, physical ability, age, religious preference, and other characteristics as relevant. (This is essentially the same worksheet used in Exercise 3.3. If worksheets from that exercise are relevant, simply review and revise as needed for this exercise.)

Stakeholder Worksheet

Stakeholder:			
Criteria Used by Stakeholders to Assess the Coalition's Actual or Potential Performance	Our Sense of Their Judgment About Our Performance		
	Very Good	OK	Poor

How do they influence us?

What do we need from them?

How important are they?

☐ Extremely

☐ Reasonably

☐ Not very

☐ Not at all

Exercise 4.5. Laying the Groundwork
for a Winning Coalition, Cont'd.

2. From the worksheets and the power-versus-interest grid produced in Exercise 4.2, generate a list of potential coalition members. For each, answer these questions:

   • What can the stakeholder contribute to the coalition?
   • What might the stakeholder get from the coalition?

3. Use insights about problem framing from Exercise 4.3 to generate ideas for persuading stakeholders to join the coalition.

4. Develop strategies for organizing the coalition and keeping it intact or growing.

   • How will we deal with power differences among coalition members?
   • Which person or organization can coordinate the coalition?
   • How can we keep members informed and engaged in ongoing activities?

Based in part on Bryson, J. M., and Alston, F. *Creating and Implementing Your Strategic Plan: A Workbook for Public and Nonprofit Organizations.* San Francisco: Jossey-Bass, 2004.

Overcome Bureaucratic Resistance During Implementation

Implementation of major policy change usually requires the co-operation of bureaucratic institutions. Bureaucracies have intricate rules and procedures and entrenched personnel who may hamper any change. A prime mover in one of the cases featured in this book noted, "There are three women in charge of the budget stuff, who compete with each other to protect [the top decision maker] from the risk of making any decision that might result in an expenditure. They are protecting the importance of their jobs. . . ."

Political leaders must constantly find ways to enlist bureaucrats in their cause—for example, by appealing to a shared vision or goals (Behn, 1999). George Frederickson suggests that civil servants may respond favorably to such appeals, since they are more concerned about social justice than the general population is (Frederickson, 1997).

Institutional rules, procedures, and personnel may have to be changed, or new parallel or auxiliary organizations created as part of the implementation process. When necessary, political leaders find a way to appeal over the bureaucrats' heads to the broader public or other powerful stakeholders who support the change. For example, the advocacy coalition fighting for increased attention to AIDS on the part of U.S. public health officials in the early 1980s faced considerable barriers within the federal public health bureaucracy; they were, however, able to obtain a much more sympathetic hearing from members of Congress, and congressional pressure did force federal agencies to channel considerable resources toward AIDS research, treatment, and prevention.

Adeptly Design and Use Formal and Informal Arenas

The political practices described so far are connected to arenas in which leaders and constituents seek decisions from policy makers that will lead to effective implementation of their proposed solutions. The design and use of arenas determine both which proposals are placed on the policy-making agenda and which are incorporated into new laws, rules, regulations, projects, and programs. As noted in Resource D, the key considerations that leaders should include in their strategies for designing and using an arena are decision-making capabilities; domains; agendas; planning, budgeting, decision making, and implementation methods; and rules governing access to participation.

Decision-Making Capabilities
Political leaders identify and build relationships with the people who have clout (that is, key capabilities) in the executive, legislative, and administrative arenas that can supply the decisions they desire. These capabilities might include holding elected office, occupying a top position, showing proven ability to sway votes, or possessing the authority to approve budgets or personnel. For example, as Hively worked to secure funding for the Vital Aging Initiative, she had to ensure she sold the project to the dean of the college where she was working and to the university's provost, who could approve funds for the project. She conducted research to find out which individuals and foundations might approve grants for the initiative and presented her proposal to the appropriate decision makers. Depending on the decision maker, she

recruited particular community leaders or role models to support the proposal.

Schmidheiny wanted to affect decision making in businesses, so he recruited chief executives to serve on the World Business Council for Sustainable Development. Moreover, the council has issued specific models and guidance for business leaders who want to improve their practices; guidance also is tailored for certain industries and company sizes. The council is developing learning modules that can help member companies "embed sustainable development issues" in their core business practices (World Business Council for Sustainable Development, 2003, p. 15). Council representatives have presented their views to U.N. policy makers who are establishing global mechanisms and standards for fostering sustainable development. At the Johannesburg Summit, WBCSD President Stigson joined with Greenpeace Director Steve Sawyer to visibly urge heads of state to agree on an international framework for tackling global climate change that would be based on the Kyoto Protocol—an event clearly calculated to get worldwide mass media coverage and put public pressure on national governments. The council also is attempting to influence the next generation of business leaders by setting up Young Manager Teams that can participate in WBCSD events and help shape the council's future.

Political leaders should also remember to establish connections with powerful people who are opposed to the changes they support. Communicating with these people—Greenpeace leaders, for example, in the case of WBCSD—can reveal areas of agreement at least on procedures for hammering out solutions. As political leaders try to adjust their strategy to ongoing competition in an arena, they should keep working to find a way to tap the interests of opponents or find a way to neutralize them.

Domains

Political leaders consider carefully the domain of any arena to which they submit their proposed policies and projects. In submitting the final report of the African American Men Project, Cunningham and Milligan noted that the recommendations were directed at policy makers in many institutions whose domain included Hennepin County's young African American men. County government was first on the list, but they also named the "State of Minnesota, the City of Minneapolis, foundations, other nonprofits, businesses, and educational systems" (Hennepin County, 2002, p. 5).

Political leaders often realize the need for altering the domain of an existing arena or establishing a new arena that encompasses all or part of the public issue at hand. In a way, the African American Commission that was recommended by the final report as an advisory group to the Hennepin County Board of Commissioners would expand the board's domain to aspects of African American men's lives that were outside the scope of the county's traditional social service and public safety responsibilities.

Agendas

Political leaders understand how the decision-making agendas are set in the arena that they hope will consider their proposal, and they work to ensure that their proposals are advantageously placed on the agenda. This might require building a relationship with the powerful committee chair, who decides what proposed policy or legislation is considered by the committee. It might require working with the chairperson's aide or secretary. Political leaders recognize that their proposal must compete with other issues for a decision maker's attention; thus they emphasize why their proposal should be on the agenda (the issue is urgent, the decision makers' constituents support the proposals, the proposals fit the decision makers' priorities, the mass media are clamoring for action, and so on). Placement on the agenda can be quite important; for example, advocates of a policy proposal may want to have their proposal considered early in a meeting, so that it receives plenty of attention, rather than at the end when everyone is tired and just wants to finish the meeting.

To achieve a spot on the provost's agenda, Hively could point out that aging baby boomers represent a business opportunity for the university. She could offer research indicating that older Minnesotans are seeking opportunities for self-development, and she could present work plans that offer a promise of success and accountability. She could also show how the proposal builds on work the university has already supported and show that external funders will supplement university resources.

Planning, Budgeting, Decision Making, and Implementation Methods
Political leaders understand how to fit their proposal into the planning and budgeting process of the appropriate arena. They carefully consider what amount of money and other resources to request and when and what type of program or staffing arrangements are likely to be viewed favorably in light of those plans and budgets.

Political leaders consider whether decisions are to be made by consensus, majority vote, or executive order, and in closed or open meetings. They need to know whether preliminary decisions are made by committees before moving to a larger policy-making group. They must be aware of decision-making time frames. They must think through the merits of expanding or reframing the issue that concerns them to include other issues that are on the decision makers' agenda. They have to know which kinds of influence technique (lobbying, strategic voting, and the like) are acceptable. They must anticipate the moves and countermoves of others who are competing for decision makers' attention and votes.

The implementation plans included in a policy proposal must take account of decision makers' expectations and their institutional arrangement for handling a new program or a change in an old one. For example, a university administrator will expect results to be measured and reported, and that a new program is assigned to a department that handles similar programs.

As proposals are altered in the decision-making process, political leaders need to pay constant, even obsessive, attention to ensure the new proposals are technically and administratively workable, politically acceptable, and legally and ethically defensible, and that they encourage collective and individual behavior anticipated by the vision that animates their coalition.

As needed, political leaders also work for reform in planning, budgeting, decision-making, and implementation methods. For example, corruption may have to be rooted out, decision making made more transparent, and a committee system reshaped.

Access Rules
Political leaders understand the rules that govern who becomes a decision maker in an executive, legislative, or administrative arena and who is permitted to play another role in the arena (observer,

advocate, expert). They must often change the rules or the decision makers for their groups to gain access to policy-making positions or to the process. A constitution may have to be amended, or at least new structures put into place. For example, young African American men traditionally have had little access to the deliberations of the Hennepin County commissioners, because the formal and informal rules governing their meetings advantaged the well-educated, well-informed professional or middle-class taxpayer. Creation of the African American Men Commission, however, provides an official conduit to the commission for young men who would not normally set up appointments with county commissioners or attend their meetings.

The Vital Aging Network has launched an advocacy leadership program in cooperation with several sponsors. The program helps participants gain the capacity to advocate influentially for policies that promote vital aging.

Helpful Tools

David Chrislip and Carl Larson's *Collaborative Leadership* and Chrislip's *Collaborative Leadership Handbook* offer guidance for building and sustaining a coalition (Chrislip and Larson, 1994; Chrislip, 2002). The Wilder Foundation furnishes detailed advice for lobbying state and local government policy makers in the United States (Avner, 2002). Additional advice on building a coalition as well as lobbying can be found in Kevin Hula's *Lobbying Together* (1999) and Rinus van Schendelen's *Machiavelli in Brussels* (2002), and on the Website of the National Coalition Building Institute (www.ncbi.org). You can use Exercise 4.6 to assess the political leadership capacity of an individual, group, organization, or network.

Ethical Leadership

Once policy makers have enacted new policies, passed new laws and regulations, set up new programs and projects, or refused to do so, the policy makers' decisions are likely to be debated in a formal or informal court. Here, ethical leaders help constituents apply general rules to specific cases; resolve conflicts among competing ethical principles, laws, rules, and norms; and reward or

Exercise 4.6. Assessing Political Leadership Capacity.

You may use this exercise to rate a group, an organization, or an interorganizational network. You may reword the questions to rate your own or another individual's political leadership capacity.

If the exercise is done by a group, each member should do the ratings individually; the ratings can then be pooled to produce a group rating.

Respond to the questions by checking one of the three boxes after each.

	Poor/ Poorly	OK/ Acceptably	Good/ Well
1. How good are we at maintaining multiple channels of access and advocacy?	☐	☐	☐
2. Are we trained in bargaining and negotiation strategies (including copromotion, compromise, and competition)?	☐	☐	☐
3. How good are we at assembling and expanding formal and informal coalitions that can have needed clout in particular arenas?	☐	☐	☐
4. How good are we at assessing, developing, and employing the resources of our own coalition on behalf of change, and countering the advantages bestowed by our opponents' resources?	☐	☐	☐
5. How well do we keep coalition members involved in campaigns to adopt and implement our policy proposals?	☐	☐	☐
6. How well do we deal with bureaucratic barriers to the changes we support?	☐	☐	☐
7. How good are our relations with key decision makers in the arenas that act on our proposals for change?	☐	☐	☐
8. Do we consider a range of existing or new arenas that might enact the changes we support?	☐	☐	☐

Exercise 4.6. Assessing Political Leadership Capacity, Cont'd.

	Poor/ Poorly	OK/ Acceptably	Good/ Well
9. How good are we at getting our proposals on the agenda of policy makers?	☐	☐	☐
10. How well do we attend to planning, budgeting, decision-making, and implementation methods in shaping and promoting our proposals in arenas?	☐	☐	☐
11. How good are we at understanding and shaping access rules so that we can participate in the policy-making process?	☐	☐	☐
12. How good are we at achieving policy and implementation decisions that enact our vision of the common good?	☐	☐	☐

When you are done with the ratings:

For Working Alone

1. Develop a list of the political strengths of the individual, group, organization, or network on the basis of the items ranked *Good/Well*. Note a few of the reasons these items were ranked highly.
2. Develop a list of the political weaknesses of the group, organization, or network on the basis of the items ranked *Poor/Poorly*. Note a few of the reasons these items were given a low ranking.
3. Also note which aspects of the items rated *OK/Acceptably* need improving.
4. Identify specific actions you can take to build on the identified strengths and overcome identified weaknesses.

For Working in a Group

1. Develop a list of the political strengths of the group, organization, or network on the basis of the items that most group members rated *Good/Well*. Note a few of the reasons these items were ranked highly.

Exercise 4.6. Assessing Political Leadership Capacity, Cont'd.

2. Develop a list of the political weaknesses of the group, organization, or network on the basis of the items that a majority of the group ranked *Poor/Poorly*. Note a few of the reasons these items were given a low ranking.
3. Identify and discuss aspects of other items that need improvement.
4. Agree on specific actions the group can take to build on the identified strengths and overcome identified weaknesses.

punish the conduct of individuals and groups. Of course, all types of leadership have ethical aspects, but we define ethical leadership as sanctioning conduct and adjudicating disputes in court, because in this process the fundamental concern is with what is ethical and legitimate. These are the main skills of ethical leadership:

- Educating about ethics, constitutions, other laws, and norms
- Promoting awareness of how ethical principles, constitutions, other laws, and norms apply to specific cases
- Adapting principles, laws, and norms to changing times
- Resolving conflict among principles, laws, and norms
- Understanding the design and use of formal and informal courts

Educate About Ethics, Constitutions, Other Laws, and Norms

In court decisions, legal treatises, editorials, sermons, memos, and other communications, ethical leaders emphasize the importance of abiding by and critiquing ethical principles, laws, and norms. They explain how ethical principles, constitutions, other laws, and norms do or do not contribute to communal well-being. They specifically emphasize the ethical principles, laws, and norms that legitimate their desired policies and that can evoke broad support among stakeholders.

WBCSD President Stigson and his colleagues exhibited ethical leadership when they joined Greenpeace at the 2002 Johannesburg Summit in emphasizing the importance of international treaties and protocols that can give businesspeople and other stakeholders consistent standards and timetables for reducing emissions of greenhouse gases. In appealing to the court of public opinion in Hennepin County, Minnesota, Milligan, Cunningham, and their colleagues are emphasizing the norms of community and inclusion, personal responsibility and security, and equal treatment. Hively, Hal Freshley, Darlene Schroeder, and their supporters are appealing to the court of public opinion throughout Minnesota by emphasizing norms of self-determination, self-sufficiency, community involvement, productivity, intergenerational mutuality, and nondiscrimination.

Obviously, it's important that ethical leaders uphold the principles, laws, and norms they espouse in their own behavior. When protestors appeared at Shell's annual shareholders meeting in 2003 to criticize the company's environmental record, they indicated that company chairman and WBCSD leader Phil Watts and his colleagues at Shell need to do more to walk their talk. You may want to complete Exercise 4.7 to identify your role models for ethical leadership and develop ideas for overcoming barriers to it.

Promote Awareness of How Ethical Principles, Constitutions, Other Laws, and Norms Apply

Ethical principles such as the importance of respecting human dignity offer only general guidance. A constitution is usually a broad framework establishing basic organizational purposes, structures, and procedures. Laws, though more narrowly drawn, still typically apply to broad classes of people or actions; moreover, they frequently emerge from the legislative process containing purposeful omissions and generalities that were necessary to obtain enough votes for passage (Posner, 1985). Therefore, ethical principles,

---

Exercise 4.7. Identifying Ethical Role Models, and Overcoming Barriers to Ethical Leadership.

1. Who are your role models for ethical leadership?
2. What ethical principles do they espouse or live out?
3. What draws you to these people?
4. What are the main barriers to practicing ethical leadership?
5. How can you overcome these barriers?

---

constitutional provisions, and other laws (including formal codes of ethics) require authoritative interpretation in order to decide whether and how they apply to a specific case. Judges, jurors, attorneys, and other interested parties all contribute to that interpretation. Outside the formal courts, leaders must typically apply norms rather than laws. Norms may be written (as in a published code of ethics) or unwritten.

Ethical leaders also consider how sanctions should be applied in a specific case. Laws often make available some guidance about (or a range of punishments for) violation of the law; they may even guarantee rewards (such as tax breaks) for those who comply with the law. Ethical leaders make the case for specific sanctions that are needed to give force to principles, laws, and norms.

Adapt Principles, Laws, and Norms to Changing Times

Although principles, laws, and norms have lasting force, they are the product of historical social issues and forces (when *historical* includes the recent past). As conditions change, new issues emerge and old ones change. Thus existing principles, laws, and norms must change, and ethical leaders help constituents understand the need for change and the type of change needed. Mounting evidence of global climate change caused by greenhouse emissions calls into question a regime of disparate national laws regulating polluters—a regime based on principles of national sovereignty. WBCSD officials are calling on national government officials to cede some of their sovereignty to an international body that would set global standards for reducing greenhouse emissions and increasing use of renewable energy.

Often, as in the WBCSD example, ethical leaders are urging policy makers in an executive, legislative, or administrative arena to alter the law. However, the leaders often must ask a formal court to mandate a change because vested interests that tend to oppose change hold sway over the executive, legislative, and administrative arena (Van Horn, Baumer, and Gormley, 2001). (This assumes that the court is reasonably independent of the arena.) In the area of constitutional law, in particular, the courts—as the "keepers" of constitutions—are usually the most legitimate venue for reinterpreting a constitution in light of societal changes.

Resolve Conflicts Among Principles, Laws, and Norms

When applied to a specific case, principles, laws, and norms often conflict with each other. Ethical leaders help constituents decide how to resolve such conflict. They can make a case for why one principle, law, or norm should trump another. For example, if a law contravenes a constitutional provision, they emphasize the need to uphold the constitution above all other laws. They can offer a balancing approach; for example, by guaranteeing business owners considerable autonomy in how they achieve government-mandated emission controls. Thus the principle of liberty is balanced with the principle of environmental stewardship. Ethical leaders also are able to reinterpret conflict to suggest how competing principles, laws, or norms might be reconciled. For example, WBCSD members remind businesspeople that they will have neither autonomy nor security if the world's natural resources are destroyed. Thus environmental stewardship is cast ultimately as a way to guarantee business viability.

Understand the Design and Use of Formal and Informal Courts

The setting for the ethical practices described here is a formal or informal court. Ethical leaders know that the design and use of these settings critically affect which policies and behaviors are subjected to judicial scrutiny and which sanctions are meted out. Courts often determine which adopted policies, programs, and projects are actually implemented and which are halted entirely or rendered ineffectual. As noted in Resource D, the key considerations that leaders should include in their strategies for designing and using courts are conflict management and sanctioning capabilities, rules governing conflict resolution, jurisdiction, conflict management methods, and rules governing access.

Conflict Management and Sanctioning Capabilities

Ethical leaders identify those (including themselves) who have the authority and skills needed to resolve residual conflict and make binding decisions about applying ethical principles, laws, and norms as well as sanctioning conduct. They may consider these judges' record of wise and fair decisions or their level of training in strategizing about whether and how to attempt to argue a case before them. Ethical leaders may need to work for increased judicial authority—for example, the ability to levy higher fines or sentences for violations of a law. They may need to help some publics (customers of polluting industries, for instance) apply the sanctions they control (such as purchasing power). They may need to help people in their coalition apply peer pressure or acquire additional skills in conflict management or legal procedures. The organizers of the African American Men Project are relying on the sanctioning capacity of the African American community itself to affect the behavior of young African American men. The project planners are sponsoring a Dream Assessment Initiative, in which "dream assessors" encourage students in grades five through twelve to define their dreams and aspirations, and develop a plan to make their dream a reality. Additionally, the project is working with Brother Achievement, which is training hundreds of mentors to work with young African American men.

Leaders recognize that policy makers (whether on a board, in a legislature, or administrators or executives) act as judges when they consider whether or not a recipient of funds is complying with policies and contracts. They can apply sanctions, as in giving more money or refusing to do so. Thus the African American Men Project and Vital Aging Network have included accountability mechanisms in their work programs to help funders judge their accomplishment and accept them as legitimate.

Rules Governing Conflict Resolution

Ethical leaders analyze the rules (such as due process) that govern the courts acting on the cases that concern them. They help constituents develop strategies for taking advantage of the rules or altering them. For example, WBCSD officials are helping shape a number of Voluntary Environmental Initiatives (see Christmann and Taylor, 2002) that serve as an informal court judging whether a corporation is living up to agreed-upon environmental standards. WBCSD recognizes the importance of using independent verification of company reports so that the findings of a court will be seen as legitimate. An obvious impetus for establishing voluntary initiatives is the desire to avoid litigation in many national courts, where rules require or allow a lengthy and costly process, and sanctions can be severe.

The African American Men Project is working with the Hennepin County courts system to alter formal and informal rules that make it difficult for young men involved with the criminal justice system to escape it. For example, the project advocates developing or continuing educational programs and networks to help these young men become productive citizens. The project is also working with the National Leadership Institute on a process for expunging the criminal records of men who have been released from prison and completed probation and parole.

Jurisdiction

Ethical leaders recognize that a dispute over the legitimacy or application of an enacted policy will be channeled to courts on the basis of jurisdiction (that is, whether the authority of the court covers the substance or location of the dispute). They may have to move through a hierarchy of courts, in which successive courts have authority over the ones below them. They may strive to alter a court's jurisdiction or create a new court (such as the Voluntary Environmental Initiatives just mentioned) that will have jurisdiction over the cases that concern them.

Conflict Management Methods

In designing and using courts, ethical leaders strive, if possible, to use the conflict resolution methods that are most likely to produce outcomes that are the intended objectives of the policies, programs, and projects they support. For example, relying on legal findings by formal judges or members of a jury may be highly effective, if the judgment is legitimate and enforceable. Leaders also recognize the merit of using other methods, such as mediation, to avoid some of the cost (to pocketbooks and relationships) of adversarial proceedings. Members of the African American Men Project are working with a committee of judges, corrections officials, and others to develop a community response to "liveability crimes," such as street corner drug sales and prostitution, in poor neighborhoods. The solutions might include informal sanctions by community residents, mediation among neighbors, or restitution agreements.

Rules Governing Access

A formal court usually has precise rules about selecting judges and juries, qualifications of lawyers and other officers of the court, types of cases it will consider, and in what format. Informal rules, such as a requirement that substantial funds be devoted to arguing a court case, also determine who has access to a formal court. Ethical leaders help constituents alter or take advantage of these rules so they can obtain a favorable verdict for their policy or program.

Helpful Tools

We recommend two exercises for helping you or your group practice ethical leadership. Exercise 4.8 helps you analyze the ethical principles, laws, and norms that apply to the policies you support. Exercise 4.9 helps you assess the ethical leadership of an individual, group, organization, or network.

Exercise 4.8. Analyzing Ethical Principles, Laws, and Norms.

---

1. What ethical principles bestow legitimacy on the policies supported by our group or coalition?
2. How are these principles connected to "higher law," such as widely shared religious beliefs, or international treaties and protocols?
3. What are we doing to enact these principles in our own words and deeds?
4. What laws and court decisions support our desired policies?
5. What norms might we expect key stakeholder groups to apply in support of our desired policies?
6. What conflicts exist among ethical principles, laws, and norms that are applicable to our desired policies?
7. How might we deal with these conflicts?
8. How might pertinent ethical principles, laws, and norms need to be reinterpreted or updated to apply to the current issues that concern us?

Exercise 4.9. Assessing Ethical Leadership Capacity.

You may use this exercise to rate a group, an organization, or an inter-organizational network. You may reword the questions to rate your own or another individual's ethical capacity.

If the exercise is done by a group, each member should fill in the ratings individually; the ratings can then be pooled to produce a group rating.

Respond to the questions by checking one of the three boxes after each.

	Poor/ Poorly	OK/ Acceptably	Good/ Well
1. How good are we at educating others about ethical principles, laws, and norms that legitimate the policies we support?	☐	☐	☐
2. How well do we "walk the talk" (match our own behavior to the principles we espouse)?	☐	☐	☐
3. Are we succeeding in helping others understand how principles, laws, and norms apply to specific cases?	☐	☐	☐
4. How good are we at explaining why and how existing principles, laws, and norms should be adapted to changing times?	☐	☐	☐
5. How good are we at identifying and suggesting ways to resolve conflict among ethical principles, laws, and norms?	☐	☐	☐
6. How good are we at building and activating conflict management and sanctioning capabilities?	☐	☐	☐
7. How well do we understand the rules governing the courts that matter to us?	☐	☐	☐
8. How good are our strategies for taking advantage of those rules or altering them?	☐	☐	☐

Exercise 4.9. Assessing Ethical Leadership Capacity, Cont'd.

	Poor/ Poorly	OK/ Acceptably	Good/ Well
9. How good are we at finding or creating courts with the appropriate jurisdiction for the conflicts that concern us?	☐	☐	☐
10. How good are we at assessing the merits of methods for resolving disputes in formal and informal courts?	☐	☐	☐
11. How good are we at taking advantage of or altering rules governing access to courts?	☐	☐	☐

When you are done with the ratings:

For Working Alone

1. Develop a list of the ethical strengths of the individual, group, organization, or network on the basis of the items ranked *Good/Well.* Note a few of the reasons these items were ranked highly.
2. Develop a list of the ethical weaknesses of the group, organization, or network on the basis of the items ranked *Poor/Poorly.* Note a few of the reasons these items were given a low ranking.
3. Also note which aspects of the items rated *OK/Acceptably* need improving.
4. Identify specific actions you can take to build on the identified strengths and overcome identified weaknesses.

For Working in a Group

1. Develop a list of the ethical strengths of the group, organization, or network on the basis of the items that most group members rated *Good/Well.* Note a few of the reasons these items were ranked highly.
2. Develop a list of the ethical weaknesses of the group, organization, or network on the basis of the items that a majority of the group ranked *Poor/Poorly.* Note a few of the reasons these items were given a low ranking.
3. Identify and discuss aspects of other items that need improvement.
4. Agree on specific actions the group can take to build on the identified strengths and overcome identified weaknesses.

Summary

Visionary leaders focus on creation and communication of shared meaning in formal and informal forums. To do this, they seize opportunities to be interpreters and direction givers in a situation of uncertainty or difficulty, offer a compelling vision of the future, postpone a full-fledged vision during crisis, and adeptly design and use forums. Political leaders focus on making and implementing legislative, executive, and administrative policy decisions in formal and informal arenas. They mediate and shape conflict within and among constituencies; build winning, sustainable coalitions; overcome bureaucratic resistance; and adeptly design and use arenas. Ethical leaders educate others about ethics, constitutions, other laws, and norms; promote awareness of how ethical principles, constitutions, other laws, and norms apply to specific cases; adapt principles, laws, and norms to changing times; resolve conflict among principles, laws, and norms; and adeptly design and use courts.

The next chapter turns to the work of policy entrepreneurship—coordination of leadership tasks in the course of a major policy change effort. We also focus on discerning the common good.

Chapter Five

Policy Entrepreneurship and the Common Good

The quintessential problem of politics [is] how to judge
rightly the lesser evil, the relatively best, the ends that
justify the means and the means themselves. . . .
MARY DIETZ

The common good . . . is good human life of the
multitude, of a multitude of persons; it is their
communion in good living.
JACQUES MARITAIN

We now turn to policy entrepreneurship, or coordination of leadership tasks over the course of a policy change cycle. Leaders who are policy entrepreneurs—such as Marcus Conant, Stephan Schmidheiny, Gary Cunningham, Jan Hively, and many of their colleagues—are catalysts of systemic change (Roberts and King, 1996). Policy entrepreneurs "introduce, translate, and implement an innovative idea into public practice" (1996, p. 10). Like entrepreneurs in the business realm, they are inventive, energetic, and persistent in overcoming systemic barriers. They can work inside or outside government organizations; unlike Nancy Roberts and Paula King (1996), we do not reserve the term *policy entrepreneur* for nongovernmental leaders.

The essential requirements of policy entrepreneurship are a systemic understanding of policy change and a focus on enacting the common good. This chapter offers an overview of these two requirements; subsequent chapters are devoted to individual phases of the policy change cycle.

Before going further, we should note that public policy has both substantive and symbolic aspects. It can be defined as *substantive decisions, commitments, and implementing actions by those who have governance responsibilities (including, but going beyond government), as interpreted by various stakeholders.* Thus public policy is what the affected people think it is, and based on what the substantive content symbolizes to them. Public policies may be called policies, plans, programs, projects, decisions, actions, budgets, rules, or regulations. Moreover, they may emerge deliberately or as the result of mutual adjustment among partisans (Lindblom, 1959; Mintzberg and Waters, 1985). Exhibit 5.1 presents brief definitions of public policy and other key terms in this chapter.

Understanding Policy Change

The policy change process can be described as a seven-phase cycle (Figure 5.1), in which a shifting set of change advocates work in multiple forums, arenas, and courts to remedy a public problem. The phases are interconnected and build on each other, but policy entrepreneurs are seldom able to march through them in an orderly, sequential fashion. In the case of a highly complex public problem such as AIDS or global warming, the cycle (and "re-cycling") may extend over decades. The effort to enact solutions for less complex problems, such as homelessness in a particular city, may be successful in a much shorter period. No matter what, the same set of leaders and constituents who began a change effort may not be able to see the effort all the way through the cycle. Moreover, new leaders and constituencies are likely to join the process all along the way. Wise leaders attend to timing and are prepared to handle disruptions and delays throughout the process.

The policy change cycle is an orienting framework rather than a precise causal model (Sabatier, 1991). It contains a set of repeating and intersecting loops that highlight the frequency and pervasiveness of feedback throughout the cycle. The phases of the cycle and their central actions are on page 160.

Exhibit 5.1. Policy Entrepreneurship
and the Common Good: Some Definitions.

Policy entrepreneurship	Coordination of leadership tasks over the course of a policy change cycle; policy entrepreneurs catalyze systemic change.
Public policy	Substantive decisions, commitments, and actions by those who have governance responsibilities, as they are interpreted by various stakeholders.
Key stakeholders	Stakeholders who are most affected by a public problem or who control the most important resources needed to remedy the problem.
Issue creation	The process of placing a public problem together with at least one solution (that has pros and cons from the standpoint of various stakeholders) on the public agenda.
Public agenda	The matters of current concern to a broad range of citizens and community members.
Policy makers' agenda	The list of proposed policies, projects, and plans under consideration by policy makers.
Advocacy coalition	Stakeholders who accept a shared problem frame and support a set of related solutions that require action by a range of policy makers. The coalition is likely to include one or more formal groups that make an explicit commitment to pressure policy makers to adopt the groups' policy proposals.
Policy subsystem	Policy regime that operates behind the scenes, or "off-cycle."
Common good	An actual or potential regime of mutual gain produced through careful stakeholder analysis and substantial involvement.

Figure 5.1. Policy Change Cycle.

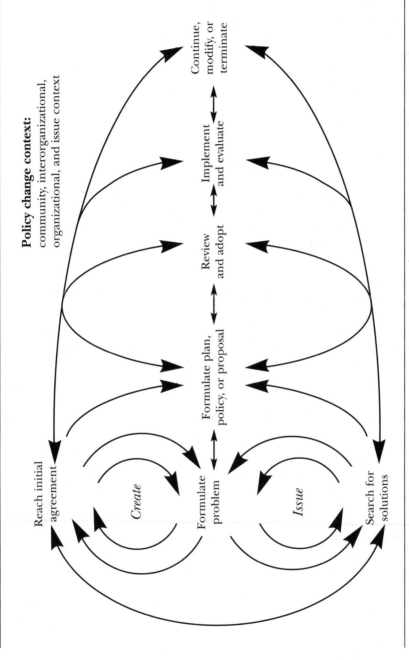

Policy change context:
community, interorganizational, organizational, and issue context

Reach initial agreement

Formulate plan, policy, or proposal

Review and adopt

Implement and evaluate

Continue, modify, or terminate

Formulate problem

Search for solutions

Create

Issue

1. *Initial agreement:* Agree to do something about an undesirable condition, or "plan for planning"

2. *Problem formulation:* Fully define the problem; consider alternative problem frames

3. *Search for solutions:* Consider a broad range of solutions; develop consensus on preferred solutions

4. *Policy or plan formulation:* Incorporate preferred solutions into winning proposals for new policies, plans, programs, proposals, budgets, decisions, projects, rules, and so on; proposals must be technically and administratively feasible, politically acceptable, and morally and legally defensible

5. *Proposal review and adoption:* Bargain, negotiate, and compromise with decision makers; maintain supportive coalition

6. *Implementation and evaluation:* Incorporate formally adopted solutions throughout relevant systems, and assess effects

7. *Continuation, modification, or termination:* Review implemented policies to decide how to proceed

Designing and using forums (and visionary leadership) is most important in the first three phases, designing and using arenas (and political leadership) is most important in the middle, and designing and using courts (and ethical leadership) is most important toward the end of the cycle. Leadership in context and personal leadership are important at the outset; team and organizational leadership are vital throughout.

Policy entrepreneurs may become involved at any phase of a change cycle. Those dealing with emergent problems, such as the early AIDS crisis, must devote lots of attention to the first three phases, which constitute issue creation. If, as in the World Business Council case, leaders become involved after an issue is already well defined and new policies, programs, and projects are already being considered or implemented in arenas, they have to devote attention to the middle phases. They may also recycle through earlier phases to involve new constituents or develop alternatives to solutions that are under consideration.

If policy regimes are already fully implemented yet unable to remedy the problems they are supposed to address, leaders will focus on the last phase of the change cycle to determine whether the regime merits minor renovation, major overhaul, or destruction. For major overhaul or destruction, the change advocates may have to circle back to issue creation and involve new groups, redefine the problem, and search for new solutions. For example, when Hively and her colleagues became concerned about the lack of resources and support systems to help older adults lead productive lives, they were, in effect, pointing to the deficiencies of existing policy regimes (such as Medicaid and Medicare) that defined older adults as either frail dependents or self-centered retirees.

Before describing each phase, we want to examine policy making as a type of "organized anarchy" and emphasize the importance of managing ideas, analyzing and involving stakeholders, and designing institutions throughout the change cycle. Policy innovation simply won't happen without introducing compelling new ideas and additional players into the policy process. Nor is it likely to happen without altering or replacing existing institutional or shared-power arrangements.

Understanding the Policy Process as Organized Anarchy

The phrase *organized anarchy* has been used to describe the disorder, confusion, ambiguity, and randomness that accompany much decision making in large, "loosely coupled" organizations (Cohen, March, and Olsen, 1972). The term applies, perhaps with even more force, to the shared-power, interorganizational, interinstitutional policy environments where no one is in complete charge, and many are partly in charge.

Several scholars (see Cohen, March, and Olsen, 1972; Pfeffer, 1992; and Kingdon, 1995) emphasize the "anarchic" qualities of an organized anarchy:

- Goals and preferences are fairly consistent, at least for a time, within an individual, group, organization, or coalition. Goals and preferences are, however, inconsistent and pluralistic across individuals, groups, organizations, and coalitions.
- The position of an interest group and the composition of a coalition can change, sometimes quickly.
- Conflict is legitimate and expected as part of the free play of the political marketplace. Struggle, conflict, and winners and losers are normal.

- Information is used and withheld strategically.
- Within a social group, people hold consistent (often ideological) beliefs about the connection between actions and outcomes. Across groups, however, there may be considerable disagreement about the action-outcome relationship.
- The decision process often appears disorderly because of the clash of shifting coalitions and interest groups.
- Decisions result from the negotiation, bargaining, and interplay among coalitions and interest groups, indicating that these groups find it necessary to share power.

Despite this evidence of anarchy, there are points of stability and predictability in the policy process. Indeed, a shared-power arrangement is typically designed to furnish some of this stability. The basic organizing features of the policy process are the rules, resources, and transformation procedures that structure, enable, and legitimate specific actions. (These rules, resources, and procedures link action and underlying social structure in the "second dimension of power," described in Resource D). Thus the shared-power world is not as anarchic as it may seem at first. It has many predictable features that policy entrepreneurs can use to achieve desirable change (Feldman, 2000). Moreover, the anarchic features open up innumerable opportunities to alter shared-power arrangements and create new ones (Huxham and Beech, 2003).

Policy analysts identify two types of policy change: "off-cycle," or incremental change resulting from ongoing, routine, behind-the-scenes decision making in established policy regimes; and "on-cycle," major change efforts that move onto the public agenda and force policy makers to thoroughly rethink and restructure existing policy regimes or develop new ones. Policy entrepreneurs attend most to on-cycle decision-making processes (represented by the policy change cycle), but they also need to understand off-cycle processes.

For example, in the African American Men case, policy entrepreneurs must understand the off-cycle decision-making process in education and criminal justice systems as they try to introduce mentoring programs for African American boys into the public schools, or to establish a process for expunging the records of ex-prisoners who have successfully completed probation and parole.

Managing Ideas

Practical people often underestimate the power of ideas, but as Guy Peters notes, "Shaping the nature of issues and policy problems is a basic aspect of the policy process, and the fundamental coordination issues arise from conflicts over ideas rather than from organizational interests" (1996b, p. 76). The idea or ideas promoted by policy entrepreneurs must compete with opposing ideas that are incorporated into existing policy regimes related to the problem at hand. These regimes are what Frank Baumgartner and Bryan Jones (1993) call policy subsystems, which operate behind the scenes, or off-cycle. Policy makers have already enacted major policies and established programs and regulatory mechanisms on the basis of a set of ideas about a public problem and optimal solutions. Participants in a shared-power arrangement are implementing those policies, programs, and regulations more or less in line with policy makers' intentions. Off-cycle policy and decision making are not part of the policy makers' agenda because day-to-day bureaucratic decision making—though it may have widespread indirect effects—does not directly affect most people, and therefore few take an interest in it. Moreover, policy subsystems have numerous built-in reinforcing and stabilizing mechanisms (Baumgartner and Jones, 1993). Change occurs, but it is incremental. Advocates of major change often must call established policy subsystems into question, because the systems are failing to deal with the problem at hand (even though they are expected to deal with this kind of problem), because the systems' efforts to remedy the problem are largely ineffectual, or because they are causing the problem.

Let's take a look at our four cases. Doctors and public health workers who became concerned in the early 1980s about the deaths of gay men from a mysterious disease were themselves already operating within a public health policy system, consisting of numerous interacting subsystems. In the system, local health departments administered vaccination programs, inspected restaurants, collected statistics about diseases, and the like. Nonprofit organizations pooled government and foundation funding to campaign against unhealthy lifestyles. The national government administered a host of research programs, operated hospitals and clinics, and investigated disease outbreaks. Nonprofit and for-profit hospitals and clinics treated patients and offered their own health education programs. Universities conducted medical research and operated teaching hospitals. Journalists specialized in health reportage; think tanks analyzed health policy.

Clearly, the system embraced a host of organizations (business, government, and nonprofit) and organized and unorganized constituencies (from newborns to cancer patients, from hospital associations to mental health support groups). It could accommodate problems that fit existing categories and required minimal reallocation of resources. Physicians, gay activists, and public health officials concerned about the emerging AIDS crisis realized after some initial effort that the new disease could not be dealt with through existing policy subsystems. These policy entrepreneurs began insisting that the local and national health policy makers put the new disease on their agenda and substantially redirect resources to investigate, treat, and prevent it.

The founders of the World Business Council for Sustainable Development were confronted with multiple policy systems and subsystems at the global, national, and industry levels. For example, the U.N. Development Programme and a multitude of nonprofits, national governments, and businesses were engaged in a development policy system that included subsystems focusing on specific aspects of development, such as farming. Other pertinent policy systems aimed at environmental protection or market regulation. None of these systems, however, were marshaling adequate business support for combining economic development and environmental protection.

The organizers of the African American Men Project (AAMP) had to deal with state and local policy systems related to education, criminal justice, housing, health care, and families. Within a given policy system, they called for changes in particular subsystems—such as physician education—that had an impact on the well-being of African American men. Jan Hively, Hal Freshley, and Darlene Schroeder created the Vital Aging Initiative to shake up the aging policy system of Minnesota and the United States. The system overlaps with health policy systems, education policy systems, and employment regulation systems; it embraces numerous policy subsystems, such as the Medicaid program.

To call policy subsystems into question, policy entrepreneurs present compelling ideas or explanations of the problem that concerns them. Marcus Conant, Michael Gottlieb, and Linda Laubenstein emphasized the idea that the disease affecting gay men was a medical problem, to be dealt with through the accepted protocols of epidemiology and infectious disease. Thus they redefined the mysterious as something familiar. They also defined a problem affecting a large number of gay men as a public responsibility. Change advocates also engage in other types of redefinition:

- Something previously thought of as good may be redefined as bad (for example, nuclear power is redefined as a threat to human health, or productive factories are redefined as contributors to global warming).
- Something previously thought of as bad is redefined as good (old age is redefined as productive maturity).
- The familiar is redefined as mysterious (the previous understanding of what causes a public problem is disproved, and the problem again becomes a mystery to be explored).
- Something thought of as a personal failure is redefined as a public, or communal responsibility (as with the switch from defining smoking as a personal choice to making it a public health issue).

If you are concerned about a public problem, you might use Exercise 5.1 to sort out your own ideas about the problem. What are the causes of the problem? What potential remedies should be considered, given the hypothesized causes? Which policy subsystems might be expected to deal with the problem? What redefinitions of the problem might be necessary to change existing subsystems or establish new ones? What opposing policy ideas am I likely to encounter? What is the "ideal" outcome of a change effort, and what does it imply about the problem? For example, does my desired outcome help me see that some other problem is more important?

In addition to problem definition, the policy change process may also be driven by "problem finding." In other words, change advocates may be vested in a preferred solution and seek connections

Exercise 5.1. Thinking About a Public Problem.

Focus on a public problem that concerns you.

1. What are the causes of the problem?
2. What potential remedies should be considered, given the hypothesized causes?
3. What policy subsystems might be expected to deal with the problem?
4. What redefinitions of the problem might be necessary to change existing subsystems or establish new ones?
5. What opposing policy ideas am I likely to encounter?
6. What is the "ideal" outcome of a change effort, and what does that imply about the problem?

As you become involved in efforts to remedy the problem, you may wish to revise your answers from time to time.

---

to problems that need solving. The solution may have resulted from a policy system that was designed to remedy some other problem that has now been resolved or diminished in importance. The advocates promote ideas that forge new connections between their preferred solution and one or more public problems.

Analyzing and Managing Stakeholders

Any ideas about how a problem should be understood and remedied must be developed and refined in concert with an array of stakeholders, since successful navigation of the policy change cycle requires the inspiration and mobilization of enough key stakeholders to adopt policy changes and protect them during implementation. Recall that a stakeholder is any person, group, or organization that is affected by a public problem, has partial responsibility to act on it, or has resources needed to resolve it. Key stakeholders are those most affected by the problem (regardless of their formal power) and those who control the most important resources needed to remedy the problem.

A stakeholder group consists of people who generally share an orientation to a problem and potential solutions. Specific individuals, however, may have weaker or stronger ties to the group. Indeed, individuals are likely to belong to more than one stakeholder group. Moreover, as philosopher Hannah Arendt has pointed out, it is important to remember that each citizen has a unique view of a public problem. She argues, "For though the common [i.e., public] world is the common meeting ground for all, those who are present have different locations in it, and the location of one can no more coincide with the location of another than the location of two objects. . . . Everybody sees and hears from a different position" (Arendt, 1958, p. 57).

Policy entrepreneurs need to keep this plurality of citizens in mind as they seek to draw individuals and groups into any new advocacy coalition that seeks to overcome the power of an existing coalition sustaining the current policy regime. Subsequent chapters suggest a variety of methods and tools appropriate to the various phases of the policy change cycle to analyze the interests, views, and power of stakeholders and involve them in the change process. Members of the mass media may be especially important since they have the capacity to magnify messages that policy entrepreneurs want to deliver.

Deciding who should be involved, how, and when in doing stakeholder analysis is a key strategic choice, one in which the devil and the angels are in the details. In general, particular people should be involved if they have information that cannot be gained otherwise, or if their participation is necessary to ensure successful implementation of initiatives built on the analysis (Thomas, 1993, 1995). In other words, involving people early on may be a key strategic step in building a supportive coalition needed later.

For entrepreneurs working inside government, stakeholder involvement may come under the heading of public participation. Entrepreneurs working outside government can also use an official public participation event such as a public hearing to promote their policy ideas.

Entrepreneurs must often strike a balance between too much and too little participation. The balance depends on the situation, and there are no hard and fast rules (let alone good empirical evidence) on when, where, how, and why to draw the line. Entrepreneurs should consider the important trade-offs between early and late participation and one or more of these desirable outcomes: representation, accountability, analysis quality, analysis credibility, analysis legitimacy, and the ability to act on the basis of the analysis.

These trade-offs have to be thought through. The challenge may be, for example, "how to get everyone in on the act and still get some action" (Cleveland, 2002), or how to avoid cooptation (Selznick, 1949) to the point that the change advocates' mission is unduly compromised. Or the challenge may be how to have enough stakeholder representatives so that stakeholder interests and perspectives are not misunderstood (Taylor, 1998). Fortunately, the supposed choice actually can be approached as a sequence of choices, in which first an individual or small planning group begins the effort and then others are added later as the advisability of doing so becomes apparent (Finn, 1996; Bryson, 2004a).

Designing Institutions

A policy regime or subsystem is a set of institutions that we see as relatively stable patterns of formal and informal rules, regulations, customs, norms, sanctions, and expectations, governing—or setting strong incentives for—behavior. An institution is also a system of power relations and supporting communication patterns; it represents what E. E. Schattschneider (1975) calls a "mobilization of bias" that may or may not enhance the common good.

An institution is a powerful means of coordinating the actions of diverse individuals and groups. Policy entrepreneurs understand that they must design appropriate institutions if they are to ensure some permanency, or "institutionalization," of desired changes. They often need to alter existing institutions and create new ones. Because of institutions' power and persistence, policy entrepreneurs have the responsibility to assess carefully whether an institution will be a vehicle for enacting the common good. Note that an institution may be formal or informal. Policy design typically is about formal institutions directly and informal institutions (such as the family) indirectly. Wise policy makers also know that formal institutions won't work without informal institutional supports (Ostrom, 1990; Scott, 1998).

The World Business Council for Sustainable Development, for example, emphasizes the importance of institutional design as it argues in favor of the Kyoto Protocol, or promotes the Global Compact (a U.N.-sponsored initiative in which participating corporations commit themselves to protect human rights and the environment), or helps establish certification programs for sustainable development practices. The council is also engaged in an effort to redesign markets generally, as through accounting and reporting methods that would assign costs to waste and pollution.

To take another example, the African American Men Project is itself a new institution with elaborate mechanisms for governance and oversight of initiatives. The project also aims to change major institutions, such as the public schools, city and county government, the court system, public libraries, radio and television programming, and the job market.

Exploring the Phases of the Change Cycle

Although ideas, stakeholders, and institutions are important throughout the policy change process, each phase offers particular challenges or opportunities for developing and refining policy ideas, analyzing and involving stakeholders, and altering institutions. Before describing each phase, we want to highlight the way the first three phases interact to produce public issues. The three phases together constitute *issue creation,* in which a public problem and at least one solution (with pros and cons from the standpoint of various stakeholders) gain a place on the *public agenda.* An issue is on the public agenda once it has become a subject of discussion among a broad cross-section of a community (of place or of interest). Typically, to gain a place on the agenda, policy entrepreneurs must help diverse stakeholder groups develop a new appreciation of the nature and importance of a problem and its potential solutions. Usually the three phases are highly interactive. Various agreements are struck, as problem formulations and solutions are tried out and assessed in an effort to push or block change. If policy entrepreneurs are unsuccessful in placing the issue on the public agenda, it remains a "nonissue" as far as the general community is concerned (Gaventa, 1980; Cobb and Ross, 1997).

Issues—linked problems and solutions—drive the political decision-making, or policy-making, process. Unfortunately, all too often in this process the real problems and the best solutions get lost (if ever they were "found"). Instead, a vaguely specified problem searches for possible policy options; policy advocates try to find a problem their solution might solve; and politicians seek both problems and solutions that might advance a career, further some group's goals, or be in the public interest. Hence visionary leadership becomes particularly important during the process of issue creation. A good idea can give the issue momentum; it is a compelling way of defining or framing the problem and attendant solutions so that key stakeholders are convinced the issue can and must be addressed by policy makers.

Initial Agreement

The purpose of the first phase of the policy change cycle is to develop an understanding among an initial group of key decision makers or opinion leaders about the need to respond to an undesirable condition and develop a basic response strategy. Policy entrepreneurs may initiate this phase with a simple conversation or small meeting with people they think may share their concern or have helpful insights. An example is the conversation between Mark Stenglein and Gary Cunningham that would ultimately lead to the AAMP. Before long, though, policy entrepreneurs must expand the circle to include at least some key stakeholders—those most affected by the problem and those with crucial resources for resolving the problem. (Guidelines for deciding whom to involve and how are offered in Chapter Six.) Policy entrepreneurs need visionary leadership skills as they organize forums (face-to-face and virtual) in which key stakeholders (many of whom represent a group of stakeholders) can develop at least a preliminary shared understanding of the problem and why doing something about it is important, and possibly urgent. The policy entrepreneurs must also convince stakeholders that their participation is vital and is likely to lead to personal and societal benefits.

Policy entrepreneurs have to practice leadership in context; that is, they must examine the policy environment in order to decide whether the time is right to try to launch a change effort. Timing may not be everything, but if it is off then a change effort may have difficulty gaining momentum beyond a small group of people. Thus policy entrepreneurs stay alert for subtle signals of change and any more visible "focusing event" (such as a disaster, official report of a new threat, a scientific breakthrough, a journalistic exposé)—evidence that existing policy regimes are being questioned. Focusing events are also likely to attract media attention to the problem and thus may help policy entrepreneurs involve additional stakeholders in the initial agreement. A focusing event can contribute to a window of policy-making opportunity, in which public concern about a problem comes together with promising solutions and political shifts to make policy change possible (Kingdon, 1995). (For further discussion of focusing events and related phenomena, see Baumgartner and Jones, 1993.) In the AIDS case, for example, as physicians and public health workers fought to get the epidemic that was affecting gay men on the public agenda in the early 1980s, they were attuned to scattered reports of a similar disease among drug addicts, Haitian immigrants, and hemophiliacs. These reports activated some additional stakeholders but did not attract the media attention that such subsequent focusing events as candlelight marches and the death of Rock Hudson would receive.

The desired outcome of this phase is one or more initial agreements that can guide a developing group of change advocates as they proceed through the policy change process. At the very least, the group should agree on the purpose and worth of the effort and outline a plan for planning. The agreement should be recorded in some way so that it can be a reference for future work. Subsequent agreements are likely to be struck later in the change process as more stakeholders become involved, and as an array of possible problem definitions and solutions becomes clear.

Problem Formulation

In this phase, policy entrepreneurs organize additional forums to deepen shared understanding of the problem that concerns them and to set direction for the next phases. They take a diagnostic stance, gathering information about how the problem manifests itself and about likely causes of or contributors to the problem. Information gathering can happen through stakeholder consultation (such as the stakeholder dialogues sponsored by the World Business Council for Sustainable Development), action research (such as that conducted for the African American Men Project and the Vital Aging Network), or professional conferences (such as gatherings of AIDS researchers).

Attention to framing is especially important in this phase. Policy entrepreneurs ensure there are opportunities for stakeholders to consider how they and others are framing the problem. They also help potential supporters of change understand the power of framing (the ability of a problem frame to exclude some solutions and privilege others). Thus Hively and her colleagues in the Vital Aging Initiative explicitly attacked the framing of older adults as frail dependents, which can only lead to a solution search that focuses on services and social welfare policy. Instead, they insisted on framing older adults as diverse, productive citizens. This view directed the search for a solution toward programs of empowerment and elimination of barriers to employment. Additionally, policy entrepreneurs emphasize the power of broader, more complex frames to "open up the search for solutions" (Nutt, 2002, p. 112) and attract a wider array of stakeholders. For example, the AAMP began with a narrow employment frame: the problem was that young African American men did not have jobs. Soon, however, county commissioners and staff began to focus more broadly. Once the project steering committee was established, the members understood that the "current social and economic situation of many young African American men does not stem from a single cause, but from a multitude of interrelated ones" (Hennepin County, 2002, p. 2). The committee then decided to focus on housing, family structure, health, education, economic status, community and civic involvement, and criminal justice.

Attention to frames can also constrain a group's habitual rush to a solution and help it think about the outcomes or objectives desired (Nutt, 2002; Nadler and Hibino, 1998). Chapter Seven includes exercises that can help a group identify its problem frames. Included is one adapted from Paul Nutt's work that helps individuals move from solution preferences to objectives.

Problem framing also relates to what Frank Baumgartner and Bryan Jones call policy image, which combines empirical information and emotional appeal (Baumgartner and Jones, 1993). For example, framing older adults as frail dependents is likely to prompt attention to statistics about disease and longevity or health care costs; it rouses emotions of compassion and responsibility on the positive side, but quite likely pity and resentment on the negative side. Thus policy entrepreneurs should think about not just the solutions themselves that flow from a problem frame but also the nonrational responses that may suffuse the ensuing debate about the solutions.

Policy entrepreneurs should also consider whether particular problem frames activate partisan agendas. In the United States, for example, using a government-failure frame (to explain something like the spread of the AIDS epidemic) activates long-standing disagreement between the Republican and Democratic parties about the amount and purpose of government expenditures.

Framing a problem as a crisis may also have unanticipated side effects. Stakeholders are certainly motivated to do something about the problem; reporters may begin covering it. At the same time, a crisis atmosphere can drive out thorough consideration of solutions. Journalists may even exacerbate the crisis as they seek out opposing views of what is causing the problem and thus promote controversy that sells newspapers or attracts viewers.

Search for Solutions

In this phase, policy entrepreneurs organize forums to consider solutions that might achieve the desired outcomes identified in the previous phase. In searching for solutions, forum participants can use three basic approaches: adapting solutions they know about, searching for solutions that exist but are not known to the group, and developing innovative solutions (Nutt, 2002). Organizers of the AAMP, for example, have developed a mentoring project called Brother Achievement (adapted from a program called Public Achievement) that coaches young people in citizenship.

Beyond identifying or developing solutions, the policy entrepreneurs also consider which solutions are likely to elicit interest and support from key stakeholders and the broader public. This analysis is helpful in placing the problem, and one or more promising solutions, on the public's agenda, thus creating a public issue that can attract the attention of policy makers and other affected parties who will then influence the formulation, adoption, and implementation of specific policies. It may also be possible to place an issue on the policy makers' agenda without gaining widespread public attention (Baumgartner and Jones, 1993). In the case of the AAMP, county commissioners were involved from the outset; thus the recommendations of the project steering committee were virtually ensured a place on the county board's agenda. Of course, many of the recommendations would require action by other policy makers, so supporters of the project planned a variety of forums that would attract additional stakeholders as well as media coverage that would influence decision making by state legislators, school board members, corporate boards, nonprofit leaders, and foundation grant makers.

At the conclusion of this phase, a strong advocacy coalition should be developing. Members of the group accept a shared problem frame and support a set of related solutions that require action by a range of policy makers. The coalition is likely to include a formal advocacy group and outside supporters—journalists, elected officials, public administrators, party officials—who are not members of the formal group. Our definition of an advocacy coalition is more inclusive than the one offered by Paul Sabatier and Hank Jenkins-Smith, theirs being "an advocacy coalition consists of actors from a variety of public and private institutions at all levels of government who share a set of basic beliefs (policy goals plus causal and other perceptions) and who seek to manipulate the rules, budgets, and personnel of governmental institutions in order to achieve these goals over time" (1993, p. 5). We would include nonprofit and business organizations as well as governmental institutions as objects of the coalition's effort.

Even though the emphasis in this phase is on solutions, the forums that explore solutions are also likely to spend time reconsidering problem definitions. More specific guidance about solution search strategies and coalition development is offered in Chapter Eight.

Policy or Plan Formulation

In this phase, policy entrepreneurs shift their focus from forums to arenas. Working with their advocacy coalition, they develop plans, programs, budgets, projects, decisions, and rules for review and adoption by policy-making arenas in the next phase. They attempt to design and redesign institutions (and, if the desired change is sweeping enough, entire policy regimes). Policy design must address real problems in a way that is technically and administratively feasible, politically and economically acceptable, and legally and ethically responsible (Benveniste, 1989; Kingdon, 1995). Further guidance about designing policies or plans is offered in Chapter Nine.

When more than one arena might include the problem in its domain, policy entrepreneurs consider which arena is likely to look most favorably on their proposal—a process that Frank Baumgartner and Bryan Jones (1993) call "venue shopping." Policy entrepreneurs often focus on arenas that are at multiple levels and in different realms. For example, the physicians fighting to stem the U.S. AIDS epidemic took their recommendations to local, state, and federal governments as well as to nonprofit and business arenas. Schmidheiny and his colleagues at WBCSD have focused on global and regional arenas as well. Attention to arenas may be phased, as when the initial focus in the AAMP was on the county board, which then funded further work that would include placing issues affecting African American men on other policy-making agendas. The Vital Aging Network focused initially on policy makers at the University of Minnesota and in state agencies or boards dealing with aging, but it soon sought grants from foundations and launched an educational program to help older adults press the state legislature for policy changes.

Bargaining and negotiation are common in this phase, but so is a collegial informality in which members of the advocacy coalition—elected officials, policy analysts, planners, and interest group advocates—try out alternative policies on one another, speak persuasively of the relative merits of their option, and engage in the give-and-take of a successful design session (Innes, 1996; N. C. Roberts, 1997). Policy entrepreneurs require political leadership skills, especially the skill of attending to the goals and concerns of all affected parties so as to build a coalition large and strong enough to secure adoption and implementation of a desired plan or proposal in subsequent phases.

The bargaining and negotiation, as well as the collegial give-and-take, of this phase are typically a somewhat behind-the-scenes preparation for the public battle to come in an arena. Policy entrepreneurs attempt to ensure that any proposal developed in this phase is of the kind that will survive the intense scrutiny and power plays expected in official policy-making meetings—especially those that attract television and other press coverage. If a proposal has not reached the point at which official decision makers can comfortably say yes to it under the glare of klieg lights and the scrutiny of journalists, it will be tabled for further work or buried indefinitely.

As an advocacy group converges around specific structural changes (ideas, rules, modes, media, and methods), policy entrepreneurs help the group think about how these new structures enable some behaviors and restrain others. They also help the group anticipate various stratagems that opponents may employ in the next phase, such as attacking or undermining the group; defusing, downgrading, blurring, or redefining the issue; controlling the policy makers' agenda; and strategic voting (Cobb and Elder, 1983; Riker, 1986).

Proposal Review and Adoption

In this phase, policy entrepreneurs call on their political leadership skills to persuade policy makers to adopt the policy or plan supported by their group. The first task is to place a proposed policy on the formal, or decision, agenda of the policy makers. The second is to engage in the bargaining, negotiation, and often compromise that characterize a policy-making arena without losing sight of policy objectives and alienating members of the advocacy coalition.

Crucial to policy adoption is what Guy Benveniste calls the "multiplier effect" (Benveniste, 1989, p. 27), which kicks in when stakeholders begin to perceive that a policy has a high probability of adoption. As this perception spreads, many stakeholders who were on the fence, or even against the proposed policy, join the supporting coalition. On the other hand, the same perception can cause opposition to harden if the opponents feel their fundamental beliefs or identity is threatened. A crisis may turn on the multiplier effect, changing perceptions about the costs and benefits of a proposed course of action. In the midst of crisis, advocates of change might be seen as system saviors, promising benefits to many, rather than as self-interested partisans whose proposed changes will benefit only themselves and place an undue burden on others (Wilson, 1967; Bryson, 1981).

Although implementation and evaluation are emphasized in the next phase, policy entrepreneurs should make sure that adopted policies are clear, workable, and politically acceptable to likely implementers. The new laws, regulations, or directives also should include an evaluation mechanism to help implementers ensure that problems are actually being remedied by the new policy, program, or project, and to help the implementers make needed adjustments in the initial implementation plan.

In the case of the AAMP, for example, the county commissioners were persuaded to approve the steering committee's recommendation for a permanent African American Men Commission that would include diverse stakeholders. The commission was to hammer out an action plan based on all the recommendations contained in the committee's report. It was also charged with coordinating, facilitating, and monitoring the implementation process and with publishing periodic reports on "outcomes for young African American Men in Hennepin County" (Hennepin County, 2002, p. 75). The county board also approved $500,000 in seed money to provide staffing and other support for the commission.

If change advocates fail to have their proposal adopted in this phase, they have the option of cycling back through previous phases to improve the proposal, find a more politically acceptable solution, reframe the problem, and build a stronger coalition of support. Additional guidance about proposal adoption and review is in Chapter Ten.

Implementation and Evaluation

In this phase, policy entrepreneurs attempt to ensure that adopted solutions are incorporated throughout a system, and their effects assessed. Successful implementation doesn't just happen. It requires careful planning and management; ongoing problem solving; and sufficient incentives and resources, including competent, committed people. The original leaders of the change effort may have to play new roles and allow new leaders to emerge.

The creation of the African American Men Commission attracted many additional supporters to the AAMP; in all, 130 people were appointed to the new group. The project staff organized twenty-six Saturday training sessions for all commissioners. Nine functional, or "domain," committees plus an executive committee generate many leadership opportunities for the members. Additionally, county commissioners and Minneapolis city council members are ex-officio members of the executive committee.

The initial action plans developed by the commission established objectives for projects connected to each committee domain:

fundraising, housing, family structure, health, education, economic status, community and civic involvement, criminal justice, and communications. The plans included numerous initiatives aimed at expanding the network of organizations working to improve the lives of African American men. Many were implemented almost immediately. For example, a major AAMP public conference, held just months after the county board approved the project's continuation, attracted 650 participants. Several organizations also agreed to join the project's Quality Partnerships Initiative, which brings together the AAMP, community nonprofits, faith-based organizations, and businesses to share information about their efforts to support African American men. By the time a year had elapsed from the appointment of the African American Men Commission, the AAMP was sponsoring a highly successful Day of Restoration, in which people who had piled up traffic violations could clear their records by paying fines or performing community service. The project also was preparing to launch Right Turn, which helps young men who have committed minor crimes create and implement an individual development plan.

Successful evaluation also does not just happen. Like implementation, it must be planned and supported if it is to inform judgment about program performance. Policy entrepreneurs need to keep in mind two contrasting purposes of evaluation. One is accountability to policy makers and other stakeholders, ensuring that a program or project is fulfilling policy makers' intentions and benefiting stakeholders. The second is improvement of a program or project as it is developing. Thus the Vital Aging Network's Advocacy Leadership Certificate Program includes assessment of participant learning and civic impact. Results are used to improve future renditions of the program and inform supporting organizations about the impact of their investment. Assessment of participant learning, with its focus on program improvement, is mainly what evaluation experts call "formative evaluation," and assessment of civic impact, with its focus on program results, is mainly "summative evaluation" (Patton, 1997, p. 76).

Policy entrepreneurs should beware of making evaluation so cumbersome that it hinders program development. They also need to strike a balance in deciding on the timing of evaluations. On the one hand, they should ensure that a reasonable amount of time elapses, so that a new program or project has a chance to produce results. On the other hand, they need to be wary of allowing a new practice to become so entrenched that it can't be easily altered if evaluation shows it is misguided.

In this phase, policy entrepreneurs need political leadership skills as they attempt to influence administrative policy decisions and maintain or even expand the advocacy coalition. They also require ethical leadership skills, as they appeal to formal and informal courts that can enforce the ethical principles, laws, and norms undergirding the changes being implemented. They are likely to need visionary skills as they convene forums to understand implementation difficulties and develop new processes, mechanisms, or structures for resolving the difficulties. More guidance about implementation and evaluation is offered in Chapter Eleven.

Continuation, Modification, or Termination

Once a new policy has been substantially implemented, policy entrepreneurs review it to decide whether to continue, modify, or terminate the policy. They can take advantage of the routines of politics (upcoming elections, budgeting cycles, annual reporting) to organize forums in which the review occurs. Visionary leadership skills become especially important as these entrepreneurs focus on what is really going on: What constitutes evidence of success, or of failure? Has the original problem been substantially remedied? Has it worsened? Are the costs of the new policy regime acceptable when weighed against its benefits? If the answers indicate that the new regime is generally successful, policy entrepreneurs will seek to maintain or modify the enacted policy only slightly. They should marshal supportive evidence and maintain constituency support to ward off any effort to drain resources away from the new regime. If major modifications or an entirely new policy is warranted, a whole new pass through the policy change cycle is required. Policy entrepreneurs must rally their troops to reformulate the problem concerning them so they can consider new solutions to be placed on the public agenda. More guidance about this phase is in Chapter Twelve.

A Hierarchy of Process

In addition to the distinction between off-cycle and on-cycle policy making, another useful way of viewing the phases of the policy change cycle is to assign them to different levels of the "game of politics." Each level typically involves its own participants, addressing certain kinds of challenges, with differing rhetoric, all of which together has a significant impact on the character of the action and outcomes of the game (Schattschneider, 1975, pp. 47–48; Kiser and Ostrom, 1982; Throgmorton, 1996; Flyvbjerg, 1998; Forester, 1999).

Lawrence Lynn (1987) describes three such levels of the public policy-making process: high, middle, and low. He argues that participants at each level must answer a different question. At the high level, the question is whether or not there is a public problem that requires action by policy makers, and if there is, what the purpose of that action should be. In terms of the policy change cycle, the high-level activity is principally one of issue creation. This activity, as we noted earlier, involves articulation and appreciation of emergent or developmental problems in terms of the values, norms, or goals used both to judge why the problem is a problem, and to seek optimal solutions.

In the middle level, the question is what strategies or policies should be pursued to achieve the agreed-upon purpose. The main challenges at this level are programming problems, as change advocates add detail to their preferred solutions. They have to specify policy mechanisms (taxes, subsidies, vouchers, mandated or voluntary agreements, deregulation or regulation, reliance on government service delivery or on contracts with business or nonprofit providers) and decide which government agencies, nonprofit organizations, or businesses will be responsible for applying and overseeing these mechanisms. They must also decide how statutory roles and financial, personnel, and other resources should be allocated among implementing agencies or organizations. In terms of the policy change cycle, middle-level action moves the process into the policy formulation and review and adoption phases.

At the low (or what we would call the operational) level, the questions revolve around the implementation details of plans, programs, budgets, rules, and projects. Exactly what management routine will be adopted? What schedule will be followed? What evaluation questions will be asked, and how will evaluation data be collected?

This analysis of the game of politics reinforces the importance of focusing on issue creation. It is here that stakeholders engage in passionate debate (and, ideally, considerable reflection) about values, civic responsibility, and justification for a policy decision. As Lynn notes, this debate "focuses on the right thing to do, on philosophies of government and the fundamental responsibilities of our institutions, on what kind of nation and society we should be, on social justice and our basic principles" (1987, p. 62).

Enacting the Common Good

So how do policy entrepreneurs discern and enact the common good in the policy change process, particularly if they are likely to personally identify with their causes, given the sense of importance and "rightness" they are sure to attach to the change effort? Not only that, as opposition intensifies they undoubtedly see the well-being of their own group as being synonymous with the common good and shut out any alternative version (Price, 2003; Gray, 2003). At worst, they may decide that their overwhelmingly virtuous ends justify immoral means (Price, 2003).

Before offering our own views of how policy entrepreneurs and their supporters can discern and enact the common good, we want to explore an array of conceptions of the common good, because it is a phrase that (like the word *leadership*) has a taken-for-granted quality that overlays vast differences of opinion about what it really means.

As we have considered how the common good appears in ordinary conversation, in philosophical treatises, and in political exhortations, we have noted that it may be applied at more than one level. Most often, it is connected to the condition of an entire community or society. Frequently, though, it has a much narrower application: to an organization or smaller group. Less often, the term is applied to a global region or the entire planet.

Our examination of philosophical and political pronouncements about the common good reveals that the term is actually part of a family of concepts. This "common good family" includes "the good society" (Galbraith, 1996; Bellah and others, 1991; Friedmann,

1979), "the commons" (Lohmann, 1992; Cleveland, 1990), "commonwealth" (Boyte, 1989), the "public interest" (Campbell and Marshall, 2002), and the "public good" (Campbell and Marshall, 2002). Other closely related concepts are community, the collective, and the just society. These concepts can be seen as distinct from, or in relation to, a contrasting set of concepts that include the individual, the personal, and the private.

The distinction between the two sets can be seen as central to an age-old debate about the relationship of the individual and society. The debate often stems from an understanding that what is best for a group of people or an entire society is in some way different from what might be best, or most advantageous, for a particular member of the group or society. Debate also arises from awareness that at least some people and groups will attempt to maximize their own interests at the expense of others.

Additionally, many philosophers argue that human beings can truly thrive only if they establish generally beneficial arrangements that provide services and goods that individuals are unable to obtain for themselves. These arrangements include governance mechanisms that balance individual and collective interests, sometimes by constraining and sometimes by liberating individual behavior. Debate then arises as to which governance mechanisms are best and how to provide collective goods and services. Traditionally, protection of the common good or public interest has been assigned to government. As Aristotle argued in his *Politics*, "True forms of government . . . are those in which the one, or the few, or the many, govern with a view towards the common interest; but governments which rule with a view to the private interest, whether of the one, the few, or the many, are perversions" (Aristotle, 1943, p. 139).

Guidelines for Thinking About the Common Good

Our examination of multiple views of the common good revealed four main themes that appear with a varying degree of emphasis in philosophical and political writings:

1. The relation between the individual and the community
2. The group whose common good is important

3. The content of the common good
4. The means of achieving the common good

From these themes, we have developed four guidelines for thinking about the common good:

1. Clarify your group's views of human nature and the relationship between the individual and society.
2. Decide whose common good is important.
3. Develop a general idea of what the common good might be.
4. Choose the means of achieving the common good.

Clarify Your Views on Human Nature and Society

Clearly, any conception of the common good rests on an understanding of the connection between the welfare of the individual and the society of which he or she is a part.

A minimalist stance is based on the recognition that individuals have differing goals and interests, and that some societal referee (government) is needed to deal with conflict among individuals. Government thus has the minimal (or negative) goal of preventing one person's actions from harming another. A more expansive stance is based on the recognition that society contributes to individual well-being above and beyond acting as a protector of individual freedom. Government has positive goals of supplying public goods, such as universal education, that help individuals thrive (see Berlin, 2002).

Thus one starting place for people trying to clarify their thinking about the common good is to explore how they see the relation of the individual and society, and perhaps how they view human nature. They might consider questions such as these:

- How does or should the community enhance individual development?
- Are people mainly self-interested, mainly concerned with and about others, or some mixture?
- Are people fundamentally equal?
- Is human life sacred? Less abstractly, are individual human beings sacred? Where is the line of sacredness drawn between individual human beings and human life generally?

Decide Whose Common Good Is Important

Major policy change efforts often arise from the perception that the common good of some large group, or of an entire society, is being undermined, or certainly not fulfilled. Policy entrepreneurs naturally focus on the well-being of the groups with whom they identify; it might be the advocacy coalition they've assembled, or some group within the coalition, or even some large category such as women or the poor. There are pragmatic as well as ethical reasons, however, to think more expansively. The pragmatic argument is that those whose interests are not considered in a change effort are quite unlikely to be committed members of an advocacy coalition and much more prone to join an opposing coalition. If they are not part of the coalition, they can be expected to resist the coalition's proposals. The ethical argument is that most ethical systems require adherents to consider the well-being of others. The life of every human being is deemed sacred by the majority of religions and by widely accepted treatises such as the Universal Declaration of Human Rights. Ethically, policy entrepreneurs need to ask how any proposed changes affect everyone within the political unit in which they are operating. Even more expansively, they may have to consider how the change will affect those outside the unit (even all the other citizens of the world). Indeed, they might want to include future generations in their consideration. There are, of course, practical limitations on how many stakeholder groups can be thoroughly considered and involved in a policy change effort. The stakeholder analysis methods we offer help policy entrepreneurs and their supporters think about the interests of a diverse array of stakeholders, and certainly those most affected by a public problem and proposed changes.

Many of the policy entrepreneurs in the AIDS case cared most passionately about particular groups of people: gay men, children of drug users, hemophiliacs, Haitians. At the same time, many of them were deeply concerned about all the groups that were contracting AIDS and about the threat the disease posed to everyone in the United States. Some of these leaders would eventually become involved in efforts to fight AIDS in other societies around the world.

Leaders in the World Business Council for Sustainable Development have thought expansively from the beginning because of their concern for the well-being of future generations and poorer countries. However, they have also clearly focused their efforts on business stakeholders. In the African American Men Project, Mark Stenglein possibly cared most about the interests of the voters in his district, and Gary Cunningham had a lifelong commitment to the advancement of African Americans, but both also had to care about the well-being of all Hennepin County citizens. Jan Hively and her colleagues in the Vital Aging Network may be most concerned about the effects of ageism on older adults, but they also care about younger adults and children in Minnesota.

Develop a General Idea of What the Common Good Might Be

In the simplest terms, the common good might be viewed as the flip side of "the common bad"—the public problem that a group sets out to remedy. Since the problem affects a diverse group of stakeholders, the common good might be any new arrangement that substantially reduces the harmful effects on stakeholders. More extensive notions of the common good are grounded in an idea of what it takes for human beings to flourish (and such ideas are based in turn on a view of human nature). For Immanuel Kant, Jean-Jacques Rousseau, John Kenneth Galbraith, and other philosophers, the emphasis is on freedom and equality of opportunity. Galbraith, for example, argues, "The essence of the good society can be easily stated. It is that every member, regardless of gender, race, or ethnic origin, should have access to a rewarding life. . . . There must be economic opportunity for all" (1996, p. 23).

For some, the good for an entire group is equated with the interests of an elite few (a certain class, those who control the government). The notion is captured in phrases such as *noblesse oblige, l'état c'est moi,* father knows best. The utilitarians (notably Jeremy Bentham and John Stuart Mill) are more egalitarian and offer a common sense formula—"the greatest good for the greatest number"—for deciding whether a policy is in the public interest or promotes the common good.

Others view the common good as connection to God or a communal tradition. For example, the Thomist philosopher Jacques Maritain describes a host of "material and immaterial" endowments (from public roads to cultural treasures and spiritual riches) that are vital for a society to enjoy "communion in good living" (1947, p. 41). The communitarian philosophers of recent years would fit here.

The most egalitarian philosophers—Karl Marx comes readily to mind—equate the common good with a classless society. More recently, Julius Nyerere of Tanzania combined elimination of class distinctions with communal tradition into what he called "ujamaa socialism." He sought to revive tribal traditions in which each person cared for the welfare of others in the tribe and in which each person could depend on the wealth of the community and enjoy a sense of security and hospitality (Duggan and Civille, 1976).

Another vision of the common good is the "caring community," described by philosopher Nel Noddings and planning theorist Peter Marris (Noddings, 1984; Marris, 1996). In such a community, citizens give primacy to nurturing other human beings. In this work, they draw on the moral intuition and commitment that arise from parent-child relationships or from moral education. Reciprocity governs political life (Marris, 1996).

Given these diverse views, it's not surprising that the phrase *the common good* is so full of ambiguity and dispute. The loudest debate swirls around the pros and cons of utilitarian thinking and around issues of distributive justice. Critics of utilitarian thinking want to know what happens to those not included in "the greatest number." They also want to know who decides what the greatest good is. Contemporary utilitarians offer a ready calculus known as "cost-benefit analysis"; once we determine the costs of a course of action and compare it to the worth of the outcomes, we can decide whether one course is better than some other. Cost-benefit analysis certainly is an extremely useful tool, but skeptics still question the wisdom and accuracy of even attempting to put a price on every aspect of life. Additionally, it is impossible to precisely predict costs and benefits of many proposed actions.

The most egalitarian visions of the common good require considerable redistribution of material and immaterial goods to those who are poor and disenfranchised. Obviously, those who are advantaged by existing distributions may think this is a bad idea; even if they favor a more egalitarian arrangement, they are rightly skeptical of massive government "social engineering" that is fraught with dangers to human freedom. Some philosophers—for example, Iris Marion Young—question the whole idea of *a* common good. They fear that any attempt to promote a common view of the common good will founder on the reality of power relationships, leading ultimately to the dominance of some elite's ideas (Young, 1990).

Our own general sense of the common good is captured by our definition of regimes of mutual gain: a set of principles, laws, norms, rules, and decision-making procedures that achieve lasting benefit at reasonable cost and that tap and serve the stakeholders' deepest interest in, and desire for, a better world for themselves and those they care about. This idea of mutual gain, as exemplified by the cases emphasized in this book, draws on several of these perspectives on the content of the common good. The African American Men Project has emphasized the quest for equal opportunity and for a community in which everyone cares about the well-being of everyone else. The Vital Aging Network too is fighting for equal opportunity, but in this case for older adults; Vital Aging leaders have also emphasized the societal benefits of enabling older adults to have a rewarding life. Leaders of the World Business Council for Sustainable Development talk about improving opportunities for small- and medium-sized business owners in "developing nations and nations in transition." They emphasize that businesspeople have a responsibility for caring for the environment and the world's poor, and they argue that ultimately this approach benefits business as well.

Choose the Means of Achieving the Common Good

Perhaps views vary most about how to achieve the common good. Let's consider several methods that have been widely used around the world, often together in the same society; some of them are a ready match for the general ideas of the common good noted earlier.

- *The authoritarian state,* which enforces a particular group's view of the common good throughout society.
- *The market,* which allows people to obtain goods and services through buyer-seller exchange. A market transaction is, in effect, cost-benefit analysis in action; participants decide whether to

engage in an exchange depending on the cost versus the benefit of the product or service involved. At the societal level, policy experts or government officials use a similar analysis to decide whether or not a program or project achieves the greatest good for the greatest number.

• *Representative government*, in which elected representatives hash out the common good. They are responsible for protecting minority interests and handling public needs (called commons problems) that are imperfectly handled by the market. Among the political philosophers who have elaborated this approach are Edmund Burke, John Stuart Mill, and James Madison.

• *A religious regime* that enacts and enforces policies aimed at enforcing what religious leaders deem to be God's will for human society. Examples are seventeenth-century Puritan societies in North America and the Taliban in Afghanistan.

• *Expert judgment*, in which professional policy analysts research societal issues and recommend best policies, on the basis of learning from the past and predicting the future.

• *Informed public, or civic republic*, in which citizens of a state debate, discuss, and persuade each other about the policies that government should pursue in dealing with public problems. This public deliberation also includes consideration of candidates for public office. Experts are involved, but their role is to furnish facts for the public to consider. The operations of government itself must be transparent so that citizens can evaluate their efficacy. This approach is associated with Thomas Jefferson and the pragmatist philosopher John Dewey.

• *Active citizenry, or civic engagement*, in which citizens themselves name public problems, make collective decisions about what should be done, and involve government officials and experts as needed. They carry out some decisions themselves, and they judge the results (Mathews, 1997). They perform what Harry Boyte and Nancy Kari (1996) call "public work." They form a civil society, "where all versions of the good are worked out and tested" (Walzer, 1997, p. 15). Philosopher Hannah Arendt (1958) emphasized the simultaneous equality and diversity of the participants in this society; philosopher Cornel West echoes this perspective in his call for radical democracy (Lerner, 2002). Iris Marion Young argues that this public work does not require overall agreement on the nature of the common good. Her view supports the notion that citizens can find common ground by engaging in reflective conversation, or dialogue, in which they clarify meaning, describe social relationships, and defend their ideas and principles without pressing for joint endorsement of a theory of justice or the like (Young, 1990).

• *Collaboration and organizing among the less powerful.* Those who believe enactment of the common good requires direct confrontation of the mechanisms of power, class, and privilege advance this method. West (1994) also supports it. Danish political scientist Bent Flyvbjerg advises those who find themselves left out: "Then you team up with like-minded people and you fight for what you want, utilizing the means that work in your context to undermine those who try to limit participation" (1998, p. 236). These groups may have to work for transparency in a political system or promote civic virtues (such as engaging in respectful debate). Sometimes, counsels Flyvbjerg, direct power struggle works best, sometimes changing the ground rules, and sometimes writing studies that illuminate power relations (1998). Young is among those who argue that minority groups should have the ability to make their own policy decisions. A society might consist of loosely connected publics, and the common good would be determined by the people within them; to the extent there is an overarching common good, it should include some guarantee of self-determination for these groups. Marris, meanwhile, calls for nurturing social conditions that foster a politics of reciprocity. Moral education would help citizens draw on the morality of human nurture that is preached (and often practiced) in the family realm and apply it to public policies. He champions a "grown-up moral understanding" that fuses insight about nurturing and social control and justifies social control by the principles of nurturing relationships (1996, p. 170).

The last three approaches—informed public, active citizenry, and collaboration—are often directly opposed to the others (in the case of the authoritarian state and religious regime) or highly critical of the others (in the case of the market, representative government, and expert judgment).

The Leadership for the Common Good approach emphasizes comprehensive stakeholder analysis and involvement in order to develop shared understanding and enactment of the common good. It is a means of discerning and discovering, rather than pronouncing the common good. It has close affinity with the last three approaches: informed public, active citizenry, and collaboration. The policy entrepreneurs introduced in this book have emphasized these three approaches, but they have also used several of the others.

The U.S. physicians and health professionals concerned about the emerging AIDS crisis certainly applied expert judgment in their effort to understand and stop the disease, and they appealed to other experts to get involved. When they realized that public policies had to change, they put pressure on elected officials. When those avenues proved inadequate, they turned more avidly to collaborating with gay activists and trying to convey a sense of urgency to the general public.

Schmidheiny and his colleagues in the WBCSD have promoted active citizenry among businesspeople worldwide and also participated in (and often organized) forums involving numerous other citizen groups debating how best to deal with the problems of pollution and poverty. At the same time, these leaders have promoted a market approach and emphasized that governments of all stripes must become partners in sustainable development initiatives.

In launching the AAMP, Stenglein and Cunningham turned to elected officials (the county commissioners) to sponsor the project, but the project itself has engaged diverse groups of African Americans and other community leaders and experts in deciding what should be done and taking responsibility for advancing the project. The project recruited additional experts who could conduct needed research or facilitate group decision making. Several project initiatives also emphasize empowerment of young African American men, notably through training programs and job fairs that can help these men compete in the labor market.

Hively, Freshley, Schroeder, and their colleagues in the Vital Aging Network (VAN) have convened numerous forums, especially the Vital Aging Summits, to activate citizens—chiefly older people, but also people who work with them or are related to them—to work out the best means of enabling older adults to live a productive, satisfying life. The Advocacy Leadership Certificate Program in particular aims to empower older adults to be effective policy advocates. VAN also seeks to remove barriers to older adults' participation in the labor market.

Policy entrepreneurs in all these cases have attempted to foster an informed public that may join the advocacy coalition and help press policy makers to adopt proposals for change. To do this, they have employed plays, newspapers, television, the Internet, and other media.

Exercise 5.2 can help you and your colleagues think about the common good in relation to a public problem that concerns you. The exercise includes questions about whose common good is to be emphasized, the content of the common good, and the means of achieving it.

Exercise 5.2. Thinking About the Public Interest and the Common Good.

Justification of policy change efforts is usually connected to the common good (well defined or not). How, then, can policy entrepreneurs and other citizens judge whether a proposed change will serve the common good?

It may be helpful to see the common good as a family of concepts:

- Common good
- Good society
- Commons
- Commonwealth
- Public interest
- Public good
- Just society
- Community

This family of concepts contrasts with other concepts:

- Individual
- Personal
- Private

Debate over the common good is part of an age-old debate about the relationship between the individual and society. Some philosophers are skeptical about a common good. They advocate a focus on:

- Loosely connected publics determining their own interest
- Protections that counter majoritarianism: the common good might then be protection of the ability of minority groups, in particular, to make their own policy decisions

Exercise 5.2. Thinking About the
Public Interest and the Common Good, Cont'd.

Exercise

As your group focuses on a public problem that concerns you, you may
want to develop tentative answers to these questions.

1. How do you see connections between the individual and society,
   the citizen and government:

   • What do you think an individual needs from society to flourish?
   • What is the role of government in protecting individual interests
     and common interests?

2. Whose common good will you emphasize:

   • The inhabitants of a geographic territory?
   • Citizens or residents of a state, nation, or other government?
   • Members of a group or organization?
   • Future generations?

3. Develop a general idea of what a regime of mutual gain might look
   like in this case:

   • What widespread, substantial benefit do you hope to achieve that
     could be accomplished at reasonable cost?
   • What might be the elements of a desirable regime (ideas, rules
     and norms, formal relationships, informal relationships, rights,
     responsibilities, etc.)?

4. What combination of methods will you use to achieve the common
   good?

   • Markets
   • State control
   • Informed public
   • Active citizenry
   • Expert judgment
   • Religious directives
   • Other (please specify)

The group can record its answers to the questions and refer to them as
it proceeds with the policy change effort. The answers may be revised as
the group expands and develops a deeper appreciation of the problem
and promising solutions.

Summary

This chapter has given an overview of the policy change cycle and explored several approaches to enacting the common good. The policy change cycle has been described as organized anarchy that includes many predictable features as well as constant flux. To be effective navigators of the change cycle, policy entrepreneurs must manage ideas, analyze and involve stakeholders, and wisely design institutions. To discern and foster the common good, policy entrepreneurs can help constituents think about the relationship between individuals and their communities, the groups whose well-being is most crucial, the content of the common good, and means of achieving it.

This chapter has introduced the seven phases of the policy change cycle. The remainder of this book amounts to a handbook for policy entrepreneurs seeking to operate wisely in each phase. Particular attention is given to stakeholder analysis and involvement.

The Process of Policy Entrepreneurship

The remaining chapters offer extensive practical guidance and resources for policy entrepreneurs as they move through the policy change cycle. Each chapter discusses the purpose and desired outcomes of a particular phase and offers leadership guidelines for completing the phase successfully. Methods of analyzing and organizing stakeholders are emphasized throughout.

Chapters Six through Eight emphasize the design and use of formal and informal forums. Chapter Six focuses on the initial agreement phase and offers guidance for getting a change effort off the ground. Chapter Seven explains how policy entrepreneurs help constituents appreciate and define a public problem so that it can be remedied. Considerable attention is given to reframing the problem in a way that helps numerous stakeholders join the change effort. Chapter Eight offers methods for finding solutions likely to achieve the common good. We emphasize the importance of developing a policy "story" that highlights the significance of a public problem and illuminates the pathway to a better future.

In Chapter Nine, the focus shifts to executive, legislative, and administrative arenas, as we explain how policy entrepreneurs can shape a promising solution into a proposal that can be supported by policy makers and implementers. The work of building and sustaining a supportive coalition is highlighted. The focus on arenas continues in Chapter Ten, which considers how policy entrepreneurs build additional support for their proposals and persuade policy makers to adopt them. Chapter Eleven explains how policy entrepreneurs ensure that adopted policies are actually implemented so as to honor the vision that inspired the change effort. The focus is on administrative arenas and courts.

Chapter Twelve helps policy entrepreneurs review implemented policies to know whether they should be continued, modified, or terminated. We offer specific strategies for continuing an existing policy, significantly modifying it, or bringing a policy regime to an end. Also in this chapter, we suggest how policy entrepreneurs can move on to tackle a new public problem affecting their organization or community. We end the book with a Summary and Conclusion, highlighting the main concepts in the Leadership for the Common Good framework, noting achievements of the four minicases featured throughout the book, and emphasizing the importance of widespread citizen leadership in tackling global challenges.

Chapter Six

Forging an Initial Agreement to Act

*It must be considered that there is nothing more difficult
to carry out, nor more doubtful of success, nor more
dangerous to handle, than to initiate a new order of
things. For the reformer has enemies in all those who profit
by the old order and only lukewarm defenders in all those
who would benefit by the new order; this lukewarmness
arising partly from fear of their adversaries, who have
the laws in their favor; and partly from the incredulity
of mankind, who do not truly believe in anything new
until they have had actual experience of it.*
NICCOLÒ MACHIAVELLI

*Never doubt that a small group of thoughtful, committed
citizens can change the world; indeed, it is the only thing
that ever has.*
MARGARET MEAD

As previously noted, policy entrepreneurs may get involved just
about anywhere in the policy change cycle, but they often have to
begin again at the beginning—either because an effective advocacy
coalition has dissipated (or never formed) or because an adopted
policy is inadequate in some way. Policy entrepreneurs might have
to invest a large amount of time and energy in the initial-agreement
phase, but without such investment they are likely to face tremendous difficulty in subsequent phases.

This and the chapters to come describe important outcomes
of each phase and offer leadership guidelines and tools.

Purpose and Desired Outcomes

The basic purpose of the initial-agreement phase is to develop a commitment among key stakeholders to do something about a public problem. A number of outcomes constitute the foundation for problem definition in the next phase:

- A sense among at least a small group of stakeholders that a public problem can and should be remedied through a sustained policy change effort
- Attention to what the common good might be in this change effort
- An understanding of what change might mean in practice through engaging stakeholders in a discussion of problems and solutions
- A commitment to the change effort
- One or more actual agreements among a group of stakeholders to launch or join the change effort
- Identification or recruitment of powerful sponsors, effective champions, a coordinating committee, and a planning team

This first phase and the next two—or frequently, the next three—in the change cycle often form a continuous loop, as the momentum for change builds and as what happens in one phase informs the next. The phases must be linked in this fashion to generate action and place an issue on the public agenda. Moving an issue to the public agenda principally involves bringing about a change in public perception so that a situation that was not viewed as a solvable problem is seen as an area in which action is possible. For this problem to become an issue, a viable solution must be available (Kingdon, 1995). As an example, before the formation of the business group that became the World Business Council for Sustainable Development, businesspeople typically viewed economic growth and environmental protection as opposing goals and moreover gave primacy to economic growth. The contribution of the WBCSD has been to offer a solution to the conflict between the two goals by showing how each can contribute to the other.

The three phases together constitute the issue creation process, and they clearly must be thought of as interdependent. Issue creation is high-level politics involving important elites and opinion leaders (Lynn, 1987; Sabatier, 1991; Baumgartner and Jones, 1993) in order to compete strongly for some of the limited carrying capacity of the public agenda (Hilgartner and Bosk, 1988). Sometimes issue creation involves the fourth phase as well, when a detailed policy change proposal may be necessary to galvanize action.

The initial phases are closely linked, but they must also be pulled apart, at least conceptually, to prevent premature closure, which could cause the wrong problem to be solved, produce a solution that perpetuates the problem, or create a new problem. Pulling steps apart helps leaders avoid policy blindness. This is not to say, however, that problem definition and solution should (or can) be totally ignored in the initial-agreement phase; indeed, policy entrepreneurs often entertain provisional problem definitions and possible solutions as they try to initiate change. For example, the U.S. health professionals who were trying to cope with the early AIDS crisis argued that the disease was a public health problem and that the likely solutions lay with the tried-and-true tools of epidemiology, medical research, and local regulations.

The emphasis in the initial-agreement phase is on designing and using boundary-crossing forums and informal arenas—although in a major change effort a formal arena may have to authorize initiation of significant change actions (for example, the Hennepin County Board in the African American Men case). It's important to remember that agreements formed by some people to seek change may prompt agreement among others to resist the same change.

Leadership Guidelines

This section outlines a general process in which policy entrepreneurs organize forums to achieve an initial agreement among diverse stakeholders to begin working on a public problem. It is offered as guidance only; if you are attempting to develop an initial agreement, you should develop a process for your own situation. We especially recommend consulting the visionary leadership section of Chapter Four as you plan forums in this phase.

Initial Forums

Figuring out how to make headway against a public problem involves a lot of conversation and reflection. Both are needed to build understanding and agreement on how to proceed.

Getting Started

The first step is to use personal leadership exercises (two suitable examples are "Discovering Cares and Concerns," Exercise 2.1, and "Exploring Personal Highs and Lows," Exercise 2.5) to become clearer about your own commitment to the change process and about which leadership approaches seem to work well for you. You might also use Exercises 2.6 ("Assessing Additional Strengths and Weaknesses") and 2.7 (on analyzing social group membership) to gain further insight as to the leadership skills and other resources you bring to the change effort.

The second step is to begin informal conversation to find out whether at least some other stakeholders share your concern about the problem. If there is enough shared concern, invite your contacts to participate in one or more joint conversations about the problem and a common-good approach to remedying it.

Remember: seeing and hearing is believing. You may need to foster shared concern by offering some compelling evidence of your own and if possible bringing others into direct contact with the human impact of the problem. For example, visiting patients struck by AIDS often galvanized health professionals' commitment to get involved in the fight against the disease. At Minnesota's 1998 Rural Summit, Jan Hively heard and saw for herself the predicted impact of an aging population in the state's towns and cities. She listened to a talk by the seventy-five-year-old chairman of the Minnesota Association of Counties. His own leadership role exemplified the productivity of older adults, and he described the work of others like him in his hometown of Cottonwood. He noted that more than half of the residents are over sixty-five, "and many of us have kept on working. There aren't enough younger people to fill the job openings being created through retirements."

Third, as you look ahead to a joint conversation with your contact group, you may need to think about balancing the power of the participants (Winer, 2003). Unless you undertake some power-balancing measures, a large power difference in the group might hamper the free exchange of ideas and prevent participants from building the requisite level of mutual trust. You should examine your own power position, and be prepared to bring in an outside facilitator if it might get in the way of others' engagement. You may also have to resolve questions about whether people are coming to the conversation as representatives of a group or as individuals.

Organizational consultant Michael Winer recommends balancing power by affirming specialization (acknowledging the special skills and resources each participant brings); appreciating contributions (noting how each specialization contributes to the work of the group); legitimizing involvement (having powerful figures endorse participants who may not have a formal position); protecting self-interest (acknowledging the validity of self-interest and incorporating it in the work of the group); and managing displays of power (using nametags and ground rules to diminish use of titles, dress, other accoutrements such as cell phones to communicate status; Winer, 2003). Organizers of the VAN monthly meetings ask participants to introduce themselves by name only and then mention something about their experience or aspirations that relates to the meeting topic.

Fourth, you may also need to guard against coming to the conversation with a preferred general solution. You may have seen the solution work well on other problems, or come from a community or party that supports the solution. There are symbolic and tangible steps you can take to hold the solution at arm's length. Stephan Schmidheiny and his colleagues, for example, were obviously attached to market solutions. Stakeholder consultation gave them a chance to listen to people who were not enamored of market operations.

Practice the Basics of Good Meeting Preparation and Facilitation

First, plan the meeting in advance. Establish a date, time, and place for the meeting. Clarify who the contact persons are. Be as clear as possible about the desired outcomes of the meeting. Identify participants and what their interests might be. Identify requisite material and equipment and who is responsible for it. Think carefully about the meeting agenda and the amount of time that should be devoted to each item. Plan a process for each topic. Do a sanity check: Can you do everything in the time allotted? Think about how meeting follow-up will be handled.

Second, make sure the room is arranged to serve the purpose of the meeting. For example, if the purpose is to transmit information, standard classroom seating in rows may be appropriate. If you want to promote conversation, arrange seating to make face-to-face interaction possible. If you are going to use a large-group interaction method, then find space that enables people to get up and move around easily (Bryson and Anderson, 2000).

Third, make sure the meeting is managed well. Have an experienced person chair the meeting, make use of skilled facilitators when appropriate, and be prepared to alter the agenda when necessary.

Fourth, have adequate restroom facilities and refreshments, particularly if the meeting is to last a long time.

Fifth, make sure adequate records are kept of the meeting and its products. Assign someone to take minutes, shoot photographs, or make some other record of the meeting. Be sure to save any important products created by the groups in the meeting.

Sixth, evaluate the meeting. What worked well? What did not? What improvements might be made so that a meeting of this type might be more productive and satisfying in the future?

Seventh, make available a meeting summary in an appropriate format within a reasonable time after the meeting has ended.

Focusing on the Common Good

Begin the joint conversation with an opportunity for everyone to briefly state why he or she is interested in the problem. Go over the agenda: consideration of the common good, exploration of the problem context, and a basic stakeholder analysis to guide efforts to begin building a coalition for change.

Following this, ask the group to consider what the common good might be in this change effort. You may want to use Exercise 5.2.

Exploring the Context and Personal Leadership

First, explore the context of the problem. The exercises included in the leadership-in-context section of this book (see Chapter Two) should be helpful.

Next, use the personal leadership exercises previously referred to in this chapter to help group members develop an understanding about what each person might bring to an effort to remedy the problem.

Analyzing and Involving Stakeholders

To conduct the analyses described here, the group may begin with its own knowledge, but to obtain more extensive information it could use interviews, questionnaires, focus groups, or other forms of research, such as the multi-stakeholder dialogues organized by the World Business Council on Sustainable Development (2001). In the effort to find out more about the activities and aspirations of older adults, Hively conducted a survey of fifty-five- to eighty-four-year-olds in a four-county area of Minnesota. The survey was sponsored by the Mid-Minnesota Area Agency on Aging and the Regional Development Commission; it made clear that most of the area's older adults were healthy and productive and interested in more opportunities for community service, employment, and education.

Sometimes members of the group can use stakeholder surveys that have been conducted by other groups.

Here are the steps we recommend:

1. Conduct a basic stakeholder analysis, using Exercise 6.1.

2. Construct a power-versus-interest grid (Exercise 4.2). You can skip the step of brainstorming a list of stakeholders; use the list generated in the basic stakeholder analysis of Exercise 6.1. (See the discussion in the communicative capability section, under visionary leadership, of Chapter Four.)

3. Construct a stakeholder influence diagram (Exercise 6.2). Understanding stakeholder influence diagrams should help policy entrepreneurs think about whom to involve in the initial-agreement phase and how to involve them (see next step).

4. Fill out a participation planning matrix (Exercise 6.3). By all means, list key stakeholders, and consider others as well. (Key

Exercise 6.1. The Basic Stakeholder
Analysis Technique for a Policy Change Effort.

Using the definition of stakeholder as any person, group, or organization affected by a public problem or possessing resources needed to resolve the problem, complete these steps.

1. Brainstorm the list of potential stakeholders. Along with groups and organizations, include individuals who represent those groups or who have significant resources that can be used to resolve (or exacerbate) the problem.

2. Prepare a separate flipchart sheet for each stakeholder.

3. Place a stakeholder's name at the top of each sheet and divide it into three columns, labeled "Resources," "Reasons for Involving," and "Reasons for Postponing Involvement."

4. Decide which stakeholders should be invited to the next conversation or planning meeting. Make sure the next forum is designed to ensure their participation.

Exercise 6.2. Constructing a Stakeholder Influence Diagram.

Stakeholder influence diagrams indicate how the stakeholders on a power-versus-interest grid influence one another. The technique is taken from Eden and Ackermann (1998) and begins with a power-versus-interest grid. Here are the steps in developing such a diagram:

1. The planning team should start with a power-versus-interest grid and then for each stakeholder on the grid suggest lines of influence from one stakeholder to another.
2. A facilitator should draw in the lines with a soft-lead pencil.
3. Two-way influences are possible, but an attempt should be made to identify the primary direction in which influence flows between stakeholders.
4. Engage in a dialogue about which influence relationships exist, which are most important, and what the primary direction of influence is.
5. Once final agreement is reached, the pencil lines should be made permanent with a marking pen.
6. The results and implications of the resulting diagram should be discussed, including identifying the most influential or central stakeholders.

Source: Eden and Ackermann (1998), pp. 349–350; see also Finn (1996) and Bryson, Cunningham, and Lokkesmoe (2002).

Exercise 6.3. Participation Planning Matrix.

The matrix prompts planners to think about responding to or engaging stakeholders in different ways over the course of a policy or strategy change effort. As a result, the benefits of taking stakeholders seriously can be had while avoiding the perils of inappropriately responding to or engaging stakeholders. The level of participation ranges from a minimum of simply informing stakeholders to empowerment (in which the stakeholders or some subset of them are given final decision-making authority). Each level has its own goal and makes a kind of promise—implicitly if not explicitly. For example, informing carries with it the promise that "we will keep you informed." At the other extreme, empowerment as a strategy carries with it the promise that "we will implement what you decide."

Here is the process for filling out the matrix:

1. Begin using this matrix relatively early in any change effort.
2. Fill out the matrix with stakeholders' names in the appropriate boxes, and then develop an action plan for how to follow through with each stakeholder.
3. Revise the matrix as the change effort unfolds.

Exercise 6.3. Participation Planning Matrix, Cont'd.

Participation Planning Matrix

Policy Change Activity	Stakeholders to Approach, by Which Means:				
	Inform	Consult	Involve	Collaborate	Empower
	Promise: We will keep you informed.	Promise: We will keep you informed, listen to you, and provide feedback on how your input influenced the decision.	Promise: We will work with you to ensure your concerns are considered and reflected in the alternatives considered, and provide feedback on how your input influenced the decision.	Promise: We will incorporate your advice and recommendation to the maximum extent possible.	Promise: We will implement what you decide.
Initial organizing					
Creating ideas for strategic interventions (including problem formulation and search for solutions)					
Building a winning coalition around proposal development review and adoption					
Implementing, monitoring, and evaluating strategic interventions					

Source: Adapted from the International Association for Public Participation's Public Participation Spectrum of levels of public participation (http://www.iaps.org/practitioner tools/spectrum.html) and Bryson's Strategy Change Cycle (1995).

stakeholders are those most affected by the problem at hand, or those with critical resources for resolving it.) As you fill out the matrix, pay attention to the power-versus-interest grid constructed here in step two. Think about the need to balance power in a face-to-face forum. Powerful politicians, government administrators, chief executives, and mass media journalists undoubtedly need to be thoroughly involved at some point. These people can provide important links to their colleagues, constituents, and audiences, and they can inform change advocates about key decision points and strategies for influencing the decision. Policy makers can also furnish such critical resources as legitimacy, staff assignments, budgets, and a meeting place. On the other hand, their presence in an initial planning session may completely stifle the free exchange of views. Thus the planning matrix recognizes that the level of participation may vary with the phase of the policy change cycle.

5. If the group wants to proceed, plan one or more follow-up formal forums that include at least the stakeholders you listed in the "involve," "collaborate," and "empower" categories.

Follow-up Forum

This meeting can be viewed as the more public beginning of the change effort. You may want to hold the meeting in conjunction with a highly visible forum organized by some other group (for example, a U.N. conference) or simply organize a freestanding educational event that sets the background for the problem and highlights the reasons a change initiative should be undertaken. We recommend that the participants (that is, the meeting organizers and other invited stakeholders) also undertake a stakeholder analysis. This may be repetitious for several participants but necessary in order to build shared understanding and commitment.

1. The assembled group should be asked to brainstorm the list of stakeholders who might need to be involved in the change effort. (To reduce duplication of previous effort, bring the stakeholder list generated at the earlier meeting and ask the group to add to it.) Again, the basic-analysis technique, power-versus-interest grid, stakeholder influence diagram, or participation planning matrix might be used as a starting point for understanding and involving an array of stakeholders.

2. After this analysis has been completed, the group should be encouraged to think carefully about who is not at this meeting but should be subsequently (Finn, 1996). The group should consider actual or potential stakeholder power, legitimacy, and attention-getting capacity (Mitchell, Agle, and Wood, 1997). The group should carefully think through the positive and negative consequences of involving—or not involving—other stakeholders or their representatives, and in what way to do so.

3. The group should decide whether to proceed to a "full group" forum, or series of forums, where group members work with additional stakeholders to engage in further stakeholder analysis and set up a more formal structure to undertake a full-fledged change effort. If group members decide to proceed, they should empower a planning group to put together ensuing forums.

Full-Group Forums

Planners ideally should try to bring together all the participants in the previous meeting along with additional stakeholders the group believes should be included in a full-fledged change effort. A personal invitation should be sent to key individual stakeholders in addition to general invitations to selected stakeholder groups. If a combined forum is not practical, the group can hold several forums to attract the additional stakeholders and then integrate the results of all the forums. The aim of the full-group forum is to engage in a final round of stakeholder analysis and gain agreement on an organizational structure to undertake the change effort. These forums are useful for assessing and building commitment to the change effort. Policy entrepreneurs summon their visionary leadership skills to convince newcomers that change is needed and possible, and that everyone present can and should contribute to shaping the effort.

First, the previous stakeholder analyses may need to be repeated, at least in part, with the full group present so as to get everyone on the same page or "bought in," and to make any required corrections or modifications to prior analyses.

Second, if the full group has sufficient enthusiasm and commitment for undertaking the change effort, the conveners should gather their ideas for naming the effort and organizing various groups that will have some role in the change effort. These groups include sponsors and champions, a coordinating group, a planning team, and various advisory or support groups (Bryson and Roering, 1988; Friend and Hickling, 1997).

The conveners might suggest a name for the change effort and ask for other ideas or modifications. They can use focus groups to consider names or simply have people submit suggestions on note cards. Remember that the name can be quite important in framing the desired change.

Third, the conveners should explain the roles of individuals and groups typically involved in a successful change effort. Sponsors are people with enough status and authority to ensure the process will move ahead; champions are people who have a high level of personal commitment to the process and will consistently follow through on process details.

Sponsors typically do not have to commit a lot of their time to the effort, but they can be counted on to come through when needed, especially at a high-visibility juncture. In the campaign against AIDS, for example, the sponsorship of Elizabeth Taylor and other stars drew media coverage to fundraising events; other important sponsors were two congressmen, Henry Waxman and Philip Burton. The champions were the health professionals, congressional aides, and gay activists who marshaled evidence, rallied supporters, and organized an array of forums to alter the existing policy regime.

In the African American Men Project, Hennepin County commissioners Mark Stenglein and Peter McLaughlin and County Administrator Sandra Vargas were important sponsors, while Gary Cunningham, Shane Price (the current AAMP coordinator), V. J. Smith (a grassroots activist), and others were champions. Herman Milligan Jr., former Minneapolis Mayor Sharon Sayles Belton, and other prominent African American community leaders were sponsors. Champions can be policy entrepreneurs themselves, or "process" champions who do not have any preconceived notion about a desirable solution. Rather, they are committed to the process of policy change because they believe that something must be done and that a policy change effort is likely to produce a desirable solution.

The coordinating committee (possibly called a steering group, task force, or some other title) maintains momentum and serves to buffer, consult, bargain, and negotiate among the organizations and individuals affected by the change effort. Without such a mechanism, the effort is likely to flounder or fall apart completely (Trist, 1983; Bardach, 1998; Borins, 1998). Guidance about the composition and function of the coordinating committee is included in Exhibit 6.1. It is important to decide whether committee members will serve as individuals or as representatives of an organization. The organizers of the Vital Aging Network decided to invite participants as individuals. Jan Hively explained that if someone from the Senior Federation, for example, were invited as an organizational representative, he or she would have to engage in a lengthy process of gaining the federation's buy-in. Instead, the VAN organizers have sought organizational buy-in only for specific

---

**Exhibit 6.1. Characteristics of Effective
Coordinating Committees and Other Policy-Making Bodies.**

A well-functioning *coordinating committee* is usually crucial for any major policy change effort. The committee typically includes representatives of key stakeholder groups, top-level decision makers, technical and professional opinion leaders, process experts, and critics. The committee and any other policy board that is involved should:

- Focus most of their attention on their policy-making role
- Develop a mission statement that clearly states their purposes as a policy-making body
- Establish a set of policy objectives for the change effort
- Concentrate their resources to be more effective as policy makers
- Control the change process mainly through the questions they ask of the people they are coordinating, such questions taking the general form of "How does this recommendation [whether a proposal, strategy, or budget] serve our purposes, values, or policies?"
- Use staff to help them be better policy makers
- Rely on various media (press releases, newsletters, television, e-mail) to transmit information to key stakeholders and the general public
- Hold periodic retreats to develop policies, plans, strategies, and programs for subsequent years
- Appropriately monitor pertinent performance data

References: Carver (1990), Eadie (1994), and Houle (1989).

projects. Of course, participants in a steering committee should recognize that their participation may affect their organization. Even if people do not serve as an organizational representative, they are not shorn of association with their organization. They and others will view their organization as a potential resource for the committee's work.

In addition, once the change effort has expanded beyond a small group, then a planning team, or at least a project coordinator, will almost always be necessary to prepare for coordinating committee meetings and other events. The planning team may include some coordinating committee members, and certainly champions and other workhorses committed to keeping the effort moving. This entrepreneurial team carries the change effort through subsequent phases of the policy change cycle, even though membership is likely to change as time goes by. Specific working groups may be needed. A group might be assigned to draft an initial agreement for consideration by the coordinating committee; other groups may be assigned specific research tasks. For example, in the AAMP various working groups organized stakeholder consultation and expert panels and compiled research on the experience of African American men.

Fourth, the participants may also want to assess stakeholder attitudes toward the status quo, using Exercise 6.4. The exercise should reveal whether stakeholders already have enough interest in doing something about the public problem or opportunity, whether they need to see the problem or opportunity as more important, or whether political changes are necessary, which might mean changes in elected officials, partisan distribution in an elected body, pressure group activity, or public opinion.

Crafting an Actual Agreement

An informal understanding may suffice as long as only a few individuals or groups are involved in the early stages of mobilizing action, few resources are needed, and the situation is relatively straightforward. However, a detailed, jointly negotiated agreement is indicated as the number of groups increases, significant resource commitments become necessary, or the situation grows more com-

Exercise 6.4. Assessing Stakeholder Attitudes Toward the Status Quo.

This exercise helps a group assess how satisfied stakeholders are with the way a public problem or opportunity is being handled now and what it would take to raise dissatisfaction with the status quo to a critical level.

1. At the top of a flipchart sheet, write the question, How well does the status quo satisfy stakeholder goals and expectations?
2. Down the left side of the sheet, list the stakeholders involved in efforts to remedy the problem or take advantage of the opportunity. Add more sheets if needed.
3. Ask the group to decide whether the status quo performs poorly, adequately, or very well against each stakeholder's goals and expectations, and note the group's assessment next to the stakeholder.
4. Once completed, the exercise can be the basis for discussing strengths and weaknesses of the existing policy regime (or non-system), the nature of existing and potential stakeholder coalitions, and the opportunities and threats to those coalitions.

plex. As noted above, a small group can be appointed to draft an agreement for submission to the coordinating committee.

A full-fledged initial agreement should include:

- A compelling statement of the need to respond to the problem.
- A list of the stakeholders whose support or acquiescence is necessary to build a winning coalition.
- A general strategy and next steps. The next steps should focus on the problem definition phase; the planning team may want to organize a retreat, conference, or formal discussion session (see Resource F). The team will probably conduct additional research to formulate the problem and explore solutions more thoroughly, to create enough of a preliminary issue to mobilize action (and further initial agreements) among a wider circle of participants.
- Guidance about the optimal design and use of forums, arenas, and courts.
- Preferred form and timing of early reports.

- The role, function, and membership of any individual, group, or committee empowered to oversee the effort of the planning team. Characteristics of effective policy-making bodies are outlined in Exhibit 6.1. The agreement may name a project coordinator (often a champion-in-chief) or include plans for naming someone to the position.

- Commitment of resources (time and attention of key decision makers and opinion leaders, staff time, and money) to begin the endeavor.

The agreement could be a written memorandum, or a chart with supporting text; it should be distributed to the coordinating committee and planning team. If outside consultants are to be used, a formal contract is desirable. Note that considerable research and consultation may be needed to put together agreement components. For example, the drafters should talk to trusted informants about the best way to approach a pertinent public agency, legislature, or civil or administrative court. They should also consider decision-making arenas that aren't already tied to a failing solution, so that change advocates can engage in what Frank Baumgartner and Bryan Jones (1993) call venue shopping, or seeking out the arena most favorable to a proposed solution.

Using their visionary skills, policy entrepreneurs might think of the initial agreement as outlining an anticipated story of policy change. A good initial agreement names the actors, outlines the plot that is about to unfold, designates the stage on which it will be played, demarcates specific acts and scenes, describes the general character of the story and the themes to be followed, and suggests how the endeavor will be underwritten. The story metaphor is appropriate as well as useful, given how dramatic many change efforts become, but policy entrepreneurs should recognize how difficult it is to stick to the script in a situation where no one is in charge (Mangham and Overington, 1987; Bryant, 2003). In particular, the initial agreement is likely to point out that there is no single "director" but many, and much of the "story" is made up as events unfold unpredictably (and perhaps dangerously). As leaders direct these dramatic processes, they must be prepared for their well-crafted play to change suddenly into improvisational theater, or even theater of the absurd! An initial agreement that has delineated themes, actors, and plots helps leaders know when it is time for key decision makers to rewrite their script for a happier ending.

Applying their political skills, policy entrepreneurs may highlight the gamelike quality of the policy change cycle, likening the change cycle to chess, in which a player must understand the purpose of the game, the rules, and the function of each piece, as well as the likely strategies of the opponent. A player must also have an excellent strategic sense, think many moves ahead, and know what it takes to win (Behn, 1983). Perhaps the best description of this way of thinking comes from one of novelist Amy Tan's characters:

> I studied each chess piece, trying to absorb the power each contained.
>
> I learned about opening moves and why it's important to control the center early on; the shortest distance between two points is straight down the middle. I learned about the middle game and why tactics between two adversaries are like clashing ideas; the one who plays better has the clearest plans for both attacking and getting out of traps. I learned why it is essential in the endgame to have foresight, a mathematical understanding of all possible moves, and patience; all weaknesses and advantages become evident to a strong adversary and are obscured to a tiring opponent. I discovered that for the whole game one must gather invisible strengths and see the endgame before the game begins. [Tan, 1989, pp. 95–96]

The policy change cycle is far more complicated than chess, and the desirable conclusion is one in which everyone benefits. Nevertheless, the imagery is helpful, because more often than not policy entrepreneurs encounter clever opponents who design their own strategies in order to oppose important policy changes.

The entrepreneurial team might strategize how to include attention to leadership (especially leadership in context and personal, team, organizational, and visionary leadership) in a forum for developing additional agreement and proceeding with the phases of problem formulation and search for solutions. If the team is especially ambitious, it can plan a leadership development program to be available to participants in the change effort.

Building commitment for the long haul is also important, since accomplishing a major policy change can take a decade or more (Sabatier and Jenkins-Smith, 1993). The team should urge forum participants to take the long view, yet at the same time inculcate a sense that the journey will be invigorating and filled with ample opportunity for achieving milestones along the way.

Additionally, the planning team should outline a media strategy for the entire change process. Their action plans for the initial-agreement phase should include:

- Identifying mass media that reach the general public as well as the decision makers whose public support is valuable
- Identifying alternative media (neighborhood newspapers, public radio, professional journals, and the like) that reach specialized audiences, since most audiences may be characterized as cognitive misers (Nelson, 1984; Sabatier, 1991)
- Deciding whether and how to create new media
- Compiling, in useful form, media addresses, telephone and fax numbers, publication dates, deadlines, newscast schedules, format requirements, names and contact information for reporters interested in the general topic of concern, and the names of editors or news directors who may make decisions about when and how to cover the change effort
- Anticipating the change project's reports, speeches, and other activities and deciding how they should be publicized; options include press releases, photographs, articles for in-house publications, listservs, Websites, audiotapes, and videotapes
- Deciding which interpretive schemes should be emphasized in any initial public utterance or report
- Determining what resources are needed
- Identifying supporters who are especially knowledgeable, articulate, and possibly attention-getting as potential spokespersons
- Deciding whether to publicize an initial agreement, through press releases and public ceremonies, for example; doing so makes sense when the agreement includes enough advocates (especially well-known and respected ones) to signal the effort's importance and potential success
- Preparing for the effort to become public, even if participants agree not to publicize an initial agreement

If an initial agreement cannot be reached the first time through, policy entrepreneurs may want to try again, wait for an appropriate focusing event, foster political change to make the climate more receptive, engage in further problem formulation or solution-search activity, or focus on an area in which key decision makers can reach agreement. Announcement of the agreement may itself be a focusing event.

Summary

A successful initial-agreement phase results in a shared commitment among at least some key stakeholders to undertake a policy change effort to remedy a public problem. A formal initial agreement can be a guide for working through the ensuing phases of the policy change cycle. It can help foster group identity, clarify individual and group roles in the change process, tap resources, and offer a compelling sense of the importance of the problem and the possibility of problem-solving actions that will achieve the common good. We turn now to the problem-formulation phase, in which the nascent advocacy coalition prompts public deliberation on the causes and interpretation of the problem at hand and develops direction for a solution search.

Chapter Seven

Developing an Effective Problem Definition to Guide Action

It is not difficult to tally preferences in this era of instantaneous electronic polling and sophisticated marketing techniques for discovering what people want and how much they want it. It is a considerable challenge, however, to engage the public in rethinking how certain problems are defined, alternative solutions envisioned, and responsibilities for action allocated.
ROBERT REICH

The world is made of stories, not atoms.
MURIEL RUKEYSER

As they work in the problem-formulation phase, wise policy entrepreneurs know that much has to be done to cultivate a sense of urgency and possibility among ever-broader groups of stakeholders. These leaders must be willing to hold their own problem definitions or favored problem frames lightly and promote a deeper investigation of the causes, effects, and possible interpretations of the problem (Nutt, 2002). As part of this work, they may need to reframe the problem as an opportunity to achieve beneficial societal goals.

Leaders exercise extraordinary power over policy change processes when they help people see a new problem, or see an old problem in a new way. As John Kingdon notes, this change in people's perspective is "a major conceptual and political accomplishment" (1995, p. 115) because how a problem is formulated has a powerful impact on how it is addressed, and indeed whether it is addressed at all.

Purpose and Desired Outcomes

The primary purpose of the problem-formulation phase of the policy change cycle is to develop widespread awareness and appreciation of an important public problem, along with a sense that it can be solved. A secondary purpose is to specify directions for the rest of the cycle that help ensure proposed and adopted solutions actually address the problem and are technically and administratively workable, politically acceptable, and legally and ethically defensible.

These are the desired outcomes for this phase:

- Clear and apt identification of the nature and range of the problems for which solutions might be sought
- Clarification of differences among stakeholders in relation to the problem and its effects
- Criteria for measuring stakeholder satisfaction with proposed solutions
- Attention to stakeholder feelings and attitudes
- Agreement on which existing and new organizations are needed to respond to particular problems
- Direction and plan for solution search
- Sense of the outlines of a coalition that can support the change effort through subsequent phases
- A clear problem statement

Especially in the problem-formulation and search-for-solution phases, policy entrepreneurs engage in what Paul Sabatier and Hank Jenkins-Smith call "policy-oriented learning," which they define as "an ongoing process of search and adaptation motivated by the desire to realize core policy beliefs" (1993, p. 44). In the process, stakeholder beliefs may be altered. Robert Reich argues that policy making "should entail creation of contexts in which the public can critically evaluate and revise what it believes" (1987, p. 8).

Awareness and Appreciation of Public Problems

In Chapter One, we say that public problems are complex, affect diverse stakeholders, defy simple or easy solutions, and are likely to require collaborative solutions. Usually these problems affect an entire geographic community or community of interest. The problems are important (that is, serious consequences or major lost opportunities result from not dealing with them), and—at least in principle—solutions or improvements are possible. This last point is worth making because a problem without hope of remedy is more aptly called a "condition" or "difficulty" (Wildavsky, 1979). For example, physical mortality is part of the human condition; only a tiny minority of our fellow human beings have seriously proposed that humans could live forever. Instead, policy entrepreneurs highlight such problems as inadequate health care for poor people, the inability of older adults to obtain affordable prescription drugs, and the need for hospice care for people with a terminal illness.

Several analysts refer to the "wicked" nature of public problems (Rittel and Webber, 1973). Most public problems are wicked in a number of ways:

- They have no definitive formulation, and there are many ways to frame them. The criteria used to determine what constitutes a "better" or the "best" problem definition are themselves likely to be disputed.
- The problems are not solved but re-solved, again and again. For example, problems of poverty, gender, race, war, and peace are never solved conclusively; they reemerge, in the same form or differently, with great frequency.
- Solutions to the problems are not true or false, but good or bad. Stakeholders use their own (often fundamentally conflicting) expectations or criteria to judge solutions.
- Typically, the full consequences of any solution cannot be known immediately—and may never be known. Sometimes, a solution solves a problem other than the one it was intended to solve, exacerbates the original problem, or causes a new one.
- One-shot solutions don't work. These problems require a solution process that permits midcourse correction and even substitution of a new solution when necessary.

- Each problem is unique. Although current problems and previous ones may share some aspects, the differences are likely to be significant.
- The problems may be symptoms of other problems. Wicked problems are messy; they are an interconnected set of problems (Ackoff, 1981).
- The problems can be explained in many ways, and the choice of explanation largely determines the solution chosen.
- Leaders have no inherent right to be wrong. If a chemist constructs a careful experiment and her hypothesis is disproved, helpful learning occurs nonetheless. Leaders, on the other hand, are theorists who often pay (or exact) a high price for being wrong. They bear responsibility for the consequences of their actions, and if people don't like the consequences the leaders may be punished. More importantly, the people who are affected by the leaders' actions can be hurt. Policy entrepreneurs have a dual responsibility: to seek widespread gains *and* to minimize losses for their communities.

In all four cases featured in this book, policy entrepreneurs have undertaken or overseen extensive research (1) to present evidence that the problem concerning them exists, (2) to deepen their understanding of its causes and effects, and (3) to support a particular way of framing the problem. Each effort was a kind of action research (Krueger and King, 1998; Eden and Huxham, 1996), appreciative inquiry (Cooperrider and Srivastva, 1987; Cooperrider and Bilimoria, 1993), and participatory policy analysis (Durning, 1993).

The definition of a public problem conveys a message about social significance, urgency, causal mechanisms, framing, and implications for stakeholder action (Rochefort and Cobb, 1994). Astute policy entrepreneurs attempt to build support for action by emphasizing the social impact of the problem, the likely cost of inaction, and the need to do something about the problem as soon as possible. They offer multicausal explanations and frame the problem in a way that appeals to multiple constituencies. They attend to categorization of the problem, any value judgment that may be applied to it, warning signals from indicators, troubling comparisons, triggering events, and feedback on previous efforts to deal with the problem or others like it (Kingdon, 1995). They build a compelling case for pursuing a solution, and they help their constituencies develop a direction and plan for their solution search. This work strongly affects whether uninterested stake-holders begin to realize that they do have a stake in the problem or that it should move higher in their list of concerns (Rochefort and Cobb, 1994).

Social Significance and Urgency

Policy entrepreneurs become involved in a policy change effort in the first place because they are convinced that the problem concerning them is severely threatening the well-being of (or closing off opportunities for) themselves and their fellow citizens. In the initial-agreement phase, they have convinced like-minded supporters to begin a change effort. Now they must make their case to a broader, probably more skeptical set of stakeholders. They need to marshal additional evidence that the problem exists and is causing (or is highly likely to cause) widespread losses. They have to highlight the gap between what they believe is happening, or will soon happen, and what they think can or should be done about it.

Multicausal Explanations and Complex Problem Frames

To make a plausible case that a problem can be remedied, policy entrepreneurs must also help constituents understand what is causing the problem. As we have noted, the problem is often actually a set of interconnected problems; thus investigators might have difficulty deciding what causes what. Moreover, the problem could evoke preexisting interpretive schemes, or frames that supply ready-made causal explanation.

The most important interpretive schemes for defining a public problem are stories deeply rooted in culture (Mandelbaum, 2000; Stone, 2002). These stories constitute a communal world, and the most powerful are widely shared and believed "myths" (de Neufville and Barton, 1987; Innes, 1990; Delbanco, 1999). A myth proposes an analogy to simplify a complex reality and give a rationale for perceiving and behaving in a certain way. Also, because a myth takes a dramatic form and taps deeply seated values, it generates a strong emotional response that can prompt public action. New versions of old myths, or even new myths, may be created over time, but many themes remain almost timeless in a particular culture because they are created or recreated out of the culture's fairly stable repertoire of images, symbols, characters, and action styles.

Interestingly, and perhaps fortunately for policy entrepreneurs, one society's myths may be quite different from another's. For example, the United States is often identified with what Robert Reich has called the myth of the "triumphant individual," which depicts Americans as hard-working and self-reliant conquerors of the land, competitive winners, and people responsible for their own fate (Reich, 1987). At the same time, U.S. citizens also believe in the myth of the "benevolent community," in which neighbors or other groups of citizens band together to fight off a disaster; raise a barn; or care for the destitute, sick, or vulnerable. Each myth carries a moral theme. The myth of the triumphant individual evokes individual responsibility (the buck stops here; look out for number one), whereas the myth of the benevolent community evokes communal responsibility (love thy neighbor; care for others). The myths also evoke causal attributions. In one, a person's success is due to his own efforts and his failures are due to laziness, bad luck, or incompetence. In the other, a person's success in large part is due to the support he or she receives from society; his or her difficulties, in turn, are often caused by collective failures. Which myth is evoked by a policy entrepreneur's framing of a public problem makes a big difference in whether citizens will decide that a public problem requires a communal response. Because both myths are so powerful and because each has beneficial and problematic components, wise policy entrepreneurs find a way to tap the beneficial aspects of both. During the early U.S. AIDS crisis, health care professionals emphasized communal responsibility as they tried to attract resources so as to investigate the mysterious disease affecting their patients and provide adequate care for the patients. At the same time, they highlighted individual responsibility as they called on gay men to change their behavior.

Considerable research is often needed in this phase, if stakeholders are to move beyond the simplistic causal explanations offered by cultural myths. In the early stages of the AIDS case, people who preferred the individual responsibility frame were likely to say that the toll of AIDS was due to the sexual practices of gay men. People who applied the communal responsibility frame argued that the cause was more complicated and included discrimination against gay people and failure of a public health system to take the disease seriously.

Moreover, once a problem is connected to other, possibly more familiar, ones, people are likely to think about it in the way they have thought about the related problems. They may attribute the same causes to the new problem and frame it in the same way as they do an old problem. Thus many gay activists in early 1980s reacted with outrage to warnings that a dangerous new disease was being transmitted by practices in gay bathhouses. In their eyes, the warnings signaled another effort to discriminate against gay men. In a sense, they focused on what they considered the real problem: efforts to punish gay people and control their behavior.

In thinking about problems, policy entrepreneurs should keep in mind that some formulations miss the mark. All too often, policy advocates simply frame a problem as opposition to their favored solution. Thus environmentalists might fall into the trap of asserting that the main problem they face is industries that refuse to get on the renewable-energy bandwagon. Or advocates for older adults might argue that the big problem is a health care industry that stands in the way of their favored reforms, such as low-priced prescription drugs or greater public funding of in-home care. Such problem formulations are likely to prevent advocates from in-depth exploration of the problem that their solution is intended to solve, and keep them from considering problem frames that might allow them to find common ground with diverse stakeholder groups.

Additionally, problem formulations serve differing purposes (Volkema, 1986). Some formulations clearly define the problem (rightly or wrongly) and delineate a solution set. Some simply get a group working on a problem area. Some are intended to protect or advance the interests of the people who propose them. Certainly some critics have complained that the problem frames emphasized by the WBCSD tend to project an overly benign image of polluting businesses. The WBCSD downplays environmental damage caused by business operations in favor of focusing on how businesses can become eco-efficient. By implication, the problem seems to be that businesses just need more information and encouragement in order to improve their operations (Najam, 1999–2000).

We cannot overemphasize the importance of ideas about the causes of a public problem (Mandelbaum, 2000; Stone, 2002). As Rochefort and Cobb note, "To name a problem's cause is to dispel its disconcerting mystery and to turn in the direction of certain kinds of remedies and away from others" (1994, p. 163). They add, "A decision about problem causality can be a linchpin to a whole set of interdependent propositions that construct an edifice of understanding about a particular issue." A focus on one or two causes may certainly be attractive, because a course of action then seems simpler. Rochefort and Cobb, however, argue that "depending on the circumstances, multicausal explanations and the multipronged solutions they engender can also be among the most sophisticated policy endeavors and also those that have the greatest chance of building support" for tackling complex public problems (p. 17). Wise policy entrepreneurs consult diverse stakeholders in order to obtain as many views as possible about the causes of the problem concerning them.

Rochefort and Cobb also note that using levels of analysis— from individuals to social systems and dominant cultural beliefs— enhances the opportunity for effective intervention into public problems. In the AIDS case, public health officials who wanted to stop risky sexual behavior needed to understand how diverse individuals would react to educational campaigns; they had to consider how gay-rights organizations and family-values organizations, among others, would respond; they had to recognize that dominant U.S. cultural beliefs included both a commitment to personal privacy and tolerance of sexual behavior among consenting adults alongside continued antagonism toward homosexuality.

Policy entrepreneurs also should consider how the different sectors affect the problem at hand. That is, they should investigate the failures and successes of government agencies, businesses, and nonprofit organizations in dealing with the problem.

Categorization, Value Judgments, Warning Signals, Troubling Comparisons, Triggering Events, and Feedback

Problem framing inevitably leads to, and flows out of, decisions about which category "contains" the problem (Weick and Sutcliffe, 2001; Stone, 2002). Analysis cannot proceed, nor can action be mobilized, until a public problem has been placed in the proper category. For example, is the need for enabling older adults to lead satisfying, productive lives an economic problem, a health problem, or a discrimination problem?

Values tell people what is worthwhile and important. When faced with a complex, problematic situation, an individual is likely to assess how it relates to what he or she values. A Minnesotan nearing retirement, for example, is likely to place a high value on her future economic security. When she learns that combating discrimination against older workers is one of the aims of the Vital Aging Network, she is likely to think VAN has something to offer her. The political importance of values is clarified by David Easton's classic statement that "politics is the authoritative allocation of values" (1965, p. 21). Politics defines which values are supported and which are not, which public actions are justified and which not. Not all values are equal; some are more important and worthwhile than others, and politics determines which is which.

Categories and values, in turn, shape indicators and comparisons that people use to assess the health of a system, signal the existence of a problem, gauge the size of the problem, and trace its development (Kingdon, 1995; Stone, 2002). Various organizations and people around the world routinely monitor thousands of indicators. For example, indicators of climate change have helped a large and increasing number of the world's citizens realize that the problem of global warming exists and will have alarming, widespread consequences. Studies of the age composition of the Minnesota workforce have alerted planners in government, business, and nonprofit organizations to a looming shortage of experienced managers as baby boomers retire. Statistics about high school graduation rates, incarceration, home ownership, and mortality were used to supply evidence that young African American men in Hennepin County were being cut off from opportunities to build a satisfying, productive life.

Once indicators are established, comparison is possible, and one of the standard routines of politics is to compare how one group or program is doing in relation to others. Organizations, cities, states, and nations compare themselves to similar organizations, cities, states, and nations; women compare their status to that of men; working-class families compare their opportunities to those of the well-to-do. Thus, indicators of the status of African American men in Hennepin County were often dismaying enough in their own right, but when they were compared with those for "white" citizens they were even more distressing. Sometimes the comparison stimulates local pride or self-interest that prompts action on a problem. Hennepin County officials want indicators about the state of their county to look good in comparison to those of other large urban counties.

Warning signals and troubling comparisons may not be enough to prompt action. Sometimes a triggering or focusing event—a dramatic investigation, crisis, or disaster; a powerful symbol; the personal experience of a key leader—is necessary to focus public attention on a problem (Kingdon, 1995). In the AIDS case, the stories of hospital patients who developed AIDS as a result of blood transfusions and the death of Rock Hudson brought such a focus.

Feedback about a program is another important source of information about the existence, or nonexistence, of a problem (Kingdon, 1995). Feedback can come from a systematic monitoring or evaluation study, complaint, report of an administrator or frontline worker, or a news report. If feedback indicates that a stated policy or goal is not being met, costs are excessive, or unanticipated and undesirable consequences are occurring, chances are decision makers will decide that a problem exists.

Clarification of Relevant Differences Among Stakeholders

Each stakeholder group is likely to view a public problem in its own way by virtue of how the problem affects group members, what opportunities it offers them, what demands it may make upon them, and how it relates to their ideas about how the world works or should work. Clearly, as demonstrated by the power-versus-interest analysis described in the previous chapter, stakeholders have varying levels of interest in changing the status quo and differing capabilities for contributing to or blocking a change effort. Stakeholder analysis in this phase should focus on how stakeholder groups are framing the problem, which frames might appeal to an array of stakeholder groups, and how the differing power of stakeholders needs to be taken into account.

Criteria for Measuring Stakeholder Satisfaction

In the initial-agreement phase, policy entrepreneurs can identify stakeholder goals and expectations in order to clarify how much appeal a change effort is likely to have. In this phase, policy entrepreneurs should understand and specify general outcomes or goals that these stakeholders seek so as to know how best to set directions for a solution search in the next phase.

Attention to Stakeholder Feelings and Attitudes

How a public problem is defined affects stakeholders' emotional as well as logical response to a change effort (Patterson, Grenny, McMillan, and Switzler, 2002). Stakeholders often react to the symbolic nature of problem definition. For example, if environmentalists claim that polluted waterways result from corporate malevolence, corporate directors, executives, and managers are likely to react defensively. To the corporate stakeholders, this problem definition symbolizes an antibusiness attitude on the part of environmentalists. Similarly, if corporate spokespeople define pollution as simply a byproduct of development, environmentalists may erupt in anger over corporate insensitivity. Indeed, as Rochefort and Cobb (1994) point out, symbolic assessment affects rational assessment.

Agreement on Responsible Organizations

The coordinating committee should agree on which individuals, groups, or organizations should respond to which parts of the public problem they are tackling. A problem rarely corresponds to a preexisting organizational domain, so change advocates must agree on what existing organizations will do and which new organizations are needed. A temporary organization of some sort—a task force, formal or informal committee, special-purpose grouping of organizations—is likely to be necessary to consider the problem holistically and to ensure that causes, rather than mere symptoms, are addressed (Trist, 1983).

Direction and Plan for Solution Search

As already noted, how a public problem is framed determines the general range of desired outcomes and range of solutions pursued. The plan for further specifying promising solutions should include specific desired outcomes; it should foster opportunities (and assign responsibility) for assessing the technical and administrative feasibility, legality, political acceptability, and ethical implications of potential solutions.

Developing the Outlines of a Supportive Coalition

The stakeholder analyses and forums that are conducted in this phase reveal which problem definitions are likely to appeal to key stakeholders. Policy entrepreneurs should construct problem definitions that reveal the intersection between their desired outcomes and stakeholder interests. Stakeholders who can see how their interests are served by a change effort are likely to agree to join a coalition supporting the change.

Clear Problem Statement

Once the entrepreneurial team has agreed on how it intends to frame the problem and on what evidence and arguments should be marshaled to bolster support for responding to the problem, the team should develop a clear, written problem statement (unless there are compelling reasons not to do so). The statement can take the form of an official report, a needs assessment, a press release, and so on. The group might draw on or refer to other reports compiled by think tanks, academic researchers, or the news media. The statement and relevant supporting documentation help set the direction for the search for solutions, bring focus to stakeholders' subsequent action and involvement, and also instill a measure of accountability in the process. At the very least, the problem statement might serve as a trial balloon to help leaders gauge public interest in pursuing a policy change (Benveniste, 1989).

Leadership Guidelines

In the problem-formulation phase of policy change, visionary leadership skills continue to be especially important, as the entrepreneurial team stimulates and guides public deliberation about the nature of a public problem and a process for remedying it. The team focuses on creating and communicating shared problem definitions and appreciations that can inspire and motivate subsequent action. Leadership guidelines for this phase fall into four groups: maintenance and expansion of the nascent advocacy coalition; problem formulation; report preparation, review, and dissemination; and caveats.

Advocacy Coalition

Think ahead about the advocacy coalition that will be needed to support specific proposals for change in the proposal-adoption phase. Seek to add new participants in this phase by, for example, convening a forum to deal with the part of the problem concerning them. As the coalition expands, you should pay continued attention to the various tensions inherent in collaborative work, around shared purpose, trust, power, membership, environmental pressures, procedures, and leadership styles (Huxham, 2003). You may need to make special efforts to bring new participants fully on board—for example, by connecting them to people who joined the coalition much earlier, providing them with written or other documentation of previous work, and giving them significant assignments. You may want to prompt discussion of overarching concepts such as leadership for the common good and public work, and offer training in such skills as focus group research (Krueger and King, 1998) and one-on-one interviewing (Boyte, 2004).

Problem Formulation

Problem formulation typically involves a search process in order to gain a fuller understanding of what is really going on in the area of concern.

Use a Two-Step Process Where Feasible

The starting point is to determine if a two-step problem-formulation process is desirable. When the real nature of a public problem is unclear, a two-step research process is advisable. In the first step, the entrepreneurial team conducts exploratory research into possible causes of the problem, stakeholders and their views, and effects of the problem. In the second step, the team undertakes more detailed research. The team should be careful to give adequate attention to the more open-ended first step, because without it important aspects of the problem and the impact on stake-holders may be ignored.

Exploratory research includes:

• Identifying key organizations, persons, or other information sources and developing a strategy for obtaining necessary information from them.

• Using exploratory techniques for obtaining information from the sources, such as on-site observation, unstructured interviews, focus group discussions (Krueger and King, 1998), nominal group technique (Delbecq, Van de Ven, and Gustafson, 1975), and the snowcard technique. Reviewing previous studies may also be quite useful.

• Attending to interpretive schemes or problem frames, stories, gaps, categories, values, indicators, comparisons, triggering events, and feedback. Discussing these factors and noting similarities and differences across groups, as well as what seems to be missing that might significantly affect problem formulation, are also recommended. The team should pay attention to people's stories. Rather than asking informants to define the problem, researchers can ask them to talk about their experiences that relate to the problem. After these stories are collected, the team can construct a timeline of key events and record answers to the journalist's questions (what, when, where, how, and why). Constructing such an "issue history" helps guarantee that the right problem gets solved in the right way. As time allows, the team should explore other aspects of relevant history, in particular the history underlying important presumptions and the history of relevant organizations or institutions (Neustadt and May, 1986).

Exploratory research sets the stage for more detailed research, which includes these steps:

• Identifying information sources and developing a research strategy for obtaining information from them. If necessary, plan to hire experts who are knowledgeable about the problem area or appropriate research methods and who are credible to key stakeholders. Organizers of the African American Men Project did this. The project benefited not only from the experts' knowledge but also from their credibility in the eyes of various stakeholder groups. Using experts from several disciplines is usually a good idea, especially in any area where policy experts from various fields disagree. The areas of disagreement are likely to be where the "real" problem is found.

• Using structured techniques to collect information (survey research, structured interviews, structured group meetings, detailed analysis of literature and data).

• Analyzing and discussing the findings, including similarities and differences across groups and possible prompts to further action by these groups. In particular, focus on whether the problem appears to be important enough, from the standpoint of key stakeholders, to make policy change necessary and its implementation likely.

Look at the Role of Sectors in Formulating a Problem

Consider what the information you have gathered indicates about government, market, and nonprofit successes and failures. Identify how these sectors are part of the problem as well as part of potential solutions.

Favor Forums in This Phase

Be sure the emphasis in this phase is on designing and using forums, with a secondary emphasis on arenas. A combination of special-purpose forums and general forums is likely to work best. In general these forums should bridge organizational boundaries so discussion can foster shared meanings that can guide collective action in subsequent phases.

Special-purpose forums can be convened by a task force or other working group to gain insight into specific aspects of a problem or to consult groups of stakeholders. For example, the Business Council for Sustainable Development (BCSD) organized multiple task forces (on issues such as sustainable management of commercial forests) in preparation for the 1992 Earth Summit. Organizers and supporters of the AAMP conducted focus groups of African American men; sponsored a roundtable discussion among five prominent sociologists and psychologists on the emotional, spiritual, and psychological well-being of African American men;

and held meetings with leaders from government, business, and the philanthropic and spiritual communities.

A general forum can be used to bring together and integrate the results of special-purpose forums and to publicize the emerging or agreed-upon problem definition. For example, the BCSD established a liaison group, which held frequent meetings to consider the results of the issue-focused task forces. The AAMP sponsored a community town hall early on to discuss the experience of African American men; project supporters made presentations at the Juneteenth Festival, the Eleventh Annual Festival of Fathers, and a variety of other community events and meetings.

As you plan the forums, use and update the participation planning matrix (Exercise 6.3) developed in the initial-agreement phase to decide who should participate in the forums. Remember the advice in Chapter Four about ensuring these forums are accessible for those who should participate. The power-versus-interest grid (Exercise 4.2) developed in the initial-agreement phase can also help forum organizers strategize about how to strengthen the voice of people who have high interest in the change effort but little power, and how to awaken the interest of influential people who could use their power on behalf of beneficial change.

Focus on Problems and Desired Outcomes

Be sure the focus is on the problem or need and desired outcomes, not solutions. Leaders must constantly ask themselves and the others involved whether they are focusing on the problem or whether they have become captives of a particular solution. If they have succeeded in fostering among their supporters a belief that the problem is important and urgent, they may feel tremendous pressure to converge quickly on a specific solution (Nutt, 2002). Policy entrepreneurs may therefore need to summon strength and courage to follow this guideline. As Nancy Roberts suggests, giving adequate time for stakeholders to work on problem definition may be particularly difficult for a public official who is expected to solve the problem expeditiously (Roberts, 1997, 2002). Policy entrepreneurs should keep in mind that effort spent on problem identification is a key determinant of a change effort's success. One study found that change efforts are significantly more likely to succeed when participants engage in extensive problem definition (Bryson, Bromily, and Jung, 1990). In contrast, the amount of effort devoted to searching for solutions did not significantly increase the likelihood of success. Other studies have reached much the same conclusion (Nutt, 2002).

Participants in forums during this phase should be encouraged to identify specific behaviors, exchanges, or transactions "on the ground" that are either problematic or desirable. Thus, in a way, the focus is on the end of the policy change cycle—that is, on the desired outcomes of proposed policy change, or on harmful or ineffective behavior linked to previously implemented policies. In a shared-power, no-one-in-charge situation, leaders are far more likely to effect useful policy change if they "map backward" from desired behavior to proposed policy changes than if they "map forward" (Elmore, 1982).

Despite the need to emphasize problems rather than solutions in this phase, policy entrepreneurs recognize that negotiation over problem definition also involves discussion of the potential course of action or solution (Nutt, 2002). Problem formulation cannot be completely divorced from the search for a solution. Indeed, policy entrepreneurs may have to explore several solution options before an effective and final problem definition can be formulated. Additionally, the problem formulation can always be refined after solutions are under consideration. You can use Exercise 7.1 to help your group move from a focus on solutions to desired outcomes that can guide problem formulation.

Exercise 7.2 can be helpful in identifying the type of outcome preferred by key stakeholders, and the power base the stakeholders could draw on as supporters or opponents of change. A planning team can use the exercise to produce a diagram of "bases of power and directions of interest" (goals) for each stakeholder. The technique is an adaptation of Colin Eden and Fran Ackermann's "star diagrams" (1998; see also Bryson, Cunningham, and Lokkesmoe, 2002; and Bryson, 2004).

A diagram of this kind indicates the sources of power available to the stakeholder, as well as the goals or interests the stakeholder seeks to achieve or serve (see Figure 7.1). Power can come from access to or control over various support mechanisms, such as money and votes, or from access to or control over various sanc-

Exercise 7.1. Developing Objectives
from Preferred Solutions for a Problem.

This exercise builds on humans' natural tendency to jump to solutions. The facilitator helps the group see that many narrow solutions can fit into broad-scale objectives, whereas a narrow objective limits the number of solutions that might be considered.

Part One

Directions for a group:

1. Work silently and individually.
2. Take out a sheet of paper and divide it into two columns.
3. In the left-hand column, write down solutions to the problem being dealt with.
4. In the right-hand column, record the results you expect from each solution.

Part Two

1. The facilitator collects the solutions in round-robin fashion and records them on a flipchart sheet.
2. The facilitator collects the expected results round-robin and records them on a second flipchart sheet.
3. The facilitator helps the group rank the expected results (for example, by giving each participant three or more colored dots and asking the person to place a dot by his or her top three results).
4. The facilitator then helps the group decide which solutions could fit with their favored results. The facilitator explains that these favored results are, in effect, the group's objectives.

Source: Adapted from Nutt (2002).

tions, such as regulatory authority or a vote of no confidence (Eden and Ackermann, 1998).

Exercise 7.3 can be used to determine which interests or themes stakeholders have in common. In this exercise the planning team examines the diagrams of bases of power and directions of interest, constructed in Exercise 7.2, to identify which interests are sought by a significant number of stakeholders. These "supra-interests" are given a thematic label that captures or integrates the interests they include. After identifying the themes, the team constructs a map of

Exercise 7.2. Constructing a Diagram of
Bases of Power and Directions of Interest (Goals).

1. Construct a diagram of bases of power and directions of interest (goals) for key stakeholders.

   • Attach a flipchart to a wall. Write the stakeholder's name in the middle of the sheet.
   • The planning team then brainstorms possible bases of power for the stakeholder, and the facilitator writes them on the bottom half of the sheet.
   • On the basis of discussion within the group, arrows are drawn on the diagram from the power base to the stakeholder, and between power bases to indicate how one power base is linked to another.
   • The planning team then brainstorms goals or interests they believe the stakeholder has. The facilitator writes them on the top half of the sheet. Arrows are drawn from the stakeholder to the goals or interests. Arrows are also used to link goals and interests when appropriate.

2. Thoroughly discuss each diagram and its implications for problem formulation.

Figure 7.1. Diagram of Bases of Power and Directions of Interest.

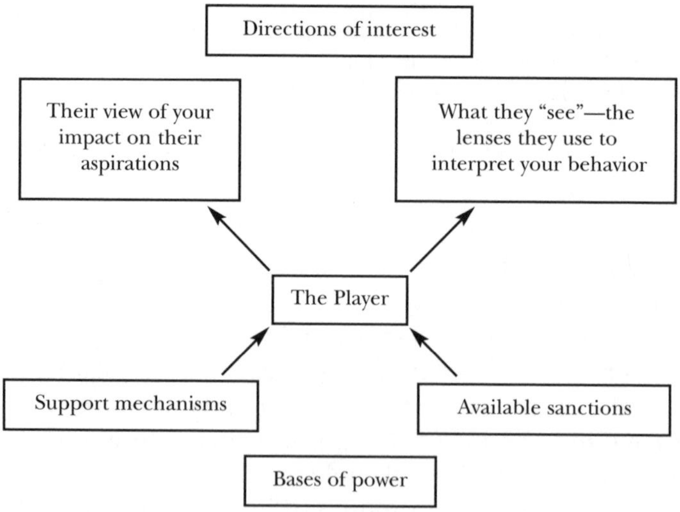

Source: Bryson, Cunningham, and Lokkesmoe (2002); adapted from Eden and Ackermann (1998).

Exercise 7.3. Constructing a Map of the
Common Good and Structure of a Winning Argument.

An individual can perform this exercise, but greater understanding and more accurate or useful outcomes are likely to result from group work.

1. Start by constructing a diagram of bases of power and directions of interest for each key stakeholder.
2. Once all of the diagrams have been created, search for common themes that unite the individual stakeholders' interests. These common themes are called *supra-interests*.
3. Decide on a label that appears to capture or integrate the specific interests that make it up. Identification of common themes is an exercise calling for creativity, discernment, and judgment.
4. After identifying these common themes, construct a map that indicates what appear to be the strongest relationships among the supra-interests. The final map represents the supra-interests that tie together the individual stakeholders' interests as well as what the relationships among the supra-interests appear to be.
5. Discuss what the common good (the supra-interests) appear to be for this group of stakeholders. Talk about how arguments probably will need to be structured to tap into the interests of enough stakeholders to create a winning coalition.

relationships among the supra-interests. This map is called the "common good and structure of a winning argument," because it suggests what the common good is for a group of stakeholders as well as how arguments will have to be structured to tap into the interests of enough stakeholders that a winning coalition can be created (Bryson, Cunningham, and Lokkesmoe, 2002).

Frame Problems in Need of Solution

Focus on interpretive schemes that frame problems so they can be solved. The way a problem is framed structures stakeholders' views of and interest in the problem, the debate surrounding possible solutions, and the coalitions that develop to oppose or support those solutions. Therefore policy entrepreneurs must articulate the view of the world that lies behind their problem definition and make sure this worldview is one that draws significant support from key stakeholders. The worldview a leader should seek is one that calls up widely shared concepts of what constitutes the common good or public interest (Stone, 2002). Further, it clarifies how the problematic situation violates a widely shared vision of how society ought to be, and it taps constituents' deeply held values and aspirations in such a way that they see the problem as a challenge to be overcome and an opportunity to call upon their best selves to realize the kind of world they want to create.

Policy entrepreneurs can use Exercise 4.3 ("Analyzing Interpretive Schemes, or Problem Frames") to identify how stakeholders are framing or likely to frame the problem. Remember that how a stakeholder frames a problem may arise from its connection to other problems or issues (Rochefort and Cobb, 1994). This exercise can be used in conjunction with the diagrams of bases of power and direction of interests to analyze stakeholder support for changes associated with a particular framing of the problem. In the final step, in which participants seek to develop a more comprehensive frame, the map of supra-interests can be helpful in identifying a frame that resonates with stakeholders' shared goals (Bryson, Cunningham, and Lokkesmoe, 2002).

Unravel Old Frames

Actively seek to undo old problem frames that hamper progress toward the outcomes you seek. The organizers of the Vital Aging Network, for example, intentionally set out to dismantle the notion that older adults are frail and dependent. They use data to bolster a more complex view of older people, and they host events that showcase people who are active in their community for decades after they turn sixty.

Report Preparation, Review, and Dissemination

Policy entrepreneurs should strategize about the best format for reporting findings on the problem that concerns them and how to promote an optimal problem frame in a report. They should be sure to leave adequate time for reviewing initial drafts and be willing to prune some problem dimensions or connections. They should also develop a strategy for sustaining media attention to the problem.

Preliminary Report

A working group should bring together the planning team's research and distill the findings into a draft report that outlines problem dimensions and makes recommendations for next steps. The draft should define the problem neither too broadly nor too narrowly and rigidly. Definitions that are too broad offer little guidance for the solution-search phase. Those that are too narrow are likely to focus on symptoms and not causes, and definitions that are too rigid destroy needed flexibility. A calculated degree of vagueness in problem definition is necessary to garner broad stakeholder support for working on the problem; room for revision allows policy entrepreneurs to respond to unforeseen changes in the situation.

You can use several techniques to arrive at an optimal problem statement:

- Break the problem into manageable subproblems that are amenable to "small win" strategies or solutions (Weick, 1984).
- At the same time, treat the subproblems as a system so that adopted strategies have a better chance of being effective (Senge, 1990; Oshry, 1995).
- Indicate the complexity of the problem (Bryson, Ackermann, Eden, and Finn, 2004).
- Be clear as to what is known and unknown about the problem (Dror, 1987).
- Check for unwarranted assumptions (Senge, 1990; Argyris, 1982).

The statement should emphasize the problem frame that seems best calculated to gain stakeholder support for an effective solution, and it should impart direction for next steps, such as listing goals, outcomes, or benchmarks that indicate progress on resolving the problem and general ideas for how the solution search should unfold.

A template for a draft and final report is presented in Exhibit 7.1.

Review Process

The draft report should be reviewed by planning team members; key decision makers, including the coordinating committee; relevant governing boards; and other selected stakeholders. The review should follow a "SWiM" approach, highlighting strengths, weaknesses, and modifications that would improve the document. Page 238 gives a possible agenda for the review sessions.

Exhibit 7.1. Generic Problem Statement Format.

- Title page, indicating content and sponsorship of the study
- Executive summary, highlighting problems or needs, desired outcomes, and recommendations
- Table of contents
- Statement of purpose and sponsorship, along with brief historical background
- Review of relevant literature
- Study design and methodology, including brief description of research staff and their qualifications
- Data sources, including people, organizations, and data banks
- Data analysis
- Findings
- Conclusions and recommendations for further action
- Appendices

1. Overview of the document
2. General comments on the document and reactions to it
3. Brainstormed list of strengths
4. Brainstormed list of weaknesses
5. Brainstormed list of modifications that would improve on the strengths and overcome the weaknesses
6. Agreement on next steps to complete the document

By focusing initially on the strengths of the document and asking for modifications, a process such as this forestalls the all-too-likely scenario in which reviewers tear apart the original document and offer little or no help in improving it.

Defer Other Problems

Policy entrepreneurs often need to resist the temptation to include other important and somewhat related problems in their change effort. For example, some participants in community forums sponsored by the AAMP argued that difficulties faced by African American children and young women ought to be a part of the project. The organizers, however, argued that a focus on better outcomes for young African American men would ultimately help their children as well as young African American women. In some cases, policy entrepreneurs may be able to refer related problems to other groups or organizations that are responsible for them.

Final Report

After review and revision of the draft report, the coordinating committee should decide whether the final report is to be widely disseminated or simply remain a working document until combined with the results of the next phase into a single report that defines the problem and recommends specific solutions. If the committee decides to publish the report, the committee should think carefully about how to present it so that stakeholders commit to efforts to overcome the problem and achieve a better future. The report may need to be prepared in versions tailored to specific audiences; usually the design of the report should be attention-getting and accessible. Various art forms may be used to enact, dramatize, or "real-ize" the interpretation of the report's findings. For example, to dramatize the problem of domestic abuse in the United States, organizers of the Silent Witness Project displayed life-size silhouettes representing women who had been killed by their abusers. Another group demonstrated the human toll of handguns by lining up row after row of empty pairs of shoes to represent all the men, women, and children who had been killed with handguns in a year. An Israeli-Palestinian peace group displays coffins at its presentations to remind the audience of deaths resulting from the Israel-Palestine conflict.

Art can also be celebratory and suggest that policy entrepreneurs' desired outcomes are being, or might be, achieved. For example, a mural might depict sustainable development, a film might portray strong African American families, or an exhibit could highlight older adults' contributions to their community.

Media Strategy

The release of the report is an occasion for attracting media attention to the problem and efforts to do something about it. Publication of the report may also be timed to coincide with some other event, such as the Earth Summit in the World Business Council case. Change advocates should supply interested journalists with background data, human interest angles, and promising leads. The difficulty may lie in sustaining media attention; in the AIDS case, for example, in the summer of 1982 *CBS Evening News* carried a major story featuring Bobbi Campbell, Larry Kramer, and public health official Jim Curran. Host Dan Rather noted that federal officials were calling the disease an epidemic. Anti-AIDS campaigners might have expected major newspapers, magazines, and broadcasters to follow up with intensive coverage, but they did not. *Newsweek* finally carried a cover story on the disease in April 1983.

Strategize about how to keep the problem concerning you in the news and how to tell the causal story that supports needed change. Because so many citizens depend on the mass news media for information, they may think that because a problem is not in the news very often it is sporadic and thus not important; moreover, their understanding of the problem is likely to be superficial since news reports don't generally highlight the causes of a problem (Rochefort and Cobb, 1994).

Caveats for Policy Entrepreneurs

Four cautions are called for. First, remember that the term *problem* can be problematic. Use language that empowers people to take responsible action to improve their situation. If *problem* induces a sense of oppression and defeat, use another term, such as *challenge* or *opportunity*. Just be sure, however, to articulate these challenges or opportunities through an inclusive and motivating interpretive scheme.

Second, remember that this phase—like every phase—can be overdone as well as underdone. Make sure that your group has done enough research and analysis to understand the problem in depth and develop an optimal problem frame. Avoid the temptation to study the problem to death since it is probably worsening anyway, and since supporters may lose some of their enthusiasm if the research drags on.

Third, do not promise stakeholders that all their problems will be solved. Such a promise, whether explicit or implied, might yield a gain in participation in the problem-formulation phase, but it is almost certain to doom policy change efforts later when those expectations are not met.

Fourth, remember that you may need to repeat parts of this phase. As you attempt to win over more stakeholders, or as new aspects of the problem emerge, your group may have to do additional research and analysis. Winning over new stakeholders can require further assurance that problems have been objectively studied; problem frames might need to be refined. At the same time, there is a limit to how much additional agreement you can achieve through more extensive problem-formulation efforts. Sometimes, your group must decide to proceed without the support of some key stakeholders.

Summary

Public problems become real when vocal and powerful people see a gap between what exists and what they think can and should be done about it. The gap is not necessarily between some ideal and reality; more often, it is simply a gap between reality and what people think they can reasonably have (Wildavsky, 1979; Nutt, 2002). How a situation is framed in the first place has the most powerful impact on how a problem is defined. Beyond that, categorization, value judgments, indicators, comparison, focusing events, and feedback also influence what is and is not considered a problem. This chapter has described how policy entrepreneurs use the problem-formulation phase to promote a shared awareness of a public problem among diverse stakeholders. As part of this phase, these entrepreneurs work with a developing advocacy coalition to present multi-faceted problem definitions that can generate widespread support for change. They also help the coalition impart a direction and plan for the solution-search phase, which is described in the next phase.

A number of benefits flow from successful problem-formulation efforts. The first is simply shared recognition and appreciation of problems and needs among a broader group of stakeholders. Second, extensive and careful problem-formulation efforts constitute a basis for effectively addressing real stakeholder concerns, and problem statements afford a rallying point. Third, in the absence of extensive and careful problem-formulation efforts, leaders never really know whether they are addressing hearsay or suspicion, vested interests, or a widely shared sense of a real need. Fourth, extensive problem-formulation efforts by change advocates avoid overreliance on technical experts, who all too often see the problem purely through the lens of their expertise. Fifth, successful problem formulation generates detailed criteria for the search for solutions. Finally, the problem statement develops a useful tension among stakeholders and an implied threat of dire consequences if nothing is done.

Chapter Eight

Searching for Solutions in Forums

Every time we hear that a possible solution simply cannot be done, we may be sure on general scientific grounds that it can. Every time we hear that a solution is not economic, we ought to ask: "for whom?"
STAFFORD BEER

We aren't lacking solutions. What we lack is the will to implement them.
MARGARET WHEATLEY

In the search-for-solutions phase, successful policy entrepreneurs use the problem definition developed in the previous phase to guide efforts to find and evaluate promising solutions. They engage stakeholders in conducting research, organizing effective forums, and championing solution ideas that can attract the support of executive, legislative, and administrative decision makers in subsequent phases. Once this phase is completed, these leaders and their supporters should have articulated a visible public issue, a public problem attached to one or more promising solutions that have pros and cons from the standpoint of key stakeholders.

Purpose and Desired Outcomes

The search-for-solutions phase of the policy change cycle has two main purposes: finding or creating solutions that effectively remedy the problem identified in the previous phase, and capturing

enough public attention to place the problem and its potential solutions—the issue, in other words—on the public agenda. In this
phase, policy entrepreneurs continue the work of constructing and
communicating a collective vision (or direction) for improving the
world. In effect, they are facilitating construction of alternative scenarios for moving from the problem-laden present, through implementing certain strategies, to a relatively problem-free future.

The problem-formulation phase turned a condition into a public problem; this phase turns a problem into an issue—a problem
connected to at least one solution that has pros and cons from the
viewpoint of various stakeholders. Creating an issue is the prime
desired outcome of the search for solutions, but there are others:

- Development of one or more conceptual frameworks for
  understanding the issue
- Identification of the goals and key components of a high-
  quality solution
- Enhancement of the quality, legitimacy, and prestige of the
  policy change endeavor
- Efficient use of people's time and other resources
- Placement of the issue on the public agenda
- Expanded advocacy coalition

Creation of a Public Issue

Policy entrepreneurs seek high-quality solutions that can attract the
support of an array of stakeholders and that are capable of remedying the problem defined in the previous phase. They are adept
in predicting how stakeholders will respond to the proposed solutions and thus able to help an advocacy coalition think through the
politics surrounding a specific proposal for enacting these solutions.

The politics surrounding public issues may be of several main
types: what James Wilson and John DiIulio (1998) call majoritarian, client, interest group, and entrepreneurial. *Majoritarian politics* results when a proposed policy offers widespread benefits and
widespread costs, and an appeal to a popular majority is necessary
for the policy to be adopted. Majoritarian politics evokes less conflict than the other types, because there is less incentive for organized interests to get involved. *Client politics* occurs when the

perceived benefits of a policy are highly concentrated on a particular group but perceived costs are distributed widely. This type of politics can become highly conflictual once the benefits are publicized and stakeholders who are expected to bear the cost become outraged. "Pork-barrel" policies are the classic example leading to client politics. An *interest group* policy provides benefits for one relatively small group and exacts costs from another group. Obviously, the politics surrounding these issues can be extremely conflictual. Finally, an *entrepreneurial* policy is one that provides perceived benefits for many stakeholders or for society as a whole, while imposing costs on a smaller number of identifiable stakeholder groups. Policy entrepreneurs should be aware of this typology; their role is especially crucial in adopting entrepreneurial policies because of the need to persuade policy makers that the policy actually will benefit a large number of stakeholders and that the concentrated costs are merited.

Robert Waste (1997) points out, however, that classifying public issues isn't always this easy, since issues tend to move around among classifications. For example, movement among categories may occur as someone radically redefines an issue or escalates the conflict associated with it, or as an event alters how people perceive the event or their stake in it. Issues may also be surrounded by conflictual politics because they are connected to other highly conflictual issues.

Policy entrepreneurs should seek to frame issues so they produce majoritarian politics if possible; thus they should strive to emphasize the benefits of the solution to society as a whole. The AIDS case is an example, because health professionals emphasized that resources were needed to understand, treat, and prevent the disease, not just to help gay men and drug users but to protect the health of the entire population. This case was easier to make once more and more groups were affected. Policy entrepreneurs also need, if possible, to keep issues from being linked to other issues that are surrounded by high antagonism among groups of warring stakeholders.

Development of Conceptual Frameworks

In the search-for-solutions phase, policy entrepreneurs explore how a public problem and promising solutions might be linked together in a way that indicates how stakeholders might move toward a better future. These leaders use the interpretive schemes they emphasized in the problem statement to frame their argument and evoke a favorable emotional response to potential solutions. They support their argument with persuasive evidence and testimonials—often personal stories—from credible, sometimes well-known individuals. They should be open to reworking and reframing their problem definition as the search for solutions turns up new information. For example, many members of the steering committee for the African American Men Project initially framed the problems affecting a large number of African American men in Hennepin County as a case of "social injustice." As they began considering the goals of a diverse array of key stakeholders, they realized that many of these stakeholders were unlikely to support solutions aimed solely or mainly at remedying injustice. As Gary Cunningham has noted, "We realized we were asking the wrong question." The question was not how to help African American men who were struggling against economic odds and institutionalized racism, but how to help African American men help themselves, and how to convince other stakeholders to do things that were in their self-interest and the interest of African American men.

Policy entrepreneurs develop a conceptual framework for the story that the advocacy coalition tells about the significance of the problem, its causes, and the pathway to change. In the AAMP case, the conceptual framework was "What's good for African American men is good for Hennepin County." The framework is helpful because it does not tie the advocacy coalition to a single solution; rather, it allows the members to embrace multiple solutions for a family of problems. A social-justice framework would have been divisive, because it all too easily evokes blame: classically, the majority population is blamed for being the oppressors and they in turn blame African American men for not succeeding. Linking benefits for African American men on the one hand and Hennepin County on the other hand sets up a different emotional dynamic. By asking, in effect, all groups in the county how they can help each other, this frame opens the way to more creative problem solving.

Identification of Solution Components

Policy entrepreneurs help supporters cast their net broadly to capture not only solutions already familiar to them but also solutions that have been tried elsewhere. Additionally, they seek innovative solutions, quite different from what has been tried before (Nutt, 2002), although innovation of this sort is typically a recombination of existing solutions (Kingdon, 1995). Every truly useful solution has to be tailored to particular circumstances (Nadler and Hibino, 1998). In practice, policy entrepreneurs help constituents find a set of solutions that include adaptation of familiar solutions, those implemented elsewhere, and innovation. A specific solution may be linked to a part of the overall problem and should be flexible enough to allow translation into a sellable proposal in the next phase. Kathleen Allen and Cynthia Cherrey (2000) recommend families of solutions that can foster systemic change.

Policy entrepreneurs should pay attention to the design of market, government, nonprofit, and community institutions that can implement and stabilize the desired changes (Brandl, 1998; Salamon, 1995; Kurland and Zeder, 2001; Weimer and Vining, 1999). They may need to develop agreement on the best use and combination of the three institutional types. For example, if the desired changes include public goods—services or products that no one can be excluded from consuming—government organizations should be involved in establishing mandates, incentives, resources, and accountability for producing those goods. This does not mean that a government agency itself has to provide the services or products. For example, governments around the world are increasingly contracting with businesses and nonprofit organizations to supply public services (Kettl, 2000). Overreliance on government control and provision of services can produce harmful effects (Scott, 1998). Overreliance on business solutions to public problems may allow profit seeking to trump the well-being of a community (Weimer and Vining, 1999). Because nonprofit organizations are so diverse (in terms of infrastructure, aims, and methods), public policy makers and managers might have trouble knowing how best to work with them and whether they are capable of delivering desired services or products (Salamon, 1995). Communities also can fail in serving public aims (Brandl, 1998).

Policy entrepreneurs may have to work hard in this phase to keep constituents from latching on to the first promising solution they encounter, a practice that Herbert Simon has called "satisficing" (Simon, 1957), or what is more commonly known as "jumping to solutions." To develop an effective family of solutions, policy entrepreneurs must sustain commitment to an expansive search strategy. Such a strategy brings benefits for the participants as they talk to people they would not ordinarily encounter, in places they would not ordinarily search. They expand their ability to communicate across boundaries, collect and synthesize information, and make considered judgments.

Efficient Use of Resources

A well-executed search makes sense even when resources are scarce, since it should ultimately save time and money through tapping existing knowledge, models, and expertise. Such a search may not be particularly cheap or quick, but it will find desirable solutions as efficiently as possible. It prevents the tendency of groups and organizations to engage in a simplistic, short, and shallow search for solutions to a problem in order to save time and money. A simplistic solution adopted in haste may be costly not just because it does a poor job of solving the problem but because it spawns unanticipated problems (Nutt, 2002). The presumed efficiency of a cheap and quick search is therefore likely to be ephemeral. For example, the Bush administration had a "solution" to Al Qaeda-backed terrorism after the tragic events of September 11, 2001, which was to invade Afghanistan a month later (where there was a real connection to this terrorism) and to invade Iraq in March 2003 (where there was little or no connection). Unfortunately, although the United States and its allies carefully planned the invasion of Iraq, they did not carefully plan what they would do after they won. In fact, they hardly planned at all for what would happen after victory, which meant the coalition moved "blind into Baghdad" (Fallows, 2004) and "botched the occupation" (Rieff, 2003). The real tragedy is that virtually all of the difficulties the coalition faced were easily known but ignored by the administration when it misdiagnosed the problem and blinded itself to important learning with a simplistic solution-search strategy.

Enhancement of Quality, Legitimacy, and Prestige

High-quality solutions are those that attack the causes of a problem, that have minimal adverse effects, and that produce widespread benefits at reasonable cost. Legitimate solutions pass legal and ethical tests. Solutions gain prestige through attachment to respected people, institutions, or processes. Policy entrepreneurs help constituents develop criteria for evaluating the quality, legitimacy, and prestige of proposed solutions. They organize forums in which stakeholders representing diverse interests can discuss and evaluate the solutions (Innes, 1996; Roberts, 1997; Margarum, 2002; Burby, 2003).

Placement of Issue on the Public Agenda

Policy entrepreneurs strive to reach an array of stakeholders through face-to-face forums as well as mass and special-interest media to convey the message that solutions exist or can be enacted to deal with an urgent and significant public problem. They hope to foster a sense among citizens that policy makers should at least consider those solutions. They may use polling data to demonstrate to policy makers that public demand for action is rising.

Expanded Advocacy Coalition

Forums convened to consider solutions in this phase (and associated media coverage) may attract new groups of stakeholders to become involved in the change effort. They may be drawn by the specific solutions being considered or by the overall sense that solutions exist to an urgent problem. Wise policy entrepreneurs find a way to help new members of the coalition become full partners in the coalition's work and ensure that old members stay on board. For example, the World Business Council on Sustainable Development launched a Young Managers Team to involve a younger generation of businesspeople in the effort to find solutions to environmental degradation. The first thirty-member team attended the 2002 Earth Summit, where they participated in a local service project and organized a dialogue with other young businesspeople, as well as representatives of government and nonprofit organizations. The WBCSD has published a report and produced a video about the team's experiences. Jan Hively ensures that new partners in the vital aging campaign receive information she collects at conferences and other sources, so they are up to date on related research and programs.

Leadership Guidelines

Policy entrepreneurs in this phase orchestrate a variety of forums that identify and evaluate potential solutions and create a public issue. They take a systems view and focus on institutional design. They make sure to bring the appropriate expertise to bear on the search for solutions. They help constituents assess solution components and continue paying attention to stakeholder interests and power bases. Finally, they help constituents construct and communicate a compelling vision of how solutions can be enacted to achieve widespread benefits.

This phase can be underdone or overdone. On the one hand, the entrepreneurial team may fail to search broadly enough for solution components, or fail to research and assess those components adequately. On the other hand, the team may keep searching too long for a perfect solution as problems worsen, casualties mount, and the advocacy unravels. The team may have to settle for a good-enough solution. It should focus energy on areas of uncertainty, such as stakeholder views or the consequences of adopting solution components. Search guidelines should be tailored to the specific situation and available resources. No matter what, the team should undertake a search strategy that pushes outside normal search channels, makes efficient use of people's time and existing knowledge sources, and increases the perceived legitimacy of the effort. In a complex situation, the search may be carried out by multiple work groups overseen by the entrepreneurial team and the coordinating committee. In a simple situation, the entrepreneurial team and coordinating committee can do their own research.

Orchestrating Forums and Managing Conflict

Policy entrepreneurs think carefully about which stakeholders to involve in particular forums. They should prevent experts from dominating the forums and be ready for increased conflict as more stakeholder groups are involved.

Create Forums to Consider Solutions

Update and use the participation planning matrix (Exercise 6.3) along with the problem statement from the previous phase to organize forums for considering solutions to the overall problem, as well as specific subproblems. As in previous phases, wise design and use of forums requires leadership by indirection—that is, managing the ideas, rules, modes, media, or methods governing the search process and those used to publicize its results. Forums are often a mix of participants in the advocacy coalition, potential members of the coalition, and stakeholders with specialized expertise about potential solutions.

Use Experts Sparingly

Be careful about relying too heavily on specialized experts, especially at the outset of this phase, since their involvement may cause premature closure around their preferred set of solutions.

Anticipate and Optimize Conflict

In the process of considering a range of solutions, the participants are likely to take up at least some that certain stakeholders view as radical and highly threatening. Controversy, of course, is not necessarily bad, since it can be used to focus attention on the problem, educate key actors and decision makers about the nature of the problem and its potential solutions, and place an issue on the public agenda. At the same time, the entrepreneurial team should avoid unnecessary controversy that may all too easily escalate to the point that compromise and mutual gain become impossible.

Remember that as more groups get involved in a forum, conflict over potential solutions is sure to increase. Take for example the efforts of public health officials in the mid-1980s to put together a blood-testing program to detect the presence of an AIDS antibody in blood donors. The blood bank industry welcomed such a program because it would enable them to allay growing fears that the nation's blood supply was spreading the virus. Some scientists, however, argued that the proposed test could still miss a significant number of carriers of the virus. Gay rights advocates, meanwhile, worried that the test results could be used by employers, insurers, and government agencies to discriminate against gay men. Even after Mervyn Silverman (as head of the U.S. Conference of Local Health Officers) put together a proposal that guaranteed confidentiality of test results, officials at the U.S. Food and Drug Administration still resisted creation of the testing program, mainly on budgetary grounds (Shilts, 1988).

Taking a Systems View and Focusing on Institutional Design

To help constituents craft the most promising solutions, policy entrepreneurs insist on thinking about systems and institutions. They seek to tap stakeholders' self-interest to ease the institutionalization of change.

Use Feedback Loops

First, to increase the chances that the solution search will get at interrelated problems, seek what Allen and Cherrey (2000) call families of solutions with abundant feedback loops. The loops should reinforce positive change, balance tendencies to reinstitute the previous status quo or produce new problems, and keep the system flexible. Such systems should make changes self-sustaining, not easily dislodged, diverted, or diminished. Peter Senge (1994) recommends identifying points of high leverage. Use oval mapping (Resource B) and future search (Resource E) to help encourage a systems view. These methods get the main participants in a system together so they can take each other's views into account and discover how elements of problem and solutions are linked.

The organizers of the Vital Aging Network have taken a systems approach by pursuing solutions, such as the Advocacy Leadership Certificate Program and the VAN Website, that are linked by their promise for empowering older adults (and their supporters) to make changes in employment, education, and health care systems.

Pay Attention to Institutional Design

In other words, consider how institutions such as schools, churches, markets, government agencies, and nonprofit service organizations should be designed in order to achieve the outcomes you desire. A starting place might be consideration of government, market, nonprofit, and community successes and failures in relation to the problem. For example, the African American Men Project final report highlighted failures in public education, the criminal justice system, public assistance programs, and the labor market in assisting African American men to be productive citizens. It also mentioned several nonprofit, government, educational, and philanthropic programs that offer significant opportunities for these men.

Recognize that any comprehensive solution set undoubtedly involves government, business, and nonprofit organizations, as well as communities. Additionally, be aware that ideologies, or at least deep preferences, revolve around the proper role of government, business, nonprofits, and communities. For example, a group like the WBCSD, not surprisingly, prefers market-oriented solutions even though it supports government regulation when necessary.

Build on Self-Interest

Try to create a solution that taps into individuals' and organizations' self-interest so that the solution can be stabilized and institutionalized. An example is the U.S. constitutional system, which gains stability through separate institutions sharing power and responsibility, thus checking each other's untoward ambitions.

Bringing Expertise to Bear on the Solution Search

Policy entrepreneurs can reap the benefits of both broad and in-depth solution-search strategies by beginning with a broad scan and proceeding to intense exploration of the most promising solutions. The process outlined here does this in a way that enables an entrepreneurial team to identify and use the expertise of stakeholders with relevant ideas and experience.

Develop Solutions Methodically

Use a three-step process to ensure that the solutions identified in the oval-mapping and future-search exercises are developed further. The process allows your team to unearth a range of solution components and then narrow them down to feasible alternatives. The process is based principally on the work of Amitai Etzioni, Andrew Delbecq, Andrew Van de Ven, David Gustafson, and John Bryson (Etzioni, 1967, 1968; Delbecq, Van de Ven, and Gustafson, 1975; Bryson and Delbecq, 1981).

The process consists of three steps:

1. A broad scan within and outside normal search channels, to gain an understanding of the possible territory within which solutions might be found
2. A narrow-gauge search within the most promising territories, to find specific solution components likely to be effective, ethical, and acceptable to key stakeholders
3. Detailed exploration of identified solution components

In step one, participants identify potential sources of broad conceptualizers and then select the conceptualizers themselves—the cosmopolitans who have an extensive grasp of the knowledge sources likely to yield solutions to the problem at hand. The most effective way to begin is to solicit nominations of information categories through structured or unstructured individual or group processes. For example, to get category suggestions, participants may hold extensive conversation with several people who seem to be plugged in to relevant networks. At a follow-up working session, participants can use their notes from these conversations to generate candidate categories that can be recorded on snowcards and grouped into columns by subject. (You can use a modification of the snowcard exercise in Exercise 3.1.) The column subject labels can then be the main search categories. They may include specific disciplines or skills, relevant professional organizations, other advocacy groups, appropriate technical assistance services, research services, and potential funding sources.

Once the categories have been identified, structured interview procedures or focus groups can be used to search within categories for further information. Interviews might be conducted over the telephone, in person, or via e-mail. A standard set of questions and standard method of recording answers should be used. Interviewees and focus group participants should be asked to identify names of knowledgeable people; books, reports, articles, and other documentation; relevant models or frameworks; and relevant projects or ongoing research.

The second step is to bring together information from the interviews or focus groups to determine the most promising areas for the narrow-gauge search. Go through the raw material, summarize key points, and engage in thorough (perhaps facilitated) discussion. Once these search areas are selected, familiarize yourselves with them; learn about the territory and the tribes, factions, unifiers and dividers, customs, practices, knowledge bases, worldviews, and stories to be encountered in the territory. This orientation may be gained through interviewing ten to twelve knowledgeable people identified in the broad-gauge search. After orienting yourself, organize a forum in which key stakeholders use a structured group process—such as brainstorming, the snowcard technique, or the delphi technique (sequential surveys designed to elicit areas of consensus, typically among experts)—to accomplish several objectives:

- Identify possible solution components
- Furnish resources to make the components workable (for example, technical assistance, a grant program, an industry association, or training program)
- Offer potential resources (via new legislation, new foundation funding, new for-profit endeavors, and so on)

See Exercise 8.1.

Be sure that the voices of all knowledgeable people are heard, not just those of respected professional experts or political figures. You can convene a separate forum or use a method of balancing power, such as holding a caucus in which a less-powerful group prepares a presentation for a plenary session, or ensuring visible experts and politicians are a minority in a particular forum.

If you convene a forum of experts, be sure to go over the purpose of the forum and where it fits in the change process. Make it clear that many other knowledgeable people are involved in finding and analyzing solutions. Offer the experts time for networking among themselves, since this may be a prime reason they agree to attend the forum. Be prepared to keep the experts on track through strong process facilitation. They are likely at the outset of a working session

---

Exercise 8.1. Undertaking a Solution Search Within Specified Areas.

Once your entrepreneurial team has selected an area (for example, "community building") in which to search for solutions to a problem, you can use this exercise to identify solution components.

1. Brainstorm possible solution components, beginning each with a verb (in the case of community building, examples might be "start a neighborhood association," or "organize block clubs," or "involve churches").
2. For each solution component, prepare a flipchart sheet with the solution component at the top. Divide the remainder of the sheet into two columns; label one "Resources Available to Make This Workable" and the other "Potential Resources."
3. Fill out the sheets and discuss the results. Decide which solutions to explore further.

---

to expose their biases through short (or not-so-short) normative assertions as they announce and stake out their positions. Once they are allowed to do so, they can be expected to move fairly expeditiously to furnish information about solution components and resources.

The third step is to decide which of the solution components identified in step two merit in-depth exploration. Try to obtain firsthand knowledge of how the component might work. For example, if the solution is an existing program (or an adaptation), observe it in action. Use a structured group process to explore the strengths of each component, weaknesses, and modifications that would improve applicability or performance in the situation at hand. Useful structured processes are brainstorming, the snowcard technique, delphi technique, or force field analysis (which is based on a map of forces promoting change and forces resisting change; see Johnson and Johnson, 2003).

Paying Attention to Stakeholders

Remember that the solutions developed in this phase need to garner the support of an adequate number of key stakeholders. A prime method, of course, is involving them in any forum convened to consider solutions. Use two additional methods to better understand how solutions might tap into stakeholder interests and relationships: (1) diagrams linking individual stakeholder interests to the common good, and (2) stakeholder-issue relationship diagrams.

The first of the two, diagramming individual links to the common good, begins with the diagrams of bases of power and directions of interest along with the supra-interests diagram (Exercises 7.2 and 7.3) developed in the previous phase. Develop a new diagram for each stakeholder showing how the stakeholder's diagram of bases of power and directions of interest links to the supra-interests. Developing these diagrams is a kind of marketing research into how policies need to be found, tailored, and sold (Andreasen, 1995; Kotler, Roberto, and Lee, 2002). The research is designed to understand the audiences well enough both to satisfy their interests and to advance the common good. Effective one-way and two-way communication strategies may be created through developing and testing out these diagrams with key informants in the target audience.

In addition to diagramming the links between each stakeholder's interests and the common good (or supra-interests) diagram, teams may construct stakeholder-issue interrelationship diagrams to indicate which stakeholders have an interest in which issues, and how the stakeholders might be related to others through their relationship with the issues (see Figure 8.1). The resulting diagrams help impose some important structuring on the problem area, in which a number of actual or potential areas for cooperation (or conflict) may become apparent. An arrow on the diagram indicates that a stakeholder has an interest in an issue, though the specific interest is likely to dif-

Figure 8.1. Stakeholder-Issue Interrelationship Diagram.

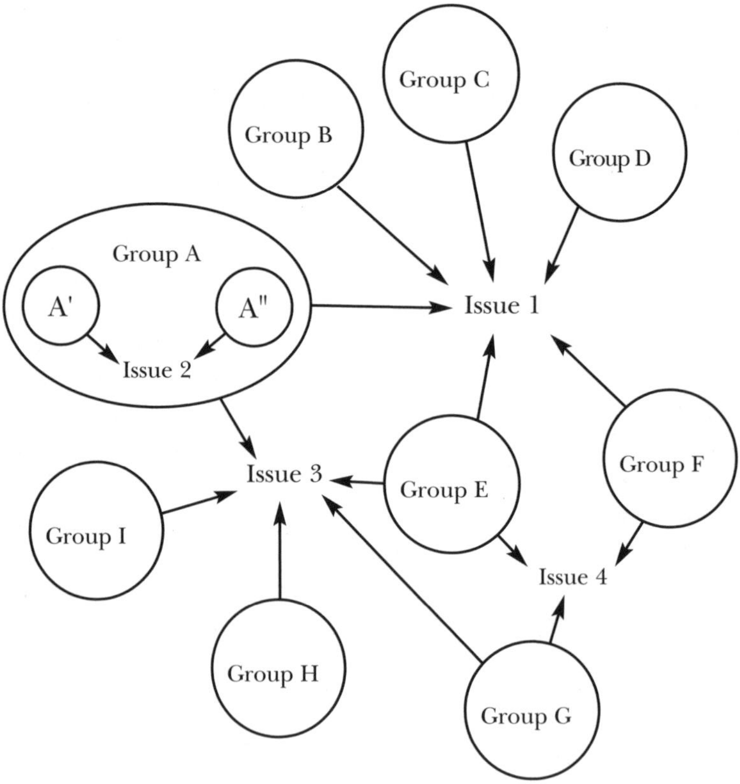

Source: Adapted from Bryant (2003), pp. 196, 264.

fer from one stakeholder to another, and the interests may well be in conflict. The arrows therefore should be labeled to indicate exactly what the interest is in each case. In Figure 8.1, stakeholders A, B, C, D, E, and F all have an interest, or stake, in issue one, while subgroups of stakeholder A have a further issue dividing them, issue two. Stakeholder A is also related to stakeholder E through their joint relationship to issue three, and to the other stakeholders on the map through their connection with issue three. In an actual case, the arrows should be labeled, so it is clear exactly what the interests are, and whether they are in conflict. Exercise 8.2 guides you through structuring a stakeholder-issue relationship diagram.

Assessing Solutions

First, take plenty of time to evaluate the technical and administrative feasibility, legality, political acceptability, and ethical implications of potential solution components. The first step is developing

Exercise 8.2. Constructing a
Stakeholder-Issue Interrelationship Diagram.

1. Start with a power-versus-interest grid and stakeholder influence diagram, and perhaps with the basic stakeholder analysis technique.
2. Tape four flipchart sheets to a wall to form a single surface two sheets high and two sheets wide.
3. Team members should brainstorm the names of stakeholders by writing names as they come to mind on a 1.5 in. × 2 in. (2.5 cm × 5 cm) self-adhesive label, one stakeholder per label. Alternatively, the names may be taken from one of the previous analyses.
4. The team also should brainstorm issues that appear to be connected to the problem concerning them. These are also placed on self-adhesive labels, preferably of another color.
5. The issues are placed on the flipchart surface, and stakeholders are arrayed around the issues. A given stakeholder may be involved in more than one issue.
6. Arrows should be drawn to indicate which stakeholders have a stake in which issues; the content of each arrow—that is, the stake or interest involved—should be identified.

A thorough discussion of each issue, stakeholder, and arrow should occur, and any implications for framing or reframing issues and management of stakeholder relationships should be noted.

evaluation criteria for each of these considerations. The second is assessing each solution component against the criteria. A thorough assessment of each component—using sound evidence—helps you decide which components should be built into a formal proposal in the next phase of the policy change cycle.

Select Evaluation Criteria

Your team can use Exercise 8.3 to choose the criteria for assessing solution components.

Criteria related to technical and administrative feasibility may include:

- High likelihood that the solution attacks the causes of the problem concerning us.
- Resources are available for implementing this solution.
- The technology (computer software, group process skills, transportation systems, administrative structures and processes, and so forth) for implementing the solution is available or easily constructed.
- High likelihood that the solution will produce desired results.
- Low likelihood that the solution will cause worse problems than the one it is designed to solve.
- High likelihood that the solution is sustainable over the long haul.

Here are possible criteria related to legality:

- Good fit with existing laws, from local to national
- Unlikely to violate human rights
- Accordance with provisions of a constitution or international treaty

These criteria are related to political acceptability:

- Good fit with the supra-interests identified in stakeholder analysis.
- Emotional or symbolic response to the solution likely to be neutral or positive among the majority of key stakeholders.
- Policy arguments and strategies can be constructed to develop support for the solution among key stakeholders and diminish the power of antagonistic stakeholders.

Exercise 8.3. Using a Multicriteria Assessment Grid.

A multicriteria assessment grid works well when you need to decide which of several options is the best choice for your purposes. You list the criteria that an option ideally should meet and then compare your options to the criteria. You choose the option that, on balance, does the best job against the criteria.

Try to have five to nine criteria. More criteria make the process too cumbersome and fewer criteria give you fewer data from which to make a choice.

Drawing a grid makes it easy to compare each option to all the criteria and to document group judgments. It is also easy to see which option meets the most criteria, so the best choice can be made.

How It Works

1. First, list your criteria. You may need to do some brainstorming initially to come up with candidate criteria. You might also consider using the snowcard technique to identify criteria.

2. Make a grid on a large sheet of paper or a flipchart. List the criteria across the top, and draw a vertical column under each. Make a "Total" column along the right-hand edge of the paper. List the options down the left side, and draw a horizontal row beside each.

3. Take one option at a time and compare it to each criterion.

   • If it meets the criterion, make a plus sign (+) in the box where the columns meet.
   • If it doesn't meet the criterion, put a minus sign (–) in the box.

   Once you've compared all the criteria, count the total pluses you marked for the option and write the number in the Total column.

4. Go on to the next option and repeat the process.

5. The option with the greatest number of pluses is probably the best option. If two or three tie, see if you can use them all, either in combination or by creating an entirely new option. This process often results in a new option that may be better than those in the original list. For example, the new option might maximize plus signs and minimize minus signs.

6. Alternatively, you might give each option a score against each criterion using a scale of 1 to 5, where 1 is very poor and 5 is excellent. For each option, add up the scores against each criterion to get a total score. The option with the highest score is probably your best option.

Source: Adapted from Kearny (1995).

- Good reason to believe a powerful, winning coalition can be formed to support the solution.

Criteria related to ethical implications may include these:

- High likelihood that the solution will improve individual lives
- High likelihood that the solution will undo a system of oppression
- High likelihood that the solution will strengthen the community
- High likelihood that the solution will benefit future generations
- High likelihood that the solution will benefit the global ecosystem
- Low likelihood that the solution will produce irreparable damage or irremediable harm to some stakeholders

Amass Evidence for Evaluation

Second, decide how much time and money to put into developing evidence that can be used to assess solution options against these criteria. Consider constructing "logic models" (Millar, Simeone, and Carnevale, 2001; Poister, 2003), which clearly articulate the presumed connection among solution inputs, processes, outputs, and outcomes (short-term, intermediate, and long-term) to help figure out what evidence is necessary in determining whether or not the logic actually holds.

For example, sophisticated computer modeling may be helpful in determining which options are most likely to produce desired outcomes, but you may have resources to develop only a fairly simple systems model on the basis of the data you have gathered. At the same time, if the consequences of choosing a poor option are going to be serious, you should strive to find the time and money for thorough analysis. Military planners in the Bush administration considered a variety of solutions in 2002 for removing Saddam Hussein from power. The option they selected—armed invasion of Iraq—resulted in a fairly quick military victory but produced additional problems for which they were ill-prepared. In this case, the consequences of not thinking through a variety of scenarios for the aftermath of war were high indeed (Rieff, 2003; Fallows, 2004).

Stafford Beer offers a compelling argument for using computer simulations to test policies: "This is to take an experimental approach to policy making, doing the experiments in the laboratory of the control room. So instead of experimenting on the poor old nation, and discovering ten years later that your policy was wrong, you can test and discard a dozen wrong policies by lunchtime without hurting anyone. After lunch maybe you will find a good policy" (1974, p. 45).

Of course, not everything can be turned into a computerized simulation. Another approach is developing action scenarios (Myers and Kitsuse, 2000; Van der Heijden and others, 2002), in which you rehearse the implications of implementing solutions. Rehearsal allows you to avoid really stupid mistakes and fine-tune solutions so they have a greater chance of success. It also keeps you from being blindsided by things that should be apparent but only become obvious after thinking through a chain of events.

There are no magic formulas for the right mix of solutions, especially what should be done by government, business, and nonprofits. Political scientist Don Kettl (2000) describes a worldwide trend of depending on government for policy making and a few core functions while farming out more and more service delivery and decision making to nonprofits, businesses, and individuals. Carol Lewis (1991) has developed an ethical analysis grid to reveal when government remedies are justified. Use of the grid helps fulfill both deontological (duty-based) and teleological (results-oriented) obligations. Results of the analysis should indicate which proposals or options for a government remedy should be eliminated or altered on ethical grounds. A somewhat modified version of the grid she proposes is found in Figure 8.2. The process for using the grid is simply to fill it out as a team and discuss the results. It may be wise to involve others in this discussion as well. In general, Lewis's admonition is to pursue the common good *and* avoid doing harm.

You may well decide that a formal collaboration among businesses, government, and nonprofits should be established to carry out some of the solutions you are considering. If formal collaboration becomes a part of the solution set, be sure to consider the transaction costs of establishing and maintaining it in your evaluation of its usefulness. (Chapter Eleven offers more guidance about managing formal collaboration.)

Figure 8.2. Ethical Analysis Grid.

Stakeholder Name and Category	Description of Stake:			
(check one)				
Internal stakeholder				
External stakeholder indirectly affected by the proposed policy change				
External stakeholder indirectly affected by the proposed policy change				
Factors and Score:	High (3)	Medium (2)	Low (1)	None (0)
Dependency of stakeholder on government (e.g., inaccessible alternative services)				
Vulnerability of stakeholder (e.g., potential injury)				
Gravity (versus triviality) of stakeholder's stake				
Likelihood remedy or relief will be unavailable				
Risk to fundamental value, such as freedom of choice, liberty, due process, etc.				
Overall negative impact of policy on stakeholder				
Total scores—Do they indicate obligatory action or relief?				

Source: Adapted from Lewis (1991), p. 122.

Don't forget that art can be part of the solution set. Fiction, film, sculpture, music, drama, and documentaries all have the power to assist and enact a new way of dealing with a public problem. The AIDS quilt that toured the United States for many years comes to mind, as do the growing number of feature films depicting the romantic lives of older adults.

Constructing and Communicating a Compelling Vision

All your research and evaluation may come to naught unless you develop a compelling vision that helps people see what a better future will be like and how to get there. We offer four suggestions for doing this.

First, remember that a compelling public vision is essentially a communal story that links past, present, and future. It helps community members think about what should be preserved and what should be created. It illuminates public problems and their causes, while projecting feasible and inspiring means of achieving solutions that can produce a better collective future. You can use such methods as future search and scenario building to develop a vision—a convincing story of why and how policy change should be enacted. Ideally, the story helps policy makers feel compelled to act on the issue and advance the common good.

Second, ensure that the vision incorporates:

- Strong images of the past, present, and future
- Empirical information (forecasts, surveys, and models) that tie the images together (Myers and Kitsuse, 2000)

The storyline of the vision should be consistent, testable, and actionable, and lead to "a morally acceptable position." Additionally, it should be beautiful—that is, full of "grace, subtlety, elegance, or interest" (Schön and Rein, 1994, pp. 4–5). Even in informal communication, Jan Hively offers such a storyline. For example, in an e-mail message to one of us, she wrote about the problem of ageism and the need for revolutionary changes:

> What's an example of ageism? The Census Bureau and all state planning agencies label all people under the age of 16 and over

the age of 65 as dependents! Even the Project 2030 Report shows
how the "Ratio of Dependency" will increase with the aging of the
population. The entire system of public services for older adults is
focused on providing health and human services to meet the needs
of the frail elderly. There is an increasing need for those services,
because of the increased longevity of the overall population, but
the fact is that over 75% of older adults report that they are healthy
and active up into their 80s. Their productivity and contributions
are limited, however, by the ageism of our culture—reflected in
their expectations for themselves, their children's expectations
for them, and the barriers set up by public and private institutions
based on societal expectations (timing of retirement packages,
organizational frameworks for volunteering, care facilities that
cultivate dependency, seniors-only retirement communities,
etc.) . . . We are seeking a revolution. The task is to shift from a
needs-based system to a strengths-based system—encouraging
vital involvement through to the last breath (Hively, personal
communication, July 2003).

This message is a good example of using just enough data to back
up one's assertions but not enough to overshadow the passion behind them.

Third, disseminate the vision through various media: reports,
speeches, books, CDs, videotapes, Websites, news coverage, posters,
performances, and other art. You might make a compilation of research data available separately, as in the AAMP. As they make
speeches, hold press conferences, and participate in debates and
discussion, members of your coalition also act as exemplars. Thus
the members of the WBCSD present themselves as the eco-efficient
businesspeople they hope will be the wave of the future. African
American men who are spreading the word about the AAMP are
examples of the African American community's contribution to
government, business, and nonprofit organizations in Hennepin
County. Several founders of the Vital Aging Network are models of
productive older adults.

A report or book outlining the vision and presenting supporting examples and other evidence is often a useful foundation for
the dissemination strategy. One or more drafts of the report should
be prepared for review by the entrepreneurial team, coordinating

committee, and other stakeholders. The report should include the vision elements noted earlier, as well as:

- The conceptual framework that links the public problem and its potential solutions
- Identification and exploration of solution components
- Existing or potential funding sources
- Recommendations for further action

The reviewers should be asked to do a SWiM analysis—that is, identify strengths, weaknesses, and modifications that would improve the report. Reviews should be extensive if the issue presented in the report is technically and politically complicated. In this case, the report should also include assurances that the solution search has been careful and rational.

Fourth, prepare a public relations and education strategy for disseminating the report. The strategy should be geared to placing and keeping the team's issue on the public agenda. Sample strategy objectives:

- Making various audiences aware that forums will be held to discuss solutions.
- Reporting on forums in which the report is discussed.
- Floating a "trial balloon" to raise consciousness of the issue and ascertain what kind of solution is likely to garner necessary support (Benveniste, 1989). A trial balloon can also stake out an extreme position in order to discover which modifications are most important to stakeholders.
- Showing how solutions will alleviate the problem and promote a better society.
- Responding to outcry from opponents who view the proposed solutions as threatening or wrong-headed.

Summary

In the search-for-solutions phase of the policy change cycle, the entrepreneurial team undertakes both broad and narrow-gauge exploration of potential solutions to the public problem defined in the previous phase. The team helps its advocacy coalition develop criteria for assessing the technical and administrative feasibility, legality, political acceptability, and ethical implications of solution components. The team emphasizes the usefulness of selecting a widely supported family of solutions that can bring strong leverage for systemic change. In particular, these policy entrepreneurs pay attention to how institutions such as schools, churches, government agencies, and nonprofit organizations should be designed or redesigned to help stabilize policy change.

Throughout this phase, policy entrepreneurs seek, through the wise design and use of forums, to raise public awareness of the problem and promising solutions. The entrepreneurs aim to expand the advocacy coalition and turn the problem into an issue— a problem connected to at least one solution that has pros and cons from the viewpoint of various stakeholders. They offer a conceptual framework for understanding the issue and develop a compelling vision to prompt enthusiasm and hope for change. Finally, they want to ensure that relevant policy makers in legislative, executive, and administrative arenas are aware of a growing demand for their attention to the issue so that they will be receptive to the specific policy proposals to be developed in the next phase.

Chapter Nine

Developing a Proposal That Can Win in Arenas

Only those policies that are widely perceived as doing both "what's right" and "what will work" will cross untroubled political waters.
DAVID ROCHEFORT AND ROGER COBB

In the policy-formulation phase, policy entrepreneurs shift their attention to formal arenas, even as they make continued use of forums and informal arenas. They make an extensive effort in forums to ensure that the solutions endorsed by their coalition in the previous phase are translated into specific policy proposals that can win approval from decision makers in formal executive, legislative, and administrative arenas. Policy entrepreneurs in this phase must combine commitment to their core ideas with the flexibility required to expand their coalition and gain the vote of policy makers.

Purpose and Desired Outcomes

The chief goal of policy entrepreneurs in this phase is to create one or more formal proposals that embody technically and administratively workable, politically acceptable, and legally and ethically defensible responses to the public issue articulated in the previous phase. The entrepreneurial team needs to exercise political leadership, along with visionary leadership, to develop the proposals and expand coalitions of support that will increase the chances that good policies or plans are ultimately adopted and implemented.

The desired outcomes of this phase include:

- A draft policy or plan (or more likely more than one) for review by official decision makers in the next phase
- A revised proposal draft incorporating constructive modifications, prompted by stakeholder interests and concerns
- Identification of necessary resources for implementing the proposal once it is adopted
- Clear indication that the necessary coalition exists to ensure adoption and implementation of the proposal
- Shared belief among involved parties that the policy change achieves their mutual goals and is a mutual endeavor

Draft Policies and Plans

In drafting a policy or plan for consideration in a formal arena, the entrepreneurial team must constantly keep in mind which arenas are likely to have not only jurisdiction over the proposed policy change but also the most favorable political dynamics: supportive people in key positions, decision making procedures that maximize the coalition's clout, and access rules that allow coalition members to be influential. The team should seek to tailor the policies and plans to the specific arenas considering them. For example, as Hively and her partners sought funding from the University of Minnesota for the Vital Aging Network, they were careful to include in their proposal evidence of how the network would fulfill the research, teaching, and service missions of the university. The steering committee of the African American Men Project, in presenting its report and recommendations to the Hennepin County Board of Commissioners, gave credit to Commissioner Stenglein for inspiring the project and acknowledged the support of the entire board. The report outlined specific steps that county government should take "to support the mutual success of young African American men and other stakeholders" (Hennepin County, 2002, p. 10). It also avoided putting the sole burden on county government by emphasizing the steps that other stakeholders—the men themselves, other government bodies, businesses, churches, nonprofits—need to take. By linking the success of young African American men to the well-being of Hennepin County, the report also appealed to the commissioners' sense of responsibility for the county as a whole.

Incorporation of Constructive Modifications

The entrepreneurial team should organize review sessions involving key stakeholders to improve the technical and administrative quality, legality, and political and ethical acceptability of the solutions developed in the previous phase. The focus on details, however, should not be overdone. The proposal must allow flexibility and adaptation during implementation, especially in the face of unforeseen difficulties.

Remember that an issue with the greatest potential benefit for key stakeholders is the one most likely to win a place on the policy makers' agenda, and the response that is most likely to be considered is the one with the least cost for key stakeholders (Light, 1991). Thus Schmidheiny and his colleagues at the World Business Council for Sustainable Development, in their campaign to persuade business policy makers to adopt sustainable development practices, deemphasize government regulation (often viewed as a costly headache for business). Instead, they highlight, for example, the possible return on investment resulting from more energy-efficient processes. The U.S. health professionals who tried in the early 1980s to convince public officials to allocate funding and staff to fight the growing AIDS epidemic emphasized the far greater costs that would occur if the epidemic were allowed to spread unchecked.

In effect, the entrepreneurial team uses the review sessions to prepare its entrepreneurial idea to compete in the political marketplace (Krieger, 1996). The team understands that the proposal will be competing with many others, and it must fit with decision makers' desires to please key stakeholders and advance their own agenda. At the same time, the team should be sure that the entrepreneurial idea remains at the core of whatever final proposal is produced.

Careful review sessions also help ensure that a draft proposal incorporates constructive, motivational symbols and avoids offensive or threatening symbolism. Careful attention to stakeholder goals and concerns helps reduce hostility and embarrassment in the formal proposal review and adoption phase. For example, in making proposals for change the World Business Council uses phrases such as eco-efficiency and "the business case for sustainable development." Instead of talking about charity projects for poor countries, the council talks about nurturing "sustainable livelihoods" in those countries.

Identification of Necessary Resources

Decision makers understandably want evidence that the supporters of policy change have thought through the staffing, equipment, transportation, supplies, and other costs of implementing the change. Policy entrepreneurs must specify those costs and indicate how much they are asking the decision makers to cover. They have to make a plausible case that other sources are going to provide the additional needed resources.

Necessary Coalition

As solutions are translated into specific proposals, policy entrepreneurs need to keep coalition members on board even if they do not like some part of a proposal. If the entrepreneurial team has worked astutely in previous phases to organize a coalition around the idea of doing something about a problem in a certain direction, rather than around specific strategies, the team should be able to retain the support of existing coalition members and attract new people to the coalition. In the AAMP, some coalition members felt, on social justice grounds, that much more public funding should flow to poor neighborhoods in Minneapolis. The steering committee's recommendations, however, put greater emphasis on using public dollars effectively and leveraging resources from nongovernment stakeholders.

The members of the entrepreneurial team may need to think through what an optimal coalition is in their case. The political science literature on policy adoption tends to emphasize the idea of a *minimum* winning coalition, since creating a larger coalition is likely to entail having to make so many concessions or trades that the proposal gets watered down to the point where it cannot achieve the original purpose (Riker, 1962, 1986). On the other hand, the literature on collaborative planning argues that a larger coalition should be pursued, since sustained implementation requires broad support and the minimum winning coalition may not do that (Margarum, 2003; Bryant, 2003). In other words, the team may have to ponder the connections between winning in the short run and winning in the long run.

Shared Belief That the Policy Change Is a Mutual Endeavor

As coalition members prepare for the tough work of championing a proposal in a formal arena, their resolve will be strengthened if they feel they helped craft the proposal. When they are involved, their sense of ownership is strong and they are knowledgeable about proposal content. In addition to holding face-to-face review sessions, policy entrepreneurs can set up an e-mail distribution list for information and solicitation of feedback on the latest proposal drafts.

Characteristics of a "Winning" Proposal

A winning proposal is not simply one that can win enough votes in a policy-making body but also one that, once implemented, actually helps remedy a public problem in a way that is just, economically efficient, and respectful of the rightful liberties of affected parties. Policy entrepreneurs should always keep in mind that a proposal that is easily adoptable may not be easily implementable. In effect, the adoption process plays out at two levels: the higher decision-making level, which is about getting a proposal on the formal agenda of policy makers and winning their approval of the proposal; and the middle decision-making level, where local officials, administrators, and managers decide how to interpret the approved policies and how to apply them. Indeed, policy makers may take the easy way out as they try to please clamoring constituents; they may pass a new law, or adopt a policy, but furnish few or no resources for implementation. The mandaters then claim victory, while the mandated cry foul (Grossback, 2002). Policy entrepreneurs therefore must ensure that their favored proposal is both adoptable *and* implementable.

A number of proposal characteristics can enhance the chance of executive, legislative, and administrative decision makers adopting and implementing a desired change:

- *Formal linkage of problems and solutions.* Attention to the public problem that first galvanized action may fade in this phase, as stakeholders debate the specifics of preferred solutions. Formal proposals should emphasize the link between solution components and an actual problem that needs solving.

- *Congruence with values held by key decision makers and other stakeholders.* Policy entrepreneurs should remember that the majority of the public, and even many decision makers, will judge the proposal mainly by its symbolic qualities (by the values and symbols associated with it). Thus how the proposal frames the public issue is vital. Values vary considerably from situation to situation, but equity, efficiency, and congruity with widely held interpretive schemes are likely to matter. Consequently, the proposal should be overtly presented as fair, resource-optimizing, and a promising vehicle for reaching a widely desired state such as "the good community" and avoiding a feared or disliked outcome such as communal instability.

- *Anticipated user or implementer support and public acquiescence.* The proposal should include evidence that proposed changes have the support of key stakeholders and that citizens generally will go along with the changes. Decision makers will be less worried about the political fallout of adopting the proposal. Policy makers are likely to be interested in the assessment of people who would be expected to administer the proposed policies, since the ultimate effectiveness has a lot to do with their administrative feasibility.

- *Clear indication that the proposal is coming from competent sources.* The decision makers' reputation, prestige, and prospects for advancement are linked to their ability to make wise judgments about possible courses of action (Neustadt, 1990). Thus decision makers are unlikely to embrace proposals championed by people they perceive to be incompetent or insufficiently skilled.

- *Local adaptation of key solution components identified in the previous phase.* The proposal should include clear evidence that proposed solution components have been tailored to the interest of the decision makers and their constituents.

- *High technical feasibility and quality.* Decision makers are likely to search for assurance that proposals are technically sound. If changes ultimately fail on technical grounds, decision makers may be able to blame technical specialists involved with the proposal's development or implementation, but they may also be blamed themselves. Meanwhile, opponents of the proposal may attack the proposal on technical grounds; thus supporters need to offer as much evidence as possible that the proposed methods and tools are likely to function well. One way to develop a defense against attack on technical or administrative grounds is to develop a logic model in advance that clearly articulates the logic connecting inputs, processes, outputs, and outcomes (Millar, Simeone, and Carnevale, 2001; Poister, 2003). Friendly allies and critics should be asked to challenge the model and suggest improvements. A strong logic model can then be used to sell the proposal (McLoughlin and Jordan, 1999).

- *Discussion of a set of alternatives.* Decision makers are wary of being trapped by advocates, planners, and technical experts. Including a set of alternatives in the proposal, along with an outline of their comparative strengths and weaknesses, indicates that decision makers are not being manipulated and gives them the chance to improve the proposal.

- *Indication of a highly favorable cost-benefit ratio for one or more alternatives.* Since decision makers are responsible to constituents for stewardship of resources, they will seek evidence that at least one of the proposed alternatives produces benefits that significantly outweigh costs.

- *Inclusion of budgetary materials and attention to budgetary concerns.* A proposed policy, project, program, or procedure may seem unreal to decision makers until it is attached to a budget. Policy entrepreneurs should ensure that their proposals include at least a tentative budget. Including general spending categories, rather than a highly detailed budget, may be best so that debate doesn't get bogged down in details and so that implementers have flexibility. If possible, budgets should include extra resources, since implementers need some budgetary leeway and since policy makers are likely to cut the requested amount.

- *Recommendation of administratively simple solutions.* As the complexity of administering a solution increases, the more likely the solution will fail (Pressman and Wildavsky, 1973). Administrators are prone to balk at adding complicated new policies, programs, or projects to their responsibilities, especially if the addition requires extensive staff retraining. Decision makers look for evidence that proposed changes will be relatively simple to administer.

Again, you can use a well-articulated logic model to show how inputs, processes (especially administrative processes), outputs, and outcomes fit together in a way that is administratively sound and workable.

• *Indications of flexibility in implementation.* Decision makers are likely to prefer solutions that can be adapted to situations and unforeseen developments and thus are more likely to actually work. Staged implementation is one method for increasing the flexibility of adopted solutions, because it facilitates learning, minimizes risk, and smoothes out resource requirements over time.

• *Guidance for implementation and evaluation.* Providing thoughtful guidance for implementation is another way of making a proposed policy, program, project, or method real in the eyes of decision makers. This also helps ensure that implementation honors the spirit of a proposal once it's adopted. Decision makers also want to know how the effectiveness of a solution will be judged in practice. Evaluation should be designed to assess whether desired results are occurring and resources are well managed. They should also be timed to allow for midcourse correction in the policy, program, project, or method being implemented.

• *Provision of adequate resources and incentives.* Savvy policy makers know that successful programs require adequate resources and incentives. Thus, proposals should generally describe what resources are needed and how they can be obtained. In crafting these proposals, policy entrepreneurs should demonstrate awareness of the decision makers' resource constraints. The proposal should also specify incentives that prompt stakeholders to comply with (or at least not undermine) proposed policies.

• *Appropriate format.* Arenas have varying requirements for the form of a proposal that they are to consider. For example, philanthropic foundations specify the contents of a grant proposal, and legislatures require a proposal to be in the form of a bill or resolution.

"Big Wins" and "Small Wins"

As the entrepreneurial team crafts its proposal, team members should think strategically about whether to pursue a big win (in which a set of solutions is implemented all at once in a visible campaign against a public problem) or a small win (in which adoption of a small-scale solution opens the door, or lays the groundwork, for a series of small victories unified by a common vision). Needless to say, small wins are more likely in a shared-power world than big wins.

Fear of major loss is a key reason most leaders shy away from attempting a big change. Instead, normal operating procedure for most organizations and organizational networks is "disjointed incrementalism" or "muddling through" (Lindblom, 1959). Incremental changes can be worthwhile, but unless they are part of a strategy of building toward a better future, they are not likely to accomplish much and may even cancel each other out (Lindblom, 1965).

A big-win strategy definitely has appeal. The prospect of a big win generates excitement and promises the satisfaction of visible, thorough triumph over a major problem (and over opponents who stand in the way). At the same time, an all-out effort to achieve a big win entails high risk; the entrepreneurial team that tries to win big can also fail big. Additionally, a highly visible big-win strategy is more likely than a small-win approach to attract the attention of opponents.

In general, policy entrepreneurs are well advised to pursue a small-win strategy that allows them to work toward major change without unacceptable risk. Karl Marx offers a helpful insight through his observation that change in degree leads to change in kind. If a series of small wins are informed by a strategic direction, the small wins can add up to a big win over time. Exercise 9.1 summarizes the difference between change in degree (small win) and change in kind (big win). A change in degree involves smooth, marginal progression in which the future is very much like the past. By contrast, a change in kind is abrupt, discontinuous, and transformational (Krieger, 1987, 1996). A change in degree assumes, and is measured against, a fixed background. By contrast, a change in kind is built on new coalitions and values. A change in degree requires little new learning and therefore is amenable to quantitative modeling, forecasting, and projection—activities that employ assumptions and data tied to the past. The sheer number of givens that must be assumed makes it unlikely that a future differing from the past will be created. By contrast, a change in kind involves qualitative models, new images, and new conceptualization. The future is invented rather than predicted.

Exercise 9.1. Pursuing a Big-Win or a Small-Win Strategy.

Big-win and small-win strategies have their own advantages and disadvantages. A series of small wins can accumulate to produce a big win, but in certain circumstances you probably should go for a big win.

A big win is a demonstrable, completed, large-scale victory.

- Advantages: policy problem and solutions thoroughly and immediately addressed
- Disadvantages: high risk of major defeat, especially because a big-win strategy may prompt intense opposition

A small win is an incremental success.

- Advantages: lower risk, possible demonstrable progress on which to build, empowering many participants, lower initial investment, allowing learning by doing, triggering resource flows
- Disadvantages: potential canceling-out effect, little momentum

To decide whether a big-win strategy should be pursued, answer these questions:

In the Current Situation:	Yes?	No?
The time is right.		
The dominant coalition supports the proposed solution.		
The solution technology is clearly understood and readily available.		
The solution will effectively address the problem.		
Resources are adequate and available.		
A clear vision guides the changes.		
A small-win strategy is undesirable or unworkable.		
Total *yes* and *no* answers		

Exercise 9.1. Pursuing a Big-Win or a Small-Win Strategy, Cont'd.

If there are six or more *yes* answers (out of seven), consider a big-win strategy. If there are fewer than six *yes* answers, seriously consider pursuing a small-win strategy.

Small wins can lead to a big win if:

- A well-articulated vision imparts a strong sense of direction.
- The overall game plan is in accordance with the vision, involves many stakeholders, can garner sufficient resources over time, and establishes milestones.
- Continuous experimentation is encouraged (for instance, through use of pilot and demonstration projects).
- Adaptation to local circumstances is possible.
- Frequent evaluation allows for learning and midcourse corrections.
- Rewards are offered for involvement and successes are publicized.

Changes in degree typically require small resource allocations and commitments, whereas changes in kind take major resources and commitments. The Kennedy administration's decision in 1961 to place a U.S. astronaut on the moon by the end of the decade would have been meaningless had not the administration and Congress committed themselves and a huge amount of resources to the decision.

Finally, a change in degree has relatively little impact, and management is charged with promoting and overseeing it. A big change typically has big impact, leadership is needed to make it happen, and the change champions are thought of as heroes and heroines. Managers of a small change receive a pat on the back; leaders of a big change receive a standing ovation and sometimes mention in the history books. Put differently, structures and systems are usually designed to produce only small changes; therefore real leadership is required to produce major change, in large part because the systems and structures themselves must be changed (Selznick, 1957; Burns, 1978, 2003).

Nevertheless, because a big win is much more difficult to achieve than a small win, policy entrepreneurs should consider how a series of small wins might be organized around a strategic direction to achieve the same effect as a big win without the concomitant risk of failure. A small-win strategy is often wise for additional reasons (Weick, 1984; Kouzes and Posner, 2002). A small win breaks a program or project into doable steps, quickly makes change real, and preserves gains. It is cheap and facilitates learning and adaptation by providing information and allowing rapid error detection and correction. It involves and empowers people, by encouraging participation, permitting immediate rewards, and boosting people's confidence and commitment.

Elements of a small-win strategy include:

• A vision that imparts direction for planning and decision making.

• An overall plan that breaks the change process down into manageable chunks.

• Continuous experimentation through, for example, pilot and demonstration projects. People should be encouraged to improvise on a general sense of direction so that the likelihood of accomplishment, learning, and reward is great (Cleveland, 2002).

• Positive incentives. The minimized personal cost of failure can help enroll people in a small-win initiative, but entrepreneurs should emphasize more positive incentives as well. Simply the availability of choice about whether to be involved, or in what way, can increase the attractiveness of the effort. Once people have committed publicly to one of the choices, they are likely to stay involved. Moreover, once the small win occurs, the choice is reinforced and people have an incentive to sign up for the next small-win campaign.

• Reliance on natural diffusion of innovation rather than on systemwide imposition of change. Policy entrepreneurs should let the benefits of change sell themselves as much as possible, and allow learning and local adaptation to occur. As changes spread, they become the accepted pattern, until relatively complete diffusion is achieved (Gladwell, 2000; Rogers, 2003).

Although the small-win strategy generally is advisable, it is not always best. In some cases, a small-win strategy is unworkable, or the problem is too urgent. U.S. physicians and other health professionals realized in the early 1980s that an all-out response to the emerging AIDS epidemic was urgently needed. They argued as forcefully as they could for a big-win strategy. They and other anti-

AIDS campaigners had to settle for small wins, which added up and eventually led to national anti-AIDS educational campaigns and substantial government funding of AIDS treatment and prevention programs.

Big-win strategies might also be pursued when the time is right—for example, when the need for action is obvious to a large coalition, the proposed solution effectively addresses the problem, solution technology is clearly understood and readily available, resources are adequate, or a clear vision is guiding the proposed changes. The Kyoto Protocol, supported by the WBCSD, is a good example of a big-win strategy to combat global warming. It commits signatory national governments to reduce greenhouse gas emissions by 5 percent, on the basis of 1990 levels, by 2012. The protocol was approved in 1997 by parties to the U.N. Framework Convention on Climate Change after years of growing scientific evidence that greenhouse gases were causing global warming. In *Walking the Talk,* Holliday, Schmidheiny, and Watts call the goal a modest one, but "a step in the right direction" (2002, p. 220). Unfortunately, the Kyoto Protocol has not been as big a win as its supporters hoped, since the United States has refused to ratify it. Even so, numerous major companies in the United States and elsewhere are proceeding with emission reduction programs that exceed the Kyoto controls, and Holliday, Schmidheiny, and Watts remain optimistic that the United States will eventually ratify. At the same time that WBCSD keeps trying for a big-win regarding climate change, the council continues to pursue small-win strategies at the local, national, regional, and industry levels.

Leadership Guidelines

The key to success in this phase is a focus on helping key decision makers say yes in the next phase, when the proposal must be adopted. Policy entrepreneurs must attend to the technical details and excellence of the proposal but also (and probably more important) must consider the interpretive schemes, goals, and concerns of key stakeholders. Simply being right about technical and administrative feasibility is not enough. A proposal must be comprehensible to key stakeholders and deemed to be in their self-interest. Attention to official decision makers is especially important, because unless they support the proposal it is unlikely to be placed on the decision agenda in the relevant arenas.

In this phase, policy entrepreneurs can take advantage of a more informal, flexible, and collegial atmosphere, compared to the formal and often adversarial process of the next phase. Anything wrong with a proposal that reaches the review-and-adoption phase can be used to kill it. Thus policy entrepreneurs attempt to uncover and fix proposal flaws in this phase, while the proposal is being drafted. These leaders should design and use forums and informal arenas to craft proposals likely to withstand the severe test of a formal policy-making arena. The leadership guidelines for this phase are divided into:

- Development and review of the draft proposal
- "Softening up" and media strategies
- Decisions about next steps

Development and Review of the Draft Proposal

Crafting a winning proposal is a process, not an event. Various choices need to be considered, and several proposal drafts are likely to be prepared and reviewed.

Choose a Big Win or a Small Win

Decide whether or not to pursue a big-win or a small-win strategy. Remember that a big win is likely to fail unless the need is obvious to a large coalition, the perceived problem and proposed solutions are clearly connected, solution technology is clearly understood and readily available, resources are identified, and a clear vision guides the changes. Use Exercise 9.1 to help your group think through which of these strategies makes the most sense.

Keep the Next Phase in Mind

Analyze the arenas that are to be important in the next phase. Consider the opportunities for venue shopping (Baumgartner and Jones, 1993). Of the arenas that might have jurisdiction over your proposed change, which are most favorable toward the change and therefore the best target of your efforts? As part of the analysis of a particular arena, ask these questions: Which committees are likely to review the proposal? What are the competing factions in the arena, and how will they view the proposal? Who are the key decision makers, and how will they view the proposal? Is an election or appointment for the arena coming up? Should the entrepreneurial team try to affect the election or appointment so as to make the political climate more favorable? Should the team try to alter hearing procedures or committee structures? The answers to such questions are important for shaping proposal content and for preparing the ground within the relevant arena. In collecting information, seek competent counsel from knowledgeable informants, in keeping with the CIA dictum that one good informant is worth a thousand theories.

Incorporate Previous Results

Draft a proposal that takes seriously the results of the previous phases. Include the problem as formulated and a tailored set of solution components that are expected to work in specific situations. Keep in mind the interpretive schemes of key stakeholders along with what you've learned about how to tap into those schemes effectively. Seek advice from key informants about the best format. Here is a possible format:

1. Title page
2. Table of contents
3. Executive summary
4. Process for developing the report
5. Problem statement
6. Key solution elements
7. Alternative solution designs in more detail
8. Summary of strengths and weaknesses of the designs
9. Recommendations and rationales
10. Budget materials
11. Appendices, which may include process details (such as who was involved and how), implementation guidance, and technical reports

The report can be drafted by the entrepreneurial team, the coordinating committee, or a smaller team that might include people from both groups.

Focus the Review on Stakeholder Goals

Set up an informal review process that focuses on the goals and concerns of key stakeholders. Update and use the participation matrix to decide which stakeholders to invite to a review session. Ideally, from five to nine people participate in a session. This number allows each person enough air time for his or her views and also gives the entrepreneurial team a sense of the group's view and where individuals fit within the larger context. The results of multiple small-group sessions can be assembled and presented to a plenary session. The small groups may be relatively homogeneous or heterogeneous. The former permit a clear picture of their common views, while the latter reveal views that recur even in disparate groups. The heterogeneous type also facilitates learning among group members.

As in the problem-formulation phase, the drafts are typically reviewed by the entrepreneurial team, the coordinating committee, a relevant governing board and members of other arenas that are to decide whether or not to adopt the proposal, and other stakeholders. The review sessions should focus on proposal strengths and modifications that improve on those strengths. The sessions can be organized in the same way as those discussed in Chapter Seven. Make sure that any draft policy or plan is viewed as a working document so that reviewers feel that the review process is authentic, not a charade. For example, you can present the proposal in outline form without expensive graphics, and stamp *DRAFT* on every page.

In relatively simple cases, the review process does not have to be extensive. Where coalition building is more difficult, arrange wider participation, allow more revision of the draft policy or plan, and give more careful attention to funder concerns and requirements; you can even repeat the process with some participants.

Be Open to Helpful Modifications

Accept as many modifications as actually improve the draft proposal. Think of a review session as a helpful source of new information, avoid defensiveness, and be open to proposal improvement. Recall what the nineteenth-century Prussian field general Helmuth von Moltke said: "Plans are nothing; planning is everything" (quoted in Linden, 2002, p. 119).

Three stakeholder analysis techniques can help your team decide which modifications improve the technical and administrative feasibility, political attractiveness, and ethical acceptability of your proposals: the stakeholder-support-versus-opposition grid, stakeholder role plays, and a grid of policy attractiveness versus stakeholder capability.

A stakeholder-support-versus-opposition grid (Exercise 9.2) groups stakeholders in one of four cells according to the importance of a stakeholder and the group's support for or opposition to specific proposals. Paul Nutt and Robert Backoff (1992) developed this technique.

Stakeholder role play has the special benefit of enhancing the entrepreneurial team's capacity to understand how other

Exercise 9.2. Constructing a
Stakeholder-Support-Versus-Opposition Grid.

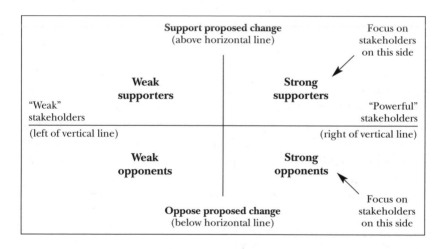

1. On flipchart sheets, construct a grid like this for each proposal being reviewed.
2. Brainstorm stakeholders' names and place them on self-adhesive labels, one name per label.
3. Place the labels on the grid in the appropriate locations.
4. Discuss what the grids reveal about the viability of specific proposals and about stakeholders requiring special attention. Discuss and deploy specific tactics on the basis of the analysis.

Exercise 9.3.　Conducting a Stakeholder Role Play.

1. The team prepares diagrams of bases of power and directions of interest if it has not done so previously.

2. Each member of the team reviews the problem-frame stakeholder maps and stakeholder-support-versus-opposition grids if they have been prepared.

3. Each member of the team assumes the role of one stakeholder.

4. With the stakeholders' diagram as a guide, each team member should answer two questions from the stakeholder's point of view about any proposal:

   • How would I react to this option?
   • What could be done to increase my support or decrease my opposition?

5. Use flipchart sheets to record the responses.

6. Do the exercise more than once, and keep modifying proposals to increase their political viability.

stakeholders think. Role play, as described by Colin Eden and Fran Ackermann (1998), builds on the information revealed in one or more diagrams of bases of power and directions of interest (see Exercise 7.2) and stakeholder problem frames (Exercise 4.3), as well as stakeholder-support-versus-opposition grids. In some cases, you may be wise to use role play to inform the search for solutions and the problem-formulation process. Directions for a stakeholder role play are in Exercise 9.3.

A grid of "policy attractiveness versus stakeholder capability" (see Exercise 9.4) compares the general attractiveness of policies, plans, proposals, or options against stakeholder capacities to implement them. The grid indicates proposals that are likely to be implemented successfully because they match stakeholder capacities, and those that are likely to fail because of lack of capacity. Proposals that are high in attractiveness and capacity certainly should be pursued. Proposals that are otherwise attractive but do not match up well with stakeholder capacities require a substantial build-up of stakeholder capability to be implemented. The entire

Exercise 9.4. Constructing a Grid of
Policy Attractiveness Versus Stakeholder Capability.

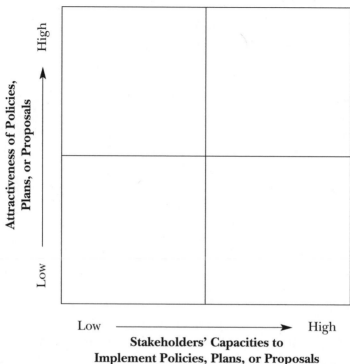

1. On flipchart sheets, construct a grid like this. Develop criteria to assess the attractiveness of proposals from low to high (in terms of mission, goals, results, outcomes, or stakeholder-related criteria) and capabilities necessary for successful implementation from low to high.
2. Have a list of proposals and a list of stakeholders ready.
3. Write proposals on self-adhesive labels of one color, one proposal per label, and place them on the grid in the appropriate position after considering both the proposal's attractiveness and the various stakeholders' capacity to implement it.
4. Discuss results and any implications for building necessary capacity among stakeholders, or for getting unattractive proposals off the agenda.
5. Record results of the discussion on flipchart sheets.

Source: Bryson, Freeman, and Roering (1986), pp. 73–76; see also Bryson (2004b).

team should discuss how to find the resources for the build-up if they want to retain the proposal. Low-attractiveness proposals are best discarded.

Consider What the Optimal Coalition Might Be

Finding the optimal coalition is a matter of matching up the problem, the proposed solution, and politics in a wise way.

Keep an Eye on What the Opponents Are Doing

Monitor opponents' attempts to develop a counterproposal or gut the proposal. Include any good ideas from the opponents' proposal in order to thwart their opportunities for coalition building. Additionally, remember that opponents may try to cut vital parts from the proposal so that even if it passes it will have little effect. Exercise extreme care to ensure that the modifications suggested by others do not render the proposal ineffective during implementation. Involving truly implacable foes in a review session is unlikely to be productive, since they may undermine the process and simply gain information that helps them organize against the proposal.

Be Prepared for Proposal Displacement

Interest groups often try to attach their favored solution to a public problem that others have placed on the agenda (Kingdon, 1995). Consequently, prepare to be vigilant once your proposal is under review in the next phase to keep it from being displaced by some interest group's favored alternative, if the alternative is at odds with your proposal. Consider drawing the group into your coalition.

Prepare a Detailed Final Draft

Prepare a more detailed and formal draft for final review in the next phase. After the informal review sessions, develop a draft that has as many characteristics of a winning proposal as seem feasible to your team. The draft should be one around which a winning coalition can organize. It should be able to withstand obstacles placed in its path, such as a veto by a chief executive or judicial review. It should accord with the state or national constitution, and its intent and effect should be supported by the relevant courts' interpretation of previous laws.

Call on Experts

In preparing the formal draft, take advantage of experts who can tailor it to the requirements of the pertinent arena. For example, legislatures typically employ legal staff who specialize in preparing bills or proposed ordinances. Be sure, though, to check the final draft to ensure that the original proposal's intent is preserved despite translation into formal or specialized language.

Explore Likely Sources for Funding

During this entire phase, your team should investigate funding possibilities in detail. A number of clues about existing or potential funding and other resources have been identified in the previous phases; here they should be pinned down. In times of resource abundance, the search may not be so crucial, but whenever resources are scarce—probably the typical circumstance—resource development is a crucial component of this phase.

Prepare a Sufficient Budget

Make sure any budget proposal necessary to implement the proposed change is prepared. For many organizations, especially in government, budget documents are *the* basic policy documents (Poister, 2003; Osborne and Hutchinson, 2004). Additionally, some arenas separate appropriations from policy approval. Winning approval of a new policy without the authorization and appropriation of necessary resources is a hollow victory.

Develop an Initial Lobbying Strategy

Plan a persuasion campaign aimed at decision makers in the next phase, and develop support within your coalition for carrying out the campaign.

"Softening Up" and Media Strategies

Winning support requires persuasion, which may take time.

Get Coalition Members on Board

Use a softening-up process to convince potential coalition members to support a big-win strategy. Proposals for change—especially ambitious ones—typically require many stakeholders to make major conceptual adjustments, and these adjustments take time (Sabatier and Jenkins-Smith, 1993). To make these stakeholders more receptive to the proposed change, marshal a variety of persuasion tools: studies, speeches, Internet messages, publicity, and draft proposals to tout the need for change and the expected improvements your proposal will bring.

A case in point is the work of the World Business Council for Sustainable Development. The notion that profit making and environmental protection are incompatible is deeply engrained. Schmidheiny and his colleagues therefore have presented counterarguments and evidence in forums around the world for more than a decade. The council's two books are replete with examples of businesses that have found a way to strengthen their bottom line through waste recovery and environmentally sensitive production processes.

Develop the Best Media Strategy for This Phase

Your team has to balance the need to sustain public momentum for change with candid give-and-take in proposal development and revision sessions. Of course, it may not always be possible to avoid news coverage of a proposal development session, especially if the proposed policy change is highly controversial. This publicity can be helpful, however, if it comes from a knowledgeable reporter, and change advocates should consider providing background sessions for reporters. The possibility that a proposal drafting session may become public gives your team even more incentive to structure the session so that acrimony, threats, and rigid position taking are discouraged. The public may feel more included in the process if at least some proposal development sessions are reported. Be prepared, however, to respond with positive counterinformation to any published reports that threaten successful proposal development.

Decisions About Next Steps

Two important decisions must be made before proceeding. First, if the necessary coalition has not formed by the end of this phase, consider cycling back through the previous phases or else dropping the project. The draft proposal review process should be designed to yield enough information to assess whether key decision makers will favor or oppose the final proposal. The more that stakeholders are openly and actively involved in the informal review sessions in this phase, the more difficult it will be for them to raise objections later.

Second, decide whether the proposal should be pressed in court rather than in an arena. The courts may be the best setting for adopting the proposal if it is justified by principles and mandates that guide the courts. On the other hand, even when you view the courts as more favorable to your cause than arenas are, you may still want to present the proposal in an arena to fan public interest and accumulate gains that might influence the courts.

Summary

In the fourth phase of the policy change cycle, policy entrepreneurs should prepare and review a policy proposal that is ready for formal review and adoption by key decision makers in the fifth phase. The proposal should therefore be a technically and administratively workable, politically acceptable, and legally and ethically defensible response to the public need that prompted the change effort in the first place. It should incorporate the vision that guides the work of the coalition formed around it. Indeed, an essential outcome of this phase is a winning coalition that can be counted on to engage in political leadership in the next phase.

Chapter Ten

Adopting Policy Proposals

*Greater than the tread of mighty armies is an idea
whose time has come.*
VICTOR HUGO

In the policy-review-and-adoption phase, policy entrepreneurs sub-mit their well-crafted policy proposal (or more likely, proposals) to official policy makers for review and possible adoption in exec-utive, legislative, or administrative arenas. They must prepare for what might be a grueling, even tumultuous process, in which pros-pects for winning or losing change by the hour, the real decision is often made outside the formal arena, and the constant need to focus on immediate details and stakeholder demands threatens at-tention to long-term consequences. Policy entrepreneurs may also decide to press their case in formal or informal courts, if arenas are unreceptive to the proposal and if the change residing at the heart of the proposal can be justified by constitutional principles, laws, or norms.

Purpose and Desired Outcomes

The purpose of the proposal-review-and-adoption phase of the pol-icy change cycle is to gain an official decision to adopt and im-plement the policy proposal that was developed and informally reviewed in the previous phase. This phase is a culmination of the efforts expended in all four of the previous phases of the policy cycle. In other words, the previous phases were designed to permit an authoritative choice among policy options in this, the fifth, phase so that the issue at hand can be addressed effectively during the sixth phase, implementation.

Policy entrepreneurs seek a number of outcomes in this phase:

- Widely shared agreement with their proposal
- A decision in the relevant arena(s) to adopt the proposal and proceed with implementation
- If needed, a decision in relevant courts to require or facilitate proposal adoption
- Provision of necessary guidance and resources for implementation
- Support of those who can strongly affect implementation success
- A widely shared sense of excitement about the new policy and its implementation
- A persistent supportive coalition that will monitor implementation
- Respectful, if not cordial relationships, among participants

Widely Shared Agreement

Ideally, some of the official policy makers are already part of the coalition that has developed the policy proposal. In this phase, policy entrepreneurs work to bring enough additional policy makers on board to obtain formal approval in the relevant arena. They seek to make their idea one whose time has come through astute use of such processes as the bandwagon effect, signing up, and exploiting a window of opportunity. These processes contribute to what John Kingdon (1995) has called "coupling," in which a public problem, solutions, and a favorable political climate come together. Kingdon has studied this process in legislative arenas; Carl Van Horn and his colleagues also emphasize the importance of coupling in decision making within corporations, public bureaucracies, and offices of an elected chief executive (Van Horn, Baumer, and Gormley, 2001). Although much of this chapter focuses on the legislative arena, policy entrepreneurs also should attempt to influence relevant executive and administrative policy makers. For example, chief executives may be able to make a significant change on their own, and they also can be powerful allies in persuading a legislative body to act.

Additionally, a chief administrator can make some important policy decisions and may have considerable sway with legislators.

The Bandwagon Effect

By playing up the strengths of their proposal, emphasizing the magnitude of support for it, and attracting favorable coverage in relevant media, policy entrepreneurs seek to generate a bandwagon, or multiplier, effect (Benveniste, 1989; Kingdon, 1995). Nonsupporters may sense that the proposal is a sure winner and decide to hop on the bandwagon so they can be part of a winning coalition.

Perception of the credibility and certainty of adoption is likely to grow as a consequence of threefold knowledge, regarding (1) the technical and administrative feasibility of the proposed change, (2) extensive support for the change among key stakeholders, and (3) the degree to which authoritative decision makers specifically support the change (Benveniste, 1989). Policy entrepreneurs should strive to increase and publicize all three kinds of knowledge.

A powerful bandwagon effect can make a proposal virtually unstoppable and is particularly important for a major policy change, which is unlikely to happen without strong and widespread support. Although previous phases should be designed to enhance the possibility of a bandwagon effect, policy entrepreneurs want it to peak at the point of a proposal-adoption decision. Once policy entrepreneurs detect this peak, they should quickly press for adoption of their proposal; otherwise crafty opponents may be able to upset the bandwagon. As John Kingdon has noted, "The really big steps are taken quickly or not at all" (1995, p. 170).

Signing Up

The softening-up process described in Chapter Nine prepares the way for building a substantial coalition and creating the bandwagon effect. Softening up, however, is different from signing up. In the softening-up process, policy entrepreneurs attempt to persuade stakeholders that policy change is needed. In the signing-up process, entrepreneurs find specific inducements to prompt specific stakeholders to support the proposal. Both the softening-up argument and the signing-up inducements must be geared to the stakeholder's interpretive schemes, values, and interests, because people choose whether or not to support a change in light of how they think it will affect what they care about.

The signing-up process often involves an interesting twist on the normal notion of costs and benefits. Policy makers may be prone to sign onto a big, pricey proposal because the high costs are actually expected to produce big benefits (Kingdon, 1995). In voting for the proposal, they position themselves to take credit for distributing those benefits or building a successful program, project, or product. Support for a very expensive proposal is more likely if it is widely perceived to be "good" policy. In 2003, the Bush administration and the U.S. Congress approved billions of dollars for the global battle against HIV/AIDS. Fighting AIDS is now widely seen as a gargantuan public problem and an issue of compassion. Small appropriations are laughable; indeed, the Bush administration was criticized for backing off its initial promise of much more generous funding. The pricey Medicare bill passed in 2003 is a similar example. The new law is a tremendous, costly expansion of Medicare benefits and payments to health care providers. It passed because Medicare is a widely supported program, and because a large number of older adults, pharmaceutical companies, and health maintenance organizations will benefit from the new policies.

Development of policy makers' support for a proposal requires cultivating networks. This is especially true in the legislative arena, but also important in the corporate or nonprofit boardroom, the executive cabinet, and administrative offices. The focus here is on the legislative arena because it is crucial in adopting policies that have general application and spur decision making in other arenas.

Policy entrepreneurs should remember that legislators must often make decisions under time pressure and without extensive knowledge. It is wise to assume that legislators know little about any bill other than one they have introduced. Legislators also are unlikely to be interested in a bill that does not relate directly to something they care about (what they likely care about is getting reelected, securing passage of one of their bills, and setting up a useful relationship). Legislative floor debate rarely sways votes. Rather, relationships (especially friendships and political connections) are critical; legislators look to these relationships and the messages conveyed through them for cues about how to vote.

Change advocates must find a way to cultivate these friendship and political networks. The networks may include factions within a legislature, but also people outside—other elected officials, civic leaders, party officials, lobbyists, and corporate executives. When a legislature shares power with an elected executive (president, governor, mayor), policy entrepreneurs should seek to win the support of the executive, since he or she has considerable power to activate the network in which legislators participate.

Legislators essentially engage in reciprocity-based decision making, in which they rely on each other and their staff members for information and support. The reciprocity may be tacit; the legislator who agrees to vote a colleague's way today may have the implicit expectation that the colleague will support her bill tomorrow. A more direct exchange is "logrolling," which James Anderson describes as "a way of gaining support from those who are indifferent or have little interest in a matter, [and which] usually encompasses a straightforward mutual exchange of support on two different topics" (1990, p. 128). Pork barrel legislation is the classic example, in which legislators vote for each other's home district projects so that everyone can bring home the bacon.

More explicit reciprocity occurs through compromise, when a legislator at odds with a colleague over the content of a bill agrees to give up something in order to obtain at least part of what he or she wants. A less savory form of explicit reciprocity (usually occurring behind closed doors) is the use of side payments, in which one legislator offers goodies—a desired committee assignment, or office space—in exchange for another's vote.

As a result of vote trading, the press of time, and the numerous details that must be addressed in major legislation, the actual legislation passed might bear little resemblance to wise public policy. As Otto von Bismarck allegedly said, "There are two things one should never see made: sausage and legislation." Therefore policy entrepreneurs must be attentive to overall legislative strategy and the details of execution; otherwise, the solutions developed in the forums of the previous phases can be lost in the legislative arena. These entrepreneurs also must not forget the desirability of finding an all-gain solution, in which all sides get what they want.

In sum, policy entrepreneurs must be wise and creative in formulating arguments and inducements to give policy makers reasons to say yes. They should cultivate relationships with and among legislators or other key decision makers, and then supply the sympathetic ones with research data, public opinion surveys, and moral and practical arguments through written and oral testimony, conversation, and printed materials. These advocates should be continuously alert to finding, inventing, or trading options for mutual gain. Policy entrepreneurs may also get involved in a campaign that decides who the policy makers will be. In a political election, they may volunteer for a particular candidate or make financial contributions to that campaign.

Similarly, when resort to formal courts is part of the change strategy, advocates should help judges say yes in light of the judges' interpretive schemes, values, and interests. Policy entrepreneurs often seek court decisions that put pressure on arenas to enact the proposals that the entrepreneurs are supporting.

Exploiting a Window of Opportunity
A window of opportunity is a time span or occasion when conditions are highly propitious for a policy proposal. A window can be opened by a growing public conviction that a problem is significant and urgent, by a political shift, or by a decision point—a time when official bodies are authorized and empowered to act. Some decision points are predictable, while others are not; regardless, policy entrepreneurs should be prepared to take advantage of them. Predictable decision points include those tied to regular reports and addresses, such as the State of the Union or State of the State; a corporation's or nonprofit's annual report; the annual or biennial budget cycle of governments, organizations, and networks; and the scheduled renewal of laws or programs. An unpredictable decision point can arise from a crisis, a sudden change in official leadership or public opinion, or an unexpected opportunity. Policy entrepreneurs make sure that at least the predictable decision points are included in the plan developed in previous phases and that the plan is also flexible enough to take advantage of unpredictable decision points. For example, U.S. advocates of safer beef slaughtering and processing pressed their case through the normal process of congressional hearings in recent years but were defeated by beef industry lobbyists. They also sued in federal court to stop the use of "downer" animals for food, but government

lawyers argued against them. A decision to dismiss the suit was under appeal, when a case of mad cow disease was reported in late 2003. The widespread news coverage of the case heightened citizen concern about slaughtering practices, revealed the impact of industry lobbyists, and opened the door for food safety advocates to press their cause in a much more favorable atmosphere.

In two similar instances, advocates of reforming the financing of U.S. election campaigns, and participants in the global anticorruption campaign, were making minor headway in recent years until, in the first case, highly visible scandals involving corporate givers emerged, and in the second case terrorist activity (prominently the September 11 attacks) caused national policy makers to insist on greater openness in financial transactions.

Decision to Adopt and Implement the Proposal

Even if problems, solutions, and politics are coupled, an advocacy coalition may still be defeated during formal adoption sessions by shrewd opponents who find a way to split the coalition or use the formal decision rules of the relevant arena to stop what otherwise would be a sure winner. In these sessions, knowledge of *heresthetics*—the name William Riker (1986) gives to the art of political manipulation—is essential. Heresthetics might also be depicted as a political martial art in which advocates and their opponents attempt to parry each other's moves with a variety of weapons (committee rules, voting procedures, calling in debts, releasing or withholding information, negative publicity).

Riker highlights three components of political manipulation: agenda control, strategic voting, and manipulation of the dimensions of an issue. *Agenda control* is a basic design element of arenas. Exercised mainly by positional leaders such as committee chairs, agenda control involves determining which items, proposals, options, or amendments will come up for consideration by the official decision-making body and at what time. In its most powerful form, agenda control can defeat what is, on paper, a certain winner, purely for procedural reasons.

Strategic voting is a practice in which individual members of a policy-making body use their voting power to accomplish long-term objectives. This practice often takes the form of "voting contrary to one's immediate tastes in order to obtain an advantage in the long run" (Riker, 1986, p. 78).

Issue dimensions can be expanded or narrowed in order to alter the composition of an advocacy coalition (Stone, 2002). Issue expansion is often a desirable option for policy entrepreneurs. For example, as the framing of AIDS in the United States expanded from a disease that affected gay men to a disease that could affect children of drug addicts, users of blood transfusions, and finally just about everyone, the coalition advocating a massive public prevention and treatment campaign expanded tremendously. Sometimes, however, expanding the dimensions of an issue can cause people to drop out of a coalition. For example, the death penalty, when framed as a deterrent to serious crime, may attract the support of many stakeholder groups that place high value on law and order. When it is reframed as state-sanctioned killing, the issue boundaries overlap with right-to-life concerns. Some of those stakeholders then may rethink their support because they have a religious conviction that life is to be preserved.

Usually, narrowing the dimensions of an issue restricts conflict and favors organized interests. Restricted conflict plays out in political subsystems, where the organized are likely to dominate the unorganized, especially those who are not even aware of the conflict. As Richard Neustadt has observed, "One never should underestimate the public's power to ignore, to acquiesce, and to forget, especially when the proceedings seem incalculable or remote from private life" (1990, p. 82). A recent example was how the danger of mad cow disease was handled in the United States before the first documented case was publicized in 2003. Before then, the issue of how to ward off the disease was dealt with largely out of the public eye by the Food and Drug Administration and congressional committees. Republicans and Democrats alike were persuaded by lobbyists for the beef industry that no major changes were needed in monitoring beef slaughter and processing. A number of nonprofit food safety groups lobbied for the changes and some beef processors and retailers altered their practices, but the conflict did not become a widespread public concern. At that juncture, the issue was effectively framed as one of economic security for beef growers and processors and for those they employed. Once the first actual case of mad cow disease emerged, the danger was reframed by press reports and by food safety groups (who suddenly had the ear of the public) as a serious public health threat. This reframing broadened the conflict and also cast the previous inaction of Congress in a new light; the failure to adopt recommended changes was now widely seen as pandering to corporate interests. As illustrated by this example, expanding conflict can improve the prospects of the weak and relatively unorganized, as well as foster greater consideration of the broader public interest, because of increased media attention to the circumstances of the affected parties and their advocates.

Another way of manipulating the dimensions of an issue is through what Deborah Stone (2002) calls *strategic release of information:* announcing research findings, issuing a report, or making a decision under conditions that bolster one's favorite policies or render it hard for opponents to respond. For example, President Bush gave the green light to the highly disputed construction of more roads in the Tongas wilderness area of Alaska during the holiday rush two days before Christmas 2003, when a majority of citizens could be counted on to be preoccupied with other matters.

In sum, policy entrepreneurs must be attentive to opportunities for agenda control, strategic voting, and manipulation of issue dimensions and information. They have to be on guard and maintain the "ability to shift from moment to moment, poking and pushing the world until it favors [their] cause" (Riker, 1986, p. 51).

Policy entrepreneurs should also remember that one arena might be overruled by another higher in the government hierarchy, or by popular referenda. Thus, if change advocates lose in a local arena, they may try again at a higher level.

Decision in Court to Require or Facilitate Adoption

Action by an arena can be shaped or overruled by a court. Throughout this phase, as in the previous phase, policy entrepreneurs make sure that changes in their proposal will stand up under scrutiny in the relevant courts. In some cases, administrative courts are extremely important, since they oversee development and application of rules and regulations designed to implement the proposed policy. Additionally, policy entrepreneurs may ask a formal court to overturn a law previously enacted by an arena, or they may seek a court decision that reshapes the way an arena functions—for example, by mandating the redrawing of electoral district boundaries or nullifying an election. Moreover policy entrepreneurs may seek to reshape the courts, as in trying to affect the appointment or election of judges.

Courts, however, face limits in making policy changes. Usually they do not attempt to implement the changes they mandate. Policy entrepreneurs should as well remember that formal court systems are often hierarchical. Change advocates who win at one level can lose on appeal to a higher court; conversely, they can lose in a lower court and win on appeal.

Provision of Guidance and Resources for Implementation

Implementers and judges look to the adopted proposal as well as to the record of policy makers' discussion of the proposal to discern the policy makers' intention for how the policy should be carried out. If guidance is inadequate, implementers can be expected to use methods with which they are familiar or spend considerable time trying to figure out what to do. Inadequate guidance also opens the door for opponents to step in with their own ideas for how the proposal should be implemented. Without thorough guidance, evaluators of policy impact might also have difficulty knowing exactly what they should evaluate.

Sometimes, the political climate is such that the only way policy entrepreneurs can win passage of their favored proposal is to keep the implementation plan ambiguous. Or the issue at the heart of the proposal might be so complex that the proposal mainly seeks authorization and funding for helping many stakeholder groups develop implementation strategies, as in the case of the African American Men Project. Here a helpful tactic is to create a commission or other group assigned to work out the implementation plan.

Meanwhile, policies that are adopted in the absence of adequate resources are little more than symbolic window dressing. Symbolic policies may be important in paving the way for future, adequately funded policies; nevertheless, to have real impact, a policy ultimately must be accompanied by needed resources for implementation.

Support of Those Who Can Affect Implementation Success

Wise policy entrepreneurs involve likely implementers of their proposal in shaping it in the first place. The concerns and capabilities of implementers still need to be considered as the proposal is modified in this phase, so that implementers remain supportive. For example, if sustainable development advocates seek to convince policy makers to pass tax incentives for reducing manufacturers' waste products, they may need to keep information flowing from people in affected businesses (especially the designers of manufacturing processes), as the policy makers debate waste reduction requirements and implementation schedules. During implementation, the policy makers themselves are likely to stay involved, either as overseers or interveners; as a result policy entrepreneurs seek to win the support of as many of the policy makers as possible, not just enough to pass the proposal.

Widely Shared Excitement About the Policy and Implementation

Once a proposal is adopted, celebratory events and messages can help sustain the momentum of change and build a bridge to the implementation phase. If a new law is passed, a president or governor may hold a signing ceremony with great fanfare. The winning advocacy coalition may hold a celebratory rally and communicate messages of triumph and great expectation through the press. They may call on citizens or organizations to join in implementing the new policy. Opponents find themselves fighting a rearguard action as the burden of proof shifts from the initiators to the opposers of the change (Wilson, 1967). Thus, the supporters of the AAMP organized major community events to announce the Hennepin County board's approval of the 2002 report and appointment of the African American Men Commission. County commissioners, other officials, and community leaders were highly visible participants. Videotapes of these events and follow-up activities were used at subsequent community gatherings to demonstrate the project's momentum and support from top officials, community leaders, and citizens.

Ideally, a renorming process begins. Assuming the new policy addresses a real public problem and is technically, administratively, politically, legally, and ethically acceptable, more and more people begin "owning" the problem and solution and expecting new behavior from themselves and others. Such ownership is extremely important if people are to commit to changes and follow through on them (Eden and Ackermann, 1998). Once the renorming is widespread, the court of public opinion will help enforce the norms.

A Persistent, Supportive Coalition to Monitor Implementation

Members of a victorious coalition are likely to feel a surge of self-confidence and self-esteem that is based on hope, faith, hard work, and task accomplishment at the end of this phase. They are also likely to feel a strong sense of connection to those who have labored alongside them in the coalition. Policy entrepreneurs should build on these good feelings to sustain the coalition for the long-term work of ensuring that adopted policies are implemented well. Members of the coalition may be understandably fatigued after a long fight and ready to declare victory and take a break. It's important, though, to remind them that their hard-won victory may be for naught if they decamp.

Respectful, Even Cordial, Participant Relationships

In the policy-review-and-adoption phase, policy entrepreneurs should strive to conduct their campaign in a way that allows their supporters and opponents alike to shake hands at the end and prepare to work together in the future. Attacking the opponents or making an effort to embarrass them in a formal review or adoption session obviously undermines this desired outcome. Maintaining civil relationships is especially important when policy entrepreneurs initially fail to win adoption of their proposal but decide to try again. They will hope to turn some opposing policy makers into supporters, a task made easier in the absence of leftover animosity (Patterson, Grenny, McMillan, and Switzler, 2002; Kegan and Lahey, 2001).

Leadership Guidelines

Success in this phase depends as much on policy entrepreneurs' ability to negotiate the intricacies of formal arenas (and in some cases courts) as on the value of the ideas contained in the proposal they are promoting. If the preceding phase has gone well, they begin this one with a well-crafted policy proposal supported by a broad coalition and attractive to relevant policy makers. They need an array of political leadership skills in order to press their proposal at the right time, guide it past procedural barriers, win over or thwart opponents, and sustain and further expand their coalition.

We group guidelines for this phase in three categories:

1. Building support
2. Providing implementation guidance and support
3. Gleaning success from failure

Building Support

Keep track of key stakeholders, especially the policy makers, throughout this phase. Organize an effective lobbying and media campaign. Use tactics such as agenda control, strategic voting, and bargaining as needed. Seek a powerful bandwagon effect.

Policy Makers Deserve Attention

Continue to pay attention to the goals, concerns, interests, beliefs, and egos of all key stakeholders, but especially of the policy makers themselves. In a government arena, party affiliation and past political alignment are important stakeholder characteristics. In government arenas, key stakeholders are likely to include top-level elected or appointed executives; legislators; directors, managers, and frontline employees and volunteers in important implementing organizations (whether government agency, business, or nonprofit); technical, professional, and interest-group opinion leaders; representatives of key constituent groups; and funding sources. In this phase, it is especially important to understand the policy makers well enough to know what type of inducement will prompt them to vote in favor of the proposal.

Assess Support and Opposition

Use the stakeholder-support-versus-opposition grid (Exercise 9.2) to assess changes in the proposal as it goes through the formal review and adoption process.

Identify Sponsors and Champions

Identify one or more policy sponsors and policy champions to gain passage in legislative and administrative arenas. In a legislature, one or more members must officially sponsor proposed legislation. In addition to formal sponsorship, someone (preferably a legislator) must champion the proposal and do the educating, networking, bargaining, and negotiating that are undoubtedly necessary to win passage of legislation. Key decision makers and opinion leaders must play similar roles in an administrative arena. Gathering more information about key stakeholders and using stakeholder support-and-opposition grids can help policy entrepreneurs identify sponsors and champions. (Sometimes policy entrepreneurs themselves are able to play these roles; Gary Cunningham was the key champion of the AAMP within Hennepin County government.)

Use Lobbying and Persuasion

Implement a lobbying strategy and persuasion campaign. Important tactics include:

• *Reducing decision-maker uncertainty about the policy proposal.* Decision makers may not be knowledgeable about the policy area connected to the proposal. Help them view your proposal positively by emphasizing compatibility with their goals, furnishing evidence of the technical quality of the proposal, and giving reassurance that it comes from competent sources. Activate members of the coalition to do behind-the-scenes work as well as public presentation. These people are often prominent, influential, and obviously connected to extensive networks that can be marshaled in support of the proposal. As an example, to obtain foundation support for the 2002 Vital Aging Summit in Minnesota, members of the summit planning committee used their personal connections and credibility with foundation directors to win donations.

• *Developing arguments and counterarguments in support of the proposal prior to formal review sessions.* Bargaining and negotiation may predominate in this phase, but persuasion still matters. You cannot be a successful bargainer or negotiator without the ability to develop a persuasive argument. Strive to articulate the logic of the proposal in a way that is convincing to key decision makers and stakeholders—or at least buys their neutrality—else the decision will go nowhere (Forester, 1999; Simons, 2001). Remember to pay attention to the egos, ideologies, and political allegiances of the policy makers (Sabatier and Jenkins-Smith, 1993). Be sure to outline the benefits of proposal adoption to various stakeholder groups and to constituencies that are important to the official decision makers, and indicate that attendant costs are reasonable. As mentioned earlier, you should be able to argue against the opponents' effort to change the dimensions of an issue. In court, arguments must show how the proposed change accords with, or indeed is required by, judicial principles and previous court decisions.

• *Organizing a well-timed demonstration of constituent support.* Demonstrations are especially important in any politically difficult situation. You can call on one or more seasoned pressure groups that are part of your coalition to begin activating members to send e-mails, write letters, show up at policy makers' offices, join rallies, and attract media coverage. Make certain, however, that pressure does not backfire. If lobbying is so intense that policy makers feel they are being browbeaten or that some key stakeholders are offended, it may actually reduce support for your proposal. For example, in March 1983, the New York AIDS Network timed its demands for well-funded city AIDS services to coincide with an explosive column by Larry Kramer in the *New York Native*. The *Native* also published a call for volunteers to be trained for civil disobedience aimed at bringing attention to the failure of city officials to take any significant action against AIDS. Kramer's column increased the polarization within the gay community—between those who denounced Kramer as an alarmist and those who sided with his claim that AIDS was now a "public health emergency" (Shilts, 1988, p. 245). New York Mayor Ed Koch responded to the calls for city-sponsored AIDS services with a new office and minor gestures of support—a minimal approach that went largely unchallenged by gay community leaders.

Use Agenda Control and Strategic Voting

Seek agenda control and strategic voting that favor the proposal. Agenda control is mainly the province of an arena's positional leaders, so they must be on board and give the proposal priority. In 1983, as chair of the Senate Committee on Labor and Human Resources Orrin Hatch used his prerogative at a crucial point in the efforts to pass a bill boosting anti-AIDS funding to send the bill directly to the Senate floor for debate. He decided against the normal practice of holding a committee hearing, because some committee members could be counted on to use the hearing to push their antigay rights agenda (Shilts, 1988). It may also be possible to end-run the agenda-control system. For example, Congressmen Henry Waxman and Phil Burton and their staffers Bill Kraus and Tim Westmoreland worked successfully in the early 1980s to secure substantial federal funding for AIDS prevention and treatment by using congressional supplemental appropriations process to counter the president's budget recommendations.

In addition to working with policy makers who can shape the decision-making agenda, pay attention to how strategic voting may affect your proposal. For example, the timing of a vote on the proposal may greatly enhance or diminish chances of the proposal's benefiting from strategic voting.

Get the Timing Right

In general, be sure that bills are introduced when competition from other pressing matters is low. This tactic helps policy makers and the press give your proposal their full attention. (In some situations, however, you may be wise to introduce a bill quietly so that it does not attract much attention.) Lobbying pressure should be exerted at the right time and in the right way; information should be circulated at the most propitious time and in the right format.

Engage Reviewers

Engage formal review bodies in a structured review session focusing on strengths, weaknesses, and modifications of the process. This is much the same as what we described in Chapter Nine. Again, be prepared to accept all modifications that actually improve the technical, administrative, political, legal, and ethical acceptability of the proposal. Remember, elected politicians favor proposals that help their constituents, avoid highly controversial issues, enhance their reputation and prospects for reelection, and achieve their concept of good public policy. Further, politicians are likely to vote in a direction consistent with the balance of opinion among their key constituents (Kingdon, 1995).

Use the formal review process to gain additional endorsement of the proposed change prior to the formal adoption process. This evidence of support can assure policy makers that they are on safe ground if they vote for the proposed change.

A review body might be a subcommittee, whose recommendations carry considerable weight with the full policy-making body. The ideal review body consists of five to nine members and has a history of constructive interaction and open communication. Lacking such a history, it may require training in effective group communication, problem solving, and conflict management.

Keep a Watchful Eye on Opponents

Much of the policy adoption process involves individuals and interest groups who want the proposed policy to fail. These opponents often hammer on the details of the proposed change, especially if passage appears likely. They know that policy intentions can be made to fail during implementation through tampering with the details during adoption. Be aware that even small changes can have a big impact, and be prepared to counter selective information, distortion, and even lies.

Try to avoid unwelcome surprises. The work in previous phases should construct an effective early warning system that eliminates unwelcome news during this phase. The systematic review process in the proposal-formulation phase and in this phase is especially helpful in uncovering troublesome concerns in advance.

Bargain and Negotiate for Support

Be prepared to bargain and negotiate over proposal features, or other issues, in exchange for political support. Bargaining and negotiation are the modus operandi in legislative bodies. The bargaining is intended to win over or placate opponents and those who are indifferent. Even a proposal that seems to have no opposition (say, one aimed at eliminating child abuse) may provoke argument over methodology, resources, and the locus of responsibility for implementation.

Finding or inventing options and inducements that can promote agreement, without sacrificing key proposal components, is a prime political leadership activity (Susskind, McKearnan, and

Thomas-Larmer, 1999; Thompson, 2001). The price of the last vote necessary for proposal adoption may be the highest, since the voter may know that without his or her support the entire proposal will be defeated (Riker, 1962). On the other hand, if a bandwagon effect occurs, relatively cost-free support may be gained as latecomers seek to avoid exclusion from the benefits of proposal adoption. No matter what, do not bargain away essentials in order to win support.

Create a Powerful Bandwagon Effect

As bargaining and negotiation continue, participants may realize that enough agreement is emerging to ensure ultimate passage. More and more of them may become convinced of the proposal's feasibility and aware of widespread stakeholder support and key decision makers' favorable attitude toward the proposal. At this point, a future different from the present gains credibility and certainty, and the bandwagon effect takes hold. Participants often "alter their behavior and responses. They will either pick preferences that have a higher probability of happening or fashion new preferences that fit their image of the future" (Benveniste, 1989, p. 130).

Announce the Proposal Publicly

Make a public announcement of the reworked proposal, at least within the affected system. The announcement may occur before or after formal adoption of the proposal. A public announcement prior to adoption may be a trial balloon to determine whether a sufficiently large supportive coalition has been formed. Or it may be designed to soften up decision makers at the same time that it solidifies or expands the coalition, perhaps triggering a powerful bandwagon effect. A preadoption announcement, however, could also allow an opposing coalition to form. A postadoption announcement informs stakeholders how things have changed and prepares them for implementation.

Use a Two-Pronged Media Strategy

First, keep the issue alive in the pertinent media so as to demonstrate to policy makers that the public is paying attention. Some of the policy makers themselves may make this task easier as they begin making newsworthy statements about the proposal. Other tactics include public rallies and press conferences to attract media attention to subcommittee hearings, procedural votes, threatened vetoes, and the final vote.

Second, communicate what is happening to your proposal as it advances through the legislative meat grinder. Maintain good press contacts so you can immediately let the public know when your proposal is being advanced, or gutted, in the legislative process.

Strike While the Iron Is Hot

When the time is right, press for formal adoption of the proposal. The time is right when the coalition is as large as it can be; the proposal is politically acceptable, technically and administratively workable, and ethically and legally defensible; and a decision point is at hand.

Decide Whether to Ask the Courts to Intervene

If your proposal is faring badly because the arena's structure or process violates laws or constitutional principles, consider asking the appropriate court to force needed change in the offending rule and methods. You may also decide to test your proposal in court if the constitution or judicial precedents offer grounds for doing so.

Providing Implementation Guidance and Support

Be sure enough resources are committed, incentives are right, and the process is well designed. Keep in mind that your ultimate goal is construction of a new policy regime.

Seek Adequate Resources

Obtain necessary resource commitments, if at all possible, prior to the formal adoption session. Gain commitment from formal decision makers and key implementers for key personnel, additional staff, training costs, conversion costs, stipends, technical assistance, contingency funds, and the like.

Align Incentives

Remember that incentives must run in the proper direction for implementation. If implementers see that they can benefit from implementation, they are more likely to facilitate it than if they see it as a kind of punishment (Weimer and Vining, 1999). Placing potential implementers in their historical context and noting important trajectories, details, and change points can help you choose preferred implementers and fashion incentives that are positive motivators rather than a punishment (Neustadt and May, 1986).

Support Movement Away from the Status Quo

Meet the conditions for effective implementation of a policy that departs substantially from the status quo. Daniel Mazmanian and Paul Sabatier (1983) argue that major policy changes are likely to be achieved if:

- The enabling legislation or other directive outlines clear and consistent policy objectives or criteria for resolving goal conflicts.
- The legislation incorporates a sound theory of what is needed to achieve the policy objective and gives implementers sufficient authority. Constructing and critiquing a logic model that captures the essence of the theory linking inputs, process, outputs, and outcomes is one way to make sure the theory is sound (Millar, Simeone, and Carnevale, 1999; Poister, 2003). Forward and backward mapping, to be discussed in the next chapter, may be helpful.
- The legislation structures the implementation process to favor success—for example, by assigning the change to a supportive and capable agency, establishing supportive decision rules, and making adequate resources available.
- Key implementers possess the necessary leadership and management skills and are committed to achieving the goals.
- A coalition of key supporters, including important legislators or chief executives, actively supports the implementation process, and the courts are supportive or neutral.
- New priorities or conflicting policies do not emerge, and underlying social conditions do not change so as to weaken the policy's political support or underlying causal theory.

Bear these conditions in mind throughout the proposal-review-and-adoption phase and carry them with you into the implementation process. If the conditions are not in place at the conclusion of this phase, you will need to strategize accordingly.

Focus on Regime Building

View the policy-adoption process as an exercise in potential regime building. Ultimately you are seeking a strong, self-sustaining regime of principles, laws, norms, expectations, and decision-making procedures that will *institutionalize* the policy changes during the implementation phase. This regime is more likely to emerge if your advocacy coalition is large, the interpretive schemes that support the new policy are widely shared, and the implementation incentives are effective.

Gleaning Success from Failure

If the outcome of this phase is disappointing, reflect on the reasons and decide whether to try again.

First, remember that *some proposals must fail at least once before they succeed.* In a politically difficult situation, initial failure is especially likely, and it may even be a necessary part of the social learning that paves the way for ultimate change. Failure can be an occasion to expand and educate key constituencies about the importance and magnitude of the public problem being addressed.

Second, *it is possible to establish a valuable principle, even though the proposal itself is defeated.* New principles may lead to standard operating procedures in the future that outweigh present losses. They may also break up an existing coalition and be the basis for new ones. A principle established in one field may spill over to others.

Third, *if adoption fails* even though the policy change process has been well designed and pursued, *consider these possibilities:*

- The time is not yet right.
- The draft policies, plans, or programs are inadequate or inappropriate.
- The problem or needs that the proposal purports to address simply are not important or urgent enough.
- The system cannot handle the magnitude of the proposed change, and the design has to be scaled back.
- The proposal must be taken to another arena or court.

Fourth, *rally the spirits of coalition members* by highlighting what they have accomplished. Additionally, if the coalition is willing to move on to another arena or court, or cycle back through previous phases, emphasize the importance of continuing to fight for change.

Summary

Formal proposal review and adoption moves the policy change process from forums to arenas and sometimes to courts. Even when the focus is on an arena, the courts must be kept in mind, because adopted changes are often challenged in the courts.

In this phase, policy entrepreneurs help official decision makers say yes to the proposed change as comfortably as possible. They use their political leadership skills as they seek to make their proposal unstoppable. To bring policy makers on board, they use such processes as the bandwagon effect, signing up, and exploiting a window of opportunity. They use their understanding of agenda control, strategic voting, issue dimensions, and information control to win passage of their proposal. They bargain and negotiate over details, while attempting to protect key provisions. They compete fiercely with opponents but hold open the possibility of working together in the future. They sustain and expand their coalition and activate coalition members to directly and indirectly lobby the policy makers. They ensure that adopted policies include adequate guidance and resources for implementation in the next phase.

If the proposal fails in an arena, policy entrepreneurs have the option of trying another arena, or pursuing change in the courts. They may also need to circle back to earlier policy change phases.

Chapter Eleven

Implementing and Evaluating New Policies, Programs, and Plans

Write the vision and make it plain, that they may run who read it.
HABABBUK 2:2

In the implementation and evaluation phase, policy entrepreneurs ensure that adopted policy changes are implemented in a way that actually achieves the vision developed in earlier phases of the policy change cycle. They must be willing to learn as they go along, since the experience of implementation is likely to deviate considerably from even the best-laid plans as fine ideas come up against organizational and human idiosyncrasies and diversity, as well as environmental changes (Pressman and Wildavsky, 1973). Policy entrepreneurs must often face the additional challenge in this phase of letting go of their creation.

Purpose and Desired Outcomes

Implementation, or operationalization, of change typically is a complex and messy process involving many actors and organizations with a host of complementary, competing, and often contradictory goals and interests (Goggin, Bowman, Lester, and O'Toole, 1990; Peters and Pierre, 1998, 2003). Clearly, policy implementation must be planned, facilitated, monitored, and evaluated.

The purpose of this phase is incorporation of the adopted policy change throughout the relevant system in a way that achieves the vision inspiring the change in the first place. Desired outcomes include:

- Reasonably smooth and rapid introduction of the adopted change in appropriate organizations and networks
- Commitment of key implementers
- Maintenance and change of coalition membership and leadership
- A "debugging" process that identifies and fixes difficulties arising as implementation proceeds
- Assurance that important features of the policy design are maintained during implementation
- A summative evaluation that ensures policy goals are in fact achieved
- Creation of a new regime to govern decision making and behavior
- Establishment or anticipation of review points during which policy maintenance, modification, or termination can be considered
- Strengthening of people and organizations involved in implementation

Introduction of Adopted Changes

Usually the arena that adopts a policy change mandates the implementation, either by issuing a directive to existing networks, organizations, and departments or by creating new organizations, networks, and departments. Policy entrepreneurs usually want to move quickly to make sure the changes are actually begun in the relevant organizational system and the start-up goes smoothly. Typically, a repertoire of strategies and tactics is necessary to bring all relevant parties on board (Bryson, 2004a; 2004b). For example, the Hennepin County Board set up the African American Men Commission, which in turn established seven committees charged with developing implementation plans in specific policy areas: families, housing, education, community civic involvement, and criminal justice; two additional committees—communications and fundraising—were expected to develop overall support for the African American Men Project. Meanwhile, the project staff began implementing such initiatives as the Right Turn Project and the Day of Restoration, as well as continuing to track and publicize AAMP's progress.

Commitment of Key Implementers

Without the commitment of key implementers, change is likely to wither on the vine. It may be given lip service but displaced by other priorities and needs. Of course, implementers who were part of the advocacy coalition that supported adoption of the change are likely to be supportive. Many, however, will not have participated in the coalition, and policy entrepreneurs and policy makers must give them incentives to allocate time, energy, and other organizational resources to implementation. In one of our four examples, implementation of the Day of Restoration developed by the AAMP required support from judges and staff in the county courts. An important incentive for these people was the prospect of saving a significant amount of time and money by clearing up traffic tickets and other violations, encouraging restorative justice, and reducing future crime.

Maintenance and Change of Coalition Membership and Leadership

In the implementation and evaluation phase, policy entrepreneurs must prepare for a shift in the composition of the advocacy coalition that supported the adopted policy change in earlier phases. Some members of the coalition may be ready to move on to another pressing social need or problem, or their job may change. Carol Johnson, an African American and superintendent of Minneapolis schools, was a strong supporter of the Dream Assessment Initiative envisioned by the AAMP, but when she accepted a new job in another city her successor was a man who had not been part of the project advocacy coalition and was not as interested in the initiative as she had been.

Some members of the advocacy coalition may want to be directly involved in implementation; others are better suited to being political guardians or monitors of the change. Leader succession may become an issue, since this phase calls for a new, more institution-building, style of leadership than in previous phases. A hand-off to new leaders may also be important in this phase simply to ensure that the change is not perpetually associated with a group of founding fathers or founding mothers and thus easily dissipated once they are no longer involved. For example, Jan Hively has been a key implementer of the Vital Aging Network and specific projects like the Vital Aging Summits in 2002 and 2004, the Leadership Advocacy Certificate Program in Vital Aging, and the Vital Force project. She announced, however, that she would step down as VAN coordinator after an initial start-up period. The coordinating work is now done by two consultants, one of whom has had a longstanding involvement with VAN; Hively, meanwhile, continues to serve on the VAN leadership group and is a driving force and key fundraiser for several of its projects.

Debugging Process

Difficulties are almost inevitable as change is introduced into an existing or new organization or department. Policy entrepreneurs should recall the well-known administrative adage of Murphy's Law: anything that can go wrong will go wrong. They should also recall the quip that Murphy was an optimist! The earlier phases of the change process should have been designed to help ensure that the proposal as adopted does not contain major flaws, but many difficulties emerge only after implementation begins. Policy entrepreneurs should ensure that a sound formative evaluation process is under way from the outset so as to help implementers identify obstacles and steer over, around, under, or through them to achieve policy goals (Bryson and Cullen, 1984; Patton, 1997). For example, the organizers of the Advocacy Leadership Certificate Program had considerable experience designing and teaching programs for adult learners. At the same time, the group had never tried offering a nine-month certificate program focusing on aging, personal renewal, community systems, and policy change to a group ranging in age from their thirties to nineties. Thus each session was formally and informally evaluated to adapt future sessions of the initial program to learner needs and plan the next year's program. The organizers also built in an evaluation of the program as a whole, to learn from the initial program and convince future participants and funders that the program was worthwhile.

Design Maintenance

The adopted policy may have been designed to address particular needs in a constructive way, but as situations change implementation can become a moving target. Policy entrepreneurs must remain alert to the possibility that design changes presented as helpful actually subvert policy aims.

Creation of a New Regime

Implementation of major changes requires creation of a new regime to govern decision making and behavior. Earlier we noted that the regime concept is taken from the field of international relations; it clearly applies to the development of effective shared-power arrangements in many, if not most, policy fields. To develop the shared set of implicit or explicit expectations that regimes embody, policy entrepreneurs should emphasize several features of regime construction, among them designing and using forums, arenas, and courts and developing supportive coalitions and practices in such a way that implementation outcomes—though not directly controlled—still effectively address the public problem of concern and satisfy key stakeholders. The new regime may also feature a widely shared "vision of success" that outlines what the world will look like if the desired changes are fully implemented.

A programmatic example is the Right Turn Project, which is bringing together community partners and public agencies to create a whole new regime for assisting young African American men who want to make a "right turn" toward a productive future. On a larger scale, the WBCSD seeks to implement new policy regimes to significantly reduce pollution and alleviate poverty around the world. Council staff and volunteers organize and promote such forums as multi-stakeholder dialogues; they participate in U.N.-sponsored forums such as the Earth Summits, produce reports, operate a large Website, and organize educational programs. They pressure national policy makers but also emphasize the possibilities for policy change in narrower arenas, such as a corporate board of directors. They highlight and encourage partnerships, notably a joint effort of Cisco Systems and the United Nations in a project called NetAid, which uses the Internet to combat poverty among the world's poorest people (Holliday, Schmidheiny, and Watts, 2002). They develop informal courts by supporting the Global Reporting Initiative, which helps companies produce sustainable development reports that can be used by various stakeholder groups to hold them accountable for goals such as environmental protection and poverty alleviation.

Summative Evaluation

Summative evaluations should occur after a policy change has been fully implemented and enough time has elapsed to know how well it is remedying the public problem or social need and to identify new problems or needs it might be generating. This evaluation focuses both on the immediate outputs and long-term outcomes and on tangible and intangible consequences of the policy change—on behaviors, products, and services as well as symbolic interpretations. Both are important in determining whether a policy change has been worth the expenditure of time and effort (Wholey, Hatry, and Newcomer, 1994). Summative evaluations are politically sensitive and constitute a link between this phase and the next. They may also be expensive and time-consuming, but without them it is hard to know whether a new policy regime is truly worthwhile.

Establishment or Anticipation of Review Points

Policy entrepreneurs should look ahead to the next phase and establish or anticipate points when stakeholders can consider whether an implemented policy should be maintained, significantly modified, or terminated. The policy change cycle is a series of loops, not a straight line. Politics, problems, and desired solutions often change things (Kingdon, 1995). There is no once-and-for-all solution, only temporary victories. Policy entrepreneurs must be alert to sources of possible challenge to an implemented solution, and they should work for maintenance of still-desirable policies; replacement with better ones, when possible or necessary; and termination of completely outmoded ones. In the case of the Vital Aging Network, future Vital Aging Summits might offer a good venue for reviewing policy implementation. The Earth Summits offer a similar opportunity for the WBCSD. The African American Men Commission might agree to engage in a thorough reassessment of its direction on the fifth and tenth anniversaries of the commission's creation.

Strengthening of People and Organizations

When the implementation process goes well, the people and organizations deemed responsible are seen as far-sighted, effective, and committed to the common good. They are likely to be trusted with additional responsibility in the future. The individuals involved are likely to experience heightened self-esteem and self-confidence (Bandura, 1997). The organizations involved are likely to enhance their capacity for future action. In addition to building a reserve of trust, they acquire an expanded repertoire of knowledge, tools, and techniques that can be applied to future changes.

Forward Mapping and Backward Mapping

Policy entrepreneurs may use two contrasting approaches, forward mapping and backward mapping (Elmore, 1982), to plan implementation. Each is a kind of logic model (Millar, Simeone, and Carnevale, 2001; Poister, 2003) or oval map (see Resource B). Forward mapping follows the rational planning model described in Chapter One. This approach "begins at the top of the process, with as clear a statement as possible of the policymaker's intent, and proceeds through a sequence of increasingly more specific steps to define what is expected of implementers at each level. At the bottom of the process, one states, again with as much precision as possible, what a satisfactory outcome would be, measured in terms of the original statement of intent" (Elmore, 1982, p. 19).

The major difficulty with forward mapping is its "implicit and unquestioned assumption that *policymakers control the organizational, political, and technological processes that affect implementation*" (Elmore, 1982, p. 20; italics in original). Forward mapping thus can be problematic in a shared-power, no-one-in-charge world, where leaders and managers can only influence, but not control, the various implementation processes, and where much of what happens during implementation "cannot be explained by the intentions and directions of policymakers" (p. 20) because implementation has more to do with the implementers' intentions and incentives than it does with the policy makers' intentions and incentives.

The alternative approach, backward mapping, begins at the very bottom of the implementation process, with "a statement of the specific behavior at the lowest level of the implementation process that generates the need for a policy" (p. 21). Backward mapping is similar to the bottom-up political decision-making model presented in Chapter One. The problem-formulation and search-for-solutions phases should lay the foundation for backward mapping in implementation. That is, participants in the problem-formulation process should focus on specific behavior and outcomes that are prompting the change effort, and participants in the search for solutions should establish objectives based on possible organizational actions at the lowest level that would minimize the problem.

Keeping these objectives in mind, implementation planners can go backward up the actual or possible structure of an implementing organization and ask two questions at each level: What is the capacity of this unit to produce the behavior envisioned by the policy change? What rules, resources, and transformation relations, broadly defined, does this unit need if it is to build or enhance that capacity? Once these questions are answered, the final stage in the process is to formulate a set of policies that direct or provide the necessary resources to the units likely to have the greatest effect. The exercise must involve explicit consideration of the design and use of new or existing forums, arenas, and courts likely to produce and protect desired changes. The source of the greatest effect, in other words, will be actors in forums, arenas, and courts—particularly those closest to the actual behaviors that are the source of the public problem—so those settings and the kind of behavior that leaders seek to enable within them must be given careful thought. For example, Hively and her collaborators have sought to understand how existing social service systems and employment policies and practices are affecting older adults; they have explored the desires and needs of older adults and their family members; they have studied the choices that older adults make about retirement, community service, and employment; and they have considered the capacity of implementing organizations such as the University of Minnesota's College of Continuing Education, the Volunteers of America, and the Humphrey Institute of Public Affairs. As a result, entities such as the VAN Website, the Advocacy Leadership Certificate Program, and the Vital Force project are all carefully designed to fit the needs of older adults and those who work with them, and to take advantage of the capabilities of the organizations involved.

Like forward mapping, backward mapping focuses on what policy entrepreneurs can do to produce desirable change. The use of backward mapping, however, does not assume that policy makers' mandates are the major influence on the behavior of various stakeholders involved in implementation. Nor does it assume that the appropriate measure of success is achievement of these mandates; rather, it assumes that the appropriate measure is a reasonable estimate of what can be done in a shared-power situation to effect desired change.

Wise policy entrepreneurs can use both backward and forward mapping to accomplish their goals. Once they have worked backward, revealing the desired behavior on the ground and the chain of influence that may produce it, they can write up the analysis in a forward fashion, as if they had used that approach. This allows them to recheck and elaborate the reasoning behind the implementation plan, as they travel back down the influence chain. This process also helps them discern whether or not the desired change is possible, using existing structures.

The bottom-up approach may be helpful even if the policy to be implemented was developed in an exclusively forward way. Even in this situation, implementers may have enough leeway to conduct a backward-mapping exercise designed to reveal a practical path to change, often through creative design and use of forums, arenas, and courts.

Vision of Success

As noted earlier, an important part of a new regime is shared expectations about what the new order will be. Such a vision is more likely to emerge from self-conscious reflection on the learning from one or more rounds of implementation practice than it is to emerge in advance. As successes build, policy entrepreneurs can weave them into a story that may include the regime's mission, basic strategies, performance criteria, important decision rules, and ethical standards. At its best, such a story is a "vision of success," a vivid description of attainable excellence (Bryson, 2004a).

A general vision, of course, is vital at the beginning of the policy change cycle, to inspire and mobilize participants in the change process. In this phase we are talking about a more detailed vision, tied to adopted policy changes in order to be useful guidance for implementation. For example, creation of the European Economic Community (EEC) was guided by Jean Monnet's vision of a "United States of Europe," articulated over most of his lifetime (Monnet, 1978). The vision of success for the *actual EEC* (now the European Union) was an emergent phenomenon derived from, and designed to influence, practical implementation of the idea. As the political and economic integration of Europe continues, Monnet's early sketch is being elaborated into an increasingly detailed portrait.

A vision of success should grow out of past decisions and actions as much as possible. These decisions and actions are often the record of a consensus about what the regime is and what it should do. Realization of a new future is easier if it can be shown to be a continuation of the past and present (Neustadt and May, 1986; Weick, 1995; Fiol, 2002). At the same time, a vision of success should not be just an extension of the present. It should be an affirmation in the present of an ideal and inspirational future. It should map back to the present to show regime participants how their daily actions can help the regime—and the participants themselves—achieve success.

A vision of success offers a number of advantages in a shared-power, no-one-in-charge situation. First, a widely accepted vision of success records enough consensus on ends and means to channel participants' efforts in a desirable direction while at the same time creating a framework for improvisation and innovation in pursuit of regime purposes. Second, the vision is the conception that precedes perception, to use Rollo May's insight (1969). People must have a conception of what success and desirable behavior look like before they actually can see them (Weick, 1995). A vision of success generates the conception that regime participants need if they are to discriminate among preferred and undesirable actions and outcomes to produce more of what is preferred, and to fashion appropriate expectations and reward systems. Third, a vision of success affirms the future in the present. It motivates adherents to live the vision in the present; they do not predict the future—a hazardous enterprise at best—but instead *make* it (Gabor, 1964).

Fourth, a clear vision of success allows people to work on behalf of regime aims without having to rely on direction from central or top decision makers. Finally, a widely shared vision of success takes on a moral quality that can infuse the regime with virtue. The normative self-regulation necessary for any moral community to survive and prosper is facilitated (Kanter, 1972; Mandelbaum, 2000). The vision of success, in other words, defines the substance and the extent of the court of public opinion within the community subscribing to the vision.

The policy entrepreneurs in all four of the cases highlighted in this book fostered a vision of success for the regimes they sought (although they were not usually produced in tangible form). In the AIDS case, the vision of success promoted by those seeking to stop the spread of AIDS was of a public health system that poured necessary resources into researching, preventing, and treating the disease. The vision also included citizens who were both aware of how AIDS spread and willing and able to practice safe sex. In their vision, AIDS might not be eradicated, but its transmission would be sharply curtailed, effective treatment would be widely available, and people with HIV would not be stigmatized and discriminated against.

In the AAMP case, the written description of the Right Turn Project begins with a future scenario of what happens when a young man is arrested for loitering and is assigned a "systems navigator," who is part of the project. The detailed scenario follows the young man as he works with the navigator and a mentor to develop and carry out a plan for paying past fines, getting stable housing and employment, and obtaining health care. The scenario also shows how neighborhood groups, church groups, government agencies, and a college offer assistance as the young man takes charge of his life.

If policy entrepreneurs cannot construct a vision of success for the new regime, it may not be essential to solidifying the regime. People do not have to agree on a vision to agree on next steps, as

U.N. diplomats, labor-management relations specialists, and used-car buyers and sellers all know (Lindblom, 1965; Thompson, 2001; Cleveland, 2002; Huxham, 2003). Simply finding ways to frame and deal with a few of the major implementation difficulties is likely to produce important progress on the social need or problem that prompted the policy change in the first place.

Managing Collaborations

In recent years, policy makers have increasingly mandated creation of formal collaboratives as a way of carrying out new policies. These collaboratives have considerable potential for focusing and aligning needed resources for achieving the policy goals—that is, for producing "collaborative advantage" (Huxham, 2003). At the same time, they can easily fall prey to "collaborative inertia" because of the built-in tension around agreeing on aims, building trust, coping with membership dynamics, managing power, and exercising leadership (Huxham, 2003). Before launching a collaboration, policy entrepreneurs should think carefully about how to deal with these tensions so that the collaborating partners achieve more together than they can separately (Huxham and Vangen, 2005).

Some of the partners might have previously collaborated informally, and those relationships can be helpful in a new formal arrangement. At the same time, formalizing relationships can bring to the fore disagreement about, for example, decision making and resource allocation that previously did not have to be explicitly addressed. Several scholars and practitioners offer helpful insights for policy entrepreneurs who are developing collaboratives for policy implementation (Ring and Van de Ven, 1994; Winer and Ray, 1994; Chrislip, 2002; Linden, 2002; Huxham, 1996, 2003; Gray, 2003; Huxham and Vangen, 2005). Chris Huxham and Siv Vangen emphasize that "single-mindedness of leaders seems to be central to collaborative success." (2000, p. 1171).

Leadership Guidelines

Policy entrepreneurs in this phase should attempt to achieve the desired outcomes we have noted and avoid the typical causes of implementation failure (Peters and Pierre, 2003), among which we highlight:

- Resistance based on attitudes and beliefs that are incompatible with the desired change; sometimes these attitudes and
  beliefs stem simply from the resisters' not having participated
  in policy development.
- Personnel problems such as inadequate numbers, over-
  commitment to other activities, inadequate orientation or
  training, poorly designed incentives, and people's uncertainty
  that involvement with implementation will help their careers.
- Incentives poorly designed to induce desired behavior on the
  part of implementing organizations.
- Implementing organization's preexisting commitment of
  resources to other priorities, and consequent absence of
  uncommitted resources to facilitate new activities; in other
  words, there is little slack in the system (Cyert and March,
  1963).
- Communication problems.
- Lack of administrative support services.
- The absence of rules, resources, and settings for resolving
  implementation problems; that is, the absence of forums,
  arenas, or courts needed to facilitate identification and resolution of these problems.
- The emergence of new political, economic, or administrative
  demands.

The overarching task of policy entrepreneurs in this phase is construction of a new policy regime. Formal and informal arenas are
likely to be especially important, along with their associated implicit
or explicit principles, norms, rules, decision-making procedures,
and incentives designed to develop a shared set of expectations
among actors about what should happen and why. Policy entrepreneurs should also attend to the design and use of formal and
informal forums to facilitate communication and to create the symbolic meanings of the regime in practice. Further, formal and informal courts are necessary for residual conflict management and
dispute resolution, along with enforcement of the underlying, and
perhaps new, norms in the system.

Additionally, policy entrepreneurs must focus on stabilization
of desired new patterns of behavior and attitude, particularly

through use of positive and negative sanctions and incentives; and continuation or creation of a coalition of implementers, advocates, and supportive interest groups.

The leadership guidelines presented here should be kept in mind as the adopted policy change moves into the implementation phase. The guidelines are divided into general guidance, communication and education, personnel, and direct versus staged implementation.

General Guidance

Policy implementation and evaluation must be thought about every bit as carefully and strategically as policy formulation.

Consciously and Deliberately Plan and Manage Implementation

An implementation planning process may or may not be mandated by the policy makers who have adopted the policy being implemented. Regardless, such planning should occur, and policy entrepreneurs should stay involved, either directly or as monitors of the planning process. This involvement is especially important when the adopted policy is more or less imposed on implementers.

Think Strategically About Implementation

How will you achieve important public purposes in practice? Implementation strategy may be defined as the *pattern* of purposes, policy statements, plans, programs, actions, decisions, or resource allocations that define what a policy is in practice, what it does, and why it does it, from the standpoint of various affected stakeholders (Bryson, 2004a; 2004b). Both forward and backward mapping approaches to implementation planning should be tried so as to find the strategies most likely to produce the outcomes envisioned by the advocates of change. Working from the top to the bottom of the implementation chain and vice versa—and then trying to reconcile the resulting differing views of what will work—is a helpful discipline. The process should include efforts to understand and accommodate the history and inclinations of key implementing individuals and organizations (Neustadt and May, 1986). Several authors offer additional detailed advice (Nutt and Backoff, 1992; Bryant, 2003; Friend and Hickling, 1997; Rosenhead and Minger, 2001; Bryson, 2004a).

Develop Strategy Documents and Action Plans

Be sure to develop strategy at four basic levels:

1. Grand strategy for the new regime as a whole
2. Strategy statements for the units (typically organizations) that make up the regime
3. Program or service strategies that prompt collaboration, coordination, and cooperation across the organization
4. Functional strategies (financial, staffing, facilities, information technology, procurement) that also facilitate interorganizational coordination

Strategies should be tied to the overall purpose of change and delineate the goals or objectives to be accomplished by the action plan. Typically, an action plan covers a period of a year or less. It outlines specific tasks, resources necessary to accomplish them, persons responsible, and a desired completion date. Without action planning, strategy is likely to remain a mere dream (Randolph and Posner, 2002). Remember to think of an action plan as building up the small wins that can nurture trust and produce large gains in the long run (see, for example, Huxham, 2003).

To guide stakeholder involvement in the action plan, you can use an implementation stakeholder grid (adapted from Meltsner, 1972; Coplin and O'Leary, 1976; Kaufman, 1986; and Christensen, 1993). The grid builds on information revealed by previously created diagrams of bases of power and directions of interest (Exercise 7.2), stakeholder-support-versus-opposition grids (Exercise 9.2), stakeholder role plays (Exercise 9.3), and grids of policy attractiveness versus stakeholder capability (Exercise 9.4). It can help your group refine strategies and develop action plans that tap stakeholder interests and resources. Exercise 11.1 explains how to develop such a grid.

Exercise 11.1. Tapping Stakeholder Interests and Resources for Policy Implementation.

1. For each implementation strategy, create a grid like the one below on either a single flipchart sheet or a wall covered with flipchart sheets.

2. Assemble previously done diagrams of bases of power and directions of interest, stakeholder-support-versus-opposition grids, stakeholder role plays, and grids of policy attractiveness versus stakeholder capability.

3. Fill out the grid of implementation strategy and action planning.

4. Discuss next steps and prepare action plans that tap supportive stakeholders' interests and resources, and deal with opposing stakeholders.

Grid of Implementation Strategy and Action Planning

Stakeholders	Stake or Interest	Resources	Action Channels Open to Stakeholder	Probability of Participation and Manner of Doing So	Influence, as a Product of Resources and Participation	Implications for Implementation Strategy	Affected Action Plan Elements
Supportive stakeholders							
Opposing stakeholders							

Start with Quick Changes

Start with changes that can be introduced easily and rapidly. As part of the action planning, identify the changes likely to encounter little resistance and pay off quickly, and make it a point to start with them. Look for the parts of the adopted policy that:

- Are conceptually clear
- Are based on a well-understood theory of cause-and-effect relationships
- Fit with the values of key implementers
- Can be made real to the bulk of implementers prior to implementation (in other words, implementers can be helped to see what they are supposed to do before they have to do it)
- Are administratively simple, with minimal bureaucracy and red tape, minor organizational restructuring, minor impact on resource allocation patterns, and minimal skill readjustments or retraining
- Allow a start-up period during which people can learn about the adopted change and engage in any necessary retraining, debugging, and development of new norms and operating routines
- Include adequate incentives to ensure that implementers wholeheartedly embrace the changes

Build in enough people, time, attention, money, administrative and support services, and other resources. Be sure that implementation plans include resources for:

- Key personnel
- "Fixers"—people who understand the relevant policy systems and how to fix things when they go wrong (Bardach, 1977)
- Additional necessary staff
- Conversion costs
- Adequate information and communication technology
- Orientation and training costs
- Technical assistance
- Inside and outside consultants

- Adequate incentives to facilitate adoption of the changes by relevant individuals and organizations
- Time, space, and mechanisms for problem solving
- Formative evaluation to facilitate implementation, and summative evaluation to determine whether or not the change produces desired results

Additionally, try to build in enough resources to allow implementers to handle unexpected contingencies, even though this may be difficult if policy makers have established a restrictive budget for the new policy. The need to have adequate resources once again points toward adequate attention to earlier phases of the policy change cycle. To garner sufficient resources, policy entrepreneurs must convince an array of stakeholders and key policy makers that a public problem is worthy of attention and the proposed solution is highly likely to produce desirable results at reasonable cost.

Develop Monitoring and Evaluation Plans

Effective monitoring and evaluation depend first of all on understanding the logic of the proposed change, so developing a logic model is the place to begin. The model helps clarify the key indicators that should be monitored. The model also allows evaluators to design evaluations to test for achievement of desired outputs and outcomes, and to gauge the soundness of the logic behind the change.

Work Quickly to Avoid Competition with New Priorities

Changing economic and political conditions can alter the priorities of those who control needed resources or the policy-making agenda. If the overall economy worsens, anticipated tax revenues, philanthropic contributions, and markets for products and services may all diminish. If a new party takes over one or more branches of government, the new officials may hold up promised funding. Sometimes even the expectation that positional leaders will be replaced or departments will be downsized is enough to paralyze implementation of a new policy, project, or proposal. So move quickly before changing conditions undermine your efforts.

Build a Protective Coalition

Maintain or develop a coalition of implementers, advocates, and interest groups who can protect change as it is institutionalized. Participants in the coalition that succeeded in having a new policy adopted may be excited about being a part of implementation, or they may want to focus on new projects at this point. Ideally, some of the originators of the new policies will stay involved, since they can be counted on to try to achieve the vision that inspired change. New individuals, groups, and organizations have to come on board, though, because their support is crucial for implementation. Policy makers may require that a formal collaboration (a type of enduring coalition) be established to carry out or oversee a policy change. Again, the collaboration should include some members of the coalition that advocated change and key implementers.

Regardless of whether a formal collaboration is established, the coalition committed to implementation is likely to experience tension around aims, trust, power, membership, and leadership style (Huxham, 2003). Power issues can be particularly prickly in this phase, since power may shift away from initial advocates to implementers. The techniques of team building in Chapter Three can be generally helpful, while visionary leadership methods described in Chapter Four can help the group develop shared purpose. Huxham (2003) emphasizes that a formal collaboration is often able to make progress on developing shared purpose by simply agreeing on some initial action and clarifying joint aims as the members move along.

You may also create a policy implementation coordinating committee as a subgroup of the collaboration. This committee could simply be a continuation of the one that coordinated the work of the advocacy coalition in the earlier phases. At least some overlap in membership between the two committees is helpful.

Ensure that Arenas Are Facilitative

Make sure that legislative, executive, and administrative arenas facilitate implementation. Maintain connections with the decision makers (board members, top executives, legislators) whose future decisions can affect the implementation effort. You are likely to need their support for supplemental policies, regulations, rules, or funding needed to implement the adopted policies. For example, when new legislation mandates a rule-making process by administrative departments, policy entrepreneurs need to understand how the process works and help the implementing coalition make sure that the process brings about the desired change expeditiously.

Evaluate the Impact of Lingering Disagreement

Think carefully about how residual disputes will be resolved and underlying norms enforced. Pay attention to the design and use of courts, including norms, conflict resolution methods, jurisdictions, access rules, and deep sources of legitimacy. The adopted policies may require that new courts (a grievance board, an ethics review commission) be set up. When new laws are being implemented, you may also have to use existing formal courts or court-related offices to clarify implementing authority, fight off any challenge to implementation, and penalize conduct that violates the law.

Be sure that new courts operate according to basic judicial principles of due process and equal protection, so the courts' decisions will not be overturned by a higher court. You may need to specify an appeal process. Rely on alternative dispute resolution techniques wherever possible, to keep conflict out of the formal courts and open up the possibility of an all-gain solution that increases the new regime's legitimacy and public acceptance of the outcomes of conflict management efforts (Fisher and Ury, 1981; Gray, 1989; Susskind, McKearnan, and Thomas-Larmer, 1999). Remember, too, that the court of public opinion has importance in reinforcing the norms in the new regime. Finally, maintaining good relations with the police may be crucial, especially if opponents are willing to use violence and intimidation to prevent policy implementation.

Hang in There!

Successful implementation in a shared-power setting typically requires a lot of time, attention, resources, and effort (Kanter, 1983; Kingdon, 1995). Moreover, implementers may need considerable courage to fight the resisters of change. The rewards, however, can be great as the implementers begin to see the beneficial effects of what they are doing.

Communication and Education

It is very easy to *under*estimate how much communication and education are likely to be needed for successful implementation. Similarly, it is very hard to *over*estimate how much will be needed.

Invest Heavily in Designing and Using Forums

Particularly when a major change is involved, stakeholders must be given the opportunity to develop, formally and informally, shared meanings and appreciations that further implementation of the policy goals (Trist, 1983; Sabatier and Jenkins-Smith, 1993; Chrislip, 2002). The stakeholders must *hear* about the new programs, projects, rules, and behaviors that are part of the developing new policy regime. Preferably, they hear the same message across multiple channels many times. Educational programs, information packets, newsletters, listservs, guidebooks, Web pages, and press releases can highlight key messages and establish a desirable frame of reference and common language for implementation efforts.

Stakeholders need to be able to talk about the change, fit it into their own interpretive schemes, adapt it to their own circumstances, and explore implications for action and the consequences of those actions (Weick, 1995; O'Toole, 1995; Bryson, Ackermann, Eden, and Finn, 2004). Ultimately, they must be convinced that the new way of doing things is better than the status quo.

Be sure to maintain contacts with the reporters, editors, and news directors who followed the earlier debate. They are unlikely to be interested in implementation details, but you can take advantage of an anniversary (a year after passage of a new law) or milestone (perhaps the first cohort to graduate from an educational program) to attract coverage.

The policy implementation coordinating group is an especially important forum. A group meeting can be the occasion for ongoing problem solving, noting milestones, taking the pulse of the project, and maintaining enthusiasm.

Deal with Resistance

Reduce any implementer resistance that is based on divergent attitudes and lack of participation. Organize orientation sessions, problem-solving teams, one-on-one coaching, and technical assistance (all supported by user-friendly written materials, Web pages, videotapes, and the like) to support enactment of the new policies. Schedule ceremonies and confer symbolic awards to reinforce desired behavior and bolster implementers' spirits over the long haul.

Consider Developing a Guiding Vision of Success

The vision should include a mission statement, the basic regime philosophy, goals, basic strategies, performance criteria, important decision rules, and ethical standards expected of all regime participants. The vision can be expressed in a written document (no more than a few pages long) and through other media such as a videotape or Website.

To begin constructing a written vision, assemble a drafting committee composed of members of the implementation coalition. Ask each committee member to prepare a draft vision, which is then discussed by the committee as a whole. After the discussion, turn over the task of drafting a shared vision of success to a member who is also a skilled writer. Additional sessions may be needed to furnish information for particular parts of the vision; for example, the committee may need to engage in stakeholder analysis to develop performance criteria.

Once a draft is prepared, convene review sessions with key stakeholders to identify the vision's strengths and modifications that will improve it. The meeting can be structured according to the agenda suggested in Chapter Nine. Remember that consensus on a vision of success is highly desirable but may not be necessary. Typically, deep-seated commitment to any vision statement emerges only over time (Senge, 1990).

If a vision of success is to help guide regime decisions and implementing actions, it must be widely disseminated and discussed. It probably should be published as a booklet and given to all key stakeholders, and it should be discussed at all orientation and training sessions aimed at implementing the new policy regime. (For additional guidance, see Angelica, 2001; Bryson and Crosby, 2003.)

Build in Regular Attention to Appropriate Indicators

The implementation plan should include regular reporting of progress in meeting regime goals. Thus the African American Men Commission must report periodically on the number of men who have made progress on (for example) specific employment, education, or health outcomes.

Personnel

You can do just about anything when the right people have the right support.

Choose Committed People

Fill policy and staff positions with highly qualified people committed to the change. Creative, skilled, experienced, resilient, committed people are necessary to create the new regime culture, systems, and structures that will focus and channel implementation efforts. If you want to attract and retain such people, be sure to:

- Offer adequate financial and psychological compensation
- Help these people see how their career can be advanced by involvement in implementation
- Provide "escape" options, such as the choice of returning to a prior job, outplacement services, or a generous severance package

Continue the Entrepreneurial Team or Establish a Successor

The team in question might be a subset of the implementation coordinating committee. The coordinating committee broadly may act as a sponsor of the implementation process, but these people are the champions. The team should include at least some of the members of the original entrepreneurial team that successfully campaigned for the adopted change. At least some of the team members should have direct implementation responsibility; for example, one of the team members may be the project manager for the implementation project. Remember too that a project manager may become powerful—a situation that could cause a clash with others on the team who might feel their control over implementation is diminished.

Ensure Access to Top Administrators During Implementation

This task is easy if the top administrators have been part of the advocacy coalition. Even if they have not, they may be open to regular communication with change advocates in order to benefit from the latter's knowledge about the new policies and to gain support for implementation plans.

Work Around or Remove Resistant People

Ease out, work around, or avoid people who are not likely to help the change effort. Policy makers often try to overcome resistance to implementation within an established organization by assigning implementation to a new unit or organization. Even so, implementers are likely to have to deal with resisters in the established organization, and sometimes within the new one as well. Options for dealing with these people include:

- Helping them get a job to which they are better suited
- Basing merit pay on achievement of implementation goals
- Buying off resisters with early retirement
- Giving them other assignments

Direct Versus Staged Implementation

Direct, full-fledged implementation of a new policy regime makes sense under some conditions, but staged implementation is often required to cope with political and technical difficulties.

Decide Whether Direct or Staged Implementation Is Better

Direct implementation is better under certain conditions: when (1) the technicalities of implementation are simple and the political atmosphere is favorable, (2) immediate action is necessary to deal with a crisis, or (3) the adopted solutions simply cannot be adopted piecemeal. In a technically and politically easy situation, direct implementation can work if enough resources are built in and implementer resistance is low. In this case, an important leadership task is to reduce resistance to change by helping implementers see how the change is in their interest. Although a crisis can have the effect of reducing resistance to change, eventually implementation leaders have to show that the implemented solution is actually beneficial. Finally, a "lumpy solution" may require direct implementation. When policy makers decided to build the Chunnel between Britain and France, they couldn't start with a little practice tunnel first and then proceed to a bigger tunnel later. They had to carry out the full plan or do nothing.

Staged implementation allows implementation to proceed in waves, in which initial adopters are followed by later adopters, and finally most of the laggards embrace the changes (Rogers, 2003). This approach is best used when technical or political difficulties hamper direct implementation.

In the case of technical difficulty, consider starting implementation with a pilot project designed to reveal the connection between the adopted solution and outcomes. The more technically difficult the situation is, the more necessary a pilot project will be to figure out which techniques work. In the case of political difficulty, consider beginning with a demonstration project to prove that solutions known to work in a benign and controlled condition can work in other settings. The more organized opposition there is to the proposed change, the more necessary a demonstration project is. At the same time, if the opposition is both organized and implacable, then direct and massive implementation may actually be best in order to overwhelm opponents, rather than give them a number of smaller targets to attack (Bryson and Delbecq, 1979; Joyce, 1999).

In the case of both technical and political difficulty, consider beginning with a pilot project followed by a demonstration project, and then transfer to the entire implementation system. In general, the more difficult the situation, the more important is a combination of educational tactics, incentives for desired changes, and development of shared commitment to the change among all interested parties.

In staged implementation, give special attention to those who implement change in the early stages. Try to attract initial implementers who have enough experience, skill, and desire to make the change work. Such people are likely to have above-average ability, firsthand experience with the need for the change, and experience with prior change efforts. They should be persuasive role models who do not charge mindlessly into every fad that comes over the horizon. Further guidance for designing effective pilot and demonstration projects and for transferring tested changes to the entire implementation system is presented in Exhibit 11.1.

Exhibit 11.1. Guidance for Pilot Projects, Demonstration Projects, and Transfer to Entire Implementation System.

Pilot Projects

- Test the scientific validity of the proposed changes, probably using experimental or quasi-experimental designs (Campbell and Stanley, 1966); that is, test whether the adopted solutions produce desired effects.
- Perform the test in a safe, controlled environment with access to a rich set of resources. Ideally, you should match a control group against an experimental group that differs from the control group *only* in experiencing the change being tested.
- Test several possible versions of the solutions and search for their strengths and weaknesses.
- Use technical specialists to evaluate cause-and-effect relations. Consider using outside experts, or an inside-outside team whose objectivity will not be questioned.
- Design tests to measure effectiveness, as well as efficiency.

Demonstration Projects

- Test for the generalizability of proposed changes for typical implementer settings, probably through use of quasi-experimental designs. True experiments are rarely possible in the field, but try to include a control group in order to determine what works under what circumstances and why.
- Test in easy, average, and difficult implementation settings to gauge the hardiness of the changes and possibilities for handling a range of implementation difficulties.
- Test several possible changes to compare their strengths and weaknesses.
- Use a two-cycle process, in which implementers learn how to work with the changes in the first cycle and the effects of changes are monitored in the second cycle.
- Include a qualitative evaluation (Patton, 1997), along with quantitative studies, to show solution strengths and weaknesses. Pay attention to outputs and outcomes.
- Remember that the demonstration stage tests the maintenance of solution design that is already known to work technically; that is, it can produce the desired effects.
- Assemble a special team, if necessary, to monitor implementation.

Exhibit 11.1. Guidance for Pilot Projects, Demonstration Projects, and Transfer to Entire Implementation System, Cont'd.

- Create opportunities for future implementers to witness the demonstrations.
- Develop a media strategy to communicate the desirability of the changes and the best way to implement them.

Transfer to Implementation System

- Commit substantial resources to communication, including cycling in observers likely to spread information about the changes and influence subsequent implementer adoptions.
- Promote the visibility of the changes.
- Produce, emphasize, and disseminate educational materials and operational guides designed to make adoption and implementation easier.
- Develop credible and easily understood models that show how the desired changes work and how they can be implemented.
- Furnish additional resources for technical assistance and problem solving.
- Provide incentives for adoption of the changes.
- Be flexible.

Summary

Policy entrepreneurs consciously, deliberately, and strategically plan and manage implementation and evaluation of the adopted policy in order to create a new policy regime. Significant elements of the new regime are new or redesigned forums, arenas, and courts; implicit or explicit principles, norms, rules, and decision-making procedures; substantive and symbolic incentives promoting the new arrangement; institutionalization of altered patterns of behavior and attitude; and continuation or creation of a supportive coalition of implementers, advocates, and other groups. The new regime may also incorporate a widely shared vision of success.

Successful implementation introduces the desired change quickly and smoothly and overcomes the typical causes of implementation failure. A combination of forward and backward mapping facilitates development of successful implementation strategies and actions. Implementation may be direct or staged. Direct implementation works better when the time is right, the need is clear to a strong coalition of implementers, agreed-upon problems and adopted solutions are clearly and logically connected, and a clear vision guides the changes. (These are the conditions that also favor a big-win strategy.) Staged implementation is advisable when policy entrepreneurs face technical and political difficulties. In this case, entrepreneurs organize a series of small wins by using pilot and/or demonstration projects followed by transfer of proven change to the entire implementation system.

Change is not complete upon adoption of a new policy by an official decision-making body. Without effectively implemented solutions, important public problems will simply fester. Implementation must be viewed as continuation of the policy change process toward its ultimate destination of successful collective action in pursuit of the common good. Effective policy entrepreneurship should be understood as a single sweeping gesture pointing from an important public problem to desirable solutions, to adopted change, to implementation of the change, and finally to outcomes that indicate the problem has been overcome.

Chapter Twelve

Reassessing Policies and Programs

In my end is my beginning.
T. S. ELIOT, *FOUR QUARTETS*

Once a policy is fully implemented, policy entrepreneurs need to anticipate the final phase of the policy change cycle: policy continuation, modification, or termination. Times change, situations change, and coalitions of interest change. A policy that works should be continued and protected through vigilance and adaptation. A policy that does not work well should be bolstered with additional resources, significantly modified or succeeded by a new policy, or terminated.

A policy ceases to work for four main reasons. First, the idea may be good but policy makers and implementers have not devoted enough resources to implementing it, and thus the impact of the policy is less than desired. Second, problems change, and an implemented solution can itself become a problem. For example, widespread Internet accessibility puts a powerful communication tool in the hands of diverse population groups, increasing their access to information about, on the one hand, employment opportunities and online courses. At the same time, widespread Internet access has offered, on the other hand, sexual predators a chance to use anonymous chat rooms to reach potential victims. Third, as problem areas become packed with policies, the interaction of these policies can produce results that no one wants. For example, public subsidy of automobile use by way of highway funding and coverage of pollution-related costs has contributed to urban sprawl, air pollution, and declining central city business districts. Fourth, the political environment may shift. As a policy becomes institutionalized, advocates may be less attentive and vocal. Supportive elected officials may be replaced by officials who are uninterested in or even hostile to the policy, and they may pass laws or appoint administrators who undermine it. For example, President George W. Bush's administration has severely and systematically weakened preexisting regulations controlling the emission of pollutants from factories and power plants.

Purpose and Desired Outcomes

The purpose of this phase of the policy change cycle is to review implemented policies, plans, or programs and to decide on one of three main courses of action: continuation of good policy, modification of less successful policy through appropriate reform, and elimination of undesirable policy. Desired outcomes include:

- Institutions that remain responsive to real needs and problems
- Resolution of residual problems that occur during sustained implementation
- Development of the energy, will, and ideas for needed reform of existing policies or for tackling the next big public problem requiring attention

Maintaining Responsive Institutions

An institution is often a permanent pattern of response to "old" problem definitions. When the problems change, the institutions often do not, and therefore they become a problem themselves (Schön, 1971; Wilson, 1989). For example, in the United States drug companies, medical researchers, and federal regulators succeeded by the 1990s in making effective drugs that can keep people with AIDS relatively healthy for a long time. Although the drugs are expensive, most people in the United States are able to afford them or obtain insurance or public assistance to pay. Once AIDS began to spread rapidly in poorer parts of the world, the need for these high-priced drugs grew and instigated the demand that drug companies change their pricing policy, and that governments overrule patent protection in some cases. Meanwhile, in the United States existing government programs that provide the drugs for low-income people are strained because AIDS patients are living longer, and because of state and federal budget cuts.

Ensuring that an institution remains responsive to real problems and needs takes effort. Periodic studies, reports, conferences, fact-finding missions, and discussion with stakeholders are necessary to stay in touch with real conditions. The design and use of forums is especially important for creating and sustaining discussion about the real problems and needs and appropriate institutional responses.

Resolving Residual Problems

Even if an implemented policy remains generally responsive to the problems that prompted it, policy entrepreneurs need to be on the alert for new difficulties that hamper the effectiveness of the policy. For example, the U.S. Medicare system continues to help older Americans obtain the health care they need. At the same time, the prescription drug coverage passed by Congress in 2003 is so costly that it is a major threat to Medicare's viability.

Tackling the Next Reform or Big Public Problem

Policy entrepreneurs can handle minor difficulties through such existing administrative mechanisms as "management by exception," administrative law courts, periodic policy review and modification exercises, and routine access to key decision makers. To achieve major reform or to tackle the next big public problem, however, they must build or renew an advocacy coalition that is committed and enthusiastic about beginning the policy change process anew. A summation of our advice for initiating the policy change process follows leadership guidelines, the next section.

Leadership Guidelines

Policy entrepreneurs should keep a number of guidelines in mind as they engage constituents in reviewing implemented policy and working to continue, modify, or terminate it. General guidelines are presented, followed by specific suggestions for policy continuation, modification, and termination (for additional details, see Hogwood and Peters, 1983).

General Guidelines

To ensure that implemented policies and institutions continue to serve public needs, policy entrepreneurs retain a focus on important goals, indicators of success and failure, contributors to inertia, and opportunities for rethinking.

Stay Focused on What Is Important

Pay attention to the needs and problems that prompted the policy change, and view policies and institutions as a means of responding to them. If the policies and institutions are no longer serving public needs, they should be altered. For example, the Vital Aging Network is critiquing public policies that attempt to respond to older adults' health care needs but mainly fund institutional care. The VAN people argue that if the policy goal is to give older adults the most appropriate care, along with minimizing costs, more of this funding should be available for in-home health care.

Focus on Indicators of Success and Failure

Pay attention to changes in the indicators that were used to argue for or against policy change in the first place; to new indicators that are important to key stakeholders and that shed light on implementation effectiveness; and to results of summative evaluation. To the extent that these indicators offer a valid sign of policy progress or failure, they can support deciding to continue, modify, or terminate a policy regime. For example, the research conducted in the African American Men Project highlighted the achievement gap between students of color and others, unemployment rates, and the level of homelessness. These indicators constituted clear evidence that existing policies, programs, and projects were not achieving their espoused goals.

Review Interpretive Schemes and Myths

Review the interpretive schemes and myths used to formulate the problem and adopted solutions. Are they still accurate and useful representations of reality? Do they embody or imply useful solutions to a public problem? Or has something changed about the reality (political, social, economic, or technological) to make these interpretations and myths a distortion of reality? If so, try to discover more appropriate myths and interpretive schemes that are more likely to promote desirable outcomes. For example, if the national vital aging movement is successful in building a new regime of educational and employment opportunities for older workers, it is possible that the public might focus so strongly on a "fountain of youth" interpretive scheme that they would thoroughly downplay a competing but valid scheme of responsibility for caring for frail elderly people.

Attend to Forums, Arenas, and Courts

Be attentive to the existing (and the new) forums, arenas, and courts in which policy is continued, modified, or terminated. These are often the same shared-power settings that were crucial during previous phases of the policy change cycle; especially if major reform or termination of the implemented policy is needed, however, you may need to create or use other forums, arenas, and courts to achieve desired outcomes in this phase. For the World Business Council for Sustainable Development, U.N. meetings—especially Earth Summits—remain important as they try to sustain support for further implementation of the global regime to control greenhouse gases. As anti-AIDS campaigners shift their attention away from the United States and Western Europe, where treatment and prevention programs are now institutionalized, in order to focus on parts of the world still struggling to cope with the pandemic, they have initiated or expanded a worldwide array of national, regional, and international forums, arenas, and courts.

Acknowledge the Staying Power of Organizations and Networks

Remember that organizations and networks often have greater staying power than any policy (Hogwood and Peters, 1983). Thus praising the intentions and goodwill of organizations and networks, while emphasizing the need to review and possibly reform their policies, is more likely to produce change than attacking the motives and goodwill of the organizations and networks themselves. You also should try to figure out how existing networks and organizations might benefit from needed reform. As noted, vital aging advocates are often harshly critical of existing government programs that have promoted nursing home care for older adults while underfunding in-home care. They would be wise to acknowledge that program administrators often share their concern for the well-being of older adults, while marshaling stories and facts about the payoff of in-home care. They should show specifically how the payoff meets administrators' and policy makers' goals of being good stewards of public funds and helping maintain the health of older adults.

You also should acknowledge that in some cases an existing organization or network is simply too resistant to change, and new organizations and networks will have to be involved in reviewing and reforming policy. Thus President Bush agreed to set up the independent September 11 investigative commission after stakeholders—prominently, the families of those who died in the September 11 terrorist attacks—forced him to concede that the existing intelligence and security agencies were unable to make needed assessments and reforms on their own.

Challenge Rules and Routines That Favor Inertia

Institutional routines and other rules embedded in established forums, arenas, and courts often give the present arrangement a taken-for-granted quality and foster equilibrium, or inertia, in a policy system (Baumgartner and Jones, 1993). Those rules and routines must be confronted and set aside in order to thoroughly review and change an implemented policy (Mangham, 1986; Feldman, 2000).

Use Existing Review Opportunities, or Create New Ones

Periodic policy reauthorization sessions and annual or biennial budget review periods create the opportunity for regular policy review. Election campaigns and changes in top elected or appointed policy makers or executives are also predictable occasions for policy review.

You can also create a policy review opportunity almost anytime, through designing and using existing or new forums. Consider arranging a conference, hearing, study commission, media event, investigative reporting, or discussion group to review and critique the policies that concern you (Bromiley and Marcus, 1987).

Convene a Review Group

The composition of this group may vary considerably with the nature of the review. Legislation and policies requiring scheduled reviews may assign them to a particular group (for example, a legislative committee, a board of directors, or an independent review board). Often, however, you can influence the composition of the group. Try to include at least some participants who do not have a vested interest in the status quo, so they can take a fresh look at the policy regime.

Stay Energized

Generate energy and enthusiasm for tackling the next big public problem. The experience, credibility, and networks that you have built in the process of working on one public problem are part of your foundation for working on a new one. Jan Hively has been able, in her vital aging work, to draw on the reputation and contacts she made as an entrepreneur in youth policy.

Policy Continuation

Focus on fine-tuning forums, arenas, and courts, and attend to a fairly narrow range of stakeholders.

Minimize Change in Forums, Arenas, and Courts

To continue an existing policy, seek little change in the design and use of forums, arenas, and courts. Any significant change is likely to undermine the regime established in the previous phase. Even so, be sure to find occasions in forums to recall or reinvigorate the vision that originally inspired and mobilized people to seek the policy change.

Attend to Certain Stakeholders

To continue or make minor changes to an existing policy, rely on implementers, supportive advocates, and focused input from consumers. Use routine surveys and discussion, focus groups, and task forces to continue fine-tuning the policy. Throwing open the door to more expansive assessment involving an array of stakeholders is likely to prompt pressure for more fundamental policy changes (Hogwood and Peters, 1983; Baumgartner and Jones, 1993; Chrislip, 2002).

Policy Modification or Succession

Design forums to alter meaning, focus on midlevel arenas, consider policy splitting or consolidation, and create parallel systems.

Change Forums, Arenas, and Courts

To facilitate the move to a significantly altered policy, significantly alter the design and use of forums, arenas, and courts. Changes in the appropriate shared-power settings allow a new set of issues, decisions, conflicts, and policy preferences to emerge.

Use Forums to Challenge Existing Meanings

Create or redesign a forum to challenge existing meanings and create new ones. Consciously estrange people from problem definitions, solution choices, or supporting political arrangements that are no longer helpful (Mangham, 1986; Fiol, 2002; Stone, 2002). Offer new interpretive schemes, myths, or stories that can be the seed crystal around which a new coalition forms in support of another configuration of policies, plans, and programs. For example, a problem reassessment may imply that a new set of categories, value judgments, indicators, comparisons, focusing events, or crises are relevant. You may help others articulate a revised vision that inspires collective action. This work begins in forums and moves toward arenas and courts.

Even if you are successful in redefining a problem, do not expect new policies to be adopted without a change in the political environment. This might be a public opinion swing, election results, administrative changes, ideological or partisan redistribution in legislative bodies, and interest group pressure campaigns. Before new proposals can be adopted, key decision makers in arenas must be receptive, and changes in politics may be a necessary precursor of this receptivity.

Major reforms may also depend on a successful search for important ideas within the relevant policy community. Recall that a policy is usually a recombination of existing ideas, or a mutation, rather than something totally new (Kingdon, 1995). Still, you need to find the right combination, one that responds effectively to the redefined problem and that is politically salable. Forums again play a crucial role as the setting within which effective solutions to a public problem are crafted.

Focus on Midlevel Arenas

The high-level political elites are unlikely to be involved in policy modification because the legitimacy of the issue has already been settled. Instead, the focus is likely to be midlevel legislative and administrative arenas and the details of program redesign being hashed and rehashed (Lynn, 1987). The people likely to have the most impact on a reform effort are current policy implementers and consumers. Precisely because the effort is unlikely to attract the interest of political elites, new interest groups, or the public at large, major reform is difficult (Hogwood and Peters, 1983; Baumgartner and Jones, 1993).

Because both implementers and beneficiaries of an existing policy are more likely to be concerned with policy details than with innovation, it may be possible to make major changes by involving at least some key policy makers who act quickly while implementers and beneficiaries are focused on the operation of current programs (Hogwood and Peters, 1983). This is always a risky strategy, however, since eventually implementers have to carry out the change. To make a substantial change, you are likely to require the support of a coalition other than the one that originally adopted and implemented the policy, and a new constellation of ideas, interests, and agreements will have to be worked out (Sabatier and Jenkins-Smith, 1993).

Consider a Move to "Split" or Consolidate Policies

Splitting or consolidating programs, projects, or administrative regimens can resolve conflict over budget allocation, implementation approach, and even leadership style. Of course, the cost of merging or breaking up a policy implementation structure should be carefully weighed against the potential gain. Pulling apart ideas that are central to the policy regime or meshing those ideas with others—a kind of reframing—can be harder than altering the implementation structure.

Build a New System

Consider building a new system without dismantling the old system. Although the result is parallel, redundant, or competing systems, net social gains may result through better market segmentation and the benefits of competition (Bendor, 1985; Osborne and Plastrik, 1997).

Policy Termination

Think of policy termination as an extreme version of policy reform. Many of the guidelines outlined under policy modification are applicable to policy termination as well (Holzer, Lee, and Newman, 2003; Nutt, 2001). Pay particular attention to the design and use of forums, arenas, and courts. You are likely to need to organize a new coalition around alternative ideas, interests, and agreements.

A substantial literature has developed on how to manage cutbacks in general. Behn (1983) argues that there are typically two stages to cutback efforts in a public organization. In the first stage, the organization borrows against the future to cover the gap between current revenues and needed expenditures. If revenues are not increased in the future, this tactic merely makes the adjustment to retrenchment or outright termination worse by postponing the second stage, or "day of reckoning," when major cuts and redesigns are made. The steps listed here would appear to be important cutback management tasks; though useful, they are obviously no panacea or quick fix (Behn, 1983; Holzer, Lee, and Newman, 2003):

- Explain the reality.
- Take a long-term view.
- Develop the support of key leaders, decision makers, and constituencies, including legislators if necessary, in the public sector.
- Emphasize mission, vision, and values.
- Develop clear guidelines and goals for making reductions.
- Emphasize the importance of focusing on results, accountability, and integrity.
- Use strategic assessment and performance measures to know what to cut and what to reward.

- Rely on transparent communications to help build understanding of the problems to be faced, and to build cooperation among affected units, unions, employees, and other stakeholders.
- Maintain morale, in part by indicating what is off-limits to being cut.
- Attract and keep quality people, which may be particularly difficult when people think the ship is sinking.
- Reinvest and redeploy staff on the basis of a strategic vision; create opportunity for innovation; emphasize continuous improvement in what remains.
- Create incentives for cooperation.
- Avoid mistakes.
- Be compassionate.
- Celebrate the actual accomplishments of the people working in the organization or with the policy or program being eliminated.

If you have necessary executive or administrative authority on your side, it may be possible to terminate a policy fairly expeditiously, using a truncated version of the policy change cycle. Research by Robert Behn and Mark Daniels indicates that in this case it is wise to put an outsider or a lame duck in charge of termination (Behn, 1978; Daniels, 1996), since these people are likely to be more willing to take a position that is unpopular with powerful constituencies of the existing policy.

Stop Resistance Quickly
Move quickly to short circuit resistance from implementers and beneficiaries of the existing policy.

Separate Stakeholders from Policies
Estrange important stakeholders from the policy (Mangham, 1986). Focus attention on the harm it does, and if possible link your effort to remedy this harm to ascendant ideologies or interpretive schemes. Thus, as vital aging advocates highlight the harm of channeling public funding mainly to nursing home and hospital care of older adults, they align their messages with the deinstitu-

tionalization ideology that has become dominant in the U.S. social policy debate in recent years. Particularly in policy termination, you should be careful to praise the accomplishments and good intentions of those who really have performed well in the existing regime.

Favor Adopting the New Over Terminating the Old

Advocate adoption of a new policy rather than termination of the old. This approach focuses on the benefits of the new policy for an array of stakeholders. You may need to include sweeteners in the new policy to quell resistance from beneficiaries of the old one. Behn (1978) also advises terminating only those portions of a policy that should end, and being willing to accept additional costs in the short run to obtain long-term savings or improvement.

Starting Anew

Assuming you are ready to move on to a new public problem affecting your organization or community, we recommend these initial strategies:

- Focus on the context and people involved.
- Outline compelling reasons to undertake the policy change effort.
- Assess leadership capabilities, and begin organizing effective teams.
- Begin laying the groundwork for a winning coalition.
- Think ahead about the process of issue creation.
- Develop a general strategy.
- Think about the costs and consequences of the policy change effort.
- Develop an action plan for obtaining an initial agreement to address the problem.
- When the going gets tough, keep in mind the benefits of the proposed policy change.
- Be willing to concede that the time may not be right for the preferred policy change.

Focus on the Context and People Involved

Remember a fundamental principle of organizing collective action: start where the affected people—the stakeholders—are (Kahn, 1991; Bobo, Kendall, and Max, 2001; Shaw, 2001; Prokosch and Raymond, 2002). Talk to them, read newspapers and magazines, read public affairs journals, listen to talk shows, log on to chat rooms, watch documentaries, pay attention to opinion polls. Keep your eyes and ears open. Prepare to connect your analysis of the problem and potential solutions, as well as the process of policy change, to their views and concerns.

You have to tailor the policy change process and your roles to the relevant communities of interest or place. The generic policy change process we have outlined must be applied with care so that it fits the situation (Christensen, 1985; Alexander, 2000).

Outline Compelling Reasons to Undertake a Policy Change Effort

By focusing on the significance and worth of the effort, you prepare yourself and others to summon the courage, strength, and endurance to undertake what is likely to be an arduous process. You also begin engaging in visionary leadership.

Assess Leadership Capabilities

Be clear about what animates you as a leader before you begin championing a policy change effort, and be candid with yourself about your own strengths and weaknesses. In assembling an initial team, be sure that members bring needed and complementary strengths that can overcome individual weaknesses, and confirm that they are willing to use their personal strengths on behalf of the policy change effort.

Begin Laying the Groundwork for a Winning Coalition

Develop a stakeholder-power-versus-interest grid (Exercise 4.2) to guide your thinking about who needs to be a part of the advocacy coalition. Certainly stakeholders who are most affected by the change effort are important, but you also have to identify powerful individuals and groups who can be sponsors and champions of the change effort.

Think Ahead About the Process of Issue Creation

This is more visionary leadership work. Recall that issue creation is the process by which a public problem and at least one solution that has pros and cons from the stakeholders' standpoint gain a place on the public agenda. We suggest that you engage an initial small group of supporters in a truncated version of the process we have described in previous chapters. Doing so helps you think ahead about what might occur once more stakeholders get involved, and to decide whether the policy change effort you are considering is likely to be worthwhile. Naturally the change effort is likely to change along the way, no matter what, but at least advance thinking can reduce unwelcome surprises.

Here is an outline for a truncated issue creation process:

- Explore various problem definitions, or formulations, to determine whether an apparent public problem really should be solved. You might have to gather data, examine the actions and results of systems already in place, and talk with many knowledgeable people.
- Consider the range of possible solutions to the problem. Which elements of various proposals already circulating in various communities might be promising?
- Specify the constellation of stakeholders that might be affected by the problem and by the change effort. Use Exercise 4.3 to assess whether you can develop problem frames that will attract the support of enough stakeholders to join a supportive advocacy coalition. The exercise should also give you an idea of how strong the opposition to proposed changes is going to be.
- Determine if an issue can be framed so that it can get on the public agenda and, at the same time, be worth the effort required to persuade relevant decision makers to adopt and implement a proposed change.

Develop a General Strategy

Use the oval-mapping process described in Resource B to elicit and connect ideas for how to proceed, and make a list of the forums, arenas, and courts in which the problem and potential solutions are currently being addressed. Refer to the map and list as you and your colleagues answer these questions:

- How is the problem being discussed (or not discussed) in existing forums? Who are the main participants, and what would they think about other ways of defining the problem and potential solutions?
- What decisions about the problem and potential solutions are being made now in existing arenas? How do these decisions alleviate or aggravate the public problem? Who are the key makers or influencers of decisions in these arenas? What would they think about new definitions of the problem and the solutions implied by those definitions?
- How is residual conflict that is related to the problem being resolved in the existing courts? What underlying norms do those courts enforce? Who are the key participants in these courts? What would they think about various problem definitions and potential solutions?
- How would existing forums, arenas, and courts have to be changed to get the problem and at least one promising solution on the public agenda? Are new forums, arenas, and courts necessary? How could advocates persuade policy makers to place a formal proposal to adopt a solution or solutions on their agenda and adopt and implement the proposal? Which new decision makers or advocates should be involved?
- In light of these analyses, what are the general outlines of a strategy for policy change?

Issue creation relies on the effective design and use of forums more than anything else, so be especially thoughtful and creative in strategizing about forums. Even when you're not sure what to do, an informal forum can be helpful. As Hubert Humphrey sagely advised, "When in doubt, talk."

Think About the Costs and Consequences of the Policy Change Effort

Develop answers to these questions:

- What are the consequences of doing nothing?
- What are the benefits and costs for particular stakeholders?
- What are the personal, team, and organizational costs (time, energy, money, attention, and alternative expenditures forgone) of the policy change effort?
- In light of predicted costs and benefits, is the change effort likely to be worthwhile?

Additionally, think about the worst-case scenario. Consider the risks of losing or ending up with a situation that is worse than the starting point. Think about how you can avoid unwanted outcomes. Set limits; decide what you are unwilling to do, even if those things appear necessary to achieve policy change. What are the personal, financial, political, ethical, legal, or other limits on what you are willing to do?

Develop an Action Plan for Obtaining an Initial Agreement

The action plan should aim at reaching the kind of initial agreement described in Chapter Six. The plan should embody a strategy for introducing the idea of policy change, developing an understanding of the change process, developing a commitment to the change effort, and reaching an actual agreement.

Keep in Mind the Benefits of the Proposed Policy Changes

When the going gets tough, recall the vision that motivates and inspires you and your colleagues. As Rosabeth Moss Kanter indicates, every innovation feels like a failure in the middle (Kanter, 1989). Reinforce and hang on to your optimism; view adversity as temporary, specific to the situation, and either someone else's fault or the result of something beyond your control (Seligman, 1998). Optimists are the dreamers whose vision and energy can inspire and mobilize others to undertake collective action in pursuit of the common good. Good leaders are *flexibly optimistic;* they envision the inspiring and even radical possibilities for change, but they also realistically assess barriers to change and action to overcome them. Flexible optimists learn to dream, in other words, with their feet on the ground.

Realize the Time May Not Be Right

A problem or need may simply not be urgent enough to command a constituency for change. A workable solution may not be available. Other existing or potential change efforts may offer unbeatable competition for citizens' and policy makers' attention. For whatever reason, be willing to concede that your cause may be lost, at least for the time being. At the same time, you can take heart from those who have championed policy changes that at one time were hopeless but eventually succeeded in great measure. We have in mind such supposedly lost causes as reduction in nuclear weapons, women's suffrage, abolition of slavery, control of landmines, environmental protection, and the fight against AIDS. The history of these change efforts emphasizes the importance of the long view and a commitment for the long haul. No virtuous cause is lost forever, so long as some people keep its flame alive.

Summary

Once a new policy regime is fully established, policy entrepreneurs should be prepared for a final phase of the policy change cycle, in which they prompt consideration of whether new policies, programs, projects, and practices warrant continuation, substantial modification, or termination. To do this, they can take advantage of regular review opportunities such as a reauthorization session or budget cycle, and create new ones through, for example, a conference, study commission, or public hearing. In this phase, they should seek to resolve residual implementation problems and keep the institutions responsive to real public needs, problems, and opportunities. As in earlier phases, they must continue paying attention to maintaining the support of a dynamic advocacy coalition and to designing appropriate forums, arenas, and courts. They also should gather needed resources for reform of the new regime or for tackling other complex public problems.

As policy entrepreneurs prepare to move onto new problems, needs, and opportunities, they should focus again on the policy change cycle as a whole and sketch out what it will take to assemble a needed advocacy coalition, create a public issue in forums, and obtain the needed decisions from arenas or courts. If the time is right, they can begin the journey of leadership for the common good all over again.

Summary and Conclusion

We have written the revised edition of *Leadership for the Common Good* in the hope of presenting a useful theoretical framework and practical guidance for those who want to inspire and mobilize others to build a better world. We assume you, the reader, are one of those people.

At this point, you should have a variety of conceptual skills and practical tools that you can use to tackle public problems that concern you and to build the leadership effectiveness of others. Let's briefly review the main concepts that make up the Leadership for the Common Good framework.

- The *shared-power world* is one in which a public problem or challenge affects numerous individuals, groups, organizations, and interorganizational networks. This view of the context of public problems reveals the importance of paying attention to an array of stakeholders, across sectors, as you try to deepen your understanding of a problem or challenge and identify promising solutions. It also highlights the existing shared-power arrangements that support the status quo and alerts you to the need to create new shared-power arrangements and alter the old ones.
- *Forums, arenas, and courts* are the shared-power settings in which leaders and constituents create and communicate shared meaning about public problems, affect the making and implementing of policy decisions, and resolve disputes and sanction conduct related to those decisions. We have argued that leaders can have their greatest impact through wise design and use of informal and formal forums, arenas, and courts.
- Eight *major leadership capabilities* are needed to achieve the common good in a shared-power world:

1. *Leadership in context:* understanding the social, political, economic, and technological givens of a problematic situation and discerning openings for change
2. *Personal leadership:* understanding self and others and deploying that understanding in a leadership endeavor
3. *Team leadership:* building productive work groups
4. *Organizational leadership:* nurturing effective and humane organizations
5. *Visionary leadership:* creating and communicating shared meaning in forums
6. *Political leadership:* making and implementing policy decisions in arenas
7. *Ethical leadership:* sanctioning conduct and resolving residual disputes in courts
8. *Policy entrepreneurship:* coordinating leadership tasks over the course of a policy change cycle

• The *policy change cycle* is the general process by which leaders and constituents tackle public problems in a shared-power world. The process involves a shifting array of leaders and followers in a variety of forums, arenas, and courts and consists of several interactive phases that can play out over the course of several years. These are the phases:

1. *Initial agreement* to do something about a public problem
2. *Problem formulation*
3. *Search for solutions*
4. *Proposal formulation*
5. *Proposal review and adoption*
6. *Implementation and evaluation*
7. *Policy continuation, modification, or termination*

• The *common good* entails widely beneficial outcomes that are never preordained but instead arrived at through mindful leadership and active followership. We describe the desired outcome of leadership for the common good as a *regime of mutual gain,* a system of policies, programs, laws, rules, and norms that yields widespread benefits at reasonable cost and taps people's deepest interest in their own well-being and that of others.

Throughout the book, we have supplied exercises that can help you and your supporters apply these concepts to whatever public problem, need, challenge, or possibility is vitally important to you. The second part of the book offers specific guidance for moving through the seven phases of the policy change cycle. We have also referred you to numerous other scholars and practitioners who offer alternative approaches and tools, or who expand on our advice.

Finally, we have used examples from four cases to illuminate leadership for the common good in practice. In each case, leaders from diverse personal and organizational backgrounds worked together to inspire and mobilize an array of stakeholders to achieve a breakthrough in thinking about a public problem and enact solutions that have far-reaching benefits.

1. In the *U.S. AIDS case*, physicians, public health workers, gay rights activists, people suffering from AIDS and their families, a few congressmen and their aides, and medical researchers strove to galvanize the medical profession, government bureaucracies, and the general public to respond to the deadly immune deficiency disease that struck first gay men and then many other groups. These leaders were able eventually to construct a regime of mutual gain. The regime is always under threat, however, as each generation has to learn or relearn the need for safe sex, and as insurance coverage for medical treatments and drugs is altered by shifting government and business policies. The HIV/AIDS epidemic continues to devastate many African countries and threatens the future of other countries around the world. Policy entrepreneurs now focus intensely on how to achieve policies that will make AIDS prevention and medication available to all who need them.

2. Through the *World Business Council for Sustainable Development,* the chief executives of major corporations have developed an innovative and effective business-oriented response to remedying environmental destruction caused by manufacturing, timber harvesting, mining, and other production processes. They and the council staff have joined many U.N. initiatives; helped spread the gospel of eco-efficiency; and launched or supported local, regional, and international projects designed to reduce pollution and waste, increase living standards, and make businesses more sustainable over the long haul. Because of the council's emphasis on voluntary

approaches and its understandable focus on business practices that foster sustainable development (rather than publicizing businesses that continue harmful practices), the council will no doubt continue to be criticized by organizations that are more focused on prompting citizen and government measures to halt environmental destruction. Yet as the common initiative with Greenpeace around the Kyoto Protocol demonstrates, the council can also find opportunities to work with corporate critics on specific initiatives.

3. In the *African American Men Project*, public officials have worked with businesspeople, nonprofit leaders, grassroots activists, educators, and researchers to connect and redefine a host of barriers faced by African American men in Hennepin County, Minnesota. The project has both revealed and expanded leadership by African American men. Moreover, these leaders are creating new narratives and groundbreaking initiatives that weave a better future for African American men into a better future for the entire county. Through such projects as Right Turn and the Day of Restoration, young African American men are increasingly able to take charge of their lives and overcome institutional barriers to their success.

4. The *Vital Aging Network* in Minnesota is part of a U.S. movement to revolutionize thinking and policy about older adulthood. The organizers of VAN brought together university administrators, educators, and nonprofit and community leaders to gather and disseminate evidence that older adults have the potential to lead productive lives into their nineties at least. They have used statewide summits, a Website, and a variety of educational programs to help empower older adults to stay healthy and productive and to advocate effectively for better public policies and community practices. VAN's organizers are laying the groundwork for a regime of mutual gain, in which older adults partner with younger generations in building communities that help all their inhabitants lead a fulfilling, dignified, and productive life. In a parallel with the AAMP, VAN has both revealed and expanded leadership on the part of older adults.

The people who exercised leadership in these cases are by no means perfect leaders. By definition, leaders will never be perfect since they are human beings. We presented these people not because they are larger-than-life heroes but because they demonstrate how personal passion connects to public issues and how the urgency, determination, and foresight of a few can spread to diverse others, who together can build an effective coalition for change.

We hope that you can see yourself in these people and that you, your friends, colleagues, and fellow citizens will find in these pages abundant reasons and resources for tackling even the most challenging public problem. The world urgently needs your leadership for the common good.

We hope as well that you believe almost anything is possible with enough leadership for the common good. As citizens of the world we have rebuilt after wars; ended depressions; virtually eliminated polio, smallpox, and river blindness; unraveled the human genome; watched a reasonably united and integrated Europe emerge; and seen democracy spread where it was thought unimaginable. Now let's think about having a good job for everyone, adequate food and housing for all, universal health care coverage, drastically reduced crime, effective educational systems, secure pensions and retirements, a dramatic reduction in greenhouse emissions, elimination of weapons of mass destruction, eradication of HIV/AIDS, realization in practice of the Universal Declaration on Human Rights, and numerous other worthy goals. Then let's get to work. We can create regimes of mutual gain by drawing on our diverse talents—and have done so again and again throughout history (Boyte and Kari, 1996; Light, 2002). With enough widespread leadership, we will do it again and again.

References

Abramson, M. A., and Lawrence, P. R. (eds.). *Transforming Organizations.* Lanham, Md.: Rowman and Littlefield, 2001.

Ackoff, R. L. "The Art and Science of Mess Management." *Interfaces,* 1981, *11*(1), 20–26.

Alexander, E. A. "Design in the Decision-Making Process." *Policy Studies,* 1982, *14*(3), 279–292.

Alexander, E. A. "Rationality Revisited: Planning Paradigms in a Post-Postmodernist Perspective." *Journal of Planning Education and Research,* 2000, *19,* 242–256.

Allen, K. E., and Cherrey, C. *Systemic Leadership: Enriching the Meaning of Our Work.* Lanham, Md.: University Press of America, 2000.

Allport, G. W. *The Nature of Prejudice.* Reading, Mass.: Addison-Wesley, 1954.

Anderson, J. E. *Public Policymaking.* Boston: Houghton Mifflin, 1990.

Anderson, M., and others. *Facilitation Resources.* St. Paul: University of Minnesota Extension Service, 1999.

Andreasen, A. R. *Marketing Social Change: Changing Behavior to Promote Health, Social Development, and the Environment.* San Francisco: Jossey-Bass, 1995.

Angelica, E. *Crafting Effective Mission and Vision Statements.* St. Paul, Minn.: Amherst H. Wilder Foundation, 2001.

Annunzio, S. *eLeadership: Proven Techniques for Creating an Environment of Speed and Flexibility in the Digital Economy.* New York: Free Press, 2001.

Antonakis, J., and Atwater, L. "Leader Distance: A Review and a Proposed Theory." *Leadership Quarterly,* 2002, *13*(6), 673–704.

Arendt, H. *The Human Condition* (2nd ed.). Chicago: University of Chicago Press, 1958.

Argyris, C. "The Executive Mind and Double-Loop Learning." *Organizational Dynamics,* Autumn 1982, pp. 5–22.

Aristotle. *Politics.* New York: Modern Library, 1943.

Avner, M. *The Lobbying and Advocacy Handbook for Nonprofit Organizations.* St. Paul, Minn.: Amherst H. Wilder Foundation, 2002.

Avolio, B. J. *Full Leadership Development: Building the Vital Forces in Organizations.* Thousand Oaks, Calif.: Sage, 1999.

Bachrach, P., and Baratz, M. S. "Two Faces of Power." *American Political Science Review*, 1962, *56*, 947–952.

Bacon, T. R. *High Impact Facilitation*. Durango, Colo.: International Learning Works, 1996.

Badaracco Jr., J. L. *Leading Quietly: An Unorthodox Guide to Doing the Right Thing*. Boston: Harvard Business School Press, 2002.

Bandura, A. *Self-Efficacy: The Exercise of Control*. New York: Freeman, 1997.

Barclay, S., and Birkland, T. "Law, Policymaking, and the Policy Process: Closing the Gaps." *Policy Studies Journal*, 1998, *26*(2), 227–243.

Bardach, E. *The Implementation Game: What Happens After a Bill Becomes Law*. Cambridge, Mass.: MIT Press, 1977.

Bardach, E. *Getting Agencies to Work Together: The Practice and Theory of Managerial Craftsmanship*. Washington, D.C.: Brookings Institution Press, 1998.

Baum, H. S. *The Organization of Hope*. Albany: State University of New York Press, 1997.

Baumgartner, F. R., and Jones, B. D. *Agendas and Instability in American Politics*. Chicago: University of Chicago Press, 1993.

Becker, E. *The Denial of Death*. New York: Free Press, 1973.

Beech, N., and Huxham, C. "Cycles of Identificationing in Collaborations." Glasgow, Scotland: University of Strathclyde Graduate School of Business, 2003.

Beer, S. *Designing Freedom*. London: Wiley, 1974.

Behn, R. D. "How to Terminate a Public Policy: A Dozen Hints for the Would Be Terminator." *Policy Analysis*, 1978, *4*(3), 393–413.

Behn, R. D. "The Fundamentals of Cutback Management." In R. J. Zeckhauser and D. Leebaert (eds.), *What Role for Government?* Durham, N.C.: Duke University Press, 1983.

Behn, R. D. "The New Public-Management Paradigm and the Search for Democratic Accountability." *International Public Management Journal*, 1999, *1*(2), 131–165.

Bellah, R. N., and others. *The Good Society*. New York: Knopf, 1991.

Bendor, J. B. *Parallel Systems: Redundancy in Government*. Berkeley: University of California Press, 1985.

Benveniste, G. *Mastering the Politics of Planning: Crafting Credible Plans and Policies That Make a Difference*. San Francisco: Jossey-Bass, 1989.

Berlin, I. *Liberty*. Oxford, England: Oxford University Press, 2002.

Blasko, L. "Billion-PC Landmark Passes Unnoticed." *Star Tribune*, July 2002, p. 8.

Boal, K. B., and Bryson, J. M. "Charismatic Leadership: A Phenomenological and Structural Approach." In J. G. Hunt, B. R. Balinga, H. P. Dachler, and C. A. Schriescheim (eds.), *Emerging Leadership Vistas*. New York: Pergamon Press, 1987.

Bobo, K., Kendall, J., and Max, S. *Organizing for Social Change: Midwest Academy Manual for Activists* (3rd ed.). Santa Ana, Calif.: Seven Locks Press, 2001.

Bok, S. *Lying: Moral Choice in Public and Private Life.* New York: Vantage, 1978.

Boler, M. *Feeling Power: Emotions and Education.* New York: Routledge, 1999.

Bolman, L. G., and Deal, T. E. *Leading with Soul: An Uncommon Journey of Spirit* (rev. ed.). San Francisco: Jossey-Bass, 2001.

Bolman, L. G., and Deal, T. E. *Reframing Organizations: Artistry, Choice, and Leadership.* San Francisco: Jossey-Bass, 2003.

Borins, S. *Innovating with Integrity: How Local Heroes Are Transforming American Government.* Washington, D.C.: Georgetown University Press, 1998.

Boyte, H. C. *Commonwealth: A Return to Citizen Politics.* New York: Free Press, 1989.

Boyte, H. C. *Everyday Politics: The Power of Public Work.* Philadelphia: University of Pennsylvania Press, 2004.

Boyte, H. C., and Kari, N. N. *Building America: The Democratic Promise of Public Work.* Philadelphia: Temple, 1996.

Brandl, J. *Money and Good Intentions Are Not Enough.* Washington, D.C.: Brookings Institution, 1998.

Braybrooke, D., and Lindblom, C. E. *A Strategy of Decision: Policy Evaluation as a Social Process.* New York: Free Press, 1963.

Bridges, W. *Making Sense of Life's Changes: Transitions.* Reading, Mass.: Addison-Wesley, 1980.

Bridges, W., and Mitchell, S. "Leading Transition: A New Model for Change." In F. Hesselbein and R. Johnston (eds.), *On Leading Change.* San Francisco: Jossey-Bass, 2002.

Brinckerhoff, P. C. *Mission-Based Marketing: How Your Not-for-Profit Can Succeed in a More Competitive World.* Hoboken, N.J.: Wiley, 1998.

Bromiley, P., and Marcus, A. "Deadlines, Routines, and Change." *Policy Sciences,* 1987, *20,* 85–103.

Brown, C. R., and Mazza, G. "Peer Training Strategies for Welcoming Diversity." In J. Dalton (ed.), *Racism on Campus: Confronting Racial Bias Through Peer Interventions.* San Francisco: Jossey-Bass, 1991.

Brown, M. E., and Gioia, D. A. "Making Things Click: Distributive Leadership in an Online Division of an Offline Organization." *Leadership Quarterly,* 2002, *13*(4), 397–419.

Brown, T. "Why Companies Don't Learn." *Industry Week,* Aug. 19, 1991, pp. 36–41.

Bryant, J. *The Six Dilemmas of Collaboration: Inter-Organizational Relationships as Drama.* Hoboken, N.J.: Wiley, 2003.

Bryson, J. M. "A Perspective on Planning and Crises in the Public Sector." *Strategic Management Journal,* 1981, *2,* 181–196.

Bryson, J. M. *Strategic Planning for Public and Nonprofit Organizations* (rev. ed.). San Francisco: Jossey-Bass, 1995.

Bryson, J. M. *Strategic Planning for Public and Nonprofit Organizations* (3rd ed.). San Francisco: Jossey-Bass, 2004a.

Bryson, J. M. "What to Do When Stakeholders Matter: Stakeholder Identification and Analysis Techniques." *Public Management Review,* 2004b, *6*(1), 21–53.

Bryson, J. M., Ackermann, F., Eden, C., and Finn, C. *Visible Thinking: Unlocking Causal Mapping for Practical Business Results.* Chichester, England: Wiley, 2004.

Bryson, J. M., and Anderson, S. R. "Applying Large-Group Interaction Methods in the Planning and Implementation of Major Change Efforts." *Public Administration Review,* 2000, *60*(2), 143–162.

Bryson, J. M., Bromiley, P., and Jung, Y. S. "Influences of the Context and Process on Project Planning Success." *Journal of Planning Education and Research,* 1990, *9*(3), 183–185.

Bryson, J. M., and Crosby, B. C. "Policy Planning and the Design and Use of Forums, Arenas, and Courts." *Environment and Planning B: Planning and Design,* 1993, *20,* 175–194.

Bryson, J. M., and Crosby, B. C. "Planning and the Design and Use of Forums, Arenas, and Courts." In R. Burchell, S. Mandelbaum, and L. Mazza (eds.), *Planning Theory for the 1990s.* New Brunswick, N.J.: Rutgers University/CIPR Press, 1996.

Bryson, J. M., and Crosby, B. C. "Retreats to Prepare Mission and Vision Statements." In C. Weisman (ed.), *Guide to Retreats for Nonprofit Organizations.* St. Louis: Robbins, 2003.

Bryson, J. M., and Cullen, J. W. "A Contingent Approach to Strategy and Tactics in Formative and Summative Evaluations." *Evaluation and Program Planning,* 1984, *7,* 276–294.

Bryson, J. M., Cunningham, G. L., and Lokkesmoe, K. J. "What to Do When Stakeholders Matter: The Case of Problem Formulation for the African American Men Project of Hennepin County, Minnesota." *Public Administration Review,* 2002, *62*(5), 568–584.

Bryson, J. M., and Delbecq, A. L. "A Contingent Approach to Strategy and Tactics in Project Planning." *Journal of the American Planning Association,* 1979, *45,* 167–179.

Bryson, J. M., and Delbecq, A. L. *A Contingent Program Planning Model.* Minneapolis: University of Minnesota, 1981.

Bryson, J. M., and Einsweiler, R. C. *Shared Power.* Lanham, Md.: University Press of America, 1991.

Bryson, J. M., Freeman, R. E., and Roering, W. D. "Strategic Planning in the Public Sector: Approaches and Directions." In B. Checkoway (ed.), *Strategic Perspectives on Planning Practice*. Lexington, Mass.: Lexington Books, 1986.

Bryson, J. M., and Roering, W. D. "Initiation of Strategic Planning by Governments." *Public Administration Review*, 1988, *48*, 995–1004.

Bunch, C. *Passionate Politics*. New York: St. Martin's Press, 1987.

Burby, R. J. "Making Plans That Matter: Citizen Involvement and Government Action." *Journal of the American Planning Association*, 2003, *69*(1), 33–49.

Burns, J. M. *Leadership*. New York: HarperCollins, 1978.

Burns, J. M. *Transforming Leadership*. New York: Atlantic Monthly Press, 2003.

Burt, G. "Towards a Theory of Volitional Strategic Change: The Role of Transitional Objects in Constancy and Change" (paper no. 2002-04, ed.). Glasgow, Scotland: University of Strathclyde Graduate School of Business, 2002.

Cameron, K. S., and Caza, A. "Organizational and Leadership Virtues." *Journal of Leadership and Organizational Studies*, 2002, *9*(1), 33–48.

Campbell, H., and Marshall, R. "Utilitarianism's Bad Breath? A Re-Evaluation of the Public Interest Justification for Planning." *Planning Theory*, 2002, *1*(2), 163–187.

Campbell, D. T., and Stanley, J. C. *Experimental and Quasi-Experimental Designs for Research*. Skokie, Ill.: Rand McNally, 1966.

Carver, J. *Boards That Make a Difference*. San Francisco: Jossey-Bass, 1990.

Cashman, K. *Leadership from the Inside Out: Becoming a Leader for Life*. Provo, Utah: Executive Excellence, 1999.

Chakrabarty, D. *Provincializing Europe: Postcolonial Thought and Historical Difference*. Princeton, N.J.: Princeton University Press, 2000.

Charan, R., Drotter, S., and Noel, J. *The Leadership Pipeline: How to Build the Leadership-Powered Company*. San Francisco: Jossey-Bass, 2001.

Chen, C. C., and Van Velsor, E. "New Directions for Research and Practice in Diversity Leadership." *Leadership Quarterly*, 1996, *7*(2), 285–302.

Chrislip, D. D. *The Collaborative Leadership Fieldbook: A Guide for Citizens and Civic Leaders*. San Francisco: Jossey-Bass, 2002.

Chrislip, D. D., and Larson, C. E. *Collaborative Leadership: How Citizens and Civic Leadership Can Make a Difference*. San Francisco: Jossey-Bass, 1994.

Christensen, K. S. "Coping with Uncertainty in Planning." *Journal of the American Planning Association*, 1985, *51*(1), 63–73.

Christensen, K. S. "Teaching Savvy." *Journal of Planning Education and Research*, 1993, *12*, 202–212.

Christmann, P., and Taylor, G. "Globalization and the Environment: Strategies for International Voluntary Environmental Initiatives." *Academy of Management Executive*, 2002, *16*(3), 121–135.

Clegg, S. *Frameworks of Power.* Thousand Oaks, Calif.: Sage, 1989.

Cleveland, H. *The Global Commons.* Lanham, Md.: University Press of America, 1990.

Cleveland, H. *Birth of a New World: An Open Moment for International Leadership.* San Francisco: Jossey-Bass, 1993.

Cleveland, H. *Nobody in Charge: Essays on the Future of Leadership.* Hoboken, N.J.: Wiley, 2002.

Cobb, R. W., and Elder, C. D. *Participation in American Politics: The Dynamics of Agenda Building* (2nd ed.). Baltimore: Johns Hopkins University Press, 1983.

Cobb, R. W., and Ross, M. H. *Cultural Strategies of Agenda Denial: Avoidance, Attack, and Redefinition.* Lawrence: University Press of Kansas, 1997.

Cohen, M. D., March, J. G., and Olsen, J. P. "A Garbage Can Model of Organization and Choice." *Administrative Science Quarterly,* 1972, *17,* 1–25.

Cohen, S., and Brand, R. *Total Quality Management in Government: A Practical Guide for the Real World.* San Francisco: Jossey-Bass, 1993.

Collins, J. C., and Porras, J. I. *Built to Last: Successful Habits of Visionary Companies.* New York: HarperBusiness, 1997.

Combs, G. M. "Meeting the Leadership Challenge of a Diverse and Pluralistic Workplace: Implications of Self-Efficacy for Diversity Training." *Journal of Leadership Studies,* 2002, *8*(4), 1–16.

Connell, B. (prod.). *Into the Bright Sunshine.* (Film.) Bethesda, Md.: Concept Associates, 1983.

Cooperrider, D. L., and Bilimoria, D. "The Challenge of Global Change for Strategic Management: Opportunities for Charting a New Course." In P. Shrivastava, A. Huff, and J. Dutton (eds.), *Organizational Dimensions of Global Change.* Greenwich, Conn.: JAI Press, 1993.

Cooperrider, D. L., and Srivastva, S. "Appreciative Inquiry in Organizational Life." In W. A. Pasmore and R. W. Woodman (eds.), *Research in Organization Development and Change* (vol. 1). Greenwich, Conn.: JAI Press, 1987.

Coplin, W., and O'Leary, M. *Everyman's Prince: A Guide to Understanding Your Political Problem.* Boston: Duxbury Press, 1976.

Crosby, B. C. *Leadership for Global Citizenship: Building Transnational Community.* Thousand Oaks, Calif.: Sage, 1999.

Crosby, B. C., Bryson, J. M., and Anderson, S. R. *Leadership for the Common Good Fieldbook.* St. Paul: University of Minnesota Extension Service, University of Minnesota, 2003.

Crossan, M. M., Lane, H. W., and White, R. E. "An Organizational Learning Framework: From Intuition to Institution." *Academy of Management Review,* 1999, *24*(3), 522–537.

Csikszentmihalyi, M. *Flow: The Psychology of Optimal Experience.* New York: HarperCollins, 1990.

Cyert, R., and March, J. *The Behavioral Theory of the Firm.* Upper Saddle River, N.J.: Prentice Hall, 1963.

Dahl, R. A. *Who Governs?* New Haven, Conn.: Yale University Press, 1961.

Daloz, L. A., Keen, J. P., Keen, C. H., and Parks, S. D. *Common Fire: Lives of Commitment in a Complex World.* Boston: Beacon Press, 1996.

Dalton, G. W., and Thompson, P. H. *Novations-Strategies for Career Management.* Glenview, Ill.: Scott, Foresman, 1986.

Daniels, M. R. "Implementing Policy Termination: Health Care Reform in Tennessee." *Policy Studies Review,* 1995–96, *14*(3/4), 353–374.

Day, D. V. "Assessment of Leadership Outcomes." In S. J. Zaccaro and R. J. Klimoski (eds.), *The Nature of Organizational Leadership: Understanding the Performance Imperatives Confronting Today's Leaders.* San Francisco: Jossey-Bass, 2001.

de Neufville, J. I., and Barton, S. E. "Myths and the Definition of Policy Problems: An Exploration of Home Ownership and Public-Private Partnerships." *Policy Sciences,* 1987, *20,* 181–206.

Delbanco, A. *The Real American Dream: A Meditation on Hope.* Cambridge, Mass.: Harvard University Press, 1999.

Delbecq, A. L., and Friedlander, F. "Strategies for Personal and Family Renewal: How a High-Survivor Group of Executives Cope with Stress and Avoid Burnout." *Journal of Management Inquiry,* 1995, *4*(3), 262–269.

Delbecq, A. L., Van de Ven, A. H., and Gustafson, D. *Group Techniques for Program Planning.* Glenview, Ill.: Scott, Foresman, 1975.

De Pree, M. *Leadership Jazz.* New York: Dell, 1992.

Dietz, M. *Turning Operations: Feminism, Arendt, and Politics.* New York: Routledge, 2002.

DiTomaso, N., and Hooijberg, R. "Diversity and the Demands of Leadership." *Leadership Quarterly,* 1996, *7*(2), 163–187.

Douglass, F. "The Significance of Emancipation in the West Indies." (Speech, Canandaigua, N.Y., Aug. 3, 1857; collected in pamphlet by author.) In J. E. Blassingame (ed.), *Frederick Douglass Papers.* Series One: Speeches, Debates, and Interviews. Vol. 3: 1855–1863. New Haven, Conn.: Yale University Press, 1985 [1857].

Drath, W. H. *The Deep Blue Sea: Rethinking the Source of Leadership.* San Francisco: Jossey-Bass, 2001.

Dror, Y. "Planning as a Mode of Policy Reasoning." In L. Guelke and R. Preston (eds.), *Abstract Thoughts, Concrete Solutions: Essays in the Honor of Peter Nash.* Waterloo, Canada: Department of Geography Publications Series, University of Waterloo, 1987.

Duggan, W. R., and Civille, J. R. *Tanzania and Nyere.* New York: Orbis, 1976.

Dunn, W. N. *Public Policy Analysis: An Introduction* (2nd ed.). Upper Saddle River, N.J.: Prentice Hall, 1994.

Durning, D. "Participatory Policy Analysis in a Social Service Agency: A Case Study." *Journal of Policy Analysis and Management,* 1993, *12*(2), 297–322.

Dutton, J. E., and others. "Leading in Times of Trauma." *Harvard Business Review,* Jan. 2002, pp. 54–61.

Eadie, D. *Boards That Work: A Practical Guide for Building Association Boards.* Washington, D.C.: American Society of Association Executives, 1994.

Easton, D. *A Systems Analysis of Political Life.* Hoboken, N.J.: Wiley, 1965.

Edelman, M. W. *The Measure of Our Success: A Letter to My Children and Yours.* New York: HarperPerennial, 1993.

Eden, C. "Problem-Solving or Problem-Finishing." M. C. Jackson and P. Keys (eds.), *New Directions in Management Science.* Aldershot, England: Gower, 1987.

Eden, C., and Ackermann, F. *Making Strategy: The Journey of Strategic Management.* London: Sage, 1998.

Eden, C., and Ackermann, F. "SODA—The Principles." In J. Rosenhead and J. Mingers (eds.), *Rational Analysis in a Problematic World Revisited.* London: Wiley, 2001.

Eden, C., and Huxham, C. "Action Research for Management Research." *British Journal of Management,* 1996, *7,* 75–86.

Eliot, T. S. *Four Quartets.* Orlando: Harcourt Brace, 1971.

Elmore, R. F. "Backward Mapping: Implementation Research and Policy Decisions." In W. Williams (ed.), *Studying Implementation: Methodological and Administrative Issues.* Chatham, N.J.: Chatham House, 1982.

Eoyang, G. H. *Coping with Chaos: Seven Simple Tools.* Cheyenne, Wyo.: Lagumo, 1997.

Etzioni, A. "Mixed Scanning: A 'Third' Approach to Decision Making." *Public Administration Review,* 1967, *27,* 385–392.

Etzioni, A. *The Active Society: A Theory of Societal and Political Processes.* London: Collier, 1968.

Fairholm, G. W. *Leadership and the Culture of Trust.* New York: Praeger, 1994.

Fallows, J. "Blind into Baghdad." Atlantic, Jan.–Feb. 2004, *293*(1), 52–74.

Feldman, M. S. "Organizational Routines as a Source of Continuous Change." *Organization Science,* 2000, *11*(6), 611–629.

Feldman, M. S., and Khademian, A. M. "To Manage Is to Govern." *Public Administration Review,* 2002, *62*(5), 541–554.

Finn, C. B. "Stakeholder Influence Mapping." In C. Huxham (ed.), *Creating Collaborative Advantage.* Thousand Oaks, Calif.: Sage, 1996.

Fiol, C. M. "Capitalizing on Paradox: The Role of Language in Transforming Organizational Identities." *Organization Science,* 2002, *13*(6), 653–666.

Fisher, R., and Ury, W. *Getting to Yes: Negotiating Agreement Without Giving In.* New York: Penguin Books, 1981.

Fisher, R., and Ury, W. *Getting to Yes: Negotiating Agreement Without Giving In* (2nd ed.). New York: Penguin Books, 1991.

Fletcher, J. K., and Kaüfer, K. "Shared Leadership: Paradox and Possibility." C. L. Pearce and J. A. Conger (eds.), *Shared Leadership: Reframing the Hows and Whys of Leadership.* Thousand Oaks, Calif.: Sage, 2003.

Flower, J. "Future Search: Power Tool for Building Healthier Communities." *Healthcare Forum Journal,* May/June 1995, 34–56.

Flyvbjerg, B. *Rationality and Power: Democracy in Practice.* Chicago: University of Chicago Press, 1998.

Forester, J. "Critical Theory and Planning Practice." *Journal of the American Planning Association,* 1980, *46*(3), 275–286.

Forester, J. *Planning in the Face of Power.* Berkeley: University of California Press, 1989.

Forester, J. *The Deliberative Practitioner.* Cambridge, Mass.: MIT Press, 1999.

Foucault, M. *Politics of Truth.* New York: Semiotext(e), 1997.

Frederickson, H. G. *The Spirit of Public Administration.* San Francisco: Jossey-Bass, 1997.

Freeley, A. J. *Argumentation and Debate.* Belmont, Calif.: Wadsworth, 1976.

Freeman, S.J.M. "Women at the Top: You've Come a Long Way, Baby." S.J.M. Freeman, S. C. Bourque, and C. M. Shelton (eds.), *Women on Power: Leadership Redefined.* Boston: Northeastern University Press, 2001.

French Jr., J.R.P., and Raven, B. "The Bases of Social Power." In D. Cartwright and A. F. Zander (eds.), *Group Dynamics: Research and Theory.* New York: HarperCollins, 1968.

Friedman, T. L. *The Lexus and the Olive Tree: Understanding Globalization.* New York: Anchor Books, 2000.

Friedmann, J. *The Good Society.* Cambridge, Mass.: MIT Press, 1979.

Friedmann, J. *Planning in the Public Domain: From Knowledge to Action.* Princeton, N.J.: Princeton University Press, 1987.

Friend, J. K., and Hickling, A. *Planning Under Pressure: The Strategic Choice Approach* (2nd ed.). Oxford, England: Heinemann, 1997.

Fukuyama, F. *Our Posthuman Future.* New York: Farrar, Straus and Giroux, 2002.

Gabor, D. *Inventing the Future.* New York: Knopf, 1964.

Galbraith, J. K. *The Good Society: The Humane Agenda.* Boston: Houghton Mifflin, 1996.

Gardner, H. *Leading Minds.* New York: Basic Books, 1995.

Gaventa, J. *Power and Powerlessness: Quiescence and Rebellion in an Appalachian Valley.* Urbana: University of Illinois Press, 1980.

Gerzon, M. *A House Divided: Six Belief Systems Struggling for America's Soul.* New York: Putnam, 1996.

Giddens, A. *Central Problems in Social Theory: Action, Structure and Contradiction in Social Analysis.* Berkeley: University of California Press, 1979.

Giddens, A. *The Constitution of Society.* Berkeley: University of California Press, 1984.

Gladwell, M. *The Tipping Point: How Little Things Can Make a Big Difference.* Boston: Little, Brown, 2000.

Goffman, I. *The Presentation of Self in Everyday Life.* New York: Anchor/Doubleday, 1959.

Goggin, M. L., Bowman, A. O., Lester, J. P., and O'Toole Jr., L. J. *Implementation Theory and Practice: Toward a Third Generation.* Glenview, Ill.: Scott, Foresman, 1990.

Goleman, D. *Emotional Intelligence.* New York: Bantam, 1995.

Goleman, D., Boyatzis, R., and McKee, A. *Primal Leadership: Realizing the Power of Emotional Intelligence.* Boston: Harvard Business School Press, 2002.

Gordon, R. D. "Conceptualizing Leadership with Respect to Its Historical-Contextual Antecedents to Power." *Leadership Quarterly,* 2002, *13*(2), 151–167.

Gray, B. *Collaborating: Finding Common Ground for Multiparty Problems.* San Francisco: Jossey-Bass, 1989.

Gray, B. "Strong Opposition: Frame-Based Resistance to Collaboration." In P. Hibbert (ed.), *Co-creating Emergent Insights: Multi-Organizational Partnerships, Alliances and Networks.* Glasgow, Scotland: University of Strathclyde Graduate School of Business, 2003.

Greenleaf, R. K. *Servant Leadership: A Journey into the Nature of Legitimate Power and Greatness.* New York: Paulist Press, 1977.

Gronn, P. "Distributed Leadership as a Unit of Analysis." *Leadership Quarterly,* 2002, *13*(4), 423–451.

Grossback, L. J. "The Problem of State-Imposed Mandates: Lessons from Minnesota's Local Governments." *State and Local Government Review,* 2002, *34*(3), 183–197.

Gutmann, A., and Thompson, D. *Ethics and Politics.* Chicago: Nelson-Hall, 1990.

Habermas, J. *Communication and the Evolution of Society.* Boston: Beacon Press, 1979.

Hagberg, J. O. "Learn to Use Your Soul in the Business World. *Minneapolis Star Tribune,* Mar. 6, 1995.

Hagberg, J. O., and Guelich, R. A. *The Critical Journey: Stages in the Life of Faith.* Salem, Wis.: Sheffield, 1995.

Hall, P. *Great Planning Disasters.* Berkeley: University of California Press, 1980.

Hall, P. *Cities of Tomorrow* (updated ed.). Oxford, England: Blackwell, 1996.

Handy, C. *Age of Uncertainty: The Changing Worlds of Organizations.* Boston: Harvard Business School Press, 1996.

Healey, P. *Collaborative Planning: Shaping Places in Fragmented Societies.* London: Macmillan, 1997.

Heenan, D. A., and Bennis, W. *Co-Leaders: The Power of Great Partnerships.* Hoboken, N.J.: Wiley, 1999.

Heifetz, R. A. *Leadership Without Easy Answers.* Cambridge, Mass.: Belknap Press, 1994.

Heifetz, R. A., and Laurie, D. L. "The Work of Leadership." *Harvard Business Review,* Jan.–Feb. 1997, pp. 124–134.

Hennepin County. *Crossroads: Choosing a New Direction* (Final Report of the African American Men Project). Minneapolis: Hennepin County Office of Planning and Development, 2002.

Henton, D., Melville, J., and Walesh, K. *Grassroots Leaders for a New Economy: How Civic Entrepreneurs Are Building Prosperous Communities.* San Francisco: Jossey-Bass, 1997.

Hesselbein, F., and Johnston, R. "Leader as Social Advocate: Building the Business by Building Community." In F. Hesselbein and R. Johnston (eds.), *On Mission and Leadership.* San Francisco: Jossey-Bass, 2002a.

Hesselbein, F., and Johnston, R. "Strategies for Change Leaders: A Conversation Between Peter F. Drucker and Peter M. Senge." In F. Hesselbein and R. Johnston (eds.), *On Leading Change.* San Francisco: Jossey-Bass, 2002b.

Hicks, D. "Spiritual and Religious Diversity in the Workplace." *Leadership Quarterly,* 2002, *13*(4), 379–396.

Hilgartner, S., and Bosk, C. L. "The Rise and Fall of Social Problems: A Public Arenas Model." *American Journal of Sociology,* 1988, *94*(1), 53–78.

Hillman, J. *The Soul's Code: In Search of Character and Calling.* New York: Warner Books, 1997.

Himmelman, A. T. "On the Theory and Practice of Transformational Collaborations: From Social Service to Social Justice." In C. Huxham (ed.), *Creating Collaborative Advantage.* Thousand Oaks, Calif.: Sage, 1996.

Hirschman, A. O. *Exit, Voice, and Loyalty: Responses to Decline in Firms, Organizations, and States.* Cambridge, Mass.: Harvard University Press, 1970.

Hively, J. "History of the Vital Aging Network." Minneapolis: Vital Aging Network, 2002.

Hock, D. "The Art of Chaordic Leadership." In F. Hesselbein and R. Johnston (eds.), *On Mission and Leadership*. San Francisco: Jossey-Bass, 2002.

Hoffman, E. *Lost in Translation: A Life in a New Language*. New York: Penguin, 1990.

Hogwood, B. W., and Peters, B. G. *Policy Dynamics*. New York: St. Martin's Press, 1983.

Holliday Jr., C. O., Schmidheiny, S., and Watts, P. *Walking the Talk: The Business Case for Sustainable Development*. San Francisco: Berrett-Koehler, 2002.

Holman, P., and Devane, T. *The Change Handbook: Group Methods for Shaping the Future*. San Francisco: Berrett-Koehler, 1999.

Holzer, M., Lee, S. H., and Newman, M. A. "Best Practices in Managing Reductions in Force." *Review of Public Personnel Administration*, 2003, *23*(1), 38–60.

Hooijberg, R., Hunt, J. G., and Dodge, G. E. "Leadership Complexity and Development of the Leaderplex Model." *Journal of Management*, 1997, *23*(3), 37–48.

Hooijberg, R., and Schneider, M. "Behavioral Complexity and Social Intelligence: How Executive Leaders Use Stakeholders to Form a Systems Perspective." In S. J. Zaccaro and R. J. Klimoski (eds.), *The Nature of Organizational Leadership: Understanding the Performance Imperatives Confronting Today's Leaders*. San Francisco: Jossey-Bass, 2001.

Hooker, C., and Csikszentmihalyi, M. "Rethinking the Motivation and Structuring of Knowledge Work." In C. L. Pearce and J. A. Conger (eds.), *Shared Leadership: Reframing the Hows and Whys of Leadership*. Thousand Oaks, Calif.: Sage, 2003.

hooks, b. *All About Love*. New York: Morrow, 2000.

Houghton, J. D., Neck, C. P., and Manz, C. C. "Self-Leadership and SuperLeadership." In C. L. Pearce and J. A. Conger (eds.), *Shared Leadership: Reframing the Hows and Whys of Leadership*. Thousand Oaks, Calif.: Sage, 2003.

Houle, C. O. *Governing Boards: Their Nature and Nurture*. San Francisco: Jossey-Bass, 1989.

House, R. J., Wright, N. S., and Aditya, R. N. "Cross-Cultural Research on Organizational Leadership." In C. Earley and M. Erez (eds.), *New Perspectives on International Industrial/Organizational Psychology*. San Francisco: Jossey-Bass, 1998.

Howard, A. "Identifying, Assessing, and Selecting Senior Leaders." In S. J. Zaccaro and R. J. Klimoski (eds.), *The Nature of Organizational*

Leadership: Understanding the Performance Imperatives Confronting Today's Leaders. San Francisco: Jossey-Bass, 2001.

Hugo, V. *Les Miserables* (C. E. Wilbur, trans.). New York: Modern Library, 1980.

Huizinga, J. "What 'Play' Is." *Parabola,* Winter 1996, pp. 59–63.

Hula, K. W. *Lobbying Together: Interest Group Coalitions in Legislative Politics.* Washington, D.C.: Georgetown University Press, 1999.

Huntington, S. P. *The Clash of Civilizations and the Remaking of World Order.* New York: Simon and Schuster, 1996.

Hutton, W. "We're All Pseudo Babies Now." *London Observer,* July 13, 2003, p. 26.

Huxham, C. (ed.). *Creating Collaborative Advantage.* Thousand Oaks, Calif.: Sage, 1996.

Huxham, C. "Theorizing Collaboration Practice." *Public Management Review,* 2003, 5(3), 401–423.

Huxham, C., and Beech, N. "Exploring the Power Infrastructure of Interorganizational Collaborations." Glasgow, Scotland: University of Strathclyde Graduate School of Business, 2003.

Huxham, C., and Vangen, S. "Leadership in the Shaping and Implementation of Collaboration Agendas: How Things Happen in a (Not Quite) Joined-up World." *Academy of Management Journal,* 2000, 43(6), 1159–1175.

Huxham, C., and Vangen, S. *Doing Things Collaboratively.* London: Routledge, 2005.

Innes, J. E. *Knowledge and Public Policy: The Search for Meaningful Indicators.* New Brunswick, N.J.: Transaction, 1990.

Innes, J. E. *Planning Through Consensus Building: A New View of the Comprehensive Planning Ideal.* Berkeley: Institute of Urban and Regional Development, University of California Press, 1994.

Innes, J. E. "Planning Through Consensus Building: A New View of the Comprehensive Planning Ideal." *Journal of the American Planning Association,* Autumn 1996, 460–472.

Innes, J. E., and Booher, D. E. "Consensus Building and Complex Adaptive Systems: A Framework for Evaluating Collaborative Planning." *Journal of the American Planning Association,* 1999a, 65(4), 412–423.

Innes, J. E., and Booher, D. E. "Consensus Building as Role Playing and Bricolage: Toward a Theory of Collaborative Planning." *Journal of the American Planning Association,* 1999b, 65(1), 9–27.

Institute for Intercultural Studies. "FAQ: What Is the Source of [Margaret Mead's] 'Never doubt. . .' quote?" July 2004 (http://www.interculturalstudies.org/IIS/faq.html).

Jacobs, R. W. *Real Time Strategic Change: How to Involve an Entire Organization in Fast and Far-Reaching Change.* San Francisco: Berrett-Koehler, 1994.

Janowitz, M. *The Last Half-Century: Societal Change and Politics in America.* Chicago: University of Chicago Press, 1978.

Jantsch, E. *Design of Evolution.* New York: Braziller, 1975.

Johnson, D. W., and Johnson, F. P. *Joining Together: Group Theory and Group Skills* (8th ed.). Boston: Allyn and Bacon, 2003.

Joyce, P. *Strategic Management for the Public Services.* Buckingham, England: Open University Press, 1999.

Kahn, S. *Organizing: A Guide for Grassroots Leaders.* New York: McGraw-Hill, 1991.

Kanter, R. M. *Commitment and Community: Communes and Utopia in Sociological Perspectives.* Cambridge, Mass.: Harvard University Press, 1972.

Kanter, R. M. *The Changemasters.* New York: Simon and Schuster, 1983.

Kanter, R. M. *When Giants Learn to Dance: Mastering the Challenge of Strategy, Management, and Careers in the 1990s.* New York: Simon and Schuster, 1989.

Kanter, R. M. *Evolve! Succeeding in the Digital Culture of Tomorrow.* Boston: Harvard Business School Press, 2001.

Kanter, R. M. "The Enduring Skills of Change Leaders." In F. Hesselbein and R. Johnston (eds.), *On Leading Change.* San Francisco: Jossey-Bass, 2002.

Kaplan, R. D. *Warrior Politics: Why Leadership Demands a Pagan Ethos.* New York: Random House, 2002.

Kaplan, R. S., and Norton, D. P. *The Balanced Scorecard: Translating Strategy into Action.* Boston: Harvard Business School Press, 1996.

Kaufman, J. L. "Making Planners More Effective Strategists." In B. Checkoway (ed.), *Strategic Perspectives on Planning Practice.* Lexington, Mass.: Lexington Books, 1986.

Kearny, L. *The Facilitator's Tool Kit: Tools and Techniques for Generating Ideas and Making Decisions in Groups.* Amherst, Mass.: HRD Press, 1995.

Kegan, R. *In Over Our Heads: The Mental Demands of Modern Life.* Cambridge, Mass.: Harvard University Press, 1994.

Kegan, R., and Lahey, L. L. *How the Way We Talk Can Change the Way We Work: Seven Languages for Transformation.* San Francisco: Jossey-Bass, 2001.

Kellerman, B. *Reinventing Leadership: Making the Connection Between Politics and Business.* Albany: State University of New York Press, 1999.

Kelley, R. *The Power of Followership.* New York: Doubleday Currency, 1992.

Kennedy, C. *Profiles in Courage for Our Time.* New York: Hyperion, 2002.

Kets de Vries, M.F.R. *Life and Death in the Executive Fast Lane.* San Francisco: Jossey-Bass, 1995.

Kets de Vries, M.F.R. "Leaders Who Make a Difference." *European Management Journal*, 1996, *14*(5), 486–493.

Kettl, D. F. *The Global Public Management Revolution: A Report on the Transformation of Governance.* Washington, D.C.: Brookings Institution, 2000.

Kettl, D. F. *Transformation of Governance: Public Administration for Twenty-First Century America.* Baltimore: Johns Hopkins University Press, 2002.

King Jr., M. L. *Stride Toward Freedom: The Montgomery Story.* San Francisco: HarperCollins, 1986.

Kingdon, J. W. *Agendas, Alternatives, and Public Policies* (rev. ed.). Boston: Little, Brown, 1995.

Kiser, L., and Ostrom, E. "The Three Worlds of Action." In E. Ostrom (ed.), *Strategies of Political Inquiry.* Thousand Oaks, Calif.: Sage, 1982.

Klandermans, B. "The Social Construction of Protest and Multiorganizational Fields." In A. D. Morris and C. M. Mueller (eds.), *Frontiers in Social Movement Theory.* New Haven, Conn.: Yale University Press, 1992.

Klein, N. *Fences and Windows: Dispatches from the Front Lines of the Globalization Debate.* New York: Picador, 2002.

Kluckhohn, F. R., and Strodtbeck, F. L. *Variations in Value Orientations.* Evanston, Ill.: Row, Peterson, 1961.

Kostner, J. *Virtual Leadership: Secrets from the Round Table for the Multi-Site Manager.* New York: Warner Books, 1994.

Kotler, P., Roberto, N., and Lee, N. *Social Marketing: Improving the Quality of Life* (2nd ed.). Thousand Oaks, Calif.: Sage, 2002.

Kotter, J. P. *Leading Change.* Boston: Harvard Business School Press, 1996.

Kouzes, J. M., and Posner, B. Z. *Credibility: How Leaders Gain and Lose It, Why People Demand It.* San Francisco: Jossey-Bass, 1993.

Kouzes, J. M., and Posner, B. Z. *Encouraging the Heart: A Leader's Guide to Rewarding and Recognizing Others.* San Francisco: Jossey-Bass, 1999.

Kouzes, J. M., and Posner, B. Z. *The Leadership Challenge: How to Get Extraordinary Things Done in Organizations* (3rd ed.). San Francisco: Jossey-Bass, 2002.

Krasner, S. D. "Structural Causes and Regime Consequences: Regimes as Intervening Variables." In S. D. Krasner (ed.), *International Regimes.* Ithaca, N.Y.: Cornell University Press, 1983.

Krieger, M. H. "Planning and Design as Theological and Religious Activities." *Environment and Planning B: Planning and Design,* 1987, *14,* 5–13.

Krieger, M. H. *Entrepreneurial Vocations: Learning from the Callings of Augustine, Moses, Mothers, Antigone, Oedipus, and Prospero.* Atlanta: Scholars Press, 1996.

Krueger, R. A., and King, J. A. *Involving Community Members in Focus Groups.* Thousand Oaks, Calif.: Sage, 1998.

Kurland, J., and Zeder, J. "Coalition-Building: The Promise of Government." *American Journal of Community*, 2001, *29*(2), 285–287.

Lader, L. *Abortion II: Making the Revolution.* Boston: Beacon Press, 1973.

Lauria, M. (ed.). *Reconstructing Urban Regime Theory.* Thousand Oaks, Calif.: Sage, 1997.

Leonard, D., and Swap, W. "How to Make Good Work Its Own Reward." In F. Hesselbein and R. Johnston (eds.), *On Creativity, Innovation and Renewal.* San Francisco: Jossey-Bass, 2002.

Lerner, M. "An Interview with Cornel West." *Tikkun,* Sept/Oct. 2002 (http://www.tikkun.org/magazine/index.cfm/action/tikkun/issue/tik0209/article/020912.html; retrieved Sept. 2, 2004).

Letts, C. W., Ryan, W. P., and Grossman, A. *High-Performance Nonprofit Organizations: Managing Upstream for Greater Impact.* Hoboken, N.J.: Wiley, 1998.

Lewis, C. W. *The Ethics Challenge in Public Service: A Problem-Solving Guide.* San Francisco: Jossey-Bass, 1991.

Light, P. C. *The President's Agenda.* Baltimore: Johns Hopkins University Press, 1991.

Light, P. C. *Sustaining Innovation: Creating Nonprofit and Government Organizations That Innovate Naturally.* San Francisco: Jossey-Bass, 1998.

Light, P. C. *Government's Greatest Achievements.* Washington, D.C.: Brookings Institution, 2002.

Lindblom, C. E. "The Science of Muddling Through." *Public Administration Review,* 1959, *19,* 79–88.

Lindblom, C. E. *The Intelligence of Democracy.* New York: Free Press, 1965.

Lindblom, C. E. *Politics and Markets.* New York: Free Press, 1977.

Linden, R. M. *Working Across Boundaries: Making Collaboration Work in Government and Nonprofit Organizations.* San Francisco: Jossey-Bass, 2002.

Lipman-Blumen, J. *Connective Leadership: Managing in a Changing World.* San Francisco: Jossey-Bass, 1996.

Locke, E. A. "Starting at the Top." In C. L. Pearce and J. A. Conger (eds.), *Shared Leadership: Reframing the Hows and Whys of Leadership.* Thousand Oaks, Calif.: Sage, 2003.

Loeb, P. R. *Soul of a Citizen: Living with Conviction in a Cynical Time.* New York: St. Martin's Press/Griffin, 1999.

Lohmann, R. A. *The Commons: New Perspectives on Nonprofit Organizations and Voluntary Action.* San Francisco: Jossey-Bass, 1992.

Lord, R. G., and Brown, D. J. "Leadership, Values, and Subordinate Self-Concepts." *Leadership Quarterly,* 2001, *12,* 133–152.

Luke, J. S. "Managing Interconnectedness." In J. M. Bryson and R. C. Einsweiler (eds.), *Shared Power.* Lanham, Md.: University Press of America, 1991.

Luke, J. S. *Catalytic Leadership: Strategies for an Interconnected World.* San Francisco: Jossey-Bass, 1998.

Lukes, S. *Power: A Radical View.* New York: Macmillan, 1974.

Lynn, L. E. *Managing Public Policy.* Boston: Little, Brown, 1987.

Mandelbaum, S. J. *Open Moral Communities.* Cambridge, Mass.: MIT Press, 2000.

Mangham, I. L. *Power in Performance in Organizations.* Oxford, England: Basil Blackwell, 1986.

Mangham, I. L., and Overington, M. A. *Organizations as Theatre: A Social Psychology of Dramatic Appearances.* Hoboken, N.J.: Wiley, 1987.

Manz, C. C., and Neck, C. P. *Mastering Self-Leadership: Empowering Yourself for Personal Excellence.* Upper Saddle River, N.J.: Prentice Hall, 1999.

Manz, C. C., and Sims, H. P. *Superleadership: Leading Others to Lead Themselves.* Upper Saddle River, N.J.: Prentice Hall, 1989.

Manz, C. C., and Sims, H. P. *The New SuperLeadership: Leading Others to Lead Themselves.* San Francisco: Berrett-Koehler, 2001.

March, J., and Simon, H. *Organizations.* Hoboken, N.J.: Wiley, 1958.

Margarum, R. D. "Collaborative Planning: Building Consensus and Building a Distinct Model for Practice." *Journal of Planning Education and Research,* 2002, *21,* 237–253.

Marion, R., and Uhl-Bien, M. "Leadership in Complex Organizations." *Leadership Quarterly,* 2001, *12*(4), 389–418.

Maritain, J. *The Person and the Common Good.* New York: Scribner, 1947.

Marris, P. *The Politics of Uncertainty: Attachment in Private and Public Life.* London: Routledge, 1996.

Mathews, D. ". . . afterthoughts." *Kettering Review,* Winter, 1997, 73–76.

May, R. *Love and Will.* New York: Norton, 1969.

Mazmanian, D. A., and Sabatier, P. A. *Implementation and Public Policy.* Glenview, Ill.: Scott, Foresman, 1983.

McKibben, B. "Buzzless Buzzword." (Op-Ed.). *New York Times,* Apr. 11, 1996.

Meadows, D. H. "Envisioning a Sustainable World." Paper presented at Third Biennial Meeting of the International Society for Ecological Economies, San Jose, Costa Rica, 1994.

Meltsner, A. J. "Political Feasibility and Policy Analysis." *Public Administration Review,* Nov.–Dec. 1972, *32,* 859–867.

Meyer, J. P., Allen, N. J., and Gellatly, I. R. "Affective and Continuance Commitment to the Organization: Evaluation of Measures and Analysis of Concurrent and Time-Lagged Relations." *Journal of Applied Psychology,* 1990, *75*(6), 710–720.

Mikolic, J. M., and others. "A New Laboratory Method for Studying Procedural Choice and Escalation in Conflict." Proceedings of the Fifth

Annual Conference of the International Association for Conflict Management, June 17–20, 1992, Minneapolis, Minn.

Millar, A., Simeone, R. S., and Carnevale, J. T. "Logic Models: A Systems Tool for Performance Management." *Evaluation and Program Planning*, 2001, *24*, 73–81.

Mintzberg, H., and Waters, J. A. "Of Strategies, Deliberate and Emergent." *Strategic Management Journal*, 1985, *6*(3), 257–272.

Mintzberg, H. "Crafting Strategy." *Harvard Business Review*, July–Aug. 1987, pp. 66–75.

Mintzberg, H. "Managing Quietly." In F. Hesselbein and R. Johnston (eds.), *On Mission and Leadership*. San Francisco: Jossey-Bass, 2002.

Mitchell, R. K., Agle, B. R., and Wood, D. J. "Toward a Theory of Stakeholder Identification and Salience: Defining the Principle of Who and What Really Counts." *Academy of Management Review*, 1997, *22*(4), 853–886.

Mitroff, I. I., and Anagnos, G. *Managing Crises Before They Happen: What Every Executive and Manager Needs to Know About Crisis Management*. New York: AMACOM, 2000.

Mitroff, I. I., and Featheringham, D. "On Systematic Problem Solving and Errors of the Third Kind." *Behavioral Science*, 1984, *19*, 383–393.

Monnet, J. *Memoirs*. New York: Doubleday, 1978.

Moore, M. H. *Creating Public Value*. Cambridge, Mass.: Harvard University Press, 1995.

Moore, M. H. "Managing for Value: Organizational Strategy in For-Profit, Nonprofit, and Governmental Organizations." *Nonprofit and Voluntary Sector Quarterly*, 2000, *29*(1), 183–204.

Morgan, G. *Creative Organizational Theory: A Resourcebook*. Thousand Oaks, Calif.: Sage, 1989.

Morgan, G. *Imagin-I-Zation*. San Francisco: Berrett-Koehler, 1997.

Morrison, A. M. *The New Leaders: Guidelines on Leadership Diversity in America*. San Francisco: Jossey-Bass, 1992.

Morse, S. W. "Leadership for an Uncertain Century." *Phi Kappa Phi Journal*, Winter 1991, pp. 2–4.

Myers, D., and Kitsuse, A. "Constructing the Future in Planning: A Survey of Tools and Theories." *Journal of Planning Education and Research*, 2000, *19*, 221–231.

Nadler, G., and Hobino, S. *Breakthrough Thinking: The Seven Principles of Creative Problem Solving* (rev. 2nd ed.). Roseville, Calif.: Prima, 1998.

Najam, A. "World Business Council for Sustainable Development: The Greening of Business or a Greenwash?" In H. O. Bergesen, G. Parmann, and O. B. Thommessen (eds.), *Yearbook of International Cooperation on Environment and Development*. London: Earthscan, 1999–2000.

Nanus, B. *Visionary Leadership: Creating a Compelling Sense of Direction for Your Organization.* San Francisco: Jossey-Bass, 1992.

Nanus, B., and Dobbs, S. M. *Leaders Who Make a Difference: Essential Strategies for Meeting the Nonprofit Challenge.* San Francisco: Jossey-Bass, 1999.

Nelson, B. J. *Making an Issue of Child Abuse.* Chicago: University of Chicago Press, 1984.

Nelson, B. J., Kaboolian, L., and Carver, K. A. *The Concord Handbook: How to Build Social Capital Across Communities.* Los Angeles: UCLA School of Planning and Social Policy Research, 2003.

Neustadt, R. E. *Presidential Power and the Modern President.* New York: Free Press, 1990.

Neustadt, R. E., and May, E. R. *Thinking in Time: The Uses of History for Decision-Makers.* New York: Free Press, 1986.

Noddings, N. *Caring: A Feminine Approach to Ethics and Moral Education.* Berkeley: University of California Press, 1984.

Nutt, P. C. "De-Development as a Way to Change Contemporary Organizations." *Research in Organizational Change and Development,* 2001, 13, 81–115.

Nutt, P. C. *Why Decisions Fail: Avoiding the Blunders and Traps That Lead to Debacles.* San Francisco: Berrett-Koehler, 2002.

Nutt, P. C., and Backoff, R. W. *Strategic Management of Public and Third Sector Organizations: A Handbook for Leaders.* San Francisco: Jossey-Bass, 1992.

Osborn, R. N., Hunt, J. G., and Jauch, L. R. "Toward a Contextual Theory of Leadership." *Leadership Quarterly,* 2002, *13*(6), 797–837.

Osborne, D., and Plastrik, P. *Banishing Bureaucracy: The Five Strategies for Reinventing Government.* Reading, Mass.: Addison-Wesley, 1997.

Oshry, B. *Seeing Systems: Unlocking the Mysteries of Organizational Life.* San Francisco: Berrett-Koehler, 1995.

Ostrom, E. *Governing the Commons.* New York: Cambridge University Press, 1990.

O'Toole, J. *Leading Change: Overcoming the Ideology of Comfort and the Tyranny of Custom.* San Francisco: Jossey-Bass, 1995.

Palmer, P. J. *Let Your Life Speak: Listening for the Voice of Vocation.* San Francisco: Jossey-Bass, 2000.

Patterson, K., Grenny, J., McMillan, R., and Switzler, A. *Crucial Conversations: Tools for Talking When Stakes Are High.* New York: McGraw-Hill, 2002.

Patton, M. Q. *Utilization-Focused Evaluation: The New Century Text* (3rd ed.). Thousand Oaks, Calif.: Sage, 1997.

Pearce, C. L., and Conger, J. A. *Shared Leadership: Reframing the Hows and Whys of Leadership.* Thousand Oaks, Calif.: Sage, 2003.

Pearce, T. *Leading Out Loud: The Authentic Speaker, the Credible Leader.* San Francisco: Jossey-Bass, 1995.

Peters, B. G. *American Public Policy: Promise and Performance* (4th ed.). Chatham, N.J.: Chatham House, 1996a.

Peters, B. G. *The Future of Governing: Four Emerging Models.* Lawrence: University Press of Kansas, 1996b.

Peters, B. G., and Pierre, J. "Governance Without Government? Rethinking Public Administration." *Journal of Public Administration Research and Theory,* 1998, *8*(2), 223–243.

Peters, B. G., and Pierre, J. (eds.). *Handbook of Public Administration.* Thousand Oaks, Calif.: Sage, 2003.

Peterson, D. B., and Hicks, M. D. *Leader as Coach: Strategies for Coaching and Developing Others.* Minneapolis: Personnel Decisions International, 1996.

Pfeffer, J. *Managing with Power: Politics and Influence in Organizations.* Boston: Harvard Business School Press, 1992.

Pinchot, G. "An Alternative to Hierarchy." In F. Hesselbein and R. Johnston (eds.), *On High-Performance Organizations.* San Francisco: Jossey-Bass, 2002.

Poister, T. H. *Measuring Performance in Public and Nonprofit Organizations.* San Francisco: Jossey-Bass, 2003.

Posner, R. A. *The Federal Courts: Crisis and Reform.* Cambridge, Mass.: Harvard University Press, 1985.

Pressman, J., and Wildavsky, A. *Implementation.* Berkeley: University of California Press, 1973.

Price, T. L. "The Ethics of Authentic Transformational Leadership." *Leadership Quarterly,* 2003, *14*(1), 67–82.

Prokosch, M., and Raymond, L. *The Global Activist's Manual: Local Ways to Change the World.* New York: Nation Books, 2002.

Pruyne, E. *Conversations on Leadership.* Cambridge, Mass.: John F. Kennedy School of Government, Harvard University, 2002.

Putnam, R. D. *Bowling Alone: The Collapse and Revival of American Community.* New York: Simon and Schuster, 2000.

Quinn, R. E. *Beyond Rational Management: Mastering the Paradoxes and Competing Demands of High Performance.* San Francisco: Jossey-Bass, 1988.

Quinn, R. E. *Change the World: How Ordinary People Can Accomplish Extraordinary Results.* San Francisco: Jossey-Bass, 2000.

Quinn, R. E., Faerman, S. R., Thompson, M. P., and Mcgrath, M. R. *Becoming a Master Manager: A Competency Framework* (reissued 2nd ed.). Hoboken, N.J.: Wiley, 1996.

Raelin, J. A. *Work-Based Learning: The New Frontier of Management Development.* Upper Saddle River, N.J.: Prentice Hall, 2000.

Randolph, W. A., and Posner, B. Z. *Checkered Flag Projects: 10 Rules for Creating and Managing Projects That Win!* Upper Saddle River, N.J.: Financial Times Prentice Hall, 2002.

Ray, K. *The Nimble Collaboration: Fine Tuning Your Collaboration for Lasting Success.* St. Paul, Minn.: Wilder Foundation, 2002.

Rees, F. *Teamwork from Start to Finish.* San Francisco: Jossey-Bass, 1997.

Reich, R. B. *Tales of a New America.* New York: Times Books, 1987.

Rieff, D. "Blueprint for a Mess." *New York Times Magazine,* Nov. 2, 2003, pp. 28–78.

Rifkin, J. *The Age of Access: The New Culture of Hypercapitalism Where All of Life Is a Paid-for Experience.* New York: Tarcher/Putnam, 2000.

Riggio, R. E., and Orr, S. S. *Improving Leadership in Nonprofit Organizations.* San Francisco: Jossey-Bass, 2004.

Riker, W. H. *The Theory of Political Coalitions.* New Haven, Conn.: Yale University Press, 1962.

Riker, W. H. *The Art of Political Manipulation.* New Haven, Conn.: Yale University Press, 1986.

Ring, P. S., and Van de Ven, A. H. "Developmental Processes of Cooperative Interorganizational Relationships." *Academy of Management Review,* 1994, *19*(1), 90–118.

Rittel, H.W.J., and Webber, M. "Dilemmas in a General Theory of Planning." *Policy Sciences,* 1973, *4*, 155–169.

Roberts, A. "Performance-Based Organizations: Assessing the Gore Plan." *Public Administration Review,* 1997, *57*(6), 465–478.

Roberts, N. C. "Public Deliberation: An Alternative Approach to Crafting Policy and Setting Direction." *Public Administration Review,* 1997, *57*(2), 124–132.

Roberts, N. C. *The Transformative Power of Dialogue.* Amsterdam, Netherlands: JAI (Elsevier Science), 2002.

Roberts, N. C., and King, P. J. *Transforming Public Policy: Dynamics of Policy Entrepreneurship and Innovation.* San Francisco: Jossey-Bass, 1996.

Rochefort, D. A., and Cobb, R. W. *The Politics of Problem Definition: Shaping the Policy Agenda.* Lawrence: University Press of Kansas, 1994.

Rogers, E. M. *Diffusion of Innovations* (5th ed.). New York: Free Press, 2003.

Rosenberg, M. *Nonviolent Communication: A Language of Compassion.* Chicago: PuddleDancer, 1999.

Rosener, J. B. *America's Competitive Secret: Utilizing Women as a Management Strategy.* New York: Oxford University Press, 1995.

Rosenhead, J., and Mingers, J. (eds.). *Rational Analysis in a Problematic World Revisited.* London: Wiley, 2001.

Rost, J. C. *Leadership for the Twenty-First Century.* New York: Praeger, 1991.

Roy, A. *Power Politics.* Cambridge, Mass.: South End Press, 2001.

Rusk, T., and Miller, P. *The Power of Ethical Persuasion.* New York: Viking, 1993.

Sabatier, P. A. "Toward Better Theories of the Policy Process." *PS: Political Science and Politics,* 1991, *24*(2), 144–156.

Sabatier, P. A., and Jenkins-Smith, H. C. *Policy Change and Learning: An Advocacy Coalition Approach.* Boulder, Colo.: Westview, 1993.

Salamon, L. *Partners in Public Service.* Baltimore: Johns Hopkins University Press, 1995.

Salovey, P., and Mayer, J. D. "Emotional Intelligence." *Imagination, Cognition and Personality,* 1990, *9*(3), 185–211.

Samovar, L., and Porter, R. *Intercultural Communications: A Reader* (7th ed.). Belmont, Calif.: Wadsworth, 1994.

Sardar, Z., and Davies, M. W. *Why Do People Hate America?* Cambridge, England: Icon Books, 2002.

Schattschneider, E. E. *The Semisovereign People: A Realist's View of Democracy in America.* Hinsdale, Ill.: Dryden Press, 1975.

Schein, E. H. *Organizational Culture and Leadership* (2nd ed.). San Francisco: Jossey-Bass, 1992.

Schein, E. H. "On Dialogue, Culture, and Organizational Learning." *Organizational Dynamics* (Autumn 1993), pp. 40–51.

Schein, E. H. *Organizational Culture and Leadership* (3rd ed.). San Francisco: Jossey-Bass, 2004.

Schmidheiny, S. *Changing Course: A Global Business Perspective on Development and the Environment.* Cambridge, Mass.: MIT Press, 1992.

Schön, D. A. *Beyond the Stable State.* London: Temple Smith, 1971.

Schön, D. A. *The Reflective Practitioner: How Professionals Think in Action.* New York: Basic Books, 1983.

Schön, D. A., and Rein, M. *Frame Reflection: Toward the Resolution of Intractable Policy Controversies.* New York: Basic Books, 1994.

Schutz, A. *The Phenomenology of the Social World.* Evanston, Ill.: Northwestern University Press, 1967.

Schwarz, R. M. *The Skilled Facilitator* (rev. ed.). San Francisco: Jossey-Bass, 2002.

Scott, J. C. *Seeing Like a State: How Certain Schemes to Improve the Human Condition Have Failed.* New Haven, Conn.: Yale University Press, 1998.

Seligman, M.E.P. *Learned Optimism.* New York: Pocket Books, 1998.

Selznick, P. *TVA and the Grassroots.* Berkeley: University of California Press, 1949.

Selznick, P. *Leadership in Administration: A Sociological Interpretation.* Berkeley: University of California Press, 1957.

Senge, P. M. "The Leader's New Work: Building Learning Organizations." *Sloan Management Review,* Fall 1990, pp. 7–23.

Senge, P. M. *The Fifth Discipline: The Art of Practice of the Learning Organization.* New York: Doubleday, 1994.

Senge, P. M., and others. *The Fifth Discipline Fieldbook: Strategies and Tools for Building a Learning Organization.* New York: Currency Doubleday, 1994.

Senge, P. M., and others. *The Dance of Change: The Challenges to Sustaining Momentum in Learning Organizations.* New York: Currency Doubleday, 1999.

Shapiro, D. A. *Choosing the Right Thing to Do.* San Francisco: Berrett-Koehler, 1999.

Shapiro, M. "Courts." In F. I. Greenstein and N. Polsby (eds.), *Handbook of Political Science: Government Institutions and Processes,* vol. 5. Reading, Mass: Addison-Wesley, 1975.

Shapiro, M. *A Comparative and Political Analysis.* Chicago: University of Chicago Press, 1981.

Shaw, R. *The Activist's Handbook: A Primer.* Berkeley: University of California Press, 2001.

Shilts, R. *And the Band Played on.* New York: St. Martin's Press, 1988.

Shulock, N. "The Paradox of Policy Analysis: If It Is Not Used, Why Do We Produce So Much of It?" *Journal of Policy Analysis and Management,* 1999, *18*(2), 226–244.

Simon, H. A. *Administrative Behavior.* New York: Macmillan, 1947.

Simon, H. A. *Administrative Behavior* (2nd ed.). New York: Macmillan, 1957.

Simons, H. W. *Persuasion in Society.* Thousand Oaks, Calif.: Sage, 2001.

Sirianni, C., and Friedland, L. *Civic Innovation in America: Community Empowerment, Public Policy, and the Movement for Civic Renewal.* Berkeley: University of California Press, 2001.

Snyder, D. P., and Edwards, G. *Rhetoric: The Language of Leadership.* Bethesda, Md.: Snyder Family Enterprise, 1997.

Sorenson, G., and Hickman, G. R. "Invisible Leadership: Acting on Behalf of a Common Purpose." In C. Cherry and L. R. Matusak (eds.), *Building Leadership Bridges 2002* (International Leadership Association). College Park, Md.: Burns Academy of Leadership, 2002.

Sosik, J. J., Avolio, B. J., and Jung, D. I. "Examining the Relationship of Self-Presentation Attributes and Impression Management to Charismatic Leadership." *Leadership Quarterly,* 2002, *13*(3), 217–242.

Stephan, W. G. "Intergroup Relations." In G. Lindzey and E. Aronson (eds.), *Handbook of Social Psychology* (3rd ed.), vol. 2. New York: Random House, 1985.

Stivers, C. "The Listening Bureaucrat: Responsiveness in Public Administration." *Public Administration Review,* 1994, *54*(4), 364–369.

Stone, D. A. *Policy Paradox and Political Reason* (rev. ed.). New York: Norton, 2002.

Susskind, L., McKearnan, S., and Thomas-Larmer, J. *The Consensus Building Handbook: A Comprehensive Guide to Reaching Agreement.* Thousand Oaks, Calif.: Sage, 1999.

Tan, A. *The Joy Luck Club.* New York: Ivy Books, 1989.

Taylor, H. R. "Power at Work." In A. D. Timpe (ed.), *Leadership.* New York: Facts on File, 1987.

Taylor, N. "Mistaken Interests and the Discourse Model of Planning." *Journal of the American Planning Association,* 1998, *64*(1), 64–75.

Terry, R. W. *Authentic Leadership: Courage in Action.* San Francisco: Jossey-Bass, 1993.

Terry, R. W. *Seven Zones for Leadership: Acting Authentically in Stability and Chaos.* Palo Alto, Calif.: Davies-Black, 2001.

Thomas, J. C. "Public Involvement and Governmental Effectiveness: A Decision-Making Model for Public Managers." *Administration and Society,* 1993, *24*(4), 444–469.

Thomas, J. C. *Public Participation in Public Decisions.* San Francisco: Jossey-Bass, 1995.

Thompson, J. R. "The Dual Potentialities of Performance Measurement." *Public Productivity and Management Review,* 2000, *23*(3), 267–281.

Thompson, L. *The Mind and Heart of the Negotiator* (2nd ed.). Upper Saddle River, N.J.: Prentice Hall, 2001.

Throgmorton, J. A. "The Rhetoric of Policy Analysis." *Policy Sciences,* 1991, *24,* 153–179.

Throgmorton, J. A. *Planning as Persuasive Storytelling: Rhetorical Construction of Chicago's Electric Future.* Chicago: University of Chicago Press, 1996.

Throgmorton, J. A. "On the Virtues of Skillful Meandering: Acting as a Skilled-Voice-in-the-Flow of Persuasive Argumentation." *Journal of the American Planning Association,* 2000, *66*(4), 367–383.

Tornow, W. W., London, M., and CCL Associates. *Maximizing the Value of 360-Degree Feedback.* San Francisco: Jossey-Bass, 1998.

Toulmin, S. *The Uses of Argument.* New York: Cambridge University Press, 1958.

Trist, E. "Referent Organizations and the Development of Interorganizational Domains." *Human Relations,* 1983, *36*(3), 269–284.

Tsoukas, H. "The Firm as a Distributed Knowledge System: A Constructionist Approach." *Strategic Management Journal,* 1996, *17* (Winter special issue), 11–25.

Tuchman, B. *The March of Folly: From Troy to Vietnam.* New York: Knopf, 1984.

Useem, M. *The Leadership Moment.* New York: Times Business, 1998.

Vaill, P. B. *Learning as a Way of Being: Strategies for Survival in a World of Permanent Whitewater.* San Francisco: Jossey-Bass, 1996.

Van de Ven, A. H., Polley, D. E., Garud, R., and Venkataraman, S. *The Innovation Journey.* Oxford, England: Oxford University Press, 1999.

Van der Heijden, K., and others. *The Sixth Sense: Accelerating Organizational Learning with Scenarios.* Chichester, England: Wiley, 2002.

Vangen, S., and Huxham, C. "Enacting Leadership for Collaboration Advantage." *British Journal of Management,* 2003, *15*(1), 39–55.

Van Horn, C. E., Baumer, D. C., and Gormley, W. T. *Politics and Public Policy* (3rd ed.). Washington, D.C.: Congressional Quarterly Press, 2001.

van Schendelen, R. *Machiavelli in Brussels: The Art of Lobbying the EU.* Amsterdam, Netherlands: University of Amsterdam Press, 2002.

Vecchio, R. P. "Leadership and Gender Advantage." *Leadership Quarterly,* 2002, *13*(6), 643–671.

Vickers, G. *The Art of Judgment: A Study of Policy Making.* Thousand Oaks, Calif.: Sage, 1995.

Volkema, R. J. "Problem Formulation as a Purposive Activity." *Strategic Management Journal,* 1986, *7,* 267–279.

Walker, A. *By the Light of My Father's Smile.* New York: Ballantine Books, 1999.

Wallace, D., and White, J. B. "Building Integrity of Organizations." *New Management,* 1988, *6*(1), 30–35.

Walzer, M. "The Idea of a Civil Society." *Kettering Review,* Winter 1997, pp. 8–22.

Waste, R. J. *Ecology of City Policymaking.* New York: Oxford University Press, 1997.

Weber, M. *The Theory of Social and Economic Organizations.* New York: Free Press, 1947.

Weick, K. E. "Small Wins: Redefining the Scale of Social Problems." *American Psychologist,* 1984, *39*(1), 40–49.

Weick, K. E. *Sensemaking in Organizations.* Thousand Oaks, Calif.: Sage, 1995.

Weick, K. E., and Sutcliffe, K. M. *Managing the Unexpected: Assuring High Performance in an Age of Complexity.* San Francisco: Jossey-Bass, 2001.

Weick, K. E., Sutcliffe, K., and Obstfeld, D. "High Reliability: The Power of Mindfulness." In F. Hesselbein and R. Johnston (eds.), *On High Performance Organizations.* San Francisco: Jossey-Bass, 2002.

Weimer, D. L., and Vining, A. R. *Policy Analysis: Concepts and Practice* (3rd ed.). Upper Saddle River, N.J.: Prentice Hall, 1999.

Winer, M. "Balancing Power Precedes Other Group Processes in Collaborations and Partnerships." In P. Hibbert (ed.), *Co-Creating*

Emergent Insight. Glasgow, Scotland: University of Strathclyde Graduate School of Business, 2003.

Weisbord, M., and Janoff, S. *Future Search.* San Francisco: Berrett-Koehler, 1995.

Weisbord, M. R., and others. *Discovering Common Ground: How Future Search Conferences Bring People Together to Achieve Breakthrough Innovation, Empowerment, Shared Vision, and Collaborative Action.* San Francisco: Barrett-Koehler, 1993.

Weisman, C. *Secrets of Successful Retreats: The Best from the Non-Profit Pros.* St. Louis: Robbins, 2003.

West, C. *Race Matters.* New York: Vintage Books, 1994.

Wheatley, M. J. *Leadership and the New Science: Learning About Organization from an Orderly Universe.* San Francisco: Berrett-Koehler, 1999.

Wheatley, M. J. *Turning to One Another: Simple Conversations to Restore Hope to the Future.* San Francisco: Berrett-Koehler, 2002.

Wheelan, S. A. *Creating Effective Teams: A Guide for Members and Leaders.* Thousand Oaks, Calif.: Sage, 1999.

Wholey, J. S., Hatry, H. P., and Newcomer, K. E. *Handbook of Practical Program Evaluation.* San Francisco: Jossey-Bass, 1994.

Wildavsky, A. *Speaking Truth to Power: The Art and Craft of Policy Analysis.* Boston: Little, Brown, 1979.

Williamson, O. E. *The Economic Institutions of Capitalism: Firms, Markets, Relational Contracting.* New York: Free Press, 1985.

Wilson, J. Q. "Innovation in Organizations: Notes Toward a Theory." In J. D. Thompson (ed.), *Approaches to Organizational Design.* Pittsburgh: University of Pittsburgh Press, 1967.

Wilson, J. Q. *Bureaucracy: What Government Agencies Do and Why They Do It.* New York: Basic Books, 1989.

Wilson, J. Q., and DiIulio Jr., J. J. *American Government* (7th ed.). Boston: Houghton Mifflin, 1998.

Winer, M., and Ray, K. *Collaboration Handbook: Creating, Sustaining, and Enjoying the Journey.* St. Paul, Minn.: Amherst H. Wilder Foundation, 1994.

World Business Council for Sustainable Development. *Stakeholder Dialogue Toolkit.* Geneva, Switzerland: World Business Council for Sustainable Development, 2001.

World Business Council for Sustainable Development. *Annual Review 2002.* Geneva, Switzerland: World Business Council for Sustainable Development, 2003.

Young, I. M. *Justice and the Politics of Difference.* Princeton, N.J.: Princeton University Press, 1990.

Youngblood, M. D. *Life at the Edge of Chaos: Creating the Quantum Organization.* Dallas: Perceval, 1997.

Zaccaro, S. J., and Banks, D. J. "Leadership Vision, and Organizational Effectiveness." In S. J. Zaccaro and R. J. Klimoski (eds.), *The Nature of Organizational Leadership: Understanding the Performance Imperatives Confronting Today's Leaders.* San Francisco: Jossey-Bass, 2001.

Zaccaro, S. J., and Klimoski, R. J. "The Nature of Organizational Leadership." In S. J. Zaccaro and R. J. Klimoski (eds.), *The Nature of Organizational Leadership: Understanding the Performance Imperatives Confronting Today's Leaders.* San Francisco: Jossey-Bass, 2001.

Zaccaro, S. J., Rittman, A. L., and Marks, M. A. "Team Leadership." *Leadership Quarterly,* 2001, *12,* 451–483.

Zinn, H. *A People's History of the United States: 1492 to Present.* New York: HarperPerennial, 2001.

Resource A
Conflict Management

Conflict within and among groups of people is part of life. Since it cannot be avoided, leaders need to manage conflict constructively. The conflict framework developed by Tom Fiutak at the Humphrey Institute Conflict and Change Center, University of Minnesota, suggests several strategies for leaders. This framework is intended to be adjusted to the particular situation.

There are four basic steps (see Figure A.1):

1. Be rooted in reality. Work to hear differing realities of the same situation. Is this conflict about data, relationships, interests, values, or structure? What are the causes of the conflict?
2. Examine underlying assumptions; allow people to express their feelings, or vent.
3. Create options.
4. Produce action to get on with it, which involves responsibility for all parties.

Figure A.1. Conflict Framework.

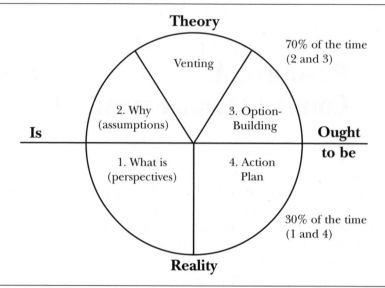

Resource B
A Guide to Oval Mapping

by John M. Bryson and Anne R. Carroll

Oval mapping goes a step beyond the snowcard technique to establish cause-and-effect or influence relationships among ideas. The process facilitator guides participants in brainstorming solutions to an issue or problem and writing their ideas on ovals, or egg-shaped cards. The ovals are then affixed to a wall, participants cluster them into groups, and the group works with the clusters to identify how the ideas are linked together by cause-and-effect or influence relations. Here is an outline of the process, which is described more fully in *Strategic Planning for Public and Nonprofit Organizations* (Bryson, 2004a).

These are the basic requirements:

- A group consisting of no more than twelve people (seven is optimal)
- A facilitator (ideally from outside the group)
- A large wall
- Flipchart sheets
- Masking tape
- Black markers
- Pencils with erasers
- Paper ovals (in yellow or another light color), approximately 7.5 inches long and 4.5 inches wide, twenty per person

1. Tape the flipchart sheets together on the wall to make a rectangular backdrop for the ovals. The rectangle should be four to six sheets wide and two or three sheets high, depending on the size

of the group. Flipchart sheets should overlap one another by one inch, so that the entire rectangle can be taken down and moved easily.

2. The facilitator asks each group member to think of solutions or responses to the problem being considered and write those ideas on the ovals, one idea per oval, using the black markers.

For example, if the problem were female illiteracy, the facilitator might pose the question, "What should we do to increase female literacy?"

The facilitator directs the group to express their solutions as imperatives—for example, "Have reading materials with female heroes." Each idea should be expressed in no more than ten words. When most members of the group are finished writing, they post their ovals on the flipchart-covered wall.

The process assumes that participants can all read and write the same language. If participants do not, an alternative process is to draw pictures that represent possible actions. The pictures can be displayed to serve as a visual backdrop for talking about the actions.

3. The facilitator then leads participants in clustering the ovals according to common themes or subjects. Within the clusters, the more general, abstract, or goal-oriented ovals are moved toward the top and the more concrete, specific, and detailed ovals toward the bottom. The facilitator asks participants to name the clusters and then places a new oval with a name above each cluster. These clusters typically represent strategic issue or option areas.

4. The facilitator works with participants to pencil in arrows indicating linkage within and between clusters. An arrow pointing upward from oval A to oval B indicates that the action described on oval A causes, influences, or precedes the action described on B; conversely the action on oval B is an effect, outcome, or follow-up to the action on A. Once the group agrees on the placement of the arrows, they can be drawn in permanently with a marker.

5. The group now has a map of clusters in which specific actions or options are located toward the bottom, strategic options are in the middle, and more goal-oriented statements are toward the top. (See the graphic representations of this arrangement in Figures B.1 and B.2, in which the oval map is now referred to as an "Action-Oriented Strategy Map"). The facilitator then encourages

the group to think further about what they hope to achieve by pursuing the strategic options on the map. The responses, or "higher," goals can be placed on new ovals at the top of the map, and arrows drawn from ovals that would contribute to those goals.

6. Finally, the group may want to decide on what it actually believes should be done, how, and why through an extended workshop process. It may wish to prioritize the actions, strategies, and goals on the map. The facilitator might give everyone five red dots to place on the five ovals considered most vital. This process can be much more elaborate, but the simple version presented here is adequate for constructing a preliminary strategic plan for what the group thinks should be done, how it should be done, and why.

The map so produced can be preserved as is, translated into an outline, or reproduced using computer graphics.

Figure B.1. Overall Logic of an Oval Map (Action-Oriented Strategy Map).

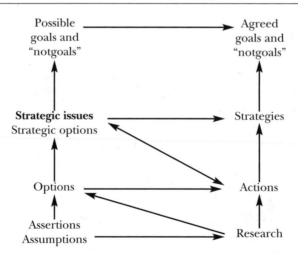

Figure B.2. Shape of an Action-Oriented Strategy Map.

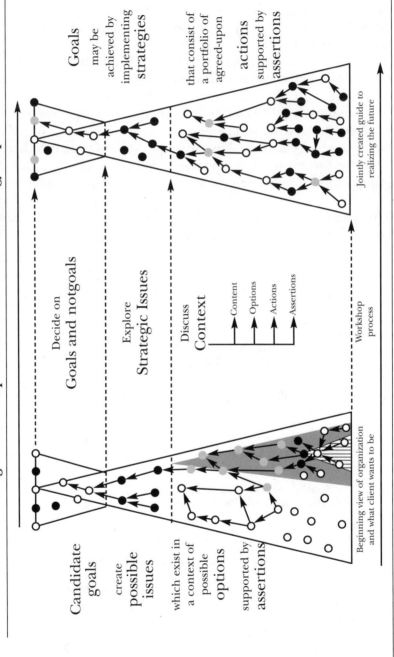

Resource C
Seven Zones

In *Seven Zones for Leadership,* Bob Terry presents a developmental typology of leadership approaches tied to the degree to which an organization's environment is "fixable and knowable." Each approach builds on the ones that precede it. Organizations in zones one and two exist in a relatively stable environment; leaders in zone-one organizations focus on honoring core values, history, and personal traits or gifts, whereas leaders in zone-two organizations ensure that people have the skills needed to accomplish functional tasks. Organizations in zone three face a more chaotic environment, so leaders focus on establishing systems that support the mission and core values while liberating human potential and promoting learning to achieve a flexible, responsive organization.

In zone four, uncertainty is even greater, and positional leaders seek to empower others in the organization in the hope of unleashing collective wisdom and action to deal with resulting problems. Large-scale interventions such as search conferences and real-time strategic change can be helpful for organizations in this zone, and Terry offers guidelines that can help leaders use these strategies effectively (see pages 206–207 in Terry, 2001).

In zone five, leaders take an even more proactive role in the face of uncertainty by helping people in the organization invent a desired future and visions of success. Leaders in this zone promote organizational competencies such as "pattern recognition, framing, outward and inward scanning, scenario writing, metaphorical thinking and generation of new insights" (Terry, 2001, p. 263).

In zone six, leaders focus on finding meaning in chaos. They help people in their organization question their assumptions and beliefs, acknowledge paradox, and become skillful improvisers.

In zone seven, leaders foster the commitment to live with paradox and act courageously in the world "to resist evil and forgive
evil doers." In this zone, leadership involves making "adept
choices" by "listening to the world's stirrings, seeking to understand them, and acting authentically in anticipation and response.
When we are adept, we live at the intersection of polarities. We can
go inside and outside, we can be centered and boundless, historically rooted and open to others, stable yet changeable, firm yet
flexible, and unified yet diverse" (Terry, 2001, p. 306).

Resource D
Forums, Arenas, and Courts

Basing our findings partly on the work of Anthony Giddens (1979, 1984), we identify three basic kinds of public action: communicating, policy making and implementing, and settling disputes and enforcing the system's underlying norms (Bryson and Crosby, 1993, 1996). Each is shaped, and biased, by three dimensions of power (Lukes, 1974), presented in Exhibit D.1.

The *first dimension* of power is emphasized by the pluralists (for example, Dahl, 1961), who argue that the power of a public actor in a democratic system varies with the issue, that there are several bases of power (wealth, status, knowledge, skill, and so on), and that there is some substitutability among power bases. In other words, winners and losers vary by issue, and society therefore is pluralist rather than elitist. The pluralists focus on observable behavior: communication, policy making and implementation, and sanctioning; key issues; observable conflict; and interests defined as policy preferences revealed by political participation.

In its *second dimension,* power is exercised more subtly, through manipulation of the vehicles of bias that affect decisions and action. As Peter Bachrach and Morton Baratz note, "To the extent that a person or group—consciously or unconsciously—reinforces barriers to public airing of policy conflicts, that person has power" (1962, p. 949). Various ideas, rules, modes, media, and methods (including "organization" in the general sense) are the principal barriers that bias attention toward some matters and away from others (Bachrach and Baratz, 1962, 1963; Schattschneider, 1975; Forester, 1989; Healey, 1997; Flyvbjerg, 1998). These barriers also can be described as asymmetrically distributed rules, resources, and transformation relations such as agenda control (Giddens, 1979),

Exhibit D.1. The Three Dimensions of Power.

Dimension	Focus	Focusing on:
1. Interaction	Behavioral	Communication, policy making and implementation, and sanctioning of conduct
		Key issues
		Observable (overt) conflict
		(Subjective) interests, seen as policy preferences revealed by political participation
2. Ideas, rules, modes, media, or methods	Qualified critique of behavioral focus	Policy decision making and nondecision making
		Issues and potential issues
		Overt and covert conflict
		(Subjective) interests, seen as policy preferences or grievances
		Ideas, rules, modes, media, or methods that influence transformation of a set of potential decisions, issues, conflicts, and policy preferences into those actually considered and those not considered
3. Deep structure	Critique of behavioral focus	Policy making and control over political agenda (not necessarily through decisions)
		Issues and potential issues
		Overt, covert, and latent conflict
		Subjective and "real" interests
		Collective basis for a set of potential decisions, issues, conflicts, and policy preferences that people might consider

Source: Adapted in part from Lukes (1974, p. 25) and Clegg (1989, p. 214).

which create decision and "nondecision" categories, and "live" issues versus "potential" issues. In other words, built-in organizational bias effectively rules out certain behaviors, which therefore will not be observed.

The *third dimension* reveals an even subtler exercise of power: the shaping of felt needs, rights, and responsibilities. These are rooted in deep, or "bedrock," social, political, and economic structures. People draw on these structures to generate the rules and resources that allow human relationships, organizations, and interorganizational networks to exist (Giddens, 1979). They are also the basis for a potential set of issues, conflicts, and policy preferences, as well as decisions that leaders and citizens might address. Yet it is ideas, rules, modes, media, and methods—the vehicles of bias—of the second dimension that influence the transformation of this potential set into the actual issues, conflicts, and policy preferences and decisions that are considered in the first dimension. The vehicles of bias also determine what remains in the second dimension as potential issues, covert conflicts, individual grievances, or nondecisions (see Figure D.1).

The three-dimensional view of power reveals how society's institutions, as embodiments of bias ultimately based on the social bedrock, lead citizens and policy makers to consider some policy decisions, issues, conflicts, and preferences while ignoring others. In the African American men case, institutional bias in government programs made it difficult for administrators to view the situation of these men holistically. In the World Business Council case, market structures have allowed businesspeople to ignore the environmental costs of production and of many resulting products.

Connections Between Public Action and Social Structure

Within and among organizations, action is linked to the three dimensions of power primarily through designing and using forums, arenas, and courts. In these shared-power settings, people interactively draw on third-dimension social structures or relationships and second-dimension organizational and interorganizational ideas, rules, modes, media, or methods to produce such instrumental effects as discussion papers, policy statements, decrees, and

Figure D.1. Dividing What Is Possible Into What Is Seen and What Is Not Seen.

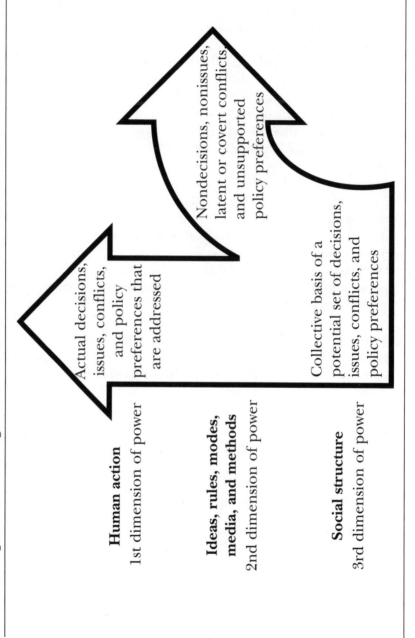

Human action
1st dimension of power

Actual decisions, issues, conflicts, and policy preferences that are addressed

Ideas, rules, modes, media, and methods
2nd dimension of power

Nondecisions, nonissues, latent or covert conflicts and unsupported policy preferences

Social structure
3rd dimension of power

Collective basis of a potential set of decisions, issues, conflicts, and policy preferences action plans. At the same time they produce instrumental effects, they also reproduce organizational or interorganizational structures, including at least partially shared understandings, social relationships, and the vehicles of bias. As these structures are reproduced, however, they also are modified, in an "ongoing strengthening, altering, or weakening of those social relations without which the production of desired results ([for example] plans, reports, recommendations) would not be possible" (Forester, 1989, p. 71; see also Giddens, 1979, pp. 49–130). In other words, people draw on structures to *create* observable action, which subsequently *recreates*, yet also reshapes, the structures that permitted the action in the first place.

The three-dimensional view emphasized here highlights the central role of ideas, rules, modes, media, and methods in governing both continuity and change in structures and social systems, from small groups to entire societies. This view also combines the two main traditions of social analysis. The first tradition focuses on patterned regularities in social interaction; structures are viewed mainly as the product of human activity. The second tradition focuses on structures as prescribed frameworks of constraint. Structures are givens, and human actors are assumed to learn, work within, and adapt to the structures. The distinction between the two traditions dissolves when one recognizes "the duality of structures," in which structures are both the medium and the outcome of human action (Giddens, 1979). Figure D.2 depicts how structuration (production and reproduction of social systems) occurs through the interaction of the three dimensions of power and in relation to the two views of society. (Anthony Giddens argues, a bit ambiguously, that there are only two dimensions of power, one corresponding to each view of society; the three-dimensional view clarifies the overlapping elements of his model.)

An appreciation of structuration implies that leaders can have their greatest influence over action and outcomes by focusing on the second dimension of power—that is, by strengthening, weakening, or altering the ideas, rules, modes, media, and methods that divide what is theoretically conceivable into what is actually possible and what is not. This is *leadership by indirection.* Instead of dictating directly what people should or should not do, or directly

Figure D.2. The Three-Dimensional View of Power in Relation to the Two Main Traditions of Social Analysis.

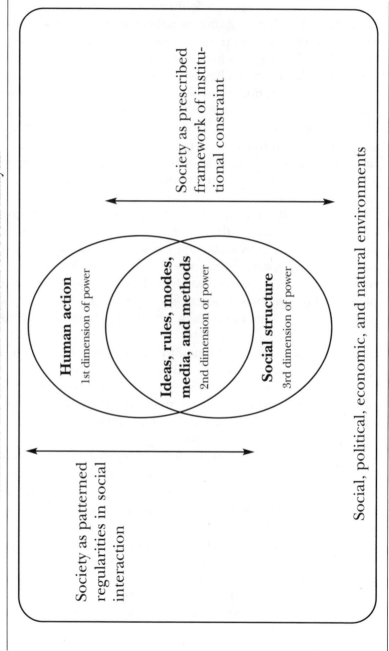

controlling the social bedrock, leaders must influence the way action and structure are created and recreated. The relevant image is not the in-charge leader, but the visionary, political, and ethical leader who is a guide, persuader, facilitator, coach, collaborator, and team player.

In other words, to raise and resolve public problems constructively, leaders must attend to human interaction, institutional arrangements, and the way in which human interaction and social structures are linked through ideas, rules, modes, media, and methods. For example, in the early years of the U.S. AIDS crisis, the people leading efforts to prevent and treat the disease had to consider the interactions of the groups being infected by the AIDS virus, their families, health professionals, university administrators, elected officials and their aides, journalists, senior bureaucrats, nonprofit advocacy and service groups, and institutions (such as "the family," the National Institutes of Health, city governments, the blood bank and bathhouse industries, and the press). They also had to attend to mediating laws, regulations, norms, interpretive schemes, research protocols, budgetary procedures, journalists' newsgathering practices, and publication rules for academic journals.

A Holistic Concept of Power

When leaders understand how three of their essential skills—communicating, policy making and implementing, and settling disputes—interact with each other and relate to the three dimensions of power, they have a holistic conception of power that can be put to practical use. To begin with, communication, policy making and implementing, and settling disputes are so important because they are the action dimensions of the three basic social practices (Giddens, 1979, 1984). We call these social practices:

- The design and use of forums (the social practice resulting in communication of meaning)
- The design and use of arenas (the social practice resulting in policy making and implementing)
- The design and use of courts (the social practice resulting in normative regulation of conduct)

(In naming the second type of social practice, we used "policy making and implementing" rather than Giddens's term *exercise of power.* In Giddens's model of social life, it is clear that what he calls the exercise of power can be meaningful only if it incorporates or comprehends the other two basic social practices.)

Although the three social practices are analytically separable, they are also in constant interaction (see Figure D.3). Thus if one is to understand policy making and implementation, one must also understand communication of meaning and normative regulation of conduct. Of course, the emphasis on each practice varies greatly with the situation.

Leaders who can locate the pertinent forums, arenas, and courts and understand and explain their operation in relation to each dimension of power have a holistic and practical grasp of the power to affect and effect change. In a forum, they must exercise visionary skills; in an arena, political skills; and in a court, conflict management and ethical skills. It may be helpful to view forums, arenas, and courts as "playgrounds" where a temporary order reigns (Huizinga, 1996). This perspective conveys a sense of the design and use of these settings as lively, participative enactment (and certainly not as a spectator sport; see also Innes and Booher, 1999).

Forums and the Three Dimensions of Power

The use of forums links speakers and audiences through dialogue, discussion, debate, and deliberation in order to create and communicate meaning (see Exhibit D.2). Forums are the principal setting within which appreciation of emergent or developmental problems and their potential solutions is either maintained or changed. Forums distribute and redistribute access to the creation and communication of meaning and thereby help maintain or change symbolic orders and modes of discourse. By discourse, we mean "historically and culturally situated speech" (Boler, 1999, p. 5).

How this happens becomes clearer when forums are viewed through the three dimensions of power. In the first dimension (action), people use symbols to engage in dialogue, discussion, debate, and deliberation on various issues. Their goal is to create shared meaning, and perhaps shared values, in the minds of the relevant groups.

Figure D.3. The Triple Three-Dimensional View of Power.

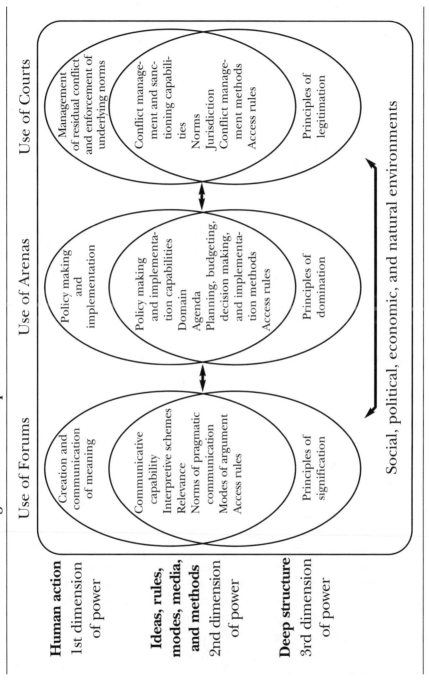

Use of Forums | Use of Arenas | Use of Courts

Human action
1st dimension of power

Creation and communication of meaning | Policy making and implementation | Management of residual conflict and enforcement of underlying norms

Ideas, rules, modes, media, and methods
2nd dimension of power

Communicative capability
Interpretive schemes
Relevance
Norms of pragmatic communication
Modes of argument
Access rules

Policy making and implementation capabilities
Domain
Agenda
Planning, budgeting, decision making, and implementation methods
Access rules

Conflict management and sanctioning capabilities
Norms
Jurisdiction
Conflict management methods
Access rules

Deep structure
3rd dimension of power

Principles of signification | Principles of domination | Principles of legitimation

Social, political, economic, and natural environments

Exhibit D.2. Designing and Using Forums.

Definition	A practice of linking speakers and audiences wherein meaning is created and communicated through discussion, debate, or deliberation.
Examples	Task forces, discussion groups, brainstorming sessions, public hearings, formal debates, newspapers, television, radio, plays, conferences, professional journals.
Policy-related role	Maintenance or change of symbolic orders and modes of discourse, especially through distribution and redistribution of access to the communication of meaning.
Structural properties	A speaker and audience (of at least one) along with a minimum set of common linguistic rules and resources.
Action	The use of symbols to create shared meaning and values among participants. Characteristic activity is discussion, debate, or deliberation.
Ideas, rules, modes, media, and methods	Communicative capability, interpretive schemes, and ways of deciding among interpretive schemes—for example, relevance, norms of pragmatic communication (speaking comprehensibly, sincerely, in context, truthfully), modes of argument, access determinants.
Effect or outcome	A potential list of decisions, issues, conflicts, or policy preferences available for discussion. In addition, a forum mediates transformation of that list into an actual list of decisions, issues, conflicts, or policy preferences to be discussed or not discussed.

The third dimension of power appears in a forum as basic signification principles, or bedrock signification structures. A forum requires a speaker and an audience, at least a partly shared set of common linguistic rules and resources, and one or more shared worldviews or ideologies. Of course, language structures accumulate through many years of human interaction and carry within them numerous biases, including biases that favor certain groups of people. Language in large part constructs human beings and their interactions (Foucault, 1997; see also Hoffman, 1990). Take, for example, meetings among physicians, gay activists, and public officials in San Francisco in the early 1980s to consider what should be done about the evidence of a new virulent disease affecting gay men. These people shared the English language, and in some cases they shared medical jargon. They shared the view that local government was at least partially responsible for protecting the health of its citizens and that citizens had a right to present their views to public officials. They also generally accepted that individuals should not be discriminated against because of their sexual orientation. Many of the gay activists shared a gay liberation ideology; many of the politicians adhered to a "liberal" political ideology.

In a forum, the most important second-dimension ideas, rules, modes, media, and methods used to link desired outcomes with deep structure are communicative capability, interpretive schemes, relevance, norms of pragmatic communication, modes of argument, and access rules. *Communicative capability* is simply the capacity to create and communicate meaning. This capability includes rhetorical skill, the ability to catch the interest of print and electronic news media, mastery of storytelling, and the potential to pull together a supportive, chanting crowd on a moment's notice. Examples would be Larry Kramer's ability to pen forceful editorials and a highly emotional play, and the ability of people at the World Business Council for Sustainable Development to write highly readable books.

Interpretive schemes (Schutz, 1967) are intersubjective organizing frameworks or schemata that people use to understand events in a meaningful way and to guide action. They include shared beliefs, expectations, and rules through which people interpret personal experiences and social knowledge. An individual's interpretation of new experiences or knowledge is thus based on the person's understanding of his or her own and others' cumulative experience; this understanding draws on ideologies, common sense, and even deeper cultural assumptions (for example, the belief, in many societies, in private property or respect for elders). In other words, each of us has a set of interpretive schemes, one or more of which are activated when we encounter and frame a new event or new information, such as evidence of a virulent new disease affecting gay men. Astute leaders think carefully about what type of interpretive scheme, or framework, they seek to activate in connection with a particular public problem (Bolman and Deal, 2003). For example, physicians and other health professionals articulated a problem frame that activated a public health framework for understanding the emerging AIDS crisis. Gay activists and bathhouse owners articulated a problem frame that activated a gay rights framework.

Inside a forum, competing, conflicting, or contradictory interpretive schemes must be partially mediated as a necessary condition for the emergence of concerted action. Norms of *relevance* and of *pragmatic communication,* as well as *modes of argument* and *access rules,* are crucial mediators among incompatible interpretive schemes. Norms of relevance were embedded in the argument between gay activists and health professionals. In San Francisco, the majority of gay activists in effect prevented concerted public health measures against the spread of HIV in the early stages by arguing that attempts to regulate sexual practices could no longer be considered relevant in an era of gay liberation (Shilts, 1988). On the other side, health professionals argued that regulation of a practice endangering a large number of citizens was certainly relevant, regardless of which groups were being regulated.

Norms of pragmatic communication include the expectation that messages will be comprehensible, sincere, appropriate to the context, and accurate. These expectations set the basic criteria for judging speech aimed at influencing the action of the listeners (see Habermas, 1979; Forester, 1989). If these criteria are violated, listeners feel confusion, distrust, lack of consent, anger, and disbelief (Forester, 1980, 1989) In the AIDS case, everyone expected the statistics produced by local health departments and the Centers for Disease Control to be reliable. Similarly, they expected truthfulness from hospitals and blood banks about the safety of the blood supply. When evidence mounted that blood bank officials and government administrators had not revealed evidence about contamination of blood supplies, public outrage mounted. An interpretive framework that accorded health professionals and administrators a high level of respect was diminished in power, as a framework emphasizing patient rights became more prominent.

Argumentation is another important means of mediating among differing interpretive schemes. William Dunn, drawing on the work of Stephen Toulmin and Austin Freeley, contends that policy arguments—those related to decisions, issues, conflicts, or policy preferences—have several elements (Dunn, 1994; Toulmin, 1958; Freeley, 1976):

- Policy-relevant information
- A policy claim, which is the conclusion of a policy argument
- A warrant, which is an assumption permitting the move from information to a claim
- Backing for the warrant, which consists of additional supporting assumptions or arguments, often based on scientific laws, the authority of experts, or ethical or moral principles
- A rebuttal, which indicates the conditions under which the original claim is unacceptable or in need of modification
- A qualifier, which expresses the degree to which the arguer is certain about the policy claim

Argumentation may be presented in a variety of formats, from reports to radio talk shows.

The design and use of forums influences which information is offered; which claims, along with which rebuttals, are accepted, and depending on which warrants and backing; how much weight is given to the qualifiers; and which formats work best (Throgmorton, 1996; Simons, 2001).

Finally, rules governing access to participation in a forum strongly influence who speaks what, where, when, why, and how, and who listens. Obviously, these rules strongly influence which decisions, conflicts, issues, and policy preferences get discussed and which do not. For example, having senior people speak first may inhibit discussion by those with less rank. Forcing people to talk about the issue at hand may make it difficult to redefine the issue. The most powerful rules are those that limit attendance at a discussion. For example, holding a meeting in a place or at a time (or at a cost) that makes attendance by interested parties difficult or impossible can silence some perspectives altogether. Formal and informal rules also govern the type of issue to be considered in a forum. National newspapers such as *Le Monde* or the *New York Times* can be expected to devote most of their attention to stories that affect a large number of people in their country or metropolis. A cabinet meeting convened by a prime minister is unlikely to discuss an issue affecting a handful of average citizens.

To sum up, the social practice we refer to as creation and communication of meaning in a forum plays four especially crucial roles in public policy making. First, this practice "creates" a public problem. Second, it defines the problem and constrains the solutions that are considered. Third, it assists formation of a coalition of stakeholders who can affect decision making in legislative, executive, and administrative arenas. Fourth, it produces and reproduces bedrock systems of communication.

In the absence of an organized forum, a public problem hardly exists. For example, individuals may become ill because they work or live near a factory emitting hazardous waste, but until a forum (such as an investigative press report or a public hearing) pools and analyzes their experience and makes it widely visible, the problem is individual, not a public concern.

Once a problem is considered in a forum, stakeholders attempt to define the problem using a number of interpretive schemes. The dominant definition that emerges from a particular forum may be the most persuasive or a blend of several interpretive schemes; regardless, this definition constrains the kind of solution considered. For example, in the early years of the AIDS crisis, the disease was defined as a "gay" problem. No one proposed widespread education about safe sex; indeed, the term *safe sex* would emerge much later as the problem definition changed in multiple forums. A "gay rights" frame was also important in constraining solutions as well. San Francisco public health officials and politicians did not recommend a return to antisodomy laws.

The participants in a forum can be the basis of a coalition developing and promoting specific proposals for new policies, programs, and projects that have to be adopted by executive, legislative, and administrative decision makers in arenas. The coalition is likely to include some of these decision makers.

Arenas and the Three Dimensions of Power

The use of arenas distributes and redistributes access to participation in policy making and implementation and thereby maintains or alters political and economic relations. An arena can be political or economic. Political arenas include the U.N. Assembly, parliaments, legislatures, city councils, corporate executive committees and boards, policy-making mechanisms of public bureaucracies, nonprofit organizations, and interorganizational networks. The market is the basic form of economic arena. Determining which decisions are handled within the market is a crucial factor in the economic patterns of most societies (Lindblom, 1977; Giddens, 1984; Williamson, 1985). For example, in the United States, collection and distribution of blood for transfusions is handled mainly by nonprofit organizations, businesses produce plasma and other blood products for medical use, and government regulators oversee the safety of the blood supply. In the United States, the actual manufacture and sale of drugs is left to commercial companies, although the national government requires strict testing before a new drug can be widely marketed. The national government and pharmaceutical companies share in funding the development of new drugs such as those needed to treat or prevent HIV infection.

The first dimension of power is manifested in an arena when people interactively use their capabilities to obtain desired outcomes—that is, adoption and implementation of their preferred policies (see Exhibit D.3). Policy making in an arena characteristically involves establishing principles, laws, rules, policies, standards, norms, or prices that apply generally to a specified population or category of actions. In addition, plans, programs, budgets, or particular recommended actions may be adopted.

The third dimension of power, the deep structure, in policy making and implementation is shaped by principles of domination. These principles are embedded in, or rationalized by, unequal distribution of resources (social position, authority, skills, intelligence, status, money) within an institutional framework. These are often referred to as the "bases of power" (French and Raven, 1968). Unequal resources generate unequal individual or group capacity to make or implement policies. The third dimension of arenas also includes the requirement of a policy maker and at least one other participant; the policy maker must be able to affect a shared resource base that renders policy making necessary and possible. In the AIDS case, the physicians advocating for an aggressive public health campaign against the new disease could draw on the social status, professional authority, and relatively high

Exhibit D.3. Designing and Using Arenas.

Definition	Participation by actors in a delimited domain of activity as part of the process of policy making and implementation.
Examples	Corporate executive committees, city councils, cartels, markets, faculty senates, boards of directors, legislatures.
Policy-related role	Maintenance or change of political and economic relations, especially through distribution and redistribution of access to the exercise of power.
Structural properties	A policy maker and at least one other participant in an institutional framework of asymmetrically distributed resources. The policy maker must be able to affect a shared resource base that makes policy making necessary.
Action	The use of actors' interacting capabilities to secure outcomes through the agency of others. Characteristic activity is policy making that establishes rules, laws, norms, principles, policies, standards, plans, or prices of general application to a specified population or category of actions.
Ideas, rules, modes, media, and methods	Capabilities and means of mediating among capabilities—for example, domains; agendas; permitted methods of planning, budgeting, decision making, and implementation; access rules.
Outcomes	Structural basis for a set of potential nondecisions and decisions about policy, and transformation of that set into actual nondecisions and decisions.

income that U.S. society accords physicians generally. At the same time, they did not have much institutional authority; top administrators and elected officials drew on their much greater institutional authority in refusing to heed the doctors' call for urgent action. Gay men, meanwhile, had low social status in U.S. society generally, but in places such as San Francisco and New York they had developed much higher status (thanks to their number, political activism, and prominence in the arts and professions). In San Francisco, they were able to draw on their political clout to have considerable effect on local government policies.

The vehicles of bias (the second dimension of power) used to link action with deep structure include decision-making capabilities; domains; agendas; planning, budgeting, decision-making, and implementation methods; and rules governing access to participation in the arenas.

The *capabilities* that a leader has available to influence a sequence of policy-related interactions depend on the rules and resources he or she can deploy. They range from verbal skill to the ability to hire and fire, to computer literacy, agenda control, and the threat of physical violence. Capability refers, in other words, to one's *potential* to affect outcomes through drawing on ideas, rules, modes, media, and methods that offer any kind of advantage. Policy making and implementation refer to the *actual* application of some of these advantages. By exercising policy-making capabilities, leaders strongly influence which decisions, issues, conflicts, and policy preferences count (and how much) in particular arenas. In the AIDS case, Congressman Henry Waxman (D-California) and his aide Tim Westmoreland were able to put the growing epidemic on the congressional agenda in the early 1980s because of their positions. Waxman was chair of the House Subcommittee on Health and the Environment, and Westmoreland was the subcommittee's counsel. Together they planned hearings on the epidemic and crafted Waxman's public remarks. As chair, Waxman had ample opportunity to express his own views and orchestrate testimony from others.

Domains, agendas, and planning, budgeting, decision-making, and implementation methods are the means by which differing or conflicting capabilities in arenas are at least partially mediated. A domain is the spatial and substantive extent of an arena's policy-making and implementation authority. Planning, budgeting, decision-making, and implementation methods are the rules used to govern the process of putting together policies, plans, and budgets; making decisions; and implementing them. The selection of methods thus constitutes one of the most important actions in any arena, because certain methods favor particular actors' capabilities and purposes (Riker, 1986; Pfeffer, 1992; Flyvbjerg, 1998; Forester, 1999). Further, rules governing *access* to arenas strongly influence which persons, groups, organizations, and capabilities are admitted to an arena and thus indirectly influence which items are considered in the policy-making and implementation process.

Congressman Waxman's subcommittee covered a specific domain: health and environmental issues within the federal government's responsibility. To channel funding toward prevention and treatment of the epidemic then identified as Gay-Related Immune Deficiency (GRID), Waxman and Westmoreland had to understand the intricacies of the federal budgeting process. When President Reagan's health budget was published in 1982, they focused on what was and was not included. Federal health programs were not to be immune from the Reagan administration's determination to reduce spending. The Centers for Disease Control were given just enough increase to cover inflation, and no line item was specifically dedicated to GRID. Waxman used his ability to convene public hearings (forums closely linked to arenas) to highlight how few resources the federal health bureaucracy was devoting to combating the epidemic. Later he and Westmoreland teamed up with another powerful congressman, Rep. Phil Burton (D-California), and his aide Bill Kraus to put together bills earmarking millions of dollars to fight the AIDS epidemic. Although the Reagan administration opposed these additions to the federal health budget, once Congress approved them "the administration would not put itself in the politically indelicate position of actually vetoing it" (Shilts, 1988, p. 187). Funding ultimately flowed to researchers; as Randy Shilts notes, the administration "would never ask for it and insist it didn't want it, but the money would be thrust upon the government anyway. It was a ritual of forced feeding" (p. 187)

Those who wanted to persuade Congress to provide more funding for AIDS research needed to understand congressional decision-making procedures and permitted methods for attempting to influence decisions. For example, funding proposals had to be put into appropriate language for bills that could be voted on.

Advocates and opponents of the proposals could try to persuade or lobby members of Congress to vote for or against the bills.

Because time is a limited resource, *agendas* are a crucial mediator among competing capabilities. Only capabilities applicable to dealing with agenda items become relevant. Thus in April 1982, when Henry Waxman came to Los Angeles to convene the first congressional hearing on the GRID epidemic, he wanted to hear from managers of federal health programs about their work only as it related to the epidemic. Additionally, the nature of an agenda item and its order on the agenda can differentially favor the relevant capabilities of competing actors or coalitions (Riker, 1986). For example, at Waxman's hearing the testimony of federal bureaucrats was followed by testimony from the president of the American Public Health Association, who was then able to poke holes in the bureaucrats' statements.

Agendas are composed of *issues,* which are points of controversy between two or more actors over procedural or substantive matters involving distribution of positions or resources (see Cobb and Elder, 1983). We define an issue more broadly as a public problem accompanied by at least one solution that has pros and cons (points of controversy) from the standpoint of various stakeholders. Complicated agenda rules can benefit a group that has considerably more political connections and financial resources than its opponents. Agenda rules can also permit some public decisions to be made with a minimum of public scrutiny.

Rules governing access to participation in an arena strongly influence who decides what, where, when, why, and how. Access may be based on formal rules, position, precedent, reputation, financial resources, or rhetorical skill. Regardless of the particular rules, the mere inclusion of some people and exclusion of others can be expected to affect what gets onto the formal agenda and, subsequently, which decisions get made on which issues and preferences. For example, Kraus and Westmoreland were among the few openly gay congressional staff members; their position as aides to two influential members of Congress gave them considerably more ability to affect federal health-related agendas than most other gay men possessed.

Most societies use rules governing access to establish hierarchies of arenas, reserving broader policy making for those nearer the top. Procedures for appealing policy decisions to a higher-level arena are also usually established. The rules of access and of appeal are basic methods of political management, allowing those further up the hierarchy to exercise greater power over those below. For example, Margaret Heckler, U.S. secretary of Health and Human Services from early 1983 to late 1985, had power to set administrative policies about federally funded medical research around the country. In turn, she followed directives from the White House and had to comply with laws passed by Congress. As another example, the California state legislature was a broader arena than the policy-making bodies of the University of California, but when Marcus Conant and Michael Gottlieb violated the rules by going around university administrators to meet with Willie Brown, the powerful speaker of the California state assembly, to appeal for AIDS research funding, they were penalized by university administrators (Shilts, 1988).

To summarize, the social practice we refer to as making and implementing executive, legislative, and administrative decisions in arenas has several main effects. This social practice shapes categories of decisions and nondecisions and deals with overt and latent conflict; it also produces and reproduces bedrock structures of domination. More specifically, this social practice determines which proposed policies, plans, programs, and projects are considered by decision makers. Of those considered, it determines which are adopted, and of those, which are implemented. Finally, an arena is the proving ground for coalitions that support or oppose particular policies, plans, programs, and projects.

Courts and the Three Dimensions of Power

A court is used to judge or evaluate decisions or conduct in relation to ethical principles, laws, or norms, usually in order to settle disputes about what conduct is permitted and how it should be sanctioned. A court distributes and redistributes access to legitimacy and therefore helps maintain or change laws or other modes of adjudicating conduct (see Exhibit D.4 and Barclay and Birkland, 1998).

Examples of formal courts are the International Court of Justice, a traffic court, an ecclesiastical court, and a military tribunal. The most important informal court is the "court of public opinion." A court that falls between the formal and the court of public

Exhibit D.4. Designing and Using Courts.

Definition	A practice of judging or evaluating policies or conduct in relation to ethical principles, laws, or norms, usually in order to settle disputes.
Examples	Court of public opinion, professional licensing bodies, deans' offices, formal courts (as examples, the Supreme Court, military tribunals, traffic courts).
Policy-related role	Maintenance or change of laws and other modes of sanctioning conduct, especially through distribution and redistribution of access to legitimacy.
Structural properties	Two disputants and a third party to resolve their disputes, plus at least partially shared norms.
Action	Moral evaluation and sanctioning of conduct, and especially conflict management and dispute resolution.
Ideas, rules, modes, media, and methods	Conflict management and sanctioning capabilities, along with differing norms as mediated by jurisdiction, conflict management methods, access rules.
Outcome	Structural basis for potentially permitted policy decisions and modes of conduct and the transformation of that set into actual policy decisions and modes of conduct that are permitted and those that are not.

opinion might be a regulatory body hearing viewpoints before issuing or changing regulations, a professional licensing board conducting a disciplinary hearing, a dean's office resolving a dispute between college departments or individual professors, a referee conducting binding arbitration, a special court-appointed master dealing with an individual case as part of a class-action settlement, or one of a host of "alternative dispute resolution" mechanisms. In each example, the emphasis is on conflict management through judging or evaluating policy decisions or conduct in relation to laws, rules, or norms. In the early years of the U.S. AIDS crisis, formal courts became involved when hemophiliacs and hospital patients who had contracted HIV through contaminated blood transfusions began suing for damages; eventually judges also had to decide what sanctions to impose on HIV carriers who knowingly exposed others to the disease and how to decide cases in which people suffering from HIV/AIDS were fired from a job or excluded from a classroom. Several disputes raged in the court of public opinion. By the mid-1980s in the United States public opinion had more or less decided that sexual practices between same-sex partners fell into the "consenting adults" category; as long as two adults agreed to some activity (that didn't harm others), they were to be let alone. The court of public opinion also favored equal opportunity for gay people (Shilts, 1988). The big disputes in the court of public opinion were over whether people with HIV/AIDS could be excluded from the workplace or classroom.

The principal activity (first dimension of power) in a court is moral evaluation and sanctioning of conduct, especially through conflict management. The disputes handled are typically "residual"; they remain after an arena has established policies and made decisions or when, for some reason, the political or economic arenas are unable to deal with them. The activity of a court either affirms or modifies policies and/or the underlying norms in the system. The deep structure (third dimension of power) of a court is two disputants plus a third party to help them resolve their dispute, along with at least partially shared principles of legitimation, to govern resolution of the dispute. Action and structure are linked through conflict management and sanctioning capabilities, rules governing conflict resolution, jurisdictions, conflict resolution methods, and access rules (second dimension of power).

Conflict management and sanctioning capabilities are vital tools that leaders bring to a court in varying degrees. Formal judges or appointed arbitrators have authority to impose fines, settlements, or other requirements such as community service or jail sentences. Wise judges and ethical leaders are skilled in identifying which ethical principles, laws, and norms apply to which cases. They are adept at applying precedents and procedures to resolve conflict among principles, laws, and norms and to maintain the legitimacy of the courts. Informal judges, such as parents resolving a dispute among their children, have authority to decide whose argument trumps the other or to develop some other settlement between differing points of view. They might also offer a reward that encourages the children to solve their own dispute. The court of public opinion enforces and reinforces informal sanctions, such as shunning and moral condemnation.

Rules governing conflict resolution may be formal, such as legal due process requirements, or informal (norms, widely applied standards of etiquette or fairness). For example, people who contracted HIV/AIDS from blood transfusions in the United States during the early 1980s had difficulty winning lawsuits against blood banks because the banks were legally protected from product liability claims. A more successful route for the plaintiffs was claiming negligence on the part of the blood banks, accusing them of violating a standard of due care as they continued to furnish blood supplies after having credible evidence that they were contaminated with HIV. Both formal and informal rules of fairness prevailed when official and unofficial judges decided that people with HIV/AIDS should not be excluded from the workplace or classroom, given that the disease could not be spread through casual contact.

Jurisdiction denotes the spatial and substantive extent of a court's authority to interpret and apply norms to resolve conflict. For example, when the U.S. Food and Drug Administration licensed the first AIDS antibody test, gay organizations petitioned a federal (rather than a local or state) court to prevent distribution of the test until safeguards were in place against the tests' being used to screen gay men generally or to discriminate against individuals who tested positive for the AIDS antibody.

Conflict management methods significantly affect the outcomes of the conflict management process, since they favor some decisions and modes of conduct and rule out others (see, for example, Fisher and Ury, 1991). The selection of methods is therefore one of a leader's most important actions in any court, since certain methods favor certain objectives. Standard methods include use of a go-between, mediation, arbitration, and substitution of law and office for consent (the traditional method in a formal court). These methods differ in the extent to which they rely on consent or coercion on the one hand and nondichotomous or dichotomous solutions on the other. In a nondichotomous solution, each party gets something; in the latter, the winner takes all (Shapiro,

1981). The attraction of a method such as mediation is that participants must consent to the process and the outcome, and that it is likely to produce a nondichotomous solution, thus reducing the likelihood that any participant feels coerced and unfairly treated. (This approach is also likely to make future interaction between the participants more amicable.) By contrast, coercion on the part of a formal court often has to be used to enforce laws and resolve disputes. The legitimacy of formal courts is highly important since it affects the willingness of plaintiffs and defendants to accept the verdict.

Formal courts can and do impose dichotomous solutions, but a wise judge also recognizes the need for all participants to feel they are treated fairly. Legal precedents and procedures offer several methods for enhancing the perception of fairness, or procedural justice. For example, a dispute over something that is indivisible—as with injury, trespass, or breach of contract—can be turned into something that is divisible (usually money). Or a dispute over right and wrong can be converted into a dispute over "balancing of equities" (Shapiro, 1975, p. 288). The use of a jury of peers also enhances defendants' perception of fairness.

Additionally, courts can channel the bulk of legal conflict into negotiation between the disputants, who are threatened with eventual court action if the negotiation fails. Even when a case is decided in a formal court, the loser typically has several channels of appeal. Moreover, the court usually has limited capability to monitor compliance with its rulings; it reintervenes to ensure compliance only at the request of one of the disputing parties (Shapiro, 1975).

Finally, rules governing *access* to participation in a court strongly influence which residual conflicts are resolved according to which norms, and therefore which actions—especially which decisions and policy preferences—are allowed and which are not. Access may be based on evidence of rule violation, demonstrated injury, formal rules (including rules of appeal), position, precedent, custom, financial resources, or some other criterion. Access rules are used by virtually all societies to establish a hierarchy of courts, reserving the most fundamental pronouncements to those at the top.

To summarize, adjudication of disputes and sanctioning of conduct in courts plays several crucial roles in public policy making.

This social practice determines how ethical principles, laws, rules, and norms are applied to disputes over policies, programs, and projects. It also decides which behaviors are permitted and rewarded and which are disallowed and punished (Barclay and Birkland, 1998).

The operation of courts also produces and reproduces the bedrock of legitimation. Courts, in effect, are a form of social control because conflict management almost invariably draws on norms held by society at large, or in the case of intraorganizational conflict resolution, by the organization itself. The use of such norms to resolve a dispute reproduces social control on the basis of those norms. For example, the people who contracted HIV/AIDS through blood transfusions in the United States were able to sue for damages in formal courts, thus giving them and their families an outlet for their outrage and offering the possibility that the underlying norms of fairness would be enforced. Recourse to the courts and outcomes that are deemed relatively fair keep U.S. citizens from turning to civil disobedience when they are injured by the operation of organizations and institutions.

Social control also results from using formal courts because they make supplementary laws. When judges and court-appointed administrators apply general rules to specific cases, they often add details that become a precedent. Courts also develop their own rules to manipulate factual issues to achieve policy goals. Presumption, burden of proof, and pro se rules are typically open to such manipulation. Appeal procedures are also a means of hierarchical social control. The possibility of appeal tells the loser in one court that he or she has access to another higher court and thus need not contemplate changing the system. Procedures for moving through the appeals hierarchy also allow judicial and political authorities time to explore the implications of basic legal changes that may be mandated by a "final" ruling of the highest court. Appeal procedures thus allow central authorities to do two things: monitor lower court operations to enforce compliance and uniformity throughout the legal system, and prepare for changes as they work their way through the system. Since the chain of appeal typically ends with the chief political authorities, appeal may thus be seen as a means of centralizing political control and change.

Summary

Public action is of three main types: communication, policy making and implementation, and settling disputes and enforcing the system's underlying norms. In turn, each social practice is shaped by the three dimensions of power. The first dimension consists of observable behavior; the second of various ideas, rules, modes, media, and methods; and the third of bedrock social, political, and economic structures.

A forum is the setting in which human beings engage in creation and communication of meaning; an arena is the setting for policy making and implementation, and a court is the setting for settling disputes and reinforcing systemic norms. By understanding how the three dimensions of power function in each setting and focusing mainly on the second dimension, policy entrepreneurs can help their advocacy coalitions achieve major progress in remedying complex public problems.

Resource E
Future Search

A visionary leadership tool used successfully in many parts of the world is the "future search" (Weisbord and others, 1993; Weisbord and Janoff, 1995), usually a three-day strategy conference involving thirty to eighty-five people. These are the main ideas of the future search:

- Bringing the whole system to the conference—that is, ensuring that a broad cross-section of stakeholders attends
- Exploring the past, current reality, and probable futures in a way that engages participants' "heads, hands, hearts, guts, and unconscious data" (Weisbord and others, 1993, p. 51)
- Generating commitment to change through self-managed dialogue

Let's consider how to conduct a future search conference on the question, "How do we ensure that all girls become literate?" This scenario is based on the approach developed by facilitators Marvin Weisbord and Sandra Janoff (Weisbord and Janoff, 1995).

Past: Step One

The conference begins in the afternoon with a review of the past. Before the conference begins, the facilitators construct three timelines on a conference room wall covered with flipchart paper. Each timeline spans the last thirty years; one is devoted to the participants' personal lives, one to the world, and one to the topic (in this example, female literacy).

Participants are asked to identify key events in their own lives, in the world, and in the cause of female literacy over the last thirty years. Participants use marking pens to record key events along each timeline; then they work in small groups of diverse stakeholders to construct a story about some part of the timelines.

Each group then has three minutes to tell the story to the larger group. When the stories are done, the facilitators ask, "What did you get out of that? What did you learn? What did you hear?" Weisbord comments: "This task has the effect of getting everybody on the same planet very quickly. We like the symbolism: the walls belong to everybody, anybody can use the markers, everybody's information is relevant, everybody has a story to tell, it's all part of a much larger picture. We don't have to say that, because people experience it in the first few hours of the conference" (Flower, 1995, p. 39).

Current Reality: Step Two

The next step in the conference is compiling a group "mind map" of current reality. It could be constructed using ovals (as in the oval mapping process of Resource B). Everyone writes on ovals the current trends he or she believes are affecting female literacy. The ovals are then attached to a wall covered with flipchart sheets, and similar ovals are clustered.

The participants explain what their ovals mean, giving concrete examples. Participants are given colored dots to place on the ovals they think are most important, and the group talks about the ones that garner the most dots. Often, says Weisbord, the map is an "overwhelming portrait of the world's troubles, as seen through the eyes of the people in this particular room at this particular time. . . . People will often report feeling down."

By the time this exercise is done, around 5:00 or 6:00 P.M., it is time to quit for the evening and let participants sleep on the results so far.

On the second day, the facilitators organize participants into small groups, but this time people who have a similar stake in the problem are grouped together. In a conference on female literacy, all the teachers would be together; the youth workers would be together; young women would be together, as would be educational administrators, and so on.

In each small group, participants reinterpret the mind map constructed the previous day. They may even revise it on new flipchart sheets, redrawing the whole map or making a minimap of the issues they consider important. Each small group then reports to the whole group on their new interpretation, their current actions on the issues they selected, and their plans for future action on the issues.

Next comes a "prouds and sorries" exercise. The facilitators ask each group to talk among themselves about their feelings about the issues that have just been highlighted. The question to the group is, "Looking at what you personally or members of your stakeholder group are doing right now about these issues, what makes you really proud? What are you doing or not doing that makes you really sorry?" Each small group summarizes its conversation for the large group. Then the whole group is asked to respond: What are their feelings, reactions, insights?

Weisbord comments on this exercise: "The point is to get people to own up, not to finger-point, not to blame, not to breastbeat, not to do anything about it, but just to be in touch with what they are proud of and what they are sorry about. This is usually a pivotal step in our conference, because of what people hear other people say. And there is an amazing release that comes from taking responsibility for your feelings" (Flower, 1995, p. 41).

Creating a Vision: Step Three

Participants are then reassembled into mixed groups and given the task of creating a vision for female literacy. They are told it is a certain day, ten years into the future. They are asked to think of their ideal scenario of what they would like to see then in terms of female literacy—what programs would be in place, and what the results would be.

The groups use flipchart sheets to write characteristics of their ideal scenarios. Then they are asked to list on additional sheets the barriers that would have to be overcome to achieve the ideal. At this point, the groups are given a lengthy lunch break (two and a half hours), during which they prepare a creative seven-minute report to present to the entire group.

Before the presentations begin, one or two people from each group are asked to take notes on common themes that emerge, especially innovative ideas for programs, projects, or policies.

Weisbord comments: "People do the most amazing presentations. All their idealism pours out. It's fun. They are often hilariously funny. Some of them are profound. Some people do ceremonies, rituals. The collective unconscious gets mobilized in a big way" (Flower, 1995, p. 42).

As the final exercise for the day, each small group compiles three flipchart sheets. On one, they list the common desires for the future they have heard in the presentations; on the second they note innovative ideas that might accomplish these desires; and on the third they note unresolved differences that emerged from the presentations.

The small groups are then paired and asked to compare and merge their lists. Each group then cuts the agreed-upon items from the old lists and places them on the wall under the headings—common futures, potential projects, unresolved differences. This exercise concludes the second day.

On the final morning, participants come back to the wall with the lists of common futures, potential projects, and unresolved differences. They rearrange the lists, grouping similar items together. Facilitators then invite the group to talk about and clarify the lists. What does everyone endorse? What should be left in the unresolved category?

Action Planning: Step Four

The conference concludes with action planning. Stakeholder groups meet to consider what they want to do immediately about female literacy, what they want do in the next six months to a year, and what they want to do in the long run. They identify needed resources, timelines, support, and action steps. They then report their conclusions to the whole group.

Next, participants meet with anyone with whom they want to work to do action planning around a particular project or interest. These common-interest groups then report to the whole group about what next steps they have agreed to. To wrap up the conference, one or more participants sum up the agreed-upon action steps—for example, a new coordinating structure that includes many of the people at the conference. Next steps might include follow-up conferences that involve the same group or additional stakeholders.

General Observations

The future search process has many variations. Participants might be asked before the conference to collect information about historical and current forces affecting the problem they are considering. Participants might be invited to a preconference session to hear presentations by experts. Such a session preceded a future search conference convened in Pakistan to develop a national conservation strategy (see Weisbord and others, 1993).

If conference participants do not read and write the same language, then skilled storytellers, translators, and artists may be able to use the process framework to help participants create a shared understanding of the problem, a desired future, ideas, and action steps for programs, policies, and projects.

Resource F
Initial Policy Retreats

An initial retreat to consider a policy change effort should begin with an introduction to the nature, purpose, and process of policy change. Key decision makers may need such an introduction—and the development of the shared understanding that comes with it—before they are willing to endorse a policy change effort that requires collective leadership and involves groups or organizations other than their own. Such an introduction is particularly important if the change will be initiated primarily by outsiders who are unfamiliar with the machinery of organizational or governmental policy making. Orientation and training methods can include lecture-discussions, case presentations by leaders who have been involved in successful and unsuccessful policy change efforts, analyses by key decision makers of written case study materials followed by group discussion, analysis of policy change, documentary film, and circulation and discussion of reading materials.

Many retreat formats are possible (Holman and Devane, 1999; Weisman, 2003). The initiators of change should carefully think through the strengths and weaknesses of any alternative format in light of their particular situation. We present one possible format for the first day of a policy retreat. This format assumes that many of those present are not seasoned veterans of a successful policy change effort.

- *Morning:* Lecture-discussion about the nature, purpose, and process of policy change. Presentation of possible "visions of success" as a consequence of policy change. Presentation of supporting studies, reports, and so forth.
- *Lunch:* Presentation from a decision maker involved in a previous policy change effort; the presentation should highlight lessons learned about how to create success and avoid failure.

• *Afternoon:* Analysis and discussion of a written policy change case study, plus instruction in any special techniques likely to facilitate movement through the change process, such as brainstorming, the snowcard process (see Exercise 3.1), simple stakeholder analysis methods, or conflict management methods (Fisher and Ury, 1981; Thompson, 2001). The case analysis should highlight the stakeholders involved; their views about appropriate problem definitions and solutions; the exercise of leadership; and design and use of forums, arenas, and courts in successful pursuit of change.

• *Evening:* Discussion of possible next steps in undertaking a policy change effort, including finalizing the agenda for the second day of the retreat.

By the end of the first day, it should be clear whether or not the key decision makers wish to proceed. If so, the second day might be organized something like this:

• *Morning:* A stakeholder analysis, followed by tentative definition of the problem(s) to be addressed.

• *Lunch:* A speaker who can present another case example; or a high-status, nonvested speaker who can emphasize the importance of collective action in the problem area; or a personal "call to action" from someone with a special message relevant to the policy area.

• *Afternoon:* Development of an initial agreement among participants that states the need to respond to the problem(s) raised and that outlines the basic initial response strategy. It is important that the session not end until agreement is reached on the immediate next steps in the process and the people responsible for each step are identified.

If the group can reach quick agreement at each point, less than two full days may be necessary. If quick agreement is not possible, more time may be necessary, and sessions may have to be spread over several weeks or even months. The more difficult the problem area for those involved or affected, and the more groups or organizations involved, the more groundwork is likely to be required to reach agreement on the purpose, timing, and length of the retreat, as well as the subsequent next steps (Bardach, 1998; Huxham, 2003).

A retreat, or series of retreats, is a valuable forum for discussion, as well as an informal arena for initial decisions about the purpose, nature, scope, and timing of a policy change effort. A retreat can also send an important signal and be a symbol that a community of place or interest is about to address one of its most important concerns, it can prompt desirable media coverage, and it can induce other stakeholders, who might have been lukewarm about the process, to participate. Additional advice on initial retreats, as well as gatherings for later phases in the policy change cycle, may be found in Holman and Devane (1999); Susskind, McKearnan, and Thomas-Larmer (1999); and Weisman (2003).

Name Index

A

Ackermann, F., 72, 122, 232, 237, 284, 301, 332
Ackoff, R. L., 10, 219
Aditya, R. N., 47
Agle, B. R., 207
Alexander, E. A., 10, 352
Allen, K. E., 80, 93, 105, 246
Allport, G. W., 63
Anagnos, G., 79
Anderson, S. R., 69, 77, 201
Andreasen, A. R., 255
Angelica, E., 81, 333
Annan, K., 126
Annunzio, S., 94, 105
Antonakis, J., 69
Arendt, H., 167, 188
Argyris, C., 237
Aristotle, 182
Atwater, L., 69
Avner, M., 143
Avolio, B. J., 95, 107

B

Backoff, R. W., 326
Bacon, T. R., 65
Bandura, A., 55, 318
Banks, D. J., 96
Bardach, E., 209, 328
Barton, S. E., 220
Baumer, D. C., 148, 291
Baumgartner, F., 163, 171, 175, 198, 280, 345, 347, 348
Beech, N., 36, 162
Beer, S., 242, 261
Behn, R. D., 89, 138, 213, 349, 351
Bellah, R. N., 19, 32, 181

Bendor, J. B., 349
Bennis, W., 98, 106
Bentham, J., 185
Benveniste, G., 174, 176, 265, 292, 307
Bergland, R., 127
Berlin, I., 183
Bilimoria, D., 219
Blasko, L., 23
Boal, K. B., 110, 112, 118, 120
Bobo, K., 352
Bok, S., 112
Boler, M., 57, 127
Bolman, L. G., 52, 53, 104, 134
Borins, S., 209
Bosk, C. L., 199
Bowman, A. O., 312
Boyatzis, R., 57
Boyte, H. C., 31, 63, 134, 182, 188, 228, 363
Brand, R., 104
Brandl, J., 246
Braybrooke, D., 11
Bridges, W., 53, 98, 99
Brinckerhoff, P. C., 105
Bromily, P., 232, 345
Brown, C. R., 68
Brown, D. J., 71
Brown, M. E., 105
Brown, T., 98
Brundtland, G. H., 3
Bryant, J., 129, 212, 271, 326
Bryson, J. M., 14, 17, 18, 39, 69, 82, 86, 87, 102, 110, 112, 118, 120, 121, 122, 168, 176, 201, 208, 232, 235, 236, 237, 252, 313, 315, 321, 325, 326, 332, 333, 336

Bunch, C., 64
Burby, R. J., 248
Burke, E., 188
Burns, J. M., 31, 36, 115, 129, 132, 277
Burt, G., 102
Burton, P., 208, 305
Bush, G. W., 341, 345

C

Cameron, K., 90, 105
Campbell, B., 239
Campbell, H., 182
Carnevale, J. T., 260, 273, 309, 318
Carver, K., 105
Cashman, K., 53
Caza, A., 90, 105
Chakrabarty, D., 44
Charan, R., 100
Chen, C. C., 74
Cherrey, C., 80, 93, 105, 246
Chrislip, D., 143, 323, 332, 347
Christensen, K. S., 326, 352
Christmann, P., 150
Civille, J. R., 186
Cleveland, H., 19, 24, 27, 29, 36, 44, 45, 55, 168, 182, 278
Clinton, B., 127
Cobb, R. W., 169, 176, 219, 220, 222, 223, 226, 236, 240, 267
Cohen, M. D., 104, 161
Collins, J., 55, 81, 87
Combs, G. M., 91
Conant, M., 5, 30, 40, 51, 89, 156, 165
Conger, J., 77, 80, 106
Connell, B., 134
Cooperrider, D. L., 219
Coplin, W., 326
Crosby, B. C., 35, 46, 52, 68, 69, 82, 87, 333
Crossan, M. M., 92, 93, 94
Csikszentmihalyi, M., 75, 77
Cullen, J. W., 315
Cunningham, G. L., 11, 12, 13, 14, 41, 57, 66, 75, 82, 112, 121, 133,
140, 147, 156, 170, 185, 190, 208, 232, 235, 236, 245, 303
Curran, J., 89, 239
Cyert, R., 324

D

Daloz, L. A., 55
Dalton, G. W., 100
Davies, M. W., 28
Day, D., 82
de Neufville, J. I., 220
De Pree, M., 95
Deal, T. E., 52, 53, 104, 134
Delbanco, A., 44, 220, 252
Delbecq, A. L., 59, 229, 336
Devane, T., 77
Dewey, J., 188
Dietz, M., 31, 32, 156
DiIulio, J., 243
DiTomaso, N., 65, 92
Dobbs, S. M., 100, 105
Dodge, G. E., 56, 57
Douglass, F., 3
Drath, W., 14, 36, 37, 56, 99, 126
Dror, Y., 237
Drotter, S., 100
Drucker, P., 98
Duggan, W. R., 186
Durning, D., 219
Dutton, J. E., 81, 101

E

Easton, D., 224
Eden, C., 10, 72, 122, 219, 232, 237, 284, 301, 332
Edwards, G., 128
Einsweiler, R., 17, 18
Elder, C. D., 176
Eliot, T. S., 340
Elmore, R. F., 232, 318
Eoyang, G. H., 105
Etzioni, A., 252

F

Faerman, S. R., 93
Fairholm, G. W., 93

Fallows, J., 247, 260
Faulkner, H., 110
Featheringham, D., 10
Feldman, M. S., 5, 89, 95, 162, 345
Finn, C. B., 168, 207, 237, 332
Fiol, C. M., 321, 347
Fisher, R., 331
Fiutak, T., 68
Fletcher, J., 68, 74, 99, 126, 127
Flyvbjerg, B., 11, 29, 122, 180, 189
Forester, J., 180, 304
Frederickson, H. G., 138
Freeman, S.J.M., 92
Freshley, H., 20, 21, 42, 147, 164, 190
Friedlander, F., 59
Friedman, T., 19, 25
Friedmann, J., 181
Friend, J. K., 208, 326
Fukuyama, F., 44

G

Gabor, D., 322
Galbraith, J. K., 185
Gardner, H., 117, 127
Garud, R., 98
Gaventa, J., 169
Gerzon, M., 123
Giddens, A., 18
Gioia, D. A., 105
Glabraith, J. K., 181
Gladwell, M., 278
Goffman, I., 57
Goggin, M. L., 312
Goleman, D., 57
Gordon, R. D., 99
Gormley, W. T., 148, 291
Gottlieb, M., 5, 30, 40, 51, 165
Gray, B., 181, 331
Greenleaf, R. K., 80
Grenny, J., 226, 301
Grossback, L. J., 271
Grossman, A., 105
Guelich, R. A., 53
Gustafson, D., 229, 252
Gutmann, A., 112

H

Hagberg, J. O., 53, 57, 58
Hall, P., 46, 134
Handy, C., 28, 29
Hatch, O., 305
Hatry, H. P., 89, 317
Heenan, D. A., 98, 106
Heifetz, R., 104
Hesselbein, F., 98, 99, 101
Hibino, S., 172, 246
Hickling, A., 208, 326
Hicks, M. D., 106
Hilgartner, S., 199
Hirschman, A. O., 18
Hively, J., 20, 21, 41, 42, 76, 87, 100, 141, 147, 156, 161, 164, 172, 185, 190, 200, 203, 209, 248, 263
Hobino, S., 10
Hock, D., 32, 106
Hogwood, B. W., 344, 347, 348
Holliday, C. O., Jr., 29, 38, 53, 54, 117, 126, 279, 317
Holman, P., 77
Holzer, M., 349
Hooijberg, R., 56, 57, 65, 92
Hooker, C., 77
hooks, b., 54
Houghton, J. D., 59, 61, 71, 74, 77
House, R. J., 47
Howard, A., 100
Hudson, R., 30, 171, 225
Hugo, V., 290
Hula, K., 143
Humphrey, H. H., 134, 354
Hunt, J. G., 56, 57, 95, 96
Huntington, S., 19
Hussein, S., 260
Hutton, W., 24
Huxham, C., 36, 72, 162, 219, 228, 323, 326, 330

I

Innes, J. E., 175, 220, 248

J

Jacobs, R. W., 55

Janowitz, M., 28
Jantsch, E., 14
Jauch, L. R., 95, 96
Jefferson, T., 188
Jenkins-Smith, H. C., 11, 134, 174, 214, 217, 288, 304, 332, 348
Johnson, C., 314
Johnson, D. W., 65, 71, 72, 77
Johnson, F. P., 65, 71, 72, 77
Johnston, R., 98, 99, 101
Jones, B., 163, 171, 175, 198, 212, 280, 345, 347, 348
Jordan, 273
Joyce, P., 336
Jung, D. I., 95
Jung, Y. S., 232

K

Kaboolian, L., 105
Kahn, S., 352
Kant, I., 185
Kanter, R. M., 56, 81, 105, 322, 331, 355
Kaplan, R. S., 89, 112
Kari, N. N., 63, 134, 188, 363
Kaüfer, K., 68, 74, 99, 126, 127
Kaufman, J. L., 326
Keen, C. H., 55
Keen, J. P., 55
Kegan, R., 56, 301
Kelley, R., 37, 106
Kendall, J., 352
Kets de Vries, M., 95, 105
Kettl, D. F., 28, 246, 261
Khademian, A. M., 5, 89, 95
King, J. A., 219, 228, 229
King, M. L., Jr., 34, 115
King, P. J., 156
Kingdon, J. W., 23, 161, 171, 174, 198, 216, 219, 224, 225, 246, 286, 291, 292, 317, 331
Kiser, L., 180
Kitsuse, A., 261, 263
Klandermans, B., 5
Klein, N., 19
Klimoski, R. J., 105

Kluckhohn, F. R., 46
Koch, E., 304
Kostner, J., 69
Kotler, P., 255
Kotter, J., 102
Kouzes, J., 34, 49, 55, 67, 75, 77, 95, 97, 101, 278
Kramer, L., 44, 51, 66, 239, 304
Krasner, S. D., 18, 19
Kraus, B., 305
Krieger, M., 55, 106, 108, 269, 275
Krueger, R. A., 219, 228, 229
Kurland, J., 246

L

Lahey, L. L., 301
Lane, H. W., 92, 93, 94
Larson, C., 143
Laubenstein, L., 5, 40, 51, 165
Lauria, M., 18
Laurie, D. L., 104
Lee, N., 255
Lee, S.-H., 349
Leonard, D., 97
Lerner, M., 188
Lester, J. P., 312
Letts, C. W., 105
Lewis, C., 261
Light, P. C., 87, 97, 269, 363
Lindblom, C. E., 10, 11, 157, 275, 323
Linden, R. M., 282, 323
Lipman-Blumen, J., 28, 80, 96, 98
Locke, E. A., 81, 98
Loeb, P. R., 52
Lohmann, R. A., 182
Lokkesmoe, K. J., 14, 76, 121, 232, 235, 236
London, M., 89
Lord, R. G., 71
Luke, J. S., 30, 54
Lynn, L., 180, 181, 198, 348

M

Mcgrath, M. R., 93
Machiavelli, N., 112, 197

McKearnan, S., 306, 331
McKee, A., 57
McKibben, B., 123
McLaughlin, K., 95
McLaughlin, P., 13, 208
McLoughlin, 273
McMillan, R., 226, 301
Madison, J., 188
Mandela, N., 127
Mandelbaum, S. J., 220, 222, 322
Mangham, I. L., 212, 345, 347, 350
Manz, C., 59, 61, 71, 74, 77
March, J. G., 161, 324
Marcus, A., 345
Margarum, R. D., 248, 271
Marion, R., 80, 93, 105
Maritain, J., 156, 185
Marks, M. A., 73
Marris, P., 5, 29, 186, 189
Marshall, R., 182
Marx, K., 186, 275
Mathews, D., 188
Max, S., 352
May, E. R., 229, 321, 326
Mayer, J. D., 57
Mazmanian, D., 309
Mazza, G., 68
Mead, M., 197
Meadows, D. H., 118
Meltsner, A. J., 326
Mikolic, J. M., 68
Mill, J. S., 185, 188
Millar, A., 260, 273, 309, 318
Miller, P., 68
Milligan, H., Jr., 13, 41, 112, 140, 147, 208
Minger, J., 326
Mintzberg, H., 157
Mitchell, G., 108
Mitchell, R. K., 207
Mitchell, S., 98
Mitroff, I. I., 10, 97
Moltke, H. von, 282
Monnet, J., 321
Moore, M., 32, 105, 106
Morgan, G., 95, 104

Morrison, A. M., 91
Myers, D., 261, 263

N

Nadler, G., 10, 172, 246
Najam, A., 222
Nanus, B., 87, 100, 105
Neck, C. P., 59, 61, 71, 77
Nelson, B. J., 105, 214
Neustadt, R. E., 229, 272, 297, 321, 326
Newcomer, K. E., 89, 317
Newman, M. A., 349
Noddings, N., 186
Noel, J., 100
Norton, D. P., 89
Nutt, P. C., 14, 115, 129, 172, 216, 231, 232, 241, 247, 326, 349
Nyerere, J., 186

O

Obstfeld, D., 93
O'Leary, M., 326
Olsen, J. P., 161
Orr, S. S., 105
Osborn, S., 95, 96
Osborne, D., 349
Oshry, B., 237
Ostrom, E., 19, 168, 180
O'Toole, J., 98, 332
O'Toole, L. J., Jr., 312
Overington, M. A., 212

P

Palmer, P., 49
Parks, S. D., 55
Patterson, K., 226, 301
Patton, M. Q., 89, 178, 315
Pearce, C., 77, 80, 106
Pearce, T., 129
Peters, B. G., 28, 312, 323, 344, 347, 348
Peterson, D., 106
Pfeffer, J., 161
Pierre, J., 312, 323
Pinchot, G., 64, 100, 101

Pistorio, P., 53–54
Plastrik, P., 349
Poister, T. H., 260, 273, 309, 318
Polley, D. E., 98
Porras, J., 55, 81, 87
Posner, B. Z., 34, 49, 55, 67, 75, 77, 95, 97, 101, 147, 278, 326
Pressman, J., 273
Price, S., 208
Price, T. L., 181
Prokosch, M., 352
Putnam, R., 30

Q
Quinn, R., 7, 44, 51, 52, 53, 54, 56, 93, 97, 104, 117

R
Raelin, J. A., 88
Randolph, W. A., 326
Rather, D., 239
Ray, K., 323
Raymond, L., 352
Rees, F., 65
Reich, R., 217, 221
Rein, M., 117, 122, 263
Rieff, D., 247, 260
Rifkin, J., 24, 25–26, 29
Riggio, R. E., 105
Riker, W. H., 176, 270, 296, 297, 298, 307
Ring, P. S., 323
Rittel, H.W.J., 218
Rittman, A. L., 73
Roberto, N., 255
Roberts, N. C., 156, 175, 231, 248
Rochefort, D. A., 219, 220, 222, 223, 226, 236, 240, 267
Roddick, A., 99, 101
Roering, W. D., 208
Rogers, E. M., 278, 336
Rosenberg, M., 68
Rosener, J. B., 91
Rosenhead, J., 326
Ross, M. H., 169
Rost, J. C., 36

Rousseau, J.-J., 185
Rukeyser, M., 216
Rusk, T., 68
Ryan, W. P., 105

S
Sabatier, P. A., 11, 134, 157, 174, 198, 214, 217, 288, 304, 309, 332, 348
Salamon, L., 246
Salovey, P., 57
Sarder, Z., 28
Sawyer, S., 140
Schattschneider, E. E., 168, 180
Schein, E. H., 47, 67, 92, 93, 95
Schmidheiny, S., 15, 38, 42, 53, 54, 79, 97, 110, 111, 113, 117, 126, 140, 156, 175, 190, 269, 279, 317
Schneider, M., 57
Schön, D., 114, 117, 122, 263
Schroeder, D., 20, 21, 42, 147, 164, 190
Schumpeter, J., 94
Schwarz, R. M., 65, 77
Scott, J. C., 168, 246
Seligman, M., 55, 355
Selznick, P., 168, 277
Senge, P. M., 67, 105, 237, 333
Shapiro, D., 54
Shaw, R., 352
Shilts, R., 49, 90, 102, 250
Silverman, M., 250
Simeone, R.S., 260, 273, 309, 318
Simon, H. A., 10, 246
Simons, H. W., 127, 128, 129, 304
Sims, H. P., 74, 77
Snyder, D. P., 128
Sosik, J. J., 95
Srivastva, S., 219
Stenglein, M., 11–12, 13, 41, 112, 133, 170, 190, 208
Stephan, W. G., 63
Stigson, B., 135, 140, 146
Stivers, C., 67
Stone, D. A., 11, 220, 222, 223, 224, 236, 297, 298, 347

Strodtbeck, F. L., 46
Suchman, 122
Susskind, L., 306, 331
Sutcliffe, K., 93, 97, 223
Swap, W., 97
Switzler, A., 226, 301

T

Tan, A., 213
Taylor, E., 127, 208
Taylor, G., 151
Taylor, H. R., 100
Taylor, N., 168
Terry, R. W., 35, 36, 49, 52, 56, 80, 81, 96, 98, 104, 105, 106
Thomas, J. C., 167
Thomas-Larmer, J., 307, 331
Thompson, D., 112
Thompson, L., 71, 133, 323
Thompson, M. P., 93
Thompson, P. H., 100
Throgmorton, J. A., 128, 129, 180
Timberlake, L., 110
Tornow, W. W., 89
Trist, E., 209, 226, 332
Tsoukas, H., 92
Tuchman, B., 44

U

Uhl-Bien, M., 80, 93, 105
Ury, W., 331
Useem, M., 74

V

Vaill, P., 28
Van de Ven, A. H., 97, 98, 102, 229, 252, 323
van der Heijden, K., 118, 261
Van Horn, C. E., 148, 291
van Schendelen, R., 143
Van Velsor, E., 74
Vangen, S., 323

Vargas, S., 208
Vecchio, R. P., 92
Venkataraman, S., 98
Vickers, G., 14
Vining, A. R., 246
Volkema, R. J., 222

W

Walker, A., 128
Waste, R., 244
Waters, J. A., 157
Watts, P., 38, 53, 54, 117, 126, 147, 279, 317
Waxman, H., 208, 305
Webber, M., 218
Weber, M., 5
Weick, K., 93, 97, 128, 223, 237, 278, 321, 332
Weimer, D. L., 246
Weisbord, M., 129
Weisman, C., 73, 87
West, C., 188, 189
Westmoreland, T., 305
Wheatley, M. J., 30, 53, 77, 87, 95, 105, 242
Wheelan, S. A., 69, 70, 71, 73
White, R. E., 92, 93, 94
Wholey, J. S., 89, 317
Wildavsky, A., 10, 218, 241, 273
Wilson, J. Q., 176, 243, 300
Winer, M., 200, 201, 323
Wood, D. J., 207
Wright, N. S., 47

Y

Young, I. M., 187, 188–189
Youngblood, M. D., 30, 105

Z

Zaccaro, S. J., 73, 96, 105
Zeder, J., 246
Zinn, H., 44

Subject Index

A

AAMP (African American Men Project): active citizenry promoted by, 190; celebratory events arranged by, 300; change advocates in the, 80; change cycle phases of, 170; coalition used by, 135, 136, 270; common good defined by, 187; compelling vision created by, 264; conceptual framework for solution used by, 245; conflict resolution/management used by, 151–152; considering domains by, 140–141; designing institutions during policy process at, 169; framing forums by, 122–123, 230–231; full-group forum participants in, 210; Hennepin County district development of, 11–14, 31, 42–43; idea management during policy process at, 164; implementation strategies used by, 299; indicators monitored by, 333, 343; institutional design report by, 251; interpretation/direction giving in, 111, 112, 113–114; introduction of adopted changes by, 313–314; leadership of, 57–58; mediating and shaping conflict within, 133; off-cycle decision-making process used in, 162; origins and goals of, 31; policies/plans drafted by, 268–269; policy implementation/evaluation by, 177–178; problem formulation during, 171, 172, 224–225; proposal review/adoption of policy by, 177; public problem breakthrough by, 362; sanctioning capabilities used in, 150; search for solutions by, 173–174; sponsors and champions of, 208, 303; stakeholder analysis by, 94; team leadership role in, 65; team member recruitment for, 66; team trust and spirit in, 75–76; vision of the future by, 117, 118–119. *See also* African American Men Commission; Hennepin County district

AAMP Day of Restoration, 178, 314
AAMP Dream Assessment Initiative, 314
AAMP Right Turn, 178, 314, 316, 322
Access rules, 128–129, 142–143
Accountability mechanisms, 150
Action plans, 326, 355
Active citizenry, 188–189
Active listening, 67–68
"Acts of appreciation," 14–15
Adaptive work, 104
Advocacy Leadership Certificate Program (VAN), 178, 190, 251, 315–316, 320
African American Men Commission, 43, 136, 143, 177, 178. *See also* AAMP (African American Men Project)
Age of Access, 44
The Age of Access (Rifkin), 25
Agenda control, 296, 304–305
Agendas, 16, 141
Agreements. *See* Initial-agreements

AIDS "buddy program" (New York), 79

AIDS crisis: attractive spokespeople used during, 127, 208; big-win strategy used during, 278–279; collaboration during, 190; common good decisions during, 184; conflict between National Institutes of Health units during, 101–102; conflict management during, 250; creating public awareness during, 171; efforts to wake up public to, 51; failure to strategically use external stakeholders during, 99; framing during, 244, 297; how culture of integrity would have benefited, 90; idea management during the, 164; initial-agreement during, 199; interpretation/direction giving during, 111; lobbying and persuasion strategies used during, 304; media strategy used during, 239–240; multicausal explanations/framing of, 221–222, 223, 225; no-one-charge organization and, 7, 8*fig*, 9–10; *The Normal Heart* (play) about, 44; organizational structure which fits the, 7; overcoming bureaucratic resistance during, 139; people propelled into leadership during, 49; policy entrepreneurs during, 160; public problem breakthrough during, 361; signing-up process response to, 293; undermining of mission accomplishment during, 88–89; "venue shopping" during, 175; vision of success during, 322; working for social change during, 30, 39–40, 42

AIDS Foundation (California), 30

AIDS Medical Foundation (New York), 79

AIDS Network (New York), 304

AIDS Research and Education Foundation (San Francisco), 79

AIDS task force (San Francisco), 89

Arenas: access rules used in, 142–143; agendas of, 141; using decision-making capabilities in, 139–140; developing a winning proposals in, 267–289; domains of, 140–141; implementation and ensuring facilitative, 330–331; planning, budgeting, decision making, and implementation used in, 142; policy modification or succession and role of, 347, 348; reassessing policies and role of, 344; as shared-power setting, 359

Argument modes, 126–128

Assessment exercises: ethical leadership capacity, 153*e*–154*e*; multi-criteria assessment grid, 259*e*; political leadership capacity, 144*e*–146*e*; stakeholder attitudes toward status quo, 211*e*; visionary leadership capacity, 130*e*–132*e*; of your organization, 103*e*–104*e*; of your team, 78*e*–79*e*

Association for Conflict Resolution, 87

Authentic Leadership (Terry), 52

Authoritarian state, 187

Authority trait, 58

Awareness of continuity/change, 39

B

Backward mapping, 318–320

Bandwagon effect, 291, 307

Bargaining for support, 306–307

BASD (Business Action for Sustainable Development), 135

Bases of power, 234*e*

BCSD (Business Council for Sustainable Development), 79, 230, 231

Behavioral complexity, 56–58

Beyond Rational Management (Quinn), 97

Big-win strategy, 274–279

Blood bank screening, 90

Blurred international boundaries, 28–29

Body Shop, 99
Bold-stroke capacity, 56
Bottom-up approach, 320
Bowling Alone (Putnam), 30
Budgeting proposal, 287

C

Capacity to govern, 28–29
"Cares and concerns" exercise, 38*e*
Catalytic Leadership (Luke), 54
CCL Associates, 89
CDC (Centers for Disease Control),
    88, 89, 102
Center for Leadership of Nonprofits,
    Philanthropy, and the Public Sec-
    tor, 35
Champions: described, 208; identify-
    ing, 303
Change: being entrepreneurial/
    experimental to facilitate, 97–98;
    eight stages of organizational,
    102; emphasizing collaboration/
    team building for, 98–100; em-
    phasizing of operating values ac-
    cording to life-cycle stage of, 97;
    monitoring internal/external
    environments for, 96; organiza-
    tional leadership's responses to
    internal/external, 96–100
Change agents/advocates: leadership
    capabilities needed by, 34–37; or-
    ganizational leadership of, 77–80;
    planning for succession, 100;
    relationships cultivated by, 294;
    responses to internal/external
    change by, 96–100; use of social
    networks by, 30–31; three crucial
    leadership tasks of, 80. *See also*
    Policy entrepreneurs
*The Change Handbook: Group Methods
    for Shaping the Future* (Holman
    and Devane), 77
Change the World (Quinn), 53
Changing Course (Schmidheiny), 110,
    112, 113
Choosing the Right Thing to Do
    (Shapiro), 54

Cisco Systems, 317
Civic engagement, 188–189
Civic republic, 188
Client politics, 243–244
Coalitions: building, 134–138*e*; de-
    veloping outlines of supportive,
    227; implementation and build-
    ing protective, 330; laying
    groundwork for winning, 352–
    353; maintaining membership/
    leadership during implementa-
    tion, 314–315; to monitor imple-
    mentation of proposal, 301;
    proposals and necessary, 270–
    271, 286, 287–288; shared belief
    in policy change as mutual en-
    deavor by, 271; solutions through
    expanded advocacy, 248. *See also*
    Relationships; Stakeholders
Cognitive complexity, 56–58
Collaboration: evaluating, 261; man-
    aged during implementation, 323
Collaborative Leadership (Chrislip and
    Larson), 143
Collaborative Leadership Handbook
    (Chrislip), 143
Common Fire (Daloz and others), 55
Common good: constructing win-
    ning argument and map of, 235*e*;
    in context of policy entrepre-
    neurship, 158*e*; described, 360;
    guidelines for thinking about
    the, 182–191; initial forum focus
    on, 202; thinking about public
    interest and the, 191*e*–192*e*
Common good guidelines: choose
    means of achieving common
    good, 187–191; clarify views on
    human nature/society, 183; de-
    cide whose common good is
    important, 184–185; develop gen-
    eral idea of what the common
    good might be, 185–187; themes
    which correlating with, 182–183
Common good leadership, 37–38
Commonalities, 61, 63
Communal stories, 117–119

Communication: compelling vision of solution, 263–265; during implementation, 332–333; opening channels of, 92–93; pragmatic, 125–126; team leadership role in fostering, 67–70. *See also* Dialogue

Communication skills: active listening and dialogue, 67–68; communicative capability, 120–122; managing conflict, 68–69; matching community style/content to group type/needs, 70; oval mapping, 69; by visionary leaders, 120–122

Communities: building inclusive, 100–102; matching group type/needs to style of, 70; offering vision of the future of, 115, 117–119; productive, 117

Compromise, 133

Conflict: anticipating and optimizing, 250; management of, 68–69, 149–150, 151–152; mediating and shaping, 129, 132–134; resolving among principle, laws, and norms, 149; rules governing resolution of, 150–151; solution search and managing, 249–250

Connections (social/professional), 58

Constituent support demonstration, 304

Constructing organizational vision of success, 88e

Coordinating committees, 209e

Copromotion, 133

"Coupling" process, 291

Courage, 55–56

Courts: conflict management methods used in, 151–152; conflict management/sanctioning capabilities used in the, 149–150; decision to require/facilitate adoption of proposal, 298–299; formal and informal, 149; jurisdiction of, 151; policy modification or succession and role of, 347; reassessing policies and role of, 344; rules governing access to, 152; rules governing conflict resolution used by, 150–151; as shared-power setting, 359; when intervention for proposal is needed by, 308

Creating Effective Teams (Wheelan), 77

Creating Public Value (Moore), 105

"Creative destruction" concept, 94

Creative Organizational Theory: A Resourcebook (Morgan), 95

The Critical Journey: Stages in the Life of Faith (Hagberg and Guelich), 53

Culture: assessing differences in, 48e; becoming a student of, 45–46; dimensions of, 46–47; low-context vs. high-context, 46; organizational, 47, 89–95; quick action prized by individualistic, 69

Culture of inclusion, 91

Culture of integrity, 90

Culture of productivity, 92

D

Decision making organizations: political decision making in, 11fig–14; rational planning used in, 10fig–11

Decision-makers: to adopt and implement proposal, 296–298; capabilities of, 139–140; implementation role played by, 303; reducing uncertainty of, 303; "winning" proposals and role of, 272–274

Democratic governance, 27

Demonstration projects, 337e–338e

Dialogue: active listening and, 67–68; generative, 126–127; persuasion as supplement to, 127; relational, 126. *See also* Communication

Dimensions of Leadership Profile, 54

Direct versus staged implementation, 335–336

Directions of interest, 234e
Diversity appreciation, 61, 63
Dominance, 37
Dream Assessment Initiative, 150

E

Earth Summit (1992), 53, 79, 115, 230, 248, 316, 318
Education during implementation, 332–333
EEC (European Economic Community), 321
Elder Advocacy Network (Minnesota), 20
eLeadership (Annunzio), 105
Emotional complexity, 56–58
Empowerment, 70–73
Encouraging the Heart (Kouzes and Posner), 77
Entrepreneurial policy, 244
Entrepreneurial Vocations (Krieger), 55
Entrepreneurialism/experimentation, 97–98
Environmental degradation, 26
Ethical analysis grid, 261, 262*fig*
Ethical leadership: analyzing ethical principles, laws, and norms, 152e; assessing capacity of, 153e–154e; defining, 108; educating about ethics, constitutions, laws and norms, 146–148; forums and arenas of, 109; helpful tools used by, 152; introduction to, 143, 146; overcoming barriers to, 147e; resolving conflicts among principles, laws, and norms, 149; understanding design/use of formal and informal courts, 149–152
Ethical principles, 147–148
Ethical role models, 147e
Evaluation: AAMP practices of, 177–178; developing plans for, 329; of impact of lingering disagreement, 331; during policy change cycle, 177–179; summative, 317. *See also* Review process
Evolve! (Kanter), 105

Experts: judgment of, 188; proposal drafting and use of, 287; solution search and use of, 250, 252–255
Exploring personal highs/lows, 50e

F

Facilitation Resources (Anderson and others), 77
Feedback: problem framing and, 223–225; solution search and, 251; 360-degree, 89
Final report, 239
Flexible optimism, 55
Follow-up forum, 206–207
Follower, 37
Followership, 37
Forums: access rules used in, 128–129; building coalitions to implement proposals from, 134–138e; communicative capability during, 120–122; created to consider solutions, 249–250; using frames and interpretive schemes for, 122–125e; initial-agreement leadership guidelines on follow-up, 206–207; initial-agreement leadership guidelines on full-group, 207–210; initial-agreement leadership guidelines on initial, 199–206; media and modes of argument used in, 126–128; norms of relevance/pragmatic communication used in, 125–126; policy modification or succession and role of, 347–348; problem formulation and use of, 230–231; reassessing policies and role of, 344; searching for solutions in, 242–266; as shared-power setting, 359; visionary leadership design and use of, 120–129
Forward mapping, 318–320
Frames: analyzing interpretive schemes or problem, 124e–125e; forum use of interpretive schemes and, 122–125e; generative problem, 117–118; living systems,

104–105; for problem formulation, 171–173; of problems in need of solution, 235–236; for public problems, 113–114, 220–223; unraveling old, 236; virtues, 105
Full-group forums, 207–210

G

Gay Men's Health Crisis (1982), 66, 79, 86
Generative dialogue, 68, 126–127
Generative problem frame, 117–118
Global arms trade, 24–25
Global Compact, 168
Global economy, 25–26
Global Reporting Initiative, 317
Global trends assessment, 45e
Greenpeace, 125, 140, 146
"Group norming," 71

H

Hennepin County district, 11–14, 31, 42–43. See also AAMP (African American Men Project)
Hierarchical organizations, 6fig
High-context culture, 46
High-reliability organizations, 93–94
Human nature/condition assumptions, 46–47, 48e
Human rights demands, 27
Humor, 54
Humphrey Institute of Public Affairs, 17, 76, 320

I

ICC (International Chamber of Commerce), 135
Implementation: avoiding competition with new priorities during, 329–330; building protective coalition during, 330; commitment of key implementers, 314; communication and education during, 332–333; creating new

regime during, 316–317; debugging process of, 315–316; deliberate planning/managing of, 325; designing maintenance of, 316; desired outcomes of, 312–313; direct versus staged, 335–336; ensuring facilitative arenas during, 330–331; establishing/anticipation of review points on, 317–318; evaluating impact of lingering disagreement during, 331; forward and backward mapping during, 318–320; general guidance for, 325–338e; introduction of adopted changes, 313–314; leadership guidelines during, 323–325; maintenance of coalition/leadership during, 314–315; managing collaborations during, 323; monitoring/evaluation plans developed for, 329; personnel used during, 334–336; pilot and demonstration projects transferred to, 337e–338e; starting with quick changes, 328–329; strategic documents/action plans developed for, 326; strategic thinking about, 325–326; strengthening of people/organizations during, 318; summative evaluation of, 317; vision of success of, 320–323. See also Proposal adoption
In-charge organization: illustrated diagram of, 6fig; overview of, 4–5
Inclusive community building, 100–102
Indicators, 333, 343
Information Revolution, 44
Informed public (or civic republic), 188
Initial forums: analyzing and involving stakeholders, 202–206; exploring context and personal leadership, 202; focusing on the common good, 202; getting

started, 200–201; practicing basics of good meeting preparation/facilitation, 201–202

Initial-agreement leadership guidelines: on follow-up forum, 206–207; on full-group forums, 207–210; on initial forums, 199–206

Initial-agreements: action plan for obtaining, 355; characteristics of full-fledged agreements, 210–215; leadership guidelines for, 199–215; overview of, 170–171; purpose and desired outcomes of, 198–199

Institute of Cultural Affairs, 68

Institutions: design of, 251–252; maintaining responsive, 341–342

Integrity, 54

Interest directions, 234e

Interest group policy, 244

International AIDS Trust, 127

International Chamber of Commerce, 126

Internet knowledge economy, 24

Interpersonal space, 46, 48e

Interpreter/direction giver tasks, 110–115

Interpretive schemes, 343–344

Iraq invasion (2003), 247

Issue creation: phase of, 169–170, 243–244; thinking ahead about process of, 353. *See also* Public issues

Issue dimensions, 297

J

Johannesburg Summit on Sustainable Development, 125, 126, 140, 146–147

Joining Together (Johnson and Johnson), 77

"Jumping to solutions," 246

K

Kaposi's Sarcoma Research and Education Foundation, 30, 97

Knowledge economy, 24

Kyoto protocols, 41, 125, 168, 279

L

Leadership: defining, 30; development of, 74; ethical, 143, 146–154e; as flexibly optimistic, 356; implementation guidelines for, 323–325; initial-agreement guidelines for, 199–215; organizational, 77, 79–106; personal, 40–61e, 202; planning for succession of, 100; policy reassessment guidelines for, 342–351; political, 129, 132–143, 144e–146e; problem formulation guidelines for, 227–240; searching for solutions in forums and guidelines for, 249–265; shared-power and need for, 29–32; studies on ethnic/gender differences in, 91–92; team, 64–77; trust and spirit of, 74–77; visionary, 108–129, 130e–132e. *See also* Policy entrepreneurs

Leadership capabilities: assessing, 352; ethical leadership, 154e; leadership for the common good, 37–38; leadership in context, 38–48e; listed, 34–35, 359–360; needed by change agents, 34–37; personal leadership, 49–61e; political leadership, 144e–146e; visionary leadership, 130e–132e

The Leadership Challenge (Kouzes and Posner), 49, 77

Leadership for the Common Good approach, 189–191

Leadership for the Common Good (Crosby), 35

Leadership in context: exercise for assessing, 43e; guidelines for facilitating, 44–48e; overview of, 38–43

Leadership exercises: analyzing ethical principles, laws, and norms, 152e; analyzing interpretive schemes or problem frames,

124*e*–125*e*; assessing cultural difference, 48*e*; assessing ethical leadership capacity, 154*e*; assessing leadership in context, 43*e*; assessing other personal strengths/weaknesses, 54–61*e*; assessing political leadership capacity, 144*e*–146*e*; assessing stakeholder attitudes toward status quo, 211*e*; assessing visionary leadership capacity, 130*e*–132*e*; assessing your organization, 103*e*–104*e*; assessing your team, 78*e*–79*e*; basic stakeholder analysis technique for policy change effort, 203*e*; conducting stakeholder role play, 284*e*; constructing diagram of power bases/interest, 234*e*; constructing organizational vision of success, 88*e*; constructing stakeholder influence diagram, 204*e*; constructing winning argument and map of common good, 235*e*; developing objectives from preferred problem solutions, 233*e*; discovering cares and concerns, 38*e*; exploring personal highs/lows, 50*e*; global trends assessment, 45*e*; identifying ethical role models/overcoming barriers to ethical leadership, 147*e*; laying groundwork for winning coalition, 137*e*–138*e*; mission development, 85*e*; multicriteria assessment grid, 259*e*; outlining/constructing personal visions, 116*e*; participation planning matrix, 204*e*–205*e*; policy attractiveness versus stakeholder capability grid, 285*e*; using power-versus-interest grid, 121*e*; pursuing a big-win or small-win strategy, 276*e*–277*e*; "snowcard" technique to identify/agree on norms, 72*e*; stakeholder identification/analysis, 83*e*–84*e*; stakeholder-issue interrelationship diagram, 257*e*; stakeholder-sup-port-versus-opposition grid, 283*e*, 302, 326; tapping stakeholder interests/resources for implementation, 327*e*; thinking about public interest and the common good, 191*e*–192*e*; thinking about public problem, 166*e*; undertaking solution search within specified areas, 254*e*

Leadership from the Inside out (Cashman), 53

Leadership for Global Citizenship (Crosby), 35, 46

Leading Out Loud (Pearce), 129

Leading with Soul (Bolman and Deal), 53

Learning: commitment to continuous, 58; policy-oriented, 217; ways of interacting and, 54–55

Learning culture, 92

The Lexus and the Olive Tree (Friedman), 25

Living systems frame, 104–105

Lobbying: right timing of, 305; strategies for effective, 287, 303–304

Lobbying Together (Hula), 143

Logic models, 260

Low-context culture, 46

M

Machiavelli in Brussels (van Schendelen), 143

Majoritarian politics, 243, 244

Managing Crises Before They Happen (Mitroff and Anagnos), 97

Managing the Unexpected (Sutcliffe), 97

"Managing for Values:" (Moore), 105–106

Mapping (forward and backward), 318–320

The market, 187–188

Media: developing strategy during proposal drafting on, 288; forum use of argument and, 126–128; public announcement of proposal through, 307; report release and strategy regarding,

239–240; two-pronged strategy for use of, 307–308

Medicare, 293

Mid-Minnesota Area Agency on Aging, 203

Minnesota Board on Aging, 20

Mission statements: aligning organization design with, 87–89; being politician/role model to facilitate, 95–96; creating, 81–82, 85e; ensuring that organizational culture supports, 89–95

Modes of argument, 126–128

Monitoring plans, 329

Moral education, 189

Multicriteria assessment grid, 259e

Multinode network organization, 5, 6fig

Mutual gain regime, 360

Myers-Briggs Type Indicator, 54

Myths, 343–344

N

National Coalition Building Institute, 68

National Coalition Building Institute Web site, 143

National Institutes of Health, 40, 79, 102

NCI (National Cancer Institute), 88, 89, 102

Negotiating for support, 306–307

NetAid, 317

Networked organizations, 5, 6fig, 7

New York Native, 304

No-one-in-charge organization: illustrated diagram of, 8fig; overview of, 7, 9; planning and decision making in, 10

The Normal Heart (Kramer, play), 44

Norms of relevance, 125–126

O

Off-cycle policy change: described, 162; managing ideas during, 163–166

Oil spills, 26

Operationalization. *See* Implementation

Opponents, 306. *See also* Resistance

Optimism, 55–56

Organizational culture: described, 47; ensuring that mission/philosophy are supported by, 89–95

Organizational leadership: attention to organizational purpose/design by, 81–96; building inclusive community, 100–102; dealing with internal/external change, 96–100; helpful tools for, 102–106; introduction to, 77, 79–80

Organizational Leadership and Culture (Schein), 95

Organizational purpose/design: aligning design with, 87–89; constructing vision embodying goals/strategies for, 87, 88e; developing goals and strategies to facilitate, 82, 86; developing mission/philosophy statements on, 81–82, 85e; leadership tasks related to, 81; stakeholder identification/analysis to facilitate, 83e–84e

Organizations: agreement on responsible, 226; assessing your, 103e–104e; continuum of sharing in, 19fig; hierarchical and networked, 6fig; high-reliability, 93–94; implementation of policy change and strengthening of, 318; planning and decision making types of, 4–5, 7, 9–14; reassessment of policies and staying power of, 344–345; virtuousness of, 90

Organized anarchy of policy process, 161–169

Outlining/constructing personal visions, 116e

Oval mapping, 69

P

Participation planning matrix, 204e–205e, 231

Personal leadership: assessing other personal strengths/weaknesses, 54–61*e*; discerning the call to leadership, 49, 51–54; explored during initial forums, 202; exploring personal highs/lows, 50*e*, practices of, 49

Personal networks/balance, 59

Personal strengths/weaknesses: authority, skills, and connections, 58; cognitive, emotional, and behavior complexity, 56–58; commitment to continuous learning, 58; exercise in assessing additional, 60*e*–61*e*; integrity and sense of humor, 54; position in social hierarchies, 59, 61; sense of self-efficacy, optimism, and courage, 55–56; supportive personal networks and balance, 59; ways of learning and interacting, 54–55

Personnel during implementation, 334–336

Persuasion campaigns, 127, 303–304

Persuasion in Society (Simons), 129

Philosophy statements: creating, 81–82; ensuring that organizational culture supports, 89–95

Pilot projects, 337*e*–338*e*

Policies: continuation of, 346–347; modification or succession of, 347–349; reassessment of, 340–356; termination of, 349–351. *See also* Public policy

Policy attractiveness versus stakeholder capability grid, 285*e*

Policy change: benefits of proposed, 355–356; costs and consequences of, 355; hierarchy of, 180–181; implementation or operationalization of, 312–339; outlining compelling reasons for, 352; shared belief in mutual endeavor of, 271; starting anew following policy reassessment, 351–356; timing of, 356; two types of,

162–163; understanding, 157, 160–161. *See also* Proposals

Policy change cycle: continuation, modification, or termination during, 179; illustrated diagram of, 159*fig*; implementation and evaluation during, 177–179; initial-agreement during, 170–171, 197–215; issue creation phase of, 169–170; phases of, 169–179, 360; policy or plan formulation during, 174–176; problem formulation during, 171–173, 216–241; proposal review and adoption during, 176–177; search for solutions during, 173–174; vision at beginning of, 321

Policy entrepreneurs: adoption/implementation of proposal role by, 296–298; big/small winning strategies pursued by, 274–279; conceptual frameworks developed by, 244–245; forward and backward mapping by, 318–320; sign-up process and role of, 292–295; social significance/urgency motivations of, 220; solution components identified by, 245–248; vision of success constructed by, 320–323; window of opportunity exploited by, 295–296. *See also* Change agents/advocates; Leadership

Policy entrepreneurship: defining common good in context of, 158*e*; enacting the common good in, 181–182; essential requirements of, 156–157; guidelines for thinking about common good during, 182–192*e*; hierarchy of process, 180–181; problem formulation and caveats for, 240–241. *See also* Public policy

Policy makers, 302

Policy process: analyzing and managing stakeholders during, 166–168; designing institutions during, 168–169; managing ideas during, 163–166; understood as organized anarchy, 161–169

Policy reassessment: desired outcomes of, 341; four reasons to, 340–341; leadership guidelines for, 342–351; maintaining responsive institutions during, 341–342; resolving residual problems through, 342; starting anew following, 351–356; tackling new reform following, 342

Policy reassessment leadership guidelines: general principles used for, 343–346; for policy continuation, 346–349; for policy termination, 349–351

Policy regime: defining, 18–19; of mutual gain, 19

Policy termination, 349–351

Policy-making bodies, 209e

Policy-oriented learning, 217

Political decision making, 11fig–14

Political leadership: adeptly designing/using formal and informal arenas, 139–143; assessing capacity of, 144e–146e; building sustainable coalitions, 134–138e; defining, 108; forums and arenas of, 109; helpful tools used by, 143; main skills of, 129; mediating/shaping conflict within and among constituencies, 129, 132–134; overcoming bureaucratic resistance during implementation, 138–139

Politics (Aristotle), 182

Pollution, 26

Population shifts, 26–27

"Pork-barrel" policies, 244

Power bases, 234e

The Power of Followership (Kelley), 37, 106

Power-versus-interest grid, 121e

Pragmatic communication, 125–126

Pragmatic idealism, 55

Preliminary reports, 236–237

Problem formulation: caveats for policy entrepreneurs, 240–241; leadership guidelines for, 227–240; overview of, 171–173; purpose and desired outcomes of, 217–227. *See also* Solutions

Problem formulation leadership guidelines: caveats for policy entrepreneurs, 240–241; constructing common good map/winning argument, 235e; constructing diagram of power bases/interest, 234e; developing objectives from preferred solutions, 233e; diagram of bases of power/interest, 234fig; focus on problems/desired outcomes, 231–233, 235; on forums used, 230–231; framing problems in need of solution, 235–236; report preparation, review, and dissemination, 236–240; on role of sectors in problem formulation, 230; for two-step process, 228–230; unraveling old frames, 236

Problem formulation purposes: attention to stakeholder feelings/attitudes and, 226; awareness/appreciation of public problems and, 218–225; clarification of relevant difference among stakeholders, 225; clarification of relevant differences among stakeholders, 225; criteria for measuring stakeholder satisfaction and, 225–226; desired outcomes for, 217

Problem statement, 227, 238e

The productive community, 117

Proposal adoption: aligning incentives for implementation of, 308–309; away from status quo support of, 309; coalition to monitor implementation of, 301; decision in court to require/facilitate, 298–299; decision to proceed with, 296–298; engage reviewers

of, 305–306; leadership guidelines for, 301–311; learning from
failure of, 310–311; maintaining
respectful participant relationships during, 301; provision of
guidance/resources for implementation of, 299; purpose and
desired outcomes of, 290–291;
regime building to facilitate, 310;
shared excitement about policy/
implementation of, 300–301; supported by those who can affect
implementation, 300; widely
shared agreement on, 291–296.
See also Implementation
Proposal adoption leadership guidelines: building support, 302–308;
gleaning success from failure,
310–311; overview of, 301–302;
providing implementation
guidance/support, 308–310
Proposal displacement, 286
Proposal leadership guidelines: developing and review of draft proposal, 280–284, 286–287; on last
proposal decisions, 288–289;
overview of, 279–280; softening
up and media strategies, 287–288
Proposals: adopting policy, 290–311;
big vs. small winning strategies
for, 274–279; characteristics of
"winning," 271–274; developing
and review of drafted, 280–284,
286–287; drafting policies and
plans for, 268–269; final draft of,
286; identification of necessary
resources in, 270, 274; incorporating constructive modifications,
269–270; leadership guidelines
for, 279–289; necessary coalitions
in, 270–271, 286, 287–288; possible format of, 281; purpose and
desired outcomes of, 267–271;
stakeholder analysis for use in,
282–286. *See also* Policy change
Public issues: creation of, 169–170,
243–244, 353; helping frame and

reframe, 113–114; stakeholder-
issue interrelationship diagram,
256*fig*, 257*e*. *See also* Issue creation
Public participation, 45
Public passion, 38
Public policy: defining aspects of,
157; drafting for proposals, 268–
269; entrepreneurial, 244; exploring phases of change cycle in,
169–179; formulation of, 174–176;
interest group, 244; understanding changes in, 157, 160–161; understanding process as organized
anarchy, 161–169. *See also* Policies;
Policy entrepreneurship
Public problems: adopting a shared-
power approach to, 16–17; appreciating solutions and, 14–17;
awareness and appreciation of,
218–225; championing new ways
of dealing with, 114–115; definitions of, 219–220; emergent or
developmental, 15; examples
of breakthroughs for, 361–362;
framing, 171–173; helping frame
and reframe, 113–114; multicausal explanations/complex
framing of, 220–223; political decision making to solve, 11*fig*–14;
rational planning used to solve,
10*fig*–11, 15–16; reassessing policies and moving on to next, 342;
thinking about, 166*e*. *See also*
Solutions

Q

Quality movement, 104
Quality Partnerships Initiative, 178

R

Rational planning: comparing political decision making to, 11*fig*–14;
described, 10*fig*–11; to solve public problems, 10*fig*–11, 15–16
Reassessing policies. *See* Policy
reassessment
Reflective Leadership Center, 35

Refugee populations, 26–27
Regime of mutual gain, 360
Regional Development Commission (Minnesota), 203
Relational dialogue, 126
Relationships: cultivated by change advocates, 294; during policy-review-and-adoption phase, 301. *See also* Coalitions
Religious regime, 188
Reports: deferring other problems in, 238; final, 239; generic problem statement format for, 238*e*; media strategy following release of, 239–240; preliminary, 236–237; review process for, 237–238
Representative government, 188
Resistance: keeping an eye on opponents and, 306; to new policy, 332–333, 335; to policy termination, 350
Resources: adopted proposal provision of guidance and, 299; efficient use of, 247; identified in proposals, 270, 274; seeking adequate, 308
Review groups, 346
Review process, 305–306, 317–318, 345. *See also* Evaluation
Rio Conference on Environment and Development, 15–16
Rural Summit (1998) [Minnesota], 200

S

"Satisficing," 246
Self-efficacy, 55–56
Self-interest, 252
Senior Federation, 209
Sense of humor, 54
September 11, 2001, 247, 296
September 11 investigative commission, 345
Seven Zones for Leadership (Terry), 105
Shared Leadership (Pearce and Conger), 77, 106
Shared-power approach: causes and consequences of, 21, 23–29; con-

tinuum of organizational sharing and, 19*fig*; defining meaning of, 17–21; in no-one-in-charge organization, 7, 8*fig*, 9; public problems solved through, 16–17; some definitions included in public problems and, 22*e*–23*e*; understanding public problems in context of, 21*fig*
Shared-power world: advantages of vision in, 321–322; declining capacity to govern/blurred boundaries in a, 28–29; definitions used in the, 22*e*–23*e*; described, 259; environmental degradation in a, 26; global arms trade/terrorism threat in a, 24–25; global economy in a, 25–26; human rights demand/democratic governance in a, 27; need for leadership in, 29–32; population shifts in a, 26–27; social change in the, 33; understanding public problems in, 21*e*; the wired and wireless, 23–24
Shell's shareholders meeting (2003), 147
Signing-up process, 292–295
Single-node network organization, 6*fig*
The Skilled Facilitator (Schwarz), 77
Skills trait, 58
Small-win strategy, 274–279
"Snowcard" technique, 71, 72*e*
Social capital, 30
Social change: African American Men Project experience with, 31, 57–58; AIDS crisis and working for, 30, 39–40, 42; Hennepin County district experience with, 11–14, 31, 42–43; role of shared-power world in, 33; using social networks to bring about, 30–31; VAN (Vital Aging Initiative) [Minnesota] and, 20–21, 31, 41–42
Social Group Membership/Bridging Differences, 62*e*

Social hierarchy position, 59, 61
Social networks: change through, 30–31; importance to quality of life, 30; supportive personal, 59
Softening-up process, 287–288, 292
Solution search components: efficient use of resources, 247; enhancement of quality, legitimacy, and prestige, 247–248; expanded advocacy coalition, 248; need to identify, 245–247; placement of issue on public agenda, 248; stakeholder-issue interrelationship diagram, 256*fig*, 257*e*
Solution search leadership guidelines: for assessing solutions, 257–263; cautions regarding, 249; for constructing/communicating compelling vision, 263–265; on using expertise, 250, 252–255; orchestrating forums and managing conflict, 249–250; paying attention to stakeholders, 255–257; using systems view/focusing on institutional design, 251–252
Solutions: AAMP search for, 173–174; appreciating public problems and, 14–17; assessing, 257–263; developing objectives from preferred problem, 233*e*; using forums to search for, 242–266; "jumping to," 246; "lumpy," 335–336; methodical development of, 252–255; policy change cycle and search for, 173–174; problems in need of framed, 235–236; undertaking solution search within specified areas, 254*e*. *See also* Problem formulation; Public problems
Solutions in forums: development of conceptual frameworks, 244–245; identification of solution components, 245–248; leadership guidelines during search for, 249–265; purpose and desired outcomes, 242–245

Soulwork, 52–53
Space (interpersonal), 46, 48*e*
Splitting/consolidating programs, 348
Sponsors: described, 208; identifying, 303
Staged versus direct implementation, 335–336
Stakeholder capability versus policy attractiveness grid, 285*e*
Stakeholder Influence Diagram, 204*e*
Stakeholder role play exercise, 284*e*
Stakeholder-issue interrelationship diagram, 256*fig*, 257*e*, 302
Stakeholder-support-versus-opposition grid, 283*e*, 326
Stakeholders: analyzing and involving in initial forums, 202–206; analyzing/managing during policy process, 166–168; assessing attitudes toward status quo, 211*e*; attention to feelings and attitudes of, 226; clarification of relevant differences among, 225; criteria for measuring satisfaction of, 225–226; emphasizing collaboration among, 98–100; examples of organizational analysis of, 94; exercise on identification/analysis of, 83*e*–84*e*; policy continuation and role of, 346–347; proposal review of goals by, 282; proposals and analysis of, 282–286; separating from terminated policies, 350–351; solution search support by, 255–257; tapping interests/resources for implementation, 327*e*. *See also* Coalitions
STMicroelectronics, 53–54
Stockholm International Peace Research Initiative, 25
Strategic release of information, 298
Strategic voting, 296–297, 304–305
Strategy documents, 326
Summative evaluations, 317
Super-Leadership (Manz and Sims), 77
SWiM appraoch, 237

T

Team flow, 75

Team leadership: building team trust and spirit, 74–77; communication fostered by, 67–70; described, 64–65; empowerment task of, 70–73; team recruitment task of, 65–66

Teams: assessing your, 78e–79e; emphasizing collaboration/team building within, 98–100; empowering members of, 70–73; fostering communication skills for, 67–70; "snowcards" to identify/agree on norms for, 71, 72e; trust and spirit of, 74–77

Terrorism threat, 24–25

360-degree feedback, 89

Time: cultural perceptions of, 46, 48e; for policy change, 356

Trust issues, 74–77

Turning to One Another (Wheatley), 53

U

U.N. Conference on Environment and Development (1992) [Earth Summit], 53, 79, 115, 230, 248, 316, 318

U.N. High Commissioner for Refugees, 26

UNCED (U.N. Conference on Environment and Development), 15–16

Universal Declaration of Human Rights, 184

University of Minnesota Extension Service, 20

University of Minnesota's College of Continuing Education, 320

U.S. Department of Health and Human Services, 79, 89

V

Value judgments, 223–225

VAN (Vital Aging Initiative) [Minnesota], 20–21, 31, 41–42; access rules used by, 143; accountability mechanisms used in, 150; active

citizenry promoted by, 190; Advocacy Leadership Certificate Program of, 178, 190, 251, 315–316, 320; building trust and spirit in, 75, 76–77; change advocates in the, 80; coalition maintained during policy implementation, 315; common good as defined by, 187; dealing with change, 96; feedback loop used by, 251; full-group forums participants in, 209–210; idea management during policy process at, 164; initial forums of, 201; interpretation/direction giving in, 111, 112, 114, 115; lobbying and persuasion strategies used by, 303; mission statement of, 82; new technologies used by, 98; planning for leadership succession by, 100; policies/plans drafted by, 268; policy reassessment by, 343; problem formulation by, 171, 224; productive-citizen frame promoted by, 123; public problem breakthrough by, 362; review point established by, 318; stakeholder analysis by, 94; team leadership role in, 65; "venue shopping" by, 175

VAN Web site, 31, 115, 129, 251, 320

"Venue shopping," 175

Vietnam War, 27

Virtues frame, 105

Vision: at beginning of policy change cycle, 321; constructing/communicating compelling solution, 263–265; developing guiding, 333; shared-power world and use of, 321–322; of successful implementation, 320–323

Visionary leadership: assessing capacity of, 130e–132e; championing new ways of dealing with public problems, 114–115; characteristics listed, 109–110; communal stories communicated by, 117–119; defining, 108; designing and using forums, 120–129; forums and arenas of, 109; helping frame and reframe public issues, 113–114; interpreter/direction giver characteristic of, 110–115; offering compelling vision of the future, 115, 117–119; outlining/constructing personal visions, 116*e*; power-versus-interest grid used by, 121*e*; responses during a crisis by, 120; revealing/naming real needs and conditions, 111–112

Visionary Leadership (Nanus), 87

Vital Aging Summit (2002), 115, 117, 315

Vital Aging Summit (2004), 315

Vital Force project, 320

Voluntary activities, 45

Volunteers of America, 320

W

Walking the Talk (Holliday, Schmidheiny, and Watts), 37–38, 112, 117, 279

WBCSD (World Business Council for Sustainable Development), 16, 31, 40–41, 65, 79–80, 113, 140; active citizenry promoted by, 190; adaptation of principles, laws, norms by, 148; big-win/small-win strategies pursued by, 279; common good decisions by, 184–185; common good as defined by, 187; compelling vision created by, 264; conflict resolution rules set up by, 150–151; constructive modifications incorporated by, 269–270; dealing with change, 96; decision-making capabilities of leadership of, 140; designing institutions during policy process at, 168–169; emphasis of operating values, 97; framing of problems by, 222; idea management during policy process at, 164; initial-agreement phase of, 198, 202; interpretation/direction giving in, 111, 113; market-oriented solutions favored by, 252; mission statement of, 82; new policy regimes implemented by, 316; policy reassessment by, 344; pragmatic communication used by, 125–126; problem formulation by, 171; public problem breakthrough by, 361–362; real needs/conditions revealed by leadership of, 111–112; resolving conflicts among ethical principles, 149; review points established by, 318; social and environmental focus of, 99; softening-up process used by, 288; stakeholder analysis by, 94; strategic directions of, 86; sustainable development frame adopted by, 123; "venue shopping" during, 175; vision of the future by, 117; Young Managers Team launched by, 248

Websites: Association for Conflict Resolution, 87; Dimensions of Leadership Profile, 54; Institute of Cultural Affairs, 68; Myers-Briggs Type Indicator, 54; National Coalition Building Institute, 143; on refugee populations, 26; Stockholm International Peace Research Initiative, 25; VAN (Vital Aging Initiative), 31, 115, 129, 251, 320; WBCSD, 82, 86

Wilder Foundation, 143

Window of opportunity, 295–296

Working with Culture (Khademian), 95

World Business Council. *See* WBCSD (World Business Council for Sustainable Development)

World Health Organization, 40

World Industry Council for the Environment, 79

World Summit on Sustainable Development (2002), 135

Y

Young Manager Teams, 140

Young Managers Team (WBCSD), 248